STERLING, ROBERT R

THEORY OF THE MEASU

KV-429-691

HF5681.V3.S83

THEORY OF THE MEASUREMENT
OF ENTERPRISE INCOME

Theory
of the Measurement
# of Enterprise
Income

ROBERT R. STERLING

THE UNIVERSITY PRESS OF KANSAS
Lawrence, Manhattan, Wichita, London

© COPYRIGHT BY THE UNIVERSITY PRESS OF KANSAS, 1970
LIBRARY OF CONGRESS CATALOG CARD NO. 69-16061
PRINTED IN THE UNITED STATES OF AMERICA

DESIGNED BY GARY GORE

329 7°

"Think as I think," said a man, "or you
are abominably wicked: You are a toad."
And after I had thought of it, I said,
"I will, then, be a toad."—*Stephen Crane*

THIS BOOK IS DEDICATED TO THOSE TOADS WHO OVER THE YEARS HAVE USED
MIMEOGRAPHED COPIES OF THIS MATERIAL AS A TEXT, ESPECIALLY TO THOSE
WHO WERE SO TOAD-LIKE AS TO DISAGREE WITH ME WHILE USING IT.

PREFACE

In the eight years since the first version of this manuscript was written and in the five years since the present version was copyrighted in mimeographed form, the scope of the theory of accounting has changed drastically. A major indication of this change is that alternative valuation methods are now considered a proper subject of accounting. Several years ago a reviewer of this book found it "interesting" but "not really an accounting book," because it was concerned with "values, not costs." Moreover, he found the title to be "misleading," since the book discussed "valuation instead of the theory of income as the title promised." Contrast that attitude to Baxter's recent statement that "the problem of valuation cries out for major debate." (Baxter, p. 214.) This book is an attempt to answer that cry: it is a debate, a polemic, about alternative valuation methods.

The change in attitude, however, has significance beyond its permitting alternative valuation methods to be debated. Accounting is now in a state of unrest, even turmoil. Unrest is not new to accounting, but this time it comes from a different source. Previously the unrest was the result of some crisis, such as an exposed financial scandal or a depressed economy or sharply rising price levels. The present unrest is not due to an external crisis; instead it is the result of a change in the accountants' view of the function of accounting. Previously accounting was viewed as a closed theoretical system in which all the events or facts to be accounted for were specified; it is now tending toward an open system in which the data to be gathered is a function of the users' needs. Accountants have always been concerned about the usefulness of the data they provide, but the kind of data provided was severely constrained. In general, the data was limited to historical costs; and then *that* data was arranged in its most useful form. This is evidenced by the criteria used in the arguments in the literature. Price-level adjustments, for example, were attacked because they were a departure from the cost basis of accounting; and they were defended as being "restated" costs. Thus, one important criterion in assessing price-level adjustments was whether or not they were a departure from historical costs. If they met this criterion, *then* usefulness was considered. Recently this procedure has been reversed: usefulness is now considered first, and the data requirements are deduced from that consideration without being limited to any particular kind of data. (This difference in outlook was, in my opinion, at the core of the so-called managerial accounting "revolution.") This book follows the latter approach: the user of the information is considered first, and the valuation method selected is a consequence of those considerations.

At the time when I originally wrote this book, I considered the most important parts to be the discussion of information and measurement theory. I now believe that the careful specification of the firm model is much more important. In the Introduction I speak of tacit premises and assumptions as being the cause of the lack of understanding and agreement. I now believe that it is the tacit firm model which is at the root of the difficulties. Perhaps there can never be agreement in the abstract on the correct method of calculating income, but maybe there can be agreement in respect to certain kinds of firms. Perhaps there can never be a set of generally accepted accounting principles that is applicable to all firms, but maybe there can be different sets of principles that are applicable to specific types of firms. If we carefully work out the implications of different firm models, perhaps we would come out with different sets of principles to which we could all agree. I happen to believe that these principles would converge, but what I believe is of little consequence; the important thing is to work through the various models and see whether or not they converge.

Of equal importance is the increased understanding and appreciation of others' arguments and positions, which can be achieved by the firm-model approach. It seems clear, for example, that one can postulate a continuing firm which is operating in two different markets (say, a retailer) and make a good case for valuing inventory at replacement cost. Under those circumstances the "opportunity cost" of a unit is the cost of replacing it, since the firm *must* restock. On the other hand, in the trader model used herein it makes little sense to talk about cost savings or replacement costs. Thus, I think the basic differences between me and, for example, Edwards and Bell, spring from the kind of firm we are talking about, not the analysis. I think this is true generally. By consciously looking for different implicit firm models, I can now return to the lifo-fifo disputes in the literature and understand the respective positions. Previously the pros and cons of that long unresolved dispute made little sense to me; and judging from their writings, it seems that the proponents never understood their opponents, because they seldom addressed themselves to each others' points. One point in the argument for lifo was the underlying assumption that the basic unit of measure was the physical units of inventory, not the dollars received and paid. The fifo proponents were counting dollars, not units. (This difference is the major reason why I go through the discussion on the selection of the valuing agent in Chapter III, although "everybody agrees" that dollars ought to be the measuring unit.) It seems to me that the lifo proponents had a firm model in mind that was closely related to the mark-up-turn-over firm model mentioned above. The fifo proponents seldom attacked the model, and often the debate degenerated to accusations about avoiding taxes. The specification of the model would have contributed to understanding, and it may have brought agreement.

Although of less importance than I originally thought, the extended discussion of information and measurement has been left intact. At the time of writing, the concepts were fairly novel in accounting, and therefore an extended discussion was needed because of their unfamiliarity. Now the terms seem to have become buzzwords in much the same way that "managerial" was a few years ago. I fear that the terms are being used in such a variety of ways that we run the danger of having them lose their meaning. Thus, the extended discussion is now needed to delineate the way in which I use the terms.

No attempt has been made to update this book in the sense of citing or critiquing the recent literature. I hope the following justification for the omission is sufficient: First, a consideration of the recent literature would necessitate substantial rewriting and an attendant delay in publication. I am anxious to get wider exposure of this work and the resultant reaction. As Keynes once said, "It is astonishing what foolish things one can temporarily believe if one thinks too long alone." (Keynes, *General Theory*, p. vii.) I have been thinking alone too long, and perhaps foolish thoughts have resulted. I solicit the reader's criticism. Second, I am convinced of the merits of the firm-model approach; and I am anxious to expose this work as one example of that approach, in the hope that it will stimulate explorations of other firm models. I view this work as a faltering step toward a definitive analysis of a highly simplified firm. Perhaps others, better qualified than I, can come closer to a definitive analysis of more complex firm models. Third, and most importantly, one must cut off his literature search at some point in time; and although there have been important recent contributions, none of those contributions has caused me to change my mind about the ideas presented herein. On the contrary, much of the recent literature has reinforced my belief in these ideas.

There are many worthy works that have appeared in the interim that would have benefited this book had they been available at the time of writing. Such works are too numerous to list, but I am particularly sorry that the works of Grady and Ijiri were not available prior to the preparation of the analysis of the Accounting Tradition (Chapters XI and XII). Grady's masterful survey would have provided a current authoritative statement of traditional accounting that is missing in my analysis. At the time I wrote Chapters XI and XII, conservatism was out of favor; therefore it was necessary for me to argue that conservatism was still operative prior to criticizing it. Grady has since, correctly in my opinion, listed conservatism as a basic concept of traditional accounting. Note also that Grady's work is a reversion to the methodology of apologetics. He has not only taken an inventory of the existing concepts, but has also attempted to rationalize and justify those concepts. Ijiri's excellent description of the structure of traditional accounting would have provided the missing framework for analysis and made many of my descriptive remarks unnecessary. Excepting the greater rigor and elegance of Ijiri's presentation, the reader will note that our description of the structure of traditional accounting is quite similar but that our evaluation of that structure is quite different. This should be an important datum because of the present tendency toward thinking that the axiomatization of a system validates the system. (Ijiri does not profess this, but there are others who seem to think that Ijiri's work somehow validates traditional accounting.) An axiomatized system permits one to validate or prove theorems *within that system*, but it does not permit one to make an evaluation of the system vis-à-vis other systems. Consider, for example, the various axiomatized geometries. Selection of one of those geometries as the "true" or "best" one requires axioms or premises other than those used in the statements of the various geometries. The same is true of accounting. That traditional accounting can be axiomatized may be very helpful in giving us insights into it, but it says nothing about the "correctness" of traditional accounting. In general, I agree with most of Grady's and Ijiri's descriptive statements but disagree with many of their evaluative statements.

Most conspicuous by its absence is a comparison to Chambers' *Accounting, Evaluation and Economic Behavior*. I agree with Chambers on most issues, and his ground-breaking book would have been a great help had it been available at the time of writing. (Unfortunately, I was not aware of his earlier work in the foreign literature.) Although there is a tendency to agree on many points, my approach is quite different from Chambers', especially in the use of an idealized firm model. His work covers many more types of firms and assets, but it does so at the expense of a detailed coverage of each. Because of the simplified firm model, my coverage can be more sharply focused and detailed, but it does so at the expense of highly limited applicability. Note also that Baxter's plea for a debate on valuation was made while he was reviewing Chambers. Thus, it appears that Chambers' work has served to open up the debate on valuation instead of resolving it. To use the current argot, this book is presented in the hope that it will "advance the dialogue."

Acknowledgment is due to J. Fagg Foster, an institutional economist who introduced me to the fascinating problems of macroeconomics and macroaccounting which led to the equally fascinating problems of microaccounting; Ralph Blodgett, a neoclassical economist who let me have the freedom to make my own mistakes while writing this as a dissertation; C. Wade Savage, a philosopher-metrician who clarified all of my ideas on measurement theory that are clear and tried to clarify those that remain muddled; Sid B. Thomas, Jr., a philosopher-axiologist who listened endlessly and argued cogently; Henry Margenau, a physicist-philosopher who generously furnished me with space and time to think and read; Norwood Russell Hanson, a philosopher of science whose tragic accident robbed the world of a noble spirit and many insights and robbed me of a mentor, research collaborator, and friend; Raymond J. Chambers and Arthur B. Thomas, who read the entire manuscript and made many valuable suggestions; the Ford Foundation, for financial support; and Margery, without whom this could have been finished ten years earlier and without whom it would have never been finished. To all of the above, my sincere thanks and the usual absolution.

R.R.S.

Lawrence, Kansas
1968

CONTENTS

xiii

2

3

xvi

1

"We have to isolate for study a few simple aspects of science just as science has to isolate a few simple aspects of the world; . . . This, admittedly, is over-simplification. But conscious and cautious over-simplification, far from being an intellectual sin, is a prerequisite for investigation. We can hardly study at once all the ways in which everything is related to everything else."

—NELSON GOODMAN

"The first problems to suggest themselves to the inquirer into nature are far too complex and difficult for any early solution, even if any satisfactorily secure conclusion can ever be drawn concerning them. What ought to be done, therefore, and what in fact is done, is at first to substitute for those problems others much simpler, much more abstract, of which there is a good prospect of finding *probable solutions. Then, the reasonably certain solutions of these last problems will throw a light more or less clear upon more concrete problems which are in certain respects more interesting."*

—CHARLES S. S. PEIRCE

I

Arguments about the "correct" method of calculating income have persisted for over a century. When an argument persists for that length of time, one may suspect that there is no possibility of resolution. In the sense that one is free to define "income" in any way that he likes, the problem is merely a definitional dispute. In the same sense that one is free to calculate any statistic he likes, there is no hope for prescribing one correct way. Yet the arguments persist, and the proponents continue to insist that one calculation is better than another. Thus, it is thought that there are criteria for choosing one method and rejecting the others. Unfortunately, those criteria are seldom made explicit. The premises, assumptions, and reasoning that underlie the arguments are so sketchy that we are led to believe that the proponents consider them to be self-evident. That they are not self-evident is indicated by the fact that the arguments seldom meet on the level of analysis. Instead they meet only at the point of the conclusion which is also, of course, the point in dispute. That this is the case is evidenced by the frequent use of such terms as "understatement" or "overstatement" to

3

describe income or assets or liabilities. It is said that method A is incorrect because it will understate income, and the reply is that method B is incorrect because it will overstate income. Obviously overstate and understate are comparative terms, but they are also pejorative terms. To understate or overstate income is to report a *false* figure. In order to know which figure is false one must know which figure is correct. Removal of the pejorative connotations leaves only the simple and obvious proposition that method A income is less than method B income. Since one cannot deduce that A or B is false from the premise that A is less than B, the arguments bypass one another. They meet only at the conclusion. In such cases there is little chance for understanding and even less chance for resolving the issue.

This book joins the argument. We intend to argue that one method of calculating income is superior to others. The difference is that we have tried to make all the assumptions explicit, insofar as we are aware of them, and we have tried to set down the reasoning in meticulous detail. It is hoped that this will allow the reader who disagrees to know precisely where we part company and precisely why we disagree or precisely where this analysis errs. The reader can then challenge the argument at the point of disagreement instead of challenging the conclusions.

In order to make the argument detailed enough for the reader to know precisely where we part company, it has been necessary to limit the consideration to a highly simplified type of firm under severely simple conditions—a wheat trader in a perfect market. Since the analysis is restricted to this type of firm, the conclusions must also, strictly speaking, be so restricted. This is a serious limitation since such firms are rare. Despite this limitation the simple firm was utilized for the following reasons:

1. It was felt that it would be more beneficial to try to settle one issue, however small, than to continue the global argument for another century.

2. Although such firms are rare, they do in fact exist. This analysis then has a domain of applicability in the real world.

3. The method of using a simple model to cast light on more complex situations has been used with great success in other disciplines. Physics, for example, considers frictionless forces, perfectly rigid

bodies, absolute zero temperatures, and other nonexistent idealized models. These models or idealized constructions are then used to develop theories that are applied to real forces, bodies, and temperatures. Perhaps it would be beneficial if accounting made use of this method. Real firms are too complex and diverse to permit a definitive analysis. Undoubtedly this complexity and diversity is a major reason why the argument over income has not been resolved. Perhaps the detailed analysis of a simple firm can be extended, *mutatis mutandis,* to the complex firms.[1]

THE STRUCTURE OF THE ARGUMENT

The argument starts from a relatively naive position. A definition of income is shown to be generally accepted, and the point of disagreement is shown to be in the implementation of that definition insofar as it concerns valuation. A wheat trader is then postulated in order to precisely state the alternative valuation methods and recast the problem at its origin. The recast problem leads to a consideration of the notions of information and measurement. From those considerations some criteria are drawn and those criteria are utilized to select the appropriate valuation method.

Part II takes a different tack. The literature concerning the alternative valuation methods is subjected to close scrutiny. Criticism is leveled from the viewpoint of the information-measurement criteria developed in Part I and also from the traditional economic viewpoint. Both Part I and Part II have the same goal—the selection of a valuation method—but the procedure varies. Part I is selection from alternative proposals; Part II is selection by elimination.

Part III relaxes the stable-price-level and perfect-market assump-

1. The author has considered two other models in some detail—the "merchandiser," or inventory holder, who buys in one market and sells in another, and the "producer," or fabricator, who buys factors of production and sells finished goods —with fairly good results. These models, however, are also oversimplified in the sense that many real firms are a combination of trader, merchandiser, and producer. This has been named the "complex firm model" and it is much more recalcitrant to a demonstrable solution. Nonetheless we remain optimistic about the firm-model approach.

tions. We will examine the problems created by an unstable price level, criticize some of the proposals made to deal with that problem, and make some recommendations. Also we will examine the problems of determining prices when the market is imperfect.

II

THE DEFINITION OF INCOME AND THE COMPETING SCHOOLS OF THOUGHT

For the purpose of this study we will use the definition presented by Hicks, Simons, Haig, Alexander, *et al.*, as the fundamental basis for our discussion of the measurement of income.

Probably the most well-known of these definitions is Hicks's:

> The purpose of income calculations in practical affairs is to give people an indication of the amount which they can consume without impoverishing themselves. Following out this idea, it would seem that we ought to define a man's income as the maximum value which he can consume during a week, and still expect to be as well off at the end of the week as he was at the beginning. Thus, when a person saves, he plans to be better off in the future; when he lives beyond his income, he plans to be worse off. Remembering that the practical purpose of income is to serve as a guide for prudent conduct, I think it is fairly clear that this is what the central meaning must be. (Hicks, p. 172.)

This definition is almost ideal for our purposes because of the explicit statement that income is to be a "guide for prudent conduct." We shall lay a considerable amount of emphasis upon income being a guide for prudent conduct, or, in the more modern and Americanized terminology, we shall emphasize that income calculations should be useful for decision-making purposes. The decisions in this paper, however, will be considerably broader than the usual decision-theory type of problem. The extant literature on "Decision Theory" is aimed primarily at managerial profit maximization;[1] the decisions which we will be concerned with will not be so restricted. We will include the decisions of other people who are interested in the enterprise.

Hicks continues to discuss several approximations to the central meaning of his definition of income. Even though we have accepted Hicks's definition, we will not necessarily concur with his analysis of approximations to the central meaning of his income concept. For example, we will specifically quarrel with his statement that "*Ex post* calculations of capital accumulation have their place in economic and statistical *history;* they are a useful measuring-rod for economic progress; but they are of no use to theoretical economists, who are trying to find out how the economic system works, because they have *no significance for conduct.*" (Hicks, p. 179, italics added. See also Hayek, pp. 336 ff.) We will argue that an interpretation of the ex post calculation is a necessary datum for correct decisions and thus that it does have "significance for conduct."

Taxation theory, with its emphasis on income tax, has of necessity been an area that has closely examined various concepts of income. One such examination in the United States was made by Haig. He defines income as the "increase or accretion in one's power to satisfy his wants in a given period in so far as that power consists of (a) money itself, or, (b) anything susceptible of valuation in terms of money." (Haig, p. 59.) It is interesting to note the striking similarity between Haig's and Hicks's concepts of income, although it is clear that their basic assumptions about the use of that income were quite different. Haig was working on a problem of getting an equitable method of levying income taxes; Hicks was concerned not with taxation but with

---

1. Much of the current literature is devoted to variants on the maximum-profit theme. Some concentrate on minimizing costs, with an assumed, often tacit, demand level. Others concentrate on time minimization, with the implicit notion of the opportunity costs attached to time. We consider these, and other like developments, to be nothing more than special cases of profit maximization.

the practical conduct of affairs. Nevertheless, they came to the same conclusions as to the definition of income. This should be an important datum bearing on the prevailing notion that there is no single measurement of income that is proper for all purposes.[2] The notion of different incomes for different purposes is quite the vogue in this day and age, but, surprisingly enough, income definitions derived for different purposes do not necessarily vary.

Simons, writing contemporaneously with both Hicks and Haig, defines income as follows:

> Personal income connotes, broadly, the exercise of control over the use of society's scarce resources. It has to do not with sensations, services, or goods but rather with rights which command prices (or to which prices may be imputed). Its calculation implies estimate (a) of the amount by which the value of a person's store of property rights would have increased, as between the beginning and end of the period, if he had consumed (destroyed) nothing, or (b) of the value of rights which he might have exercised in consumption without altering the value of his store of rights. In other words, it implies estimate of consumption and accumulation. (Simons, p. 49.)

This definition is consistent with those of Hicks and Haig. A secondary purpose of Simons' statement is to reject Fisher's concept of income. The phrase "sensations, services or goods" is obviously, albeit tacitly, a quarrel with Fisher.

This quarrel is not relevant to this study. This study is restricted to the consideration of enterprise income, while Fisher's analysis is of *personal* income. Fisher's concept is almost exclusively psychic, and since, by definition, an enterprise can have no psyche, both the problems and the method of approach are different. Fisher disqualifies himself in the consideration of enterprise income by writing: "It is

2. For example, Boulding states, "The concept of profit [income] will quite rightly differ depending upon the purpose for which we need it. The definition of profit for tax purposes, for instance, may differ considerably from the definition which is required for other forms of decision-making. What we need here is not a single definition of profit applicable to all cases, but a spectrum of definitions, in which the relationship of the various concepts is reasonably clear and in which the definition is fitted to the purpose for which it is to be used." (Boulding, "Twins," p. 45.)

interesting to observe that a corporation as such can have no net income. Since a corporation is a fictitious, not a real, person, each of its items without exception is doubly entered. Its stockholders may get income from it, but the corporation itself, considered as a separate person apart from these stockholders, receives none." (Fisher, *Interest,* p. 23. See Fisher, *Capital,* for a full explanation of "doubly entered," especially pp. 159-64.) If we were to accept Fisher's thesis, this study would end at this point; therefore it is clear that we must disagree in order to continue. The point of disagreement, however, is at the premise, not in the analysis. Fisher assumes that a psychic experience must occur before there is "income." We make no such assumption in our definition, and appeal to the linguistic fact that something called "income" has been utilized for many years, both in common parlance and scientific inquiry, as a measure of the "success" of an enterprise.

Even Fisher's disciples disagree with him on this issue. Lindahl, who has probably done more than any other single person in advancing Fisher's thesis, takes him to task: "Irving Fisher's analysis is carried out in a masterly fashion, but all his attempts to demonstrate that this concept of income is the usual one and that it is the only logical one, must be considered unsatisfactory. In neither popular nor scientific terminology are income and consumption equated. . . ." (Lindahl, p. 400.)

Lindahl, after this disagreement has been stated, proceeds to develop a theory of income based upon Fisher's analysis, particularly upon the concept of *Ertrag,* or yield. The differences between Lindahl and Hicks or Simons are concerned with the valuation of wealth, not with a different definition of income. Lindahl is in agreement with the definitions presented above; his quarrel is with the method of valuation.

In a more modern context, Alexander writes (p. 127): "A year's income is, fundamentally, the amount of wealth that a person, real or corporate, can dispose of over the course of the year and remain as well off at the end of the year as at the beginning." Again, the definition is equivalent to the several presented above except for the inconsequential change of the time period from one week to one year. As Alexander continues (p. 127): "Another set of problems, which concern the question of what is meant by 'as well off at the end of the year as at the beginning,' is the principal subject of the present monograph."

Thus, Alexander is concerning himself with the problem of valuation at two time points. His conclusion is essentially the same as Boulding's: ". . . many variant concepts [of income] can be conceived, each of which has certain advantages for a particular purpose." (Alexander, p. 127.)

The above definitions of income are all by economists. Much ado has been made in recent years about the differences between the economists' and the accountants' concepts of income. The quarrel is semantic. Accountants also accept the definition; their method of valuation is the variant.

A reference to the basic accounting equation—assets equal equities —proves the point. Accountants array the assets and liabilities of a given enterprise at a point in time and "value"[3] them. At a subsequent point in time, usually a year later, the accountants repeat the process. The difference between the proprietorship or owner's equity at these two points, properly adjusted for investment and disinvestment, is equal to the owner's income for that period. Almost every basic textbook in accounting has a problem which can be stated mathematically as:

$$A(t_i) - L(t_i) = P(t_i)$$
$$P(t_{i+1}) - P(t_i) = Y$$

where A, L, and P are Assets, Liabilities, and Proprietorship and t_i is a time index. Y is the income for the period t_i to t_{i+1}, assuming there has been no investment or disinvestment. Montgomery (p. 206) makes this explicit by remarking: "If an absolutely accurate balance sheet could be prepared at the beginning and the end of a period, the difference would represent the net profit or the net loss for the term." He rejects that method, however, because "the valuation and revaluation of capital assets involve too much speculation."

More recently and more directly Gordon has stated: ". . . *we all agree* with Hicks who defined 'a man's income as the maximum value which he can consume during a week, and still expect to be as well off

3. There is a quarrel whether the accountant "values" assets or does something else. The entire rationale of "unexpired costs" has been attacked, and the debate has been over whether "costs" are "values." Simons has taken the position that the accountant does *not* value because different costs exist for the same goods. See p. 14 *infra.*

at the end of the week as at the beginning.' Disagreement arises as to the operational meaning to be given to the phrase 'as well off.'" (Gordon, p. 606, italics added.)

In summary, the definition or concept of income as being "the difference between wealth at two points of time plus consumption" is agreed upon by almost all writers. We will utilize this definition in this study as a fundamental premise.

THE PROBLEM AND SUGGESTED SOLUTIONS

The above section pointed out the concurrence of opinion about the definition or concept of income among economists as well as between economists and accountants. The problem then is not with the definition of income, but with the application of the income concept in a specific instance. The basic disagreement centers around the phrase "as well off" in the definition. There are at least four[4] different approaches to the measurement of how "well off" a person or enterprise is: (1) the Fisher Tradition, (2) the Accounting Tradition, (3) Present Market Prices, and (4) Boulding's Constant.

The Fisher Tradition[5]

> In the absence of dividend payments and new contributions by stockholders, income is measured at the end of the period by adding up the discounted values of all net receipts which the managers then expect to earn on the firm's existing net assets and subtracting from this subjective value a similar computation made at the beginning of the period. (Edwards and Bell, pp. 24-25.)

The key word in the above quotation is "expect." In the Fisher Tradi-

---

4. There are almost as many ways of classifying income concepts as there are writers on the subject. For example, Hicks (pp. 171-77) lists three; Hansen (pp. 15 ff.) lists three different concepts of the Fisher Tradition and refers to a fourth presented by Kristenson; Kerr (pp. 40-48) lists three which are subclassifications of the Accounting Tradition; Wueller discusses a great many without ever bothering to classify them except in the most general terms. In brief, this classification is not natural or infallible, it is only convenient. However, the attempt has been to state each one broadly enough to include all the extant concepts.

5. Although, as noted above, Fisher disqualified himself from the measurement of enterprise income, Lindahl, Hansen, Canning, and others have developed a concept of income that springs directly from Fisher's *Ertrag*. Thus, we classify this concept as being in "The Fisher Tradition."

tion, expectations about the future are the basis of the measurement of income.

Since future receipts must be predicted and cannot, by definition, be measured, what one is measuring under this tradition is the owner's and/or manager's expectations or feelings about the future. In the case of personal income these feelings are part of the psychic benefits received by the individual. In the case of enterprise income, since the enterprise cannot have feelings, what one is measuring are the feelings or expectations of the managers. Thus, the measurement of well-offness is dependent upon management's prognostication of what the future holds.

Criticism of this concept usually falls into two categories: (1) it is subjective, and (2) the future is uncertain.

The first criticism—subjectivity—appears to be the crucial one for most writers. The concept is usually rejected out-of-hand, because it is subjective. This problem is considered below in connection with measurement. Suffice it to say at this point that these "subjective" valuations must be made, as will be demonstrated below, and that the distinction between objectivity and subjectivity is highly confused. We would not regard this criticism without further qualification as sufficient reason to reject the method.

The second criticism—uncertainty—is not directed against the theory per se. Instead it is concerned with the problem of applying the theory, because it requires that the future be known when the future is in fact unknown. That is, many writers seem to take the position that if the future were certain there would be no problem of income determination under the Fisher Tradition. For example, Moonitz and Jordan go through "a valuation experiment" in which they assume complete certainty of the future. They conclude as follows: "How much of the data shown for each year can be reflected in a matching of cost and revenue under the practical difficulties with which we are forced to contend under ordinary circumstances? That these difficulties stem mainly from the fact that we cannot know what the events will be during the entire future life of an enterprise is now apparent." (Moonitz and Jordan, I, 135.)

The implication is that if the future were known with certainty there would be at least fewer, and perhaps no, problems of income determination. Such a sanguine view of this method under certainty is not taken by other people who are working with the development of this theory. Hansen (pp. 39 ff.) describes several theoretical difficulties that would not disappear even under conditions of certainty. The value of the whole not equalling the sum of the values of the components is an example. We will examine the Fisher Tradition below and point up several other unresolved problems even under conditions of certainty.

The Accounting Tradition

"In keeping with the principle that accounting is primarily based on cost" (AICPA Bulletin 43, p. 28), this approach appears to be antithetical to that presented above. That is, the Fisher Tradition was concerned with future expectations; while accounting, based on historical cost, is concerned with past acts. The fact that accounting is concerned with the past is one major source of criticism. If we accept Jevons' dictum that "in commerce bygones are bygones," this criticism seems to have merit. However, if there are other purposes for the measurement of income, e.g. the administration of working capital,[6] then the criticism can be met by stating a variance in purposes of the measurement.

In addition, accounting is sometimes criticized because it is not a valuation method: "One might say that he [the accountant] often eschews valuation entirely. At least, one finds difficulty in the idea that an inventory is being 'valued' when different parts of an inventory of identical goods are priced differently—as is approved practice." (Simons, p. 80n.) This depends upon the definition of "valuation." Moonitz and Jordan take the view that the problem is one of valuation and that cost is one method of expressing value and, further, that it is the desirable method.

> Accounting literature of the past quarter-century is replete with discussions of a supposed conflict between cost and value as a leading postulate in accounting. The preceding discussion has shown that there can be no conflict because the two concepts are not co-ordinate. The concept of value is the major one; cost

6. Devine reports that the administration of working capital has been an explicit objective of income calculations. That is, income should have something to do with the ability to pay dividends. (Devine, p. 163.)

is *one* method or formula for expressing value. In many cases, cost is probably the most useful formula to follow, but it is still only one procedure. In brief, the "conflict" raises a false issue. (Moonitz and Jordan, I, 169.)

We agree. Income and wealth calculations require that objects be "valued" in the general sense of that term. The quarrel is over how they ought to be valued, and "cost" or purchase price is one method of valuation. However, this point is not crucial in this analysis. If one wants to call what the accountant does nonvaluation, it will not affect this study. For convenience, we will use the term "value" to describe all four schools and call each of them a "valuation method."

Simons objects to calling "cost" valuation because identical items receive different unit values. The deviation within the firm is Simons' concern. Accountants are also concerned with identical items receiving different values, but their emphasis is on uniformity of accounting methods. For example, Bows (p. 44) criticizes the lack of uniformity in current accounting practice by positing two identical firms and noting that a value deviation of several hundred per cent can be arrived at by using different accounting methods. In both cases—within the firm and inter-firm—there are identical items that receive different values. This is a major source of criticism of the Accounting Tradition. It prohibits comparisons. The accountant's reply is that if the accounting method is "disclosed" (the principle of full disclosure) then the figure can be made comparable. This is similar to the operationists' position and is examined below in connection with measurement theory.

The fact that two different accountants could arrive at two different costs with a variation of several hundred per cent should raise some questions about the objectivity of cost valuation. People from other disciplines are not aware of such deviations and often grant the objectivity of costs without argument. For example, Alexander, an economist, writes:

> Another very powerful factor operating on the development of accounting methods has been the attempt to minimize the accountant's responsibility for the human judgments which must be made in passing from a consideration of the accounts to the conduct of business affairs. This desire to avoid responsibility

has led accountants to set up two requirements for sound accounting that somewhat limit the choice of methods. These are the requirements of objectivity and conservatism. (Alexander, p. 128.)

It is certainly true that accountants strive for objectivity, but whether or not they achieve it is a separate question. One wonders whether nonaccountants are aware of the extent of the possible deviations in cost values and if they were aware of them, whether they would be so ready to grant that they are objective.

This point is so often misunderstood that it deserves repetition. Most writers outside the field of accounting consider that the word "cost" closes the discussion of objectivity. Nothing could be further from the truth. Most of the writing about accounting could be classified as explaining what accountants mean by cost and how it is determined. Voluminous tomes have been written concerning the definition of "cost." Paton and Paton have made the matter explicit by criticizing their colleagues as some of the worst offenders in considering cost objective. They write: "Accountants are supposed to be thoroughly familiar with this situation [difficulty of determining cost] and hence the faith that some of them seem to have in the objectivity and reliability of compiled cost data is something at which to marvel." (Paton and Paton, p. 54.) Objectivity is a key issue in the Accounting Tradition. Many people outside of accounting grant that costs are objective, and many accountants make the same claim. Other accountants disagree and marvel at their colleagues. As mentioned above, the notion of objectivity is confused, and part of the problem is in making it operational so that one can decide when something is or is not objective. See Chapter VI for a further discussion.

Market Value

The notion that present market value is the correct method of valuation is supported by Simons, Haig, and Alexander, among others. Alexander (p. 137) states: "It is probably obvious to most people that market value is the appropriate measure of well-being associated with each item of wealth in a man's possession." It certainly is not obvious to accountants that market value is the appropriate measure. Quite the contrary, accountants consider market values to be obviously inappropriate. Paton and Littleton (pp. 123-24, italics added) contrast "estimated current market values" to the "*standard* scheme of income determination" and argue that "such procedure would be entirely futile from the standpoint of the measurement of periodic income." To Paton and Littleton, and to most other accountants, the matching of costs and revenues is "obviously" the appropriate measure of income. They write: "The primary purpose of accounting, as has been explained, is the measurement of periodic income by means of a systematic process of matching costs and revenues." (Paton and Littleton, p. 123.)

Some accountants have taken the position that current market value is the proper method of valuation. MacNeal set forth the position in some detail in the 1930's, and recently Edwards and Bell have developed a theory of "realizable" and "business income" which uses current market values. In a recent article Sprouse has criticized the historical cost method as being "treacherous." However, these are heterodox views. The orthodox accounting view is the cost method of valuation, as is evidenced by the great majority of the accounting literature as well as the practice of accounting.

Thus, the orthodox view in accounting is that market values are not appropriate in the measurement of income. The primary criticism is the recurrent theme of objectivity. It is thought that costs are actual facts of economic experience, while market values are merely estimates that are too subjective to be used.

A second criticism of market values stems from the notion that an increase in market value is not income because it is not "separated" or "realized." This has become legal doctrine (Eisner *v*. Macomber, 252 US 289, 1919), mainly through the efforts of Seligman who presented the following argument as a brief to the court: ". . . the real point is the separation of the increment from the capital. This separation is necessary in order to constitute income. The increment when separated is income; the increment unseparated remains capital. Separation and realization are of the essence of the transmutation of capital into income. The capital as such remains intact; the increment or capital gain when actually realized and separated constitutes income." (Seligman, p. 530.) It is not entirely clear from the general statement of the argument exactly what constitutes separation or realization.

However, in the specific examples given by Seligman it seems to turn on the receipt of something in a form different from the form of the original capital. He is specifically arguing that stock dividends are not income because the shareholder "gets only an additional evidence of his share in the undivided and unseparated assets." (Seligman, p. 535.) However, says Seligman, if the dividend were in the form of cash, stock of another corporation, or another commodity, then it would be income.

This is quite similar to the accountant's notion of realization. In the Accounting Tradition an asset must be "converted" [exchanged] to another form before income can be realized. Another similarity is the "capacity to pay" notion. Taxation theorists argue that value increments cannot be considered income because they are not in a form that would permit the payment of taxes. Accountants argue similarly that value increments are not income because they are not in a form that would permit the payment of dividends. Otherwise they seem to be identical ideas. We will discuss this further below.

Boulding's Constant

Professor Boulding seems to be in a class by himself in his suggestion for the use of a constant. While there are many other writers in economics and accounting who would agree with the basic proposition that income is essentially unmeasurable in any completely unassailable fashion, there are few who would go so far as to say that it is so arbitrary that a constant might well be used. Because of the arbitrary element, Boulding suggests a constant. He writes: "All valuation thus seems to possess a certain unavoidable arbitrary element, as long as the asset structure remains heterogeneous . . . . A possible method of escape from this dilemma is to perform all valuations at a constant valuation ratio, independent of the market price." (Boulding, *Reconstruction*, p. 45.)

Boulding is alone in this suggestion and there is no extant criticism of his method. The use of a constant is not a serious contender as a valuation method; but the argument that all methods are arbitrary is a common one. We disagree. We think there is a way to make a rational choice between valuation methods. The main reason for including Boulding's argument is to have the arbitrary school represented.

SUMMARY

There is general agreement on the definition of income among the various schools of thought: Income is the difference between wealth at two points in time plus consumption during the period. The problem centers around the method of determining the wealth or well-offness, and there are four suggested methods of valuation which yield widely varying results. Each of these methods has supporters and detractors, advantages and disadvantages. Sometimes one school will utilize a standard to judge another school when it is not entirely clear that either school would meet that standard, e.g. both Present Market Value and the Fisher Tradition are criticized by the Accounting Tradition on grounds of subjectivity, as if the cost method of valuation were completely objective; while other accountants freely admit the lack of objectivity in the cost method.

Several authors take the position that the purpose of the income measurement will determine which of the methods of valuation should be used and that there is no single correct method. Thus, the "different incomes for different purposes" notion in which more than one valuation method may be used concurrently. The extreme form of the argument that there is no single correct method is presented by Boulding. He argues that the selection process is so arbitrary that a constant valuation ratio might be used.

In the chapters that follow we will use a simple firm model to recast the problem, and we will attempt to set forth some generalized criteria which will allow us to judge the various valuation methods.

III

A DESCRIPTION OF THE FIRM AND
THE PROBLEM RECAST

THE MODEL

The firm model used in this analysis is essentially the same as the one presented by Boulding—a trader in wheat futures in a perfect market. (Boulding, *Analysis*, p. 277; *Reconstruction*, pp. 39 ff.; "Twins," pp. 44 ff.) A cursory review of the necessary assumptions and conditions will be presented below. The interested reader will find a more complete description by Boulding, especially in *Reconstruction*.

In Figure III-1 the model is presented in its entirety. Money in dollars is measured on the y-axis, and wheat in bushels on the x-axis. The simplicity of using only two commodities, although money is a "general" commodity, allows us to picture the "trader"[1] in all possible positions and also to trace the path from one position to the next. This

---

1. Boulding refers to this model as a "pure marketer." "Trader" has been selected here to differentiate between two kinds of marketers—as opposed to producers. In a later study an inventory-holding marketer—"merchandiser"—will be considered.

is one advantage of postulating such a simple firm. In a two-dimensional diagram the present position, all past positions, and all possible future positions are presented visually and cast the problem of valuation in strong relief.[2]

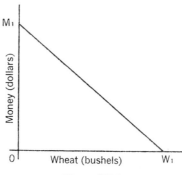

Figure III-1

The Transformation Coefficient

The line in Figure III-1 is referred to by Boulding as a "transformation coefficient." It is the same as a "market price," but Boulding prefers the more general title because it emphasizes the transformational characteristic of prices. It defines all the trader's opportunities in this market. The trader at the present moment, can move to any point on this line from M_1 to W_1 in the ratio implied by the slope of the curve. The trader cannot move to any point away from the curve and remain in the market. This is the difference between this transformation coefficient and the production-transformation function more generally used in economics.[3]

---

2. It is also possible, as Boulding shows, to present "negative wheat" and "negative money," i.e., short selling and debt, by utilizing two other quadrants. However, the existence of debt or short contracts, while real and interesting problems for other purposes, are excluded from consideration in this study because they are only tangential to the central problem.

3. The production-transformation function allows for movements to points below the curve (toward the origin) by un- or under-employment of the resources. Under- or un-employment concepts are not useful in this context of pure exchange, and the curve defines all the possibilities. If commodities are removed or destroyed it simply moves the curve back toward the origin and changes all the opportunities by the same amount.

The model further simplifies considerations by placing severe restrictions upon the activities of the trader. There are only two courses of action open to the trader: He can (1) exchange or (2) hold (the negation of, or refusal to, exchange). If he is at some point away from the axes, he can move in two directions: toward the y-axis (money) or toward the x-axis (wheat). Within the model there is no provision for additions (investment) or deductions (consumption or shifting investments). Moreover, the linearity of the curve implies, and we make explicit, that the trader is operating in a perfect market where his decisions do not affect either the present or future transformation coefficients.[4] Thus, an exhaustive statement of the trader's alternatives within this market is that he may (1) hold (maintain the status quo) or (2) exchange along an externally determined and completely defined route.

The Valuation Coefficient

In order to determine the "net worth" or "total value of assets"[5] when heterogeneous assets[6] are held, it is necessary to express one asset in terms of the other.[7] In Figure III-2 the trader has moved along a transformation curve (not shown) to point X_1, and we wish to cal-

---

4. We mean by perfect market simply that the changes in price are exogenous. The other requirements for a perfect market, such as perfect knowledge, are not germane so long as the trader cannot affect the present or future price by his actions.

5. The two terms are equal magnitudes since we have excluded debt.

6. As we will see below, heterogeneity is not the cause of the problem, but it is usually stated in this context.

7. More accurately, it is necessary to find a property common to both assets. A third unit of measure could be used, such as francs or ounces, but this would not add anything to the analysis; it would simply require a third dimension on the graph. However, it points out that we have not started from a completely naive position because we are already measuring wheat in bushels (volume) and dollars in numerosity. There is nothing inherently wrong with weighing both commodities and summing their weights. The prime problem is to decide what unit of measure to use, and the fact that we have already spoken of "valuation" and "expressing one commodity in terms of the other" further emphasizes that we had some preconceptions at the start. There is no a priori reason why one should value instead of weighing, and there is nothing in information or measurement theory that would permit one to choose. Such a choice requires exogenous criteria.

culate the value of his net worth. In order to do so we will draw off
a valuation curve (arbitrary in this case) V_m to V_w.[8]

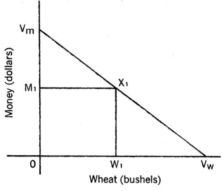

Figure III-2

The value of the enterprise can now be expressed as OV_m in money or
as OV_w in wheat. This is made up of two parts: OW_1, amount of
wheat, multiplied by the slope of the curve, and the product added to
OM_1 (muliplied by unity since money is the measuring agent in this
case) to arrive at OV_m, and the same process for OV_w if wheat were
selected as the valuing agent.

More generally, let p_m be the valuation coefficient of dollars, p_w be
the valuation coefficient of bushels of wheat, and W_i and M_i be the
respective quantities. Then

$$p_mM_i + p_wW_i = \text{Value of total assets.}$$

If $p_m = 1$ then money is defined as the valuing agent and

$$M_i + p_wW_i = V_m.$$

If $p_w = 1$ then wheat is the valuing agent and p_m is bushels per dollar
and

$$p_mM_i + W_i = V_w.$$

The problem—and it is the prime problem of this study—is that the

---

8. We also assume the valuation curve to be linear. If it is not, there are serious
difficulties, e.g. the dimension is not additive. An imperfect market presents another set of problems which are discussed in Chapter VIII.

"proper" or "correct" valuation coefficient is not immediately apparent. Indeed, it is the subject of much debate and controversy.[9]

In the preceding chapter we presented four competing methods of valuation: the Fisher Tradition; the Accounting Tradition; Present Market value; and Boulding's Constant. In terms of the model these are simply different valuation coefficients. Three of the four valuation coefficients are, have been, or are expected to be, transformation co-

Table III-1

Schools	Name of Valuation Coefficient	Relevant Transformation Coefficient
Fisher Tradition	Discounted Expectations	Future—at time of sale
Accounting Tradition	Historical Cost	Past—at time of purchase
Present Market	Current Value	Present—the existing price at time the report is prepared
Boulding's Constant	Arbitrary Constant	None

9. We can agree with Boulding when he says: "Without knowing a set of valuation coefficients, therefore, we cannot tell whether the point P is 'larger' or 'smaller' than P_1" ("Twins," p. 48); and "If, then, we are to say whether *any* given change represents a gain or a loss, and even more if we are to be able to measure the gain or loss, we must have a system of valuation" (*Reconstruction*, p. 43). However, we cannot agree with him when he says: "It is clear that, as the various transformations are made and the speculator traces out the path P_0P_1 . . . P_7, he reaches certain positions which are quite obviously superior to his starting point . . . P_5 is unquestionably a preferable position to P_0, for it represents a greater quantity of *both* assets than does P_0." (*Reconstruction*, p. 43). It is not clear, obvious, or unquestioned that simply because a position represents a greater *quantity* of both assets that it should also represent a *preferable position*.

A preferred position requires the positing of certain assumptions about the motive of the trader or his enterprise. It may be that the trader is trying to maximize something, but it is not clear that the maximization vector is necessarily in the direction of a point between the axes. The vector may be along one axis or nearer one axis than the other. Also, it is difficult to speak of a superior position without some knowledge of the trader's expectations, even if we have identified the maximization vector.

If Boulding is speaking only of a greater *quantity* representing a greater *value*, then we must agree, if the valuing agent has a constant valuation coefficient. Obviously then, a greater quantity of the valuing agent would yield a greater value so long as the other commodity's value was not less than zero.

efficients. The Fisher Tradition valuation coefficient is a future (expected) transformation coefficient. The Accounting Tradition uses a past (purchase) transformation coefficient, and the Present Market uses the present (existing) transformation coefficient.

Although other valuation coefficients have been suggested, these are the main contenders, and it is from this set that our selection will be made.[10]

Other Assumptions in the Model

The valuing agent (the commodity selected to express the total value) will be assumed to have a constant valuation coefficient (unity). This assumption implies that if money is selected as the valuing agent a stable price level is assumed. We will later relax the assumption of a stable price level. In addition, we will assume that there is no problem in ascertaining the physical quantities involved.[11]

INCOME WITHIN THE MODEL

In the analysis of the model we will use the generally accepted definition of income, viz., income is the difference between wealth at two points in time plus consumption (dividends for an enterprise). Specifically, we will value the enterprise's assets (equal to net worth) at two points and take the difference.

10. "Shadow" prices, for example, seem to be a natural outcome of linear programming; but that valuation method refers to a production process and is not applicable to the trader model.

11. The difficulty in determining physical quantities is a major problem in present accounting practice although it is not usually stated in those terms. The fundamental unit in present accounting is a "service potential" (See Paton and Littleton or Vatter) and the numerosity of those units is always difficult, and sometimes impossible, to determine. One difficulty is that these units lie in the future in the sense that they are "potential" instead of "actual." This is evidenced by an alternative formulation of the theory in which the fundamental units are called "future benefits." Exactly what is a potential service or benefit is difficult to know, especially in the case of goods which are traded. In the trader case the benefits seem to be simply the money that will be received from the sale of the goods, and the numerosity of the benefits reduces to the number of dollars that will be received. But that process reduces to the Fisher Tradition, where the prime problem is the determination of the number of dollars that will be received. We have avoided problems of this kind by arbitrarily deciding to use bushels and dollars as the units to be valued.

The limitation of "enterprise income" avoids the problem of utility measurement since, by definition, an enterprise can have no wants to be satisfied and hence no utility. If the trader's utility is relevant to the question of enterprise income, we will assume, along with Pigou and other economists, that the utility varies in the same direction as the wealth. However, only the "wealth" (value of assets of the enterprise) will be measured; any adjustment necessary because of the declining marginal utility of wealth is outside the scope of enterprise income.

Income from a Complete Exchange

If at any time the enterprise has all of its assets in the form of the valuing agent, the exchange will be defined as "complete." Following the assumption specified above—the valuing agent has a valuation coefficient of unity—the value of the enterprise is unequivocal when the exchange is complete. Hence, it follows that the measurement of the income is unequivocal between two instants when the exchange is complete at both instants.

Assume that the trader holds W_1 bushels of wheat (the valuing agent in this example) at instant t_1 and W_2 bushels at instant t_2. The income (in bushels of wheat) of the enterprise is W_2 minus W_1 for the time period t_1 to t_2. There is no problem of income determination or valuation coefficient selection when the exchange is complete. Note, however, that if the trader held M_2 dollars at t_2, then we would be unable to calculate his income from t_1 to t_2 without valuing one commodity in terms of the other. Thus, the problem of valuation coefficient selection is met even though the assets held at t_2 are homogeneous.

This is a slight disagreement with Boulding. He states that the problem arises only when heterogeneous assets are held. This may mean heterogeneous assets over time, i.e. an incomplete exchange; and if so, we agree. However, it is clear that the assets may be homogeneous at one instant in time without solving the problem of valuation. Also, if the held asset is homogeneous over time but is not in the form of the valuing agent, the problem would still arise. The point is that the asset must be homogeneous in the form of the valuing agent instantaneously *and* intertemporally before the measurement can be unequivocal.

Wheat was selected as the valuing agent in the above example, and we arrived at an unequivocal measure. However, it is obvious that the valuing agent needs to be more than a chance selection if the income calculation is to be of maximum usefulness. The selection of either commodity as the valuing agent is not dictated by the model; exogeneous criteria must be employed. The selection will be made below.

Income from an Incomplete Exchange

If the enterprise holds any portion of its total assets in a form other than the valuing agent, the exchange is defined as "incomplete." In this case, and only in this case, the problem of valuation arises. Thus, the principal problem of this study may be stated simply as the problem of valuing assets under the condition of an incomplete exchange.

It should again be noted that the problem is not one of valuing heterogeneous assets. The valuation coefficient of the valuing agent has been assumed to be unity, and hence there is no difficulty in valuation. The problem is one of valuing the *other asset(s)* in terms of the valuing agent.

This entire problem could be avoided by simply waiting until the "incomplete" exchange became "complete." Thus, the trivial solution to the problem of income measurement is evident: Wait until the exchange is complete. The problem arises only when the measurement is desired prior to the completion of the exchange. An examination of this desire—the impetus of the problem—is beyond the model and requires specific criteria. This will be discussed below.

Summary

A two-commodity trader model has been presented to facilitate discussion of the problems of income measurement. Income has been defined as the difference between wealth at two instants in time and the major problem is the selection of a valuation coefficient.

We noted that the problem of selecting a valuation coefficient arose only when the measurement was desired prior to the completion of the exchange. Two subsidiary problems were pointed out:

1. The selection of the valuing agent.
2. The impetus of the desire for the measurement.

THE NATURE OF THE ENTERPRISE

In the above section we identified two separate, although related, problems that arise because of considerations outside the model. The purpose of this section is to resolve these problems. Prior to such a resolution, a general discussion of the nature of the enterprise and the trader is necessary in order to make the assumptions, and the criteria which follow from those assumptions, explicit.

The Motive Force of the Enterprise

It is clear that the "enterprise," being an inert thing and an abstraction, can have no motive force. Any motivation imputed to the enterprise, therefore, must spring, ultimately, from humans.

The question of what motivates humans (individuals or groups) is one that is the subject of much disagreement and debate. The "economic man" has long been discredited; and utility theory has been subjected to bitter attack, concurrent with elaborate refinements. In light of this, the wonder of utility theory is not its fidelity to reality, but rather its tenacity and resilience. Since Jevons' original charge that economics must be grounded in utility, the concept has been inescapable.

The author, aware of the attacks and personally having some reservations about the adequacy of the concept, assumes that the maximand of humans, or groups of humans, is utility.

Moreover, this assumption is not restricted to the narrow notion that utility can arise only by consumption. This, in the author's opinion, is the basic flaw in the otherwise brilliant works of Fisher. It appears reasonable to assume that a man can gain satisfaction from the mere fact of being able to consume in addition to gaining satisfaction from the actual act of consumption. The act of consumption is generally agreed to be want-satisfying. The problem is one of timing: Does the expectation that one will be able to satisfy a future want (future consumption) produce the satisfaction of a present want? Fisher's answer is no; any delay in consumption must be compensated for by future consumption that is greater than the present consumption foregone. The author's answer is yes; because of the declining utility of present consumption, a delay in consumption may increase the totality of the satisfactions.

Certainly in the *reductio ad absurdum* case of zero consumption in the future with 100 per cent consumption now, there would be greater utility by waiting. It may be true that the consumers' "telescopic faculty is defective" (Pigou, p. 25), but this does not negate the fact that if a consumer decides to wait, he will increase his utility. The ability to command consumer goods in the future will avoid the disutility of anxiety in addition to the power, prestige, and security (and accompanying utility thereof) that is accorded him because of that command. Consideration of these factors can build a strong case for the willingness of a rational consumer to pay *negative* interest in order to insure future consumption. (This is exactly the situation that the Swiss Banks find themselves in today. They sometimes charge their depositors, instead of paying, interest.) Thus, the mere fact of being able to command goods and services, regardless of whether the command is ever exercised by consumption, is productive of utility.[12]

Thus, we assume that there are two (relevant) sources of utility: (1) consumption and (2) command over goods.

Selection of the Valuing Agent

Undoubtedly, it is apparent that money will be selected as the valuing agent. Nevertheless, we consider it imperative that we go through the selection process for two reasons: First, to point up the criteria used for the selection, and second, to clear up the existing confusion. Surprising as it may seem, the valuing agent is presently a hotly-debated issue, although the debate is not stated in these terms. Further, some writers shift from one valuing agent to another, apparently without ever recognizing what they have done.

The selection of the valuing agent arises from considerations outside the model. The model of the enterprise has no inherent preference for any particular position or commodity. It is indifferent. However, if the trader were indifferent, as is the model, between the two commodities, we would arrive at the anomalous position of the impossibility of losses.

Suppose that the trader enters the market with 100 bushels of wheat and "purchases" 100 dollars. If the price of money (in terms of wheat) now goes to zero, the trader still holds the 100 dollars and has suffered

12. Obviously, this cursory statement is not intended as a definitive refutation of Fisher. The intention is simply to make clear the assumptions of this study by using Fisher as a relief.

no absolute loss.[13] In the same fashion, if the trader enters the market with 100 dollars and purchases 100 bushels of wheat, and the price of wheat (in terms of money) then goes to zero, he still holds the wheat and has lost nothing.

The only thing that is being said in the above example is that the *quantity* of a commodity held is not affected by a price change. It would appear reasonable to assert that if the trader had a given amount of utility associated with a given quantity of a commodity and that quantity remained constant, then the utility would remain constant. If utility is associated with the quantity of a commodity, there is no possibility of diminishing the utility and hence no possibility of a loss.

Obviously, this is not the case. The trader undoubtedly has satisfaction from holding a consumable good, such as wheat, but due to the declining marginal utility of the consumption of a particular good, his total utility would be increased by exchanging it for some good that has a higher marginal utility.[14] Thus, the decline in price of a held good directly causes a decline in the utility of the holder. Moreover, the magnitude of decline in utility varies directly with the quantity of the commodity held; the greater the quantity held, the greater the decline in utility if the price of that commodity decreases.

It is true that a consumable commodity has an absolute floor of utility which is positive while the floor of a price is zero. Thus, in some cases, a price decrease would be greater than the utility decrease. This is a genuine problem in personal income measurement, but it is not a problem of enterprise income measurement. When this floor is reached, the "trader" would become a "consumer" of the commodity and thus subject to the Fisher analysis. This problem is avoided in the present analysis for two reasons: First, the model has restricted the activities to exchanging and holding, thereby excluding consumption; and second, we are here trading wheat *contracts* which have negligible consumption properties.

The point is a simple one. The process of exchange outside the

13. It is true that he has suffered an opportunity loss by not waiting until the dollars could be obtained without the sacrifice of the wheat, but his position has not been diminished by the price change.

14. The exchange will, of course, continue until all the marginal utilities of all goods have been equated. Cf. any basic economics text.

model increases the utility of the trader qua consumer. Money is the general expression of the ability to exchange in a market economy. In an *n* dimensional diagram, the money surface relates all the goods to money which then allows the relation of all goods to one another. Money is the single *numéraire* which performs this relational function and is therefore superior to wheat as a valuing agent.

It is true that money has no value except in exchange, but in the model the wheat contract has no value except as it relates to money. Money has value as it relates to all other wants of the trader, but wheat is one step removed from "value" to the trader qua consumer. For this reason, money is riskless (assuming a stable price level) because there can be no decline in its ability to yield utility, but wheat has a definite risk attached to it since its ability to yield utility depends on its ability to be exchanged for money.[15]

For these reasons we draw the obvious conclusion that money is the superior valuing agent. Money is the general expression of the command over goods. We assumed above that there was utility in the very act of being able to command goods, and here we find money to be the proper expression of that utility, albeit money increments may not equal utility increments.

The Maximand of the Enterprise. We assumed above that the maximand of the trader was utility. Further, we pointed out that the enterprise's motive force was provided by the trader and hence could also be stated as the maximization of utility, and then we concluded that the vehicle for maximization was money. It follows that the maximand of the enterprise is money or the ability to command money.

This conclusion is neither startling nor significantly different from the more common assumption of profit maximization. However, it does state precisely the profit maximization assumption and leaves no room for, say, the maximization of a quantity of wheat with a zero price.[16]

---

15. Again, the holding of money has an opportunity risk attached insofar as the trader might miss a profitable exchange, but there is no risk of a utility decrease if there is a stable price level.

16. Many authors state the assumption as maximization of "money profit" (Stonier and Hague, pp. 87-88) or "financial profits," and in one case at least to "make money" (Abbott, p. 137). The vast majority state the maximization of profit without a modifier, which leads Boulding to note that "the quantity which

The author is aware of the contributions by the empiricists and behaviorists to motivation theory and the consequent weakening of the strict interpretation of profit maximization. There is no quarrel with those contributions in this study. On the contrary, our total understanding has been enriched by Burnham's "separation of ownership and control," Lester's questionnaires, Simon's (p. 262) "satisficing," Boulding's insistence upon a return to utility (*Skills*, p. 28), and a host of other contributors and concepts.

Three separate (but related) arguments may still be advanced in spite of these contributions.

First, one can reasonably assume, *cet. par.*—that is, if all other things to be maximized or satisficed (e.g., leisure of trader, customer goodwill, potential entrants and competitors, taxation, empire building, management-owner-creditor-taxing-authority-consumer-labor conflicts, prestige, etc.) remain constant, it is reasonable to assume that a larger profit will be preferred to a smaller profit.

Second, if some maximand is not posited, it is difficult to make either preferential or determinate statements about the firm. That is, a theory or construct must be set up about the nature of the thing described before a *meaningful* description can be made.

Third, and most important for this study, is the fact that we made this assumption only for the purpose of selecting a valuing agent, a selection which the reader would probably have granted without the analysis. Once the valuing agent has been agreed on, the decision model that is presented below can be equally well utilized for minimizing the money profits if that is what is desired.

Presentation of the above arguments should not be interpreted as an attempt to negate other goals of the enterprise. Solvency, for example, is obviously a prerequisite for the continuity of operations. Thus, if the objective of continuity of the enterprise exists, solvency is necessarily a subobjective of continuity. Likewise, however, continuity is a subobjective of money-profit maximization. It may be necessary to

---

is supposed to be maximized does not exist!" (Boulding, *Skills*, p. 56). Perhaps profit in the abstract doesn't exist, but money increments do, and that, for better or worse, is our assumption.

make the objective more precise by adding the modifier "long-run,"[17] but the fact remains that there is "one overriding goal: the maximization of money profits." (Stigler, p. 148.)

Continuity, per se, may very well be the overriding goal of a subgroup, such as management, but it is unlikely that even the managers would continue if there were a "better" (more profitable) alternative available, *cet. par.* It is almost certain that the owners would not continue if there were, *cet. par.*, a better alternative. In short, the author casts his lot with Berle, who observes:

> . . . it is still true that a non-Statist economic organization cannot continue to exist and enjoy power (let alone enhance its position) unless it makes profits. Therefore the operation of such organizations must be directed toward reaping profits, and they must move within the general limitations of the profit system. . . . Increased capital for a corporation means increased power. Capital losses mean loss of power and eventual extinction. . . . (Berle, p. 90.)

In summary, we assume:

1. The trader's maximand is utility.
2. The *raison d'être* of the enterprise is to maximize the trader's maximand.
3. Utility varies in the same direction as the ability to command goods and services.
4. Money is the appropriate expression of the ability to command goods.
5. Therefore, the prime maximand of the enterprise is money (or ability to command money), and the correct valuing agent is money.

THE TIMING OF THE MEASUREMENT

As noted above, the problem of selecting a valuation coefficient arises only when the exchange is incomplete. The measurement can be stated as two alternative times:

1. The timing of the measurement is determined by the state of

---

17. This may become a dead issue as the distinction between the "runs" becomes less clear through further research and refinement. For example, Furubotn takes the position that the entrepreneur, in a complex industrial society, *must* constantly be working in a mixture of "runs" for his investment decision.

the exchange; i.e., income is measured (assets valued) at the time the exchange becomes complete.

2. The timing of the measurement is determined by an external desire at some particular instant in time, regardless of the state of the exchange.

Alternative one is the trivial solution: Since the valuing agent has a valuation coefficient of unity (by assumption) and the state of a completed exchange is when the assets are homogeneous in the form of the valuing agent (by definition), there is no problem in the measurement of income.

Alternative two embodies the significant problems. Indeed the underlying problem of this study can be stated as a desire for income measurement when the exchange is incomplete.

The impetus of this desire is obvious: *information is wanted.* Information is required because time has reached some specified instant, because time has elapsed since the last information was received; and therefore there is uncertainty about the events that may have occurred in the interim. Thus, the concept of income has a vital, indispensable, temporal dimension. The desire for information is the prime cause of the measurement, and this desire occurs at some instant in time. We may say, then, that time is the fundamental independent variable of the measurement of income. The advent of a specific temporal location triggers the measurement. Moreover, income is a concept bounded by time; it is a phenomenon that occurs within a time interval. Simons has cautioned against neglecting this relationship:

> The relation of the income concept to the specified time interval is fundamental—and neglect of this crucial relation has been responsible for much confusion in the relevant literature. The measurement of income implies allocation of consumption and accumulation to specified periods. In a sense, it implies the possibility of measuring the results of individual participation in economic relations *for an assigned interval* and without regard for anything which happened before the beginning of that (before the end of the previous) interval or for what may happen in subsequent periods. All data for the measurement would be found, ideally, within the period analyzed. (Simons, p. 50.)

Unfortunately, Simons' charge has been ignored or misunderstood.

Neglect of the temporal dimension is still a problem, and confusion is still the result.

Information is desired at an instant in time about the events within a time period. A measurement is made, and the results are transmitted in accordance with this desire. If the exchange is complete, there is no problem. If the exchange is incomplete, the measurement is made by means of a valuation coefficient. One overall criterion for the selection of a valuation coefficient is its "informational content." The valuation coefficient that contains the most information is the one that should be selected. Thus, our first criterion.

Criterion I: A valuation coefficient that yields more information is superior to a valuation coefficient that yields less information.

As it stands this criterion is much too general to be of use in this study. "Information" is a complex concept. In order to make the criterion applicable to the problem at hand, it is necessary to examine the concept of information in some detail. That examination is the purpose of the next chapter.

SUMMARY

The purpose of this study is to deveolp a theory of measurement of income for a trading enterprise. Hicks's definition of income is accepted by most scholars, and we will utilize it as a basic premise in this work.

The problem lies in the various implementations of the definition in the measurement of wealth. There are four competing concepts of valuation: (1) the Fisher Tradition, (2) the Accounting Tradition, (3) Market Value, and (4) Boulding's Constant.

A trading model will be utilized to analyze the problem. Such a model has the virtue of simplicity and will allow us to picture all possible positions that the trader can obtain. The activities of the trader in this model are restricted to holding or exchanging along a completely defined and externally determined route. We call this route the "transformation coefficient."

The position of the trader must be expressed as a "value" in order to determine his wealth. "Value" is the product of a quantity and a "valuation coefficient." There are four alternative valuation coefficients, three of which are transformation coefficients:

1. The Fisher Tradition—Future transformation coefficient.
2. The Accounting Tradition—Past transformation coefficient.
3. Present Market—Present transformation coefficient.
4. Boulding's Constant.

When all assets are held in the form of the valuing agent we will call this a "complete exchange." The valuing agent is assumed to have a valuation coefficient of unity, and thus the income is subject to an unequivocal measurement under conditions of a complete exchange. An incomplete exchange is defined as assets held in a form other than the valuing agent. Thus, the problem is recast as selecting the correct valuation coefficient under conditions of an incomplete exchange.

After a consideration of the nature of the enterprise, money was selected as the proper valuing agent. This was done by assuming that the trader's motivation is utility. We noted that there are two sources of utility: (1) consumption and (2) command over goods. Money is the general expression for command over goods and is the medium for obtaining consumption. The trader furnishes the motive force for the enterprise, hence the maximand of the enterprise is money profits.

An inquiry into the reason for the valuation of assets led us to the obvious conclusion that information was desired at a point in time, regardless of the state of the exchange. Thus, our first criterion for selection of a valuation coefficient is the information that it furnishes. The concept of information is the subject of the next chapter.

IV

Given Criterion I from the preceding chapter, a possible reformulation of the problem of this study is as follows:

> Determination of the informational content of the alternative valuation coefficients.

If we could determine the informational content of each valuation coefficient, the problem of this study would be solved. Thus, an examination of the concept of information is pertinent. Such an examination will necessarily be incomplete because information theory has become a separate field of study. Like other fields it has various subdivisions and one can concentrate on the linguistic, logical, engineering, physiological, sociological, etc., aspects of information. The field has been classified in various ways. Some speak of the technical, semantic, and effectiveness problems. Others divide the field into syntactics, semantics, and pragmatics. Again, as in most other fields, these divisions have overlapping boundaries. Our discussion will be concerned mainly with the effectiveness, or pragmatic, area of the field. This is the area that has to do with the "usefulness," "value," or "importance" of information, and, as might be expected by the occurrence of such terms, it is the most difficult and therefore least-developed area of information theory.

In the succeeding chapter the concept of measurement will be discussed. The two concepts—measurement and information—are difficult to separate completely, hence the discussion will overlap at several points. For purposes of clarity, however, we will attempt to separate the concepts and discuss them seriatim.

The terms "information" and "communications" are sometimes used synonymously in the literature.[1] We will break with this usage in an attempt to be more precise. We will use "communications" as a general term describing the transmission of *unevaluated* messages. "Information" will be restricted to the description of *useful* messages.

INFORMATION

If a message is to be useful there are two prerequisites: (1) verity and (2) relevance. If a message does not accurately describe reality, its usefulness is, at least, severely limited. Likewise, the message must be relevant to the problem under consideration before it can be of use to that problem.[2]

---

1. For example, Shannon and Weaver's pioneering work was entitled *The Mathematical Theory of Communication,* and Goldman's "thorough discussion of that work" was entitled *Information Theory.*

Likewise, in measurement theory the notion is that one measures in order to communicate with himself as well as with others. Churchman argues that all measurements fall in the category of communications. He writes: "Robinson Crusoe cannot bring along his hut as he searches for a flagstone for his hearth. But he does need to compare an experience on the beach with a past experience in his hut. . . . Even if there were but one mind in all the world, such a castaway would need to compare the experience of one moment and place with that of another moment and place. He would have to communicate with his own past." (Churchman, *Definitions,* p. 89.)

2. McDonough (p. 87) describes information as having two basic attributes— validity and value: "Validity implies that one can have confidence in a statement, whereas value indicates that the statement is worthwhile knowing." Validity in his context must be a synonym for "truth." This is an odd use of "validity." It usually applies to arguments, not information. Perhaps he was trying to avoid a metaphysical discussion by avoiding truth concepts. We use "verity" and explicitly skirt the metaphysics.

We disagree with McDonough when he describes "validity [verity] as the prime

Verity

The concept of verity may be described as "conformance with reality." A message is a verbal or symbolic proposition which purports to say something about the "real world." If the message describes the real world faithfully, then we will say that it is "veritable"; and this is a necessary condition for it to be termed "information." If the message does not faithfully describe the world, then it will be termed "misinformation."

Although this distinction seems clear and obvious, there are grave problems in both application and concept. There are many conflicting schools of thought concerning reality, including schools that deny that a meaningful separation between the real world and our concepts can be made. Others take the real world to be *just* the world of appearances. Sense-data or personal sensations *are* the real world under that view. Some think of theories as being models (replicas, maps) of the real world. Whitehead has complained about scientists who think of theoretical entities, constructs, and the like as being real, and he named their practice "the fallacy of misplaced concreteness." Kant believed that we could not know the real world but that we acquired knowledge through reason and then *imposed* the results of our reasoning (theories) upon the real world. Rationalists believe they can discover truth by reason alone. Empiricists of the pure or extreme variety think that they can discover connections between things in the real world without benefit of any preconceptions or theories. Conventionalists believe that one can *choose* to regard the world in any way he likes, and they demonstrate that a particular theory cannot be overthrown by observations about the real world. Thus, theories seem to have an independent existence regardless of whether or not there *is* a real world.[3] Operationalists argue that a concept is nothing more than the operation performed and that different operations therefore constitute different concepts (or dimensions). This makes "length"

---

characteristic inasmuch as it is a prerequisite to value" (p. 87). We see no reason to rank the two attributes. If it is not worthwhile to know a statement, then it is hardly information regardless of its validity.

3. See the works of Poincaré and Duhem for a full treatment of this rather startling view. Briefly the argument is that theories are in the form of "If p then

measured by a meter stick different from "length" measured by light rays, which is different from "length" measured by sound reflections, etc. Yet clearly the concept of length is the same regardless of how it is measured, as is indicated by the use of the same units in the mentioned operations.

Since Locke and Descartes scientific inquiry has been essentially dualistic. It has included both the reasoning and the world. Sometimes this is called "scientific realism," and we will follow that *assumption* in this discussion. That is, we will take the world to be more than just phenomena—objects will have qualities other than sense-data—and the message is an attempt to partially describe the real world.[4]

The import of making this assumption is that it permits us to clearly distinguish, in concept, analytic from contingent propositions. Analytic propositions are true by virtue of the constituent terms used in the proposition and by the rules of the logic employed, e.g. "fifteen is one-half of thirty" and "a bachelor is an unmarried adult male." Contingent propositions are empirical statements, and the proposition, as well as its negation, is logically possible. For example, "John is a bachelor" and "John is married" are both logically possible; and the truth value of either proposition depends upon observations.

---

q" and then "not-q" would lead to "not-p." But theories are really conjunctions of several antecedents. Thus, the form is "If p_1 and p_2, then q" and under these circumstances "not-q" leads to "not-(p_1 and p_2)" instead of "not-p_1." But "not-(p_1 and p_2)" transforms to "not-p_1 *or* not-p_2." Therefore, "not-q" does not disconfirm the theory, particularly if p_2 is taken to be a condition under which that theory applies. By this argument one can maintain that Eddington's observations did not prove Einstein right. Thus, one can still be Euclidean if he likes just by positing certain conditions or by introducing ad hoc assumptions or principles. Of course, this view is not unchallenged. Grünbaum (p. 137) speaks of the "*separately* falsifiable" geometry "as an *explanans* of the posited empirical findings."

4. Even "scientific realism" requires qualification in contemporary science, particularly in physics. Where one begins to speak of particles that are too small to have color (since they are smaller than a light wave-length) and have no determinate position or size (being subject to the uncertainty principle), etc., then one wonders whether or not such a thing is "real." In addition, there are many terms in scientific theories that are reducible to sense-data; but the reduction is so tortuous that it is hardly recognizable. Thus, an "atom" is often referred to as a theoretical entity or construct as opposed to a real thing. This has led many scientists to return to a kind of Platonic idealism in which it is claimed that scientists talk about things that are only mental constructs.

It is possible to maintain that analytic propositions have zero "informational content." If we were to receive a message that read "John is married or John is a bachelor," we could maintain that we knew that beforehand and thus no information has been received. The same is true for any purely calculational system.[5] For this reason, we will restrict our discussion to messages that are contingent propositions.

The problems of application are equally difficult and in many ways are inseparable from the conceptual problems. Reality is subject to distortion by (1) perception errors and (2) deliberate misrepresentations. Both are fundamental and both are intertwined. If one intends to misrepresent reality, he can be certain that he has succeeded only if he is certain of his perception of reality. However, it is easy to define intent to misrepresent, albeit it may be impossible to prove. Difficulties of proof aside, we submit that intent to inform rather than to deceive is a prerequisite of verity and hence of information. If the intent is to deceive, it should be named *mis*information.

Errors of perception are not so easily resolved. There has been sufficient experimentation to shake one's confidence in perception reports, regardless of the honesty of the reporter. The classic cases from psychology texts are too well known to be repeated here. Suffice it to say that the best intentions do not necessarily guarantee a veritable message.

In addition to the problems of perceiving, per se, are the problems of interpretation of the perceptions. It has been found, for example, that there are significant differences between cultures in the interpretations of the Rorschach Ink-Blot Test. Do the people of different cultures "see" different things, or do they see the same thing and "interpret" it differ-

---

5. Suppose, for example, that we define D_i as $C(1/L)$ and V_t as $C - \sum_{i=1}^{t} D_i$
If we know the values of C and L, then the report of a specific numerical value for V_t may be said to have zero informational content. It says no more than "fifteen is one-half of thirty." However, the distinction cannot be sharply drawn in all cases. If we don't know the values of C and L, then the original report of numerical values for V_t and D_i may be informative. However, the informational content of subsequent reports is suspect. The rules require that values vary with time, and thus one can predict the exact values of V_t for all subsequent time periods. The formula is the one for straight line depreciation. Accrual of interest is another example of the same thing.

ently? Obviously both see an ink blot, but then it is equally obvious
that one sees ink lines when one looks at a line drawing of a person.
Yet one says he sees a person or the representation of a person. Ptolemy
and Copernicus "saw" the same thing when they looked at the stars,
but in another sense they didn't "see" the same thing.

To say that Ptolemy was wrong and Copernicus was right, as we
often do, requires something beyond just "observing the facts." Butterfield argues convincingly that the observations will support either the
Ptolemaic or Copernican system equally well. Thus, one cannot decide
between the two on the basis of observations alone, because different
observers "see" different things or "see" the same thing but place
different "interpretations" on it. In Butterfield's terms there were two
different kinds of "thinking caps" and it was that difference that caused
the shift from geocentric to heliocentric astronomy. Thus, we now
judge Ptolemy's perceptions to be wrong because he had the wrong
kind of thinking cap, i.e. a thinking cap different from the one which
we currently wear.

There is no ultimate solution to this problem. Instead, we resolve it
by making an *assumption* that agreement among observers is the test
for verity. Then we qualify and hedge on simple agreement by speaking of "qualified" observers and of better or worse "conditions" of
observation. Thus, we make (1) a "democratic" assumption that the
modal perception and interpretation is the true one and (2) an
"authoritative" assumption that a certain group of people have superior
perception and interpretation abilities.[6] We will also accept these
criteria for the purpose of this study. However, they are small comfort
when one reflects on Cherry's wry comment: "In the Country of the
Blind the one-eyed man is *not* a king—he is a gibbering idiot." (Cherry,
p. 19.)

Our concern is with quantitative data, and thus any errors of perception would be matters of degree. If the intent is to inform, but the
reporter misperceives the data, there will be some lack of verity. The

---

6. Note that one condition of being "qualified" is that one have the *right* thinking cap or, as some say, the *right* preformed theoretical construct. The way we
judge right from wrong thinking caps is by agreement among "qualified" observers.
That is, one requirement for qualifying as an astronomer is to hold a heliocentric
view. Yet holding that view affects the perceptions that we are trying to judge.

usefulness of data that has only a degree of verity is not amenable to generalization: It would depend upon the requirements of the specific situation, i.e. upon the use to which it will be put. Note, however, that in the absence of other information the misperceived report is the only basis for action and therefore should be classified as "information." That is, some description of reality is probably better than none, even if the description has some degree of error.

Metricians often list errors of perception as one of the causes of imprecision in measurements. A more complete discussion is left to a later chapter, but in this connection we must point out that precision has little to do with verity.

"Absolute" precision is impossible to conceive, much less achieve. Limitations of precision are caused by the instrument of measurement as well as the perception of the pointer by the metrician. In addition, the limitation of the unit is crucial when the data is continuous. It is possible to conceive of an absolutely precise measurement in a given unit, but it is always possible to use smaller units or smaller fractions and hence a more precise measure. A given unit may be halved and then halved again until it becomes very small, but this unit is always subject to further fractioning and is, therefore, always imprecise in terms of a smaller unit.

This has caused some metricians to complain that no measurement is ever completely veritable, because it is never absolutely precise. We take a more generous and a more pragmatic view. The message "that water is hot" lacks precision. It may be that it is so imprecise as to be useless. The state of being useless, however, is not a result of veritableness (perhaps all would agree that it was "hot"), but a result of the lack of precision. The degree of precision required depends upon the specific situation. As a warning to a child, "hot" would be enough, but in a scientific experiment it would not be.

The same could be said of a more precise message, say, "It is 90° F." It is almost certain that the "true" temperature is different from 90.00°, and thus it may be useless for certain purposes. However, if the transmitter was trying to inform rather than deceive, we would classify the message as "veritable."

The point is that measurement messages may be veritable but not precise. The contrary condition does not hold. If the measurement is precise, it is veritable. A measurement that is both precise and veritable may still be useless, but to be useful, it must be veritable. Hence the first information proposition.

Information Proposition 1: Messages must be veritable. Verity is judged by agreement among qualified observers.

Relevance

The second attribute of information as presented by McDonough is its "value." We have here selected the word "relevance" to replace "value" because we have already overworked the latter, and more importantly, we intend to argue that relevance is a more appropriate term.

A strong case can be made that *all* information is valuable simply because it presents the individual with a more complete picture of reality. At the psychological level, an individual is receiving information at all times. He is immersed in an environment that is continually sending messages (stimuli) to his perceptors. One can argue, a priori, that it is valuable for an individual to have knowledge of his environment and therefore that all information is valuable. Gibson (p. 10) points out that "The sequence begins with the environment of the perceiver considered at the level of ecology." The individual does not utilize all the messages that are received at the ecological level, however. Most of them are shunted off as "unimportant," "uninteresting," or "irrelevant," and only a few are allowed through to the reasoning process. The response—if it is deliberate—will depend upon the selection of the "appropriate" message(s). This may be visualized in an oversimplified diagram as in Figure IV-1.

The number of appropriate messages is considerably smaller than the total number of messages sent and received. The appropriateness of the messages is determined by the problematic situation in which the organism finds itself. If the organism is hungry, it probably will not "hear" (i.e., the message will be shunted aside) the ticking of a clock. If the organism is interested in getting out of the woods when it is lost, it probably will not "perceive" the beauties of nature. One is probably capable of receiving, in some sense, all the messages, but the particular situation will determine the relevance and the irrelevant messages will be sidetracked.

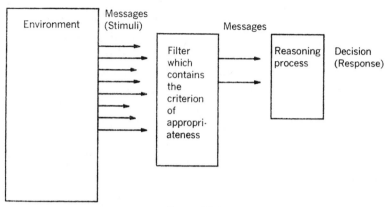

Figure IV-1

The reasoning process in the organism is set up to handle problematic situations as they occur. If there were no problems in the environment, the organism would remain in a state that would not require responses. The organism is, however, continually faced with changes in the environment and is required to adjust or respond so that it can maintain itself. Thus, we may say that all information is valuable, but that not all information is *relevant* to the particular problem at hand. Goldman writes: "The quantitative theory of information which we have been developing may appear incomplete and perhaps disappointing to the reader because it does not treat the *value* of information. There are just as many binits in the information which tells whether John Smith's wife had a boy or a girl, as in the information which tells whether your own wife had a boy or a girl." (Goldman, p. 63; a "binit" is a measurement unit of the quantity of information.) The question must be the *relevance* of the information to the receiver and his problem. If the message that Smith's wife had a boy was received by Jones, it would be difficult to argue that this information was completely valueless to Jones, but it is apparent that it is irrelevant to Jones's problem.

We can sympathize with the information theorists who did not even attempt to set forth a general theory of the "value" of information. It certainly wasn't an oversight, as Goldman's statement shows; it was simply impossible. The relevance of the information to a *particular* problem will determine its relative value to a *particular* receiver, and thus no *general* statement about value of information is possible.

Knowledge of the specific problem is required in order to ascertain relevance. That is, we must state the particular problematic situation and the desired end before we can make a judgment about relevance. This pragmatic end-directed view is the basis for our distinction between communications and information. All messages are classified as communications; information is restricted to those messages that are relevant to the solution of a particular problem. Thus, our second information proposition.

Information Proposition 2: Messages must be relevant. Relevance refers to a particular (specified) problem.

The Theory for Solution.—Knowledge of the problem is requisite for relevance judgments, but it is not sufficient. An additional requirement is necessary, viz. the theory or framework in which that problem is viewed. In the above diagram the filter-selector is controlled by the reasoning process. Messages of search must be sent to the filter-selector from the reasoning process to determine which of the substantive messages get through. The reasoning process must then set forth the criterion of relevance so that it receives messages pertinent to the problem at hand.

The above can be restated as: The mind needs a theory. One of the functions of such a theory is to select the relevant data as well as to arrange that data in a meaningful fashion. To say that the world is too complex to be perceived in its entirety has become a cliché, but it remains true. It is necessary to set up a theory that rejects the irrelevant complexities and allows one to concentrate on the communications that can be handled by the limited capacity of the mind.

Several philosophers take this one step further and argue that the conception is a prerequisite of the information. Caws (p. 8) writes: "Cassirer makes the point that all measure has to be 'conceived and sought' before it can be found in experience, i.e., one has first a concept of some quality and looks afterwards for quantitative expressions of it." The conception comes first and *then* the information. Some psychologists would argue that the "beginnings" of concept formation are from observations. Whatever the beginnings of the process may be, it seems clear that it is impossible to be a pure empiricist in the sense of collecting *all* the data and rejecting none.

Koivisto (p. 13) delineates facts and observations in his discussion of a theory: "How important a theory is to our understanding cannot be overemphasized. In fact, we cannot assert that something is a 'fact' unless we have an adequate theory. Without a theory we have only observations. . . . Facts do not consist merely in observations; they consist in a strategic combination of observation and theory." "Facts" for Koivisto do not exist separated from a theory; "observations" do, but are without value to our understanding. In our terminology the facts are "relevant information"; observations are "communications" of unevaluated data.

The functions of a theory are (1) to select the relevant information from a myriad of complex observations and (2) to arrange the information in comprehensible combinations.[7]

A particular kind of theory is one that is used in selecting from alternative courses of action. This is called a "decision-model" as well as a "decision-theory." Formally, such theories are quite simple. One

7. Of course this is a theory about theories on which disagreements are legion. There are many different schools of thought on the nature and function of theories. All of those schools, however, would accept the above proposition, except the pure empiricists. The pure empiricists would insist that the original source of the theory was from undirected observation, but they would not deny that the inductively derived theories serve as data selectors after they have been derived. The point that is important to the proposition is that theories serve as data selectors regardless of what the origins of these theories may be.

The literature on the nature of theories and their construction is vast and conflicting. Authors who have seriously attempted to come to grips with the problem invariably find themselves being required to cope with epistemology, ontology, axiology, and logic before going on to theories. In other words, consideration of theories very soon expands to considerations of the nature of the universe. For the hypothetico-deductio school, see Braithwaite; for operationalism, see Bridgman; for instrumentalism or pragmatism, see Peirce and Dewey, especially *The Quest for Certainty;* for conventionalism, see Poincaré; and so forth.

For the social sciences, see, e.g., Merton and Lazarsfield. Nagel (*Structure,* chapter 13) reviews several schools from a positivist's viewpoint. Economics has Keynes's *Scope and Method;* Schumpeter's *Doctrine and Method;* and various articles by Machlup, Koopmans, and Friedman. The exchange between Machlup and Lester, as well as the commentary by Stigler and others on that exchange, illuminates several different views as they apply to a particular problem.

is faced with a number of alternative courses of action (A_i) and a consequence (C_i) associated with each alternative. The decision theory is composed of a set of interrelated analytic and empirical propositions, together with rules for manipulating those propositions. Such manipulations permit one to say "If A_1, then C_1; if A_2, then C_2; . . ." That is, the decision theory predicts the outcome of each alternative. One then selects the consequence that most nearly conforms to his personal goal. The empirical propositions in such a theory are generalized statements about the kind of information that is relevant to the theory. In each particular problematic situation, then, one substitutes specific values for the generalized empirical propositions. These specific values are the "relevant information." Thus, the theory dictates the information to be supplied and this is the basis for our third information proposition.

Information Proposition 3: The theory concerning the solution of the problem specifies the relevant information.

COMMUNICATIONS

The quantitative theory of communications is a solution to an allocation problem. Messages are outputs that have costly inputs. The problem is to maximize the quantity of information and minimize the cost of that information. That is, the scarcity and concurrent allocation-efficiency problems are met. Shannon's work was an attempt to provide a general solution to this problem.

As Goldman points out in several places, communications theory measures "the *quantity* of information, not its *value*." (Goldman, p. 300.) More directly, communications theory assumes, for purposes of the theory, all information to be equally valuable or relevant; and it attempts to maximize the amount available. In the quote about the sex of the child (*supra*, p. 47) the *number* of binits in the message is the maximand in communications theory. No attempt is made at ordering those binits by *value* to the receivers. Despite this limitation, the concepts and terms of quantitative communications theory are helpful in the present connection.

The prime difference between communications theory, in this context, and the psychological view presented above is the spatio-temporal separation of the environment and the receiver. Contrary to the psychological situation where the receiver is immersed in the environment and continually receiving unlimited messages, the receiver in a communications setting is removed from the environment of interest and therefore is subject to a limitation on the amount of information received. It may be helpful to visualize this as follows:[8]

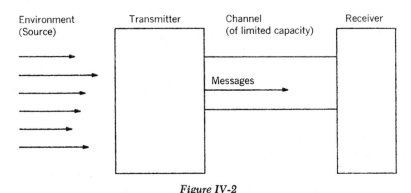

Figure IV-2

This diagram is useful because it points up two important facets in communications:

1. The limitation of the channel or, conversely, the additional cost of increasing the channel capacity.
2. The selection decision has been shifted from the receiver to the transmitter.

The limitation on information imposed by the channel capacity is all the more reason for insisting on the relevance of the information to be transmitted. Suppose that the channel was limited to x binits of information and that there were two messages to be sent, both containing exactly x binits. A choice is enforced, but there is no criterion in communication theory for making that choice. For example, if the two messages were:

8. This is a simplification of Shannon and Weaver's presentation. They set up five basic elements: (1) information source; (2) transmitter; (3) channel; (4) receiver; (5) destination. A "noise source" is sometimes added also. (Shannon and Weaver, p. 98.)

(1) The sex of Smith's child is male.
(2) The sex of Jones's child is male.

There is no way of choosing which message to transmit unless the transmitter knows the identity of the receiver and thereby infers which message is relevant. In more general terms, the transmitter needs to know the problem of the receiver before he can make an intelligent choice of the message to be transmitted.

An obvious "solution" to the problem is either to reverse the origin of the message or to select one at random and wait for the "feedback." Note, however, that this solution solves the problem by denying the existence of the problem. Admittedly, feedback is a valuable method of controlling transmissions, but it utilizes some of the channel's scarce capacity. Thus, it would require either the addition of capacity and the corollary costs, or the omission of at least part of the substantive message. The solution is trivial, because it disregards the constraints which are *the cause* of the problem.[9]

The limitation of channel capacity places an extremely heavy burden on the transmitter. This is the problem that the newscaster faces daily. He has a severely limited channel (time) and must select for transmission from a vast array of things, all of which may be classified as "news." His problem is compounded by having a great many receivers with a wide variety of interests, and hence the relative value (relevance) of the information selected will probably be different for each.

It is appropriate to reiterate that quantitative information theory is of no help in the newscaster's dilemma. For example, the probability (relative frequency) of the declaration of war is greater than the probability of snow in Miami Beach. The calculation of the quantity of information is determined by the following formula:

---

9. The author's criticism of the "different incomes for different purposes" notion stems from these considerations. If it is feasible for each receiver to feedback his particular purpose and then for the transmitter to prepare and transmit all of the information requested, there is no problem. If the channel has such a large capacity, and the corollary large costs, the non-problem has been solved. It is only when a limitation on transmissions has been set that we are required to select some data and reject some. Without this limitation *all* of the data could conceivably be transmitted, and the receiver could filter out the relevant bits. With the limitation the transmitter must filter the data; and how that is done is the problem.

$$I(x) = -\log_2 P(x)$$

Where $P(x)$ is the probability of event x occurring and $I(x)$ is the quantity of binits. (Sometimes $I(x)$ is called the value of the information, but "value" is being used in its mathematical sense; it means "quantity of binits.") Thus, the smaller the probability, the greater the quantity of binits. On this basis, the news of snow in Miami Beach would be transmitted. Obviously, something is wrong. The selection ought to be based upon "importance," which ultimately reduces to "relevance."

Also, here as above, feedback is *not* the solution. In addition to the capacity constraint, there are two other criticisms of feedback.

First, the old saw that "nothing is as dead as yesterday's news" is an indication of the time value of information. Since feedback requires the additional time necessary to transmit at least two additional messages, the value of information obtained through feedback is considerably less than that obtained in the initial transmission. It is true that feedback may aid the newscaster in developing a criterion of relevance for use in the future, but the immediate use of feedback is the result of either wrong or incomplete data in the transmission. That is, feedback is used to *correct* errors of selection, and it would be better to *avoid* errors.

The second criticism of feedback is even more fundamental. Feedback is partially a function of the information possessed by the receiver. If the receiver has inadequate information, he is very likely to ask the wrong questions. In the case of the newscaster, the receivers do not ask specific questions, such as "Was there a war declared today?" or "Was there snow in Miami Beach?" The number of such questions is infinite and the capacity is finite. The question that the receivers implicitly ask is "What's new?" and the transmitter makes the judgment. If all the transmitters decided to transmit the item about snow in Miami Beach and to omit the declaration of war, it is unlikely that any receiver would feedback a question about the unknown war. It is clear that when the receiver is spatially separated from the source, the transmitters have complete control over what they transmit and therefore have a high degree of control over the feedback. Since the receiver is spatially separated from the source, his state of knowledge is limited to the transmissions received, and it is likely that feedback will be limited to specific and relatively trivial questions to fill gaps in his knowledge. Reliance upon feedback to ensure that all relevant information is transmitted is therefore impossible.

The conclusion is inevitable: In a communications system the criterion of relevance is located at the transmission source. The transmitter must select what is to be transmitted.[10] Thus, our first communication proposition:

Communication Proposition 1: The locus of the relevance criterion is at the transmission source.

The above proposition is concerned only with the locus of the relevance criterion at the time of transmission. A legitimate question can be raised about the origin of that criterion. It is necessary for the transmitter to possess the criterion, but how does he come by it? Does he ask the receiver? If he does, he will utilize some of the scarce channel capacity, but, more importantly, he is very likely to get different answers from different receivers and thus be in no better position than before. That is, the receivers are likely to have different goals, different problems, and different decision theories, which will result in a wide variety of requests.

The "ask the receivers" notion makes the implicit assumption of *de gustibus non est disputandum,* and this should be examined. This assumption would not allow us to ask about the *origin* of the relevance

10. This is not an attempt to justify such a situation. We can note the cybernetics situation in which a low-energy information system has absolute control of a high-energy power system and join with Talcott Parsons in viewing the analogous social systems with alarm. We can join with the general outcry against the manipulation possible in the discretion allowed the transmitter and deplore the nefarious effects of an ill-motivated transmitter. The above analysis is an attempt to present the inevitable result of a limited-channel communication system. Although the purpose and methodology is different, our conclusion is, at the core, the same as Carr's (p. 69), "Propaganda is as essential a function of mass democracy as advertising of mass production." And we join with him in his reluctance to announce such a conclusion. The broad social consequences of that conclusion are beyond the scope of this study. However, the consequences for accounting are inescapable. The accounting reports are often the *sole* information that the receivers have about a firm, and this places the entire burden for the selection of data upon the accountant. The responsibility is awesome, but it cannot be avoided.

criterion that the receivers use. Instead, it takes the criterion as a given datum and proceeds from there. The notion is pervasive in present society and is given an honorific aura by associating it with other honorific terms like "democracy" and "consumer sovereignty." We could agree that if tastes were given—that is, original with the individual—a strong case could be made for not tampering with those tastes, and this could be done in the name of democracy. However, this ignores completely the philosophers', semanticists', social psychologists', sociologists', and cultural anthropologists', and others' insistence that such tastes are "socialized," "acculturized," "environmentally determined," "linguistically determined," and so on—in short, *learned* from the cultural milieu in which the individual finds himself.

The newscaster who currently spends a considerable portion of the channel capacity reporting football scores is responding to the relevance criterion of the receivers. The reason that he does not report cricket or bridge results is that the receivers are not "interested." A foreigner finds this interest in football a little strange. In another culture the capacity would be used for chess, cricket, bull fights, or opera for the same reason, i.e., receivers' interests. The result is not commonly recognized. By broadcasting football scores, the transmitter is reinforcing the interest of receivers in football. The transmitter is a significant part of the cultural milieu from which the tastes are learned. Therefore, the transmitter is, to a large extent, the determinant of tastes.

In the particular case at hand, wealth and income reports go to receivers who now have some theory. However, this theory was learned previously in some sort of an education-communication process. If we now ask the receiver what his theory is in order for the transmitter to establish a criterion of relevance, we have made a circle which is not complete, but certainly it is vicious.[11]

---

11. This circularity is contained in the suggestion that we make a survey of the receivers of financial reports and that the results of that survey be used to provide a criterion for selecting information to be transmitted in the future. The results of such a survey would very likely lend support to the continuation of whatever is now being done. We would judge that the results of such a survey could best be characterized as "give us what we have been getting." This conjecture is based on the well-known routinization theme in psychology. When people (or animals) are repetitiously subjected to something they are likely to miss it when it is removed

The moral is clear. The transmitter plays a major part in theory formation (with the attendent criterion of relevance) whether he likes it or not. He is forced into the position of making a choice between alternative roles:

1. Reinforcing the current theory by transmitting in accordance with it.
2. Changing the theory.

The escape alternative of being neutral is not available. A position of neutrality is a positive decision to continue the current situation, thereby reinforcing the current theory. The refusal to make a decision is, ipso facto, a decision to continue the status quo. Thus, the transmitter must select.

Communication Proposition 2: The transmitter must choose the appropriate theory.

Proposition 2 does not solve any problems. On the contrary, it creates very knotty problems which were previously thought to be nonexistent by the "neutrality of transmissions" notion. These problems may be roughly divided into two categories:

1. The transmitter and the receiver with different theories.
2. Receivers with a variety of theories.

In the first case, the transmitter must know or be able to determine the receiver's theory. If the transmitter does not know that the receiver has a different theory, he has no known problem. If, however, the transmitter knows that the theory of the receiver is different, the problem must be faced. The transmitter may then elect to transmit information in accordance with either:

1. The receiver's erroneous theory.[12]

---

or changed, even though it may not have been desired in the first place. Pavlov's dog adjusted to the bell and was conditioned to respond. After the experiment was over, one wonders if the dog didn't have equally as much adjustment to make because of the absence of the bell.

12. Presumably if there is a difference in theories, the transmitter considers his correct and the other erroneous. If he did not, and were rational, he would accept the receiver's theory, and there would be no difference and no problem. Therefore, we classify the receiver's theory as "erroneous" if it differs from the transmitter's theory.

2. The transmitter's correct theory.

The consequence may be:

- A. Erroneous decisions resulting from:
  1. Using the wrong information in the wrong theory.
  2. Using the right information in the wrong theory.
- B. Correct decisions which come from using the right information in the right theory.

However, consequence B has been ruled out. The receiver has the wrong theory by definition of the problem. Still, it is tempting to try to prove that the only way to get correct decisions is with correct information and thereby decide that issue. Unfortunately, the world is not that simple. It is very likely that the degree of error in the erroneous decisions varies with the information received. It is quite possible that the wrong information in the wrong theory will yield a more correct decision (i.e., a decision consonant with the desired end) than the right information in the wrong theory.[13] This is a melancholy fact that can-

---

13. It would seem that if the theory is truly wrong (as opposed to there being disagreement about the theories) then the *best* possible result would be correct decisions by chance. However, this need not be true. For example, if a witch doctor holds a demon theory of medicine, then the information specified by that theory is the wishes of the gods. It is hard to see how the witch doctor could do better than chance; i.e., the patients would recover equally as often without the witch doctor. But it may be that the incantations provide some comfort to the patient, and therefore the witch doctor does better than chance. On the other hand, the incantations may disturb the patient, and the number of recoveries may be worse than chance. It is impossible to know what the consequences would be if the wrong theory were used and the information were provided in accordance with that theory.

If a medical technician were to give the witch doctor the "right" information (blood count, X-ray films, and other reports specified by modern medical theory), the witch doctor would consider that information to be irrelevant and foolish. This probably wouldn't improve the chances of recovery but it is hard to see how it would worsen them.

As another example, suppose a physician held to a poisonous blood theory and he was given information specified by present medical theory, which included a blood count showing a dyscrasia. By letting blood or leeching in order to get rid of the poison, the physician would do worse than chance. The right information in the wrong theory decreases the number of correct decisions in this case.

These examples are intended to show that the right information in the wrong theory may yield better or worse results than the wrong information in the wrong theory. Each case requires a separate judgment.

not be avoided. No simple criterion can be laid down for the solution of the problem. Instead, it must rest in that nebulous area of personal judgment.

To further complicate the transmitter's problems, note that the receivers are often unaware that a problematic situation exists prior to the receipt of a message. Obviously then the transmitter cannot rely on the receivers' decision theories specifying the relevant data because there are no applicable decision theories to unknown problems. Moreover, sometimes information supplied in response to one problem reveals other problems that were unknown prior to the receipt of the message. Sometimes it is the solution of one problem that creates other problems; other times it is simply the gathering of information in response to one problem that reveals other problems. Consider, for example, the Bureau of Labor Statistics, which gathers and transmits large quantities of information. Often the solution of one labor problem (e.g. mobility) creates another labor problem (e.g. transportation). Sometimes labor theorists ask for breakdowns or extensions of one category of information, but find that it is not available. They complain that such breakdowns should have been made available because the problem is "obvious." The problem *is* obvious *after* the receipt of the information, but not before. That is, new problems are perceived because of information received. In order to meet the receivers' needs in such cases the transmitter must be able to anticipate the new problems and the new perceptions of old problems. Add to this already overcomplicated situation the fact that theories change over time (economic labor theory has been "revolutionized" in this century), which means that the transmitter must be able to anticipate the new theories in order to meet the receivers' needs.

Obviously this is an impossible task. Transmitters cannot anticipate new theories, nor can they anticipate new problems. However, it is equally obvious that the transmitter cannot be theoretically passive or neutral. He must fully understand the extant theories in order to make judgments about them and in order to comprehend the interrelationships of the data specified by that theory. Thus, the transmitters, at least as a group, must be theoreticians.

Communication Proposition 3: The transmitters must be actively engaged in the evaluation, refinement, and construction of decision theories applicable to the problematic situations arising from the object of concern.

Proposition 3 follows from the nonneutrality notion. Since the transmitter is in fact influential in theory formation, we believe that a conscious consideration of theories would improve the quality of communications. Of course there must be some correspondence between the decision theories used by the receivers and those used by the transmitters. The problem is one of maximizing the total information received. Once again, however, upon analysis, this raises some unresolvable problems. Is one maximizing information when the largest number of receivers can utilize the information or when a smaller number of receivers can more fully utilize the information?

Both approaches are taken in practice. Several years ago the Air Force issued a communication memorandum which forbade the use of some words (e.g., feasible, orient, secular) because some people did not understand messages that contained these words and use

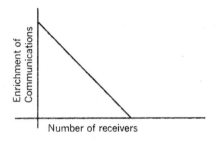

Figure IV-3

of them eliminated a number of receivers. One could push this principle to the absurd. If the number of receivers is the sole criterion, we can continue to omit "difficult" words until we have been reduced to grunts or sign language. Since a large vocabulary, including jargon, enriches the communications of some individuals, there is a sacrifice made each time a receiver is added. Conversely the enriched vocabulary decreases the number of receivers who can understand the communications. This can be visualized as in Figure IV-3.

The marginal receiver determines the level of enrichment and results in an "enrichment deficit" of all previous receivers. It would be nice now if we could measure "information" on the y-axis and pull off the marginal information curve and stop adding receivers when it crossed the x-axis. The difficulty is that enrichment is not amenable to such an analysis, and the exercise would be futile.

The curve illustrates the opposite extreme also. As communications become richer, the receivers are cut off until there is only one receiver left. Both extremes are undesirable except in rare cases. We might want to communicate to all receivers on some occasions—when issuing a civil defense warning, for example—or only to one in a highly personal situation. Unfortunately, the vast majority of communication problems fall between these extremes. Churchman makes the point nicely:

> In sum, the language of measurement does entail a decision problem. The more precise a language the less broadly is it understood. To put it otherwise—if one wanted to be cute about it—the clearer a language the more confusing it is to most people. Precise languages narrow the class of users but increase the degree of refinement that any user can attain. The proper balance between breadth and depth is the linguistic decision problem of measurement. (Churchman, *Definitions*, p. 87.)

There is no immediate solution to this problem. If the decision theory requires discriminations to be made that are so precise that they cannot be understood by the receivers, then the communications will be ineffective. But the communications will also be ineffective if the decisions are erroneous without such precise discriminations. On this point, surveys of the receivers would seem to be appropriate.[14]

14. Accountants are well aware of this problem. Such well-worn words as "depreciation," "reserve," "surplus," even "asset," are not understood in their technical accounting sense by the receivers. For this reason more descriptive terms have been adopted. However, we are not convinced that the problem has been solved by the introduction of new words. About the word "asset," for example, it is sometimes said that "unrealized appreciation [market value] would not be understood by investors," while at other times it is lamented that "investors do not understand that assets are unexpired costs, not market values." In this case we believe that the error is in the locus of the confusion. A change to "market

One implication of all these considerations is the need for the use of at least some of the channel capacity for educational purposes. If progress is going to be made, erroneous theories will have to be replaced, and the sophistication of the receivers will have to be raised. An allocation of channel capacity to this function has a high priority— higher than the communication of substantive messages if they are likely to produce dangerously erroneous decisions; perhaps not so high if they produce only slightly erroneous results. This is a difficult judgment for the transmitter.

We agree with Ogden and Richards. As early as 1923 they observed: "The old view that the only access to a subject is through prolonged study of it, has, if it be true, consequences for the immediate future which have not yet been faced. The alternative is to raise the level of communication through a direct study of its conditions, its dangers and its difficulties. The practical side of this undertaking is, if communication be taken in its widest sense, Education." (Ogden and Richards, p. x.) Thus, our fourth proposition.

Communication Proposition 4: Education has a high priority in the allocation of channel capacity.

Binit Maximization.—When all the requirements set forth above have been met, we can return to the simpler problem of maximizing the number of binits. We agree with the implicit assumption that, *cet. par.*, binits should be maximized, but we consider verity and relevance to be essential prerequisites. Recognition of these prerequisites presents us with some problems which communications theory in its present state cannot handle.

The theory in its present state is concerned with economizing channel capacity by statistical theorems. It allows one to maximize the binits transmitted under various channel conditions—noisy, lossy, etc. This is a great contribution, but we note Brillouin's warning as well as his hope.

Information has received a purely statistical definition from

---

values" would be quite confusing to accountants, because they understand accounting; but it would probably be less confusing to the receivers, because they do not understand accounting.

which all human elements are excluded: moral import, scientific
significance, artistic quality, even speculative value in business. . . . Not one of these concepts, essential though they are
to the usual meaning of the word "information" comes within
the ambit of our definition. . . . It is essential to emphasize these
restrictions, which correspond to the present state of affairs in
the theory. We may hope one day to be able to discard these
barriers, but we cannot, at the moment, foresee how it will be
possible. (Quoted by Guilbaud, p. 59.)

Unfortunately these restrictions have not always been heeded.
Guilbaud cites cases where popularizers have calculated that the
"worth" of a daily newspaper is a hundred thousand hartleys. (A
"hartley" is a unit of information. Goldman calls his units "binits";
most information theorists call them "bits.") He points out that it is
"absurd" to make such calculations and that communications theory
was not designed for this purpose. For this reason, it is clear that we
cannot meaningfully calculate the binits per message for each valuation coefficient. On the other hand, it is clear that if we could specify
the problems and theories, we could make some relational judgments
about the competing concepts. Once this has been done, we can then
maximize the information per message without cardinally measuring
the binits.

The concept is both simple and familiar: ". . . information in cybernetics is not concerned with what we actually say in our messages, but
rather with what we *could* say. What is of interest to our theory is
the *choice,* the range of possible messages." (Guilbaud, p. 59.) The
theory of choice is not an unfamiliar topic in economic tracts. Rogers
brings this even closer to home by an analogy.

Just as entropy of a source was likened to the output of a steel
mill, so, as Shannon has remarked, can capacity of a channel (in
bits/signal or bits/second) be likened to the maximum load
capacity of a conveyor belt (in tons/day). If entropy (steel
output) is below channel capacity (belt capacity) we know
that the information (steel) produced can be satisfactorily trans-
ported, provided that it is properly coded (cut up, arranged and
packed onto the moving belt). (Rogers, p. 73.)

We can speak of more or less steel without ever measuring it or even
specifying what a ton is. We can conceive of flexible capacity and

minimize it without measuring the output. This is the framework that we will utilize below when we speak of "bits of information." In our context it is an unspecified unit that we will use to order the quantity of information.

SUMMARY

It has been pointed out that a desire for information was the impetus for a measurement prior to the completion of the exchange. This necessitates a discussion of the concepts of information and communications.

We defined communications as unevaluated data, and we restricted information to useful data. Information, so defined, has two fundamental attributes. It must be veritable and relevant. Verity refers to "conformance with reality"; and this reduces to agreement among qualified observers. Relevance refers to the applicability of data to a particular problem. Theories serve the function of specifying what data is relevant.

In communications there is a spatiotemporal separation of the transmitter and receiver. This results in a shift of the data selection process from the receiver to the transmitter. Under such conditions the transmitter cannot be neutral, because the original transmission is likely to determine the scope of the feedback, and the previous transmissions have influenced the receiver's perceptions and theory formation. For these reasons, transmitters as a group must become involved in the evaluation, refinement, and construction of the appropriate decision theories. They must also devote part of their resources to the education of the receivers.

One conclusion of this discussion is that we must carefully spell out the theories appropriate to the trader model before we can make informational judgments about the various valuation coefficients. Happily, there is little controversy over the correct decision theories applicable to our simple model. We will present them below.

In this chapter we have not been able to avoid completely the province of measurement theory. A more complete discussion is the object of the next chapter.

V

MEASUREMENT

The purpose of this study is to develop a theory of the *measurement* of enterprise income. It was noted that the impetus of the measurement was a desire for information; and the first criterion of "informational content" was developed. Thus, we discovered the cause of the problem—to provide information—but we neglected the question of why one should provide "measurement-type" information. There are other kinds of information—e.g. "qualitative"—that could be provided, and there is no a priori reason for deciding on the measurement type. To examine that question and to review the concept of measurement are the purposes of this chapter.

THE DEFINITIONAL DISPUTE

A burgeoning literature on metrics has appeared in recent years. Much of it has been concerned with the proper *definition* of measurement; and a major debate has arisen. The term "measurement" is defined and used by physicists and psychologists in strikingly different ways. Anyone who expects to find a single, well-established definition of measurement is due for a disappointment. Disputes as to the possibility of measuring sensations have been sufficiently acute to cause the British Association for the Advancement of Science to appoint a special committee to study the matter. This committee devoted much of its time to a discussion of the meaning of the term "measurement." It has been said that its members "came out the same door they went in." Its reports revealed striking disagreement among its members.

In a passage that evidently refers to the work of this committee, Campbell (a physicist and committee member) says:

> A philosopher will suppose that the logical analysis of measurement is familiar to every physicist who actually measures, and he will not expect me to say anything that is not to be found in every competent textbook. He is reminded therefore that most physicists have a horror of logic and regard an accusation that their doings conform to logical principles as a personal insult. The most distinguished physicists, when they attempt logical analysis, are apt to gibber; and probably more nonsense is talked about measurement than about any other part of physics. When an international congress meets to discharge the dull but necessary duty of finding the conventions of measurement (which duty it performs admirably), a flood of incomprehensible verbiage about "units and dimensions" is let loose, which leaves everyone even more muddled than they were before. The only conclusion that can be drawn from "competent" textbooks is that there are no principles of measurement. (Campbell, *Measurement,* p. 121.)

Thus, we cannot search the literature and report the principles of measurement applicable to this study, because there are none, or, more accurately, there is no system of measurement principles which is not disputed. For this reason we will briefly review the dispute among metricians.

Opinion on measurements may be roughly divided into two categories. Following Stevens, we will call these the "broad" and the "narrow" schools (*Definitions,* p. 19). These are shorthand descriptions and should not be interpreted in any pejorative sense. The narrow school looks closely at the measurement procedures and distinguishes between "fundamental" and "derived" measurements. For example, Campbell says that length is fundamental because it does not depend upon any previous measurements, while density is derived because it is dependent upon the measurement of weight and volume. The broad school looks to the mathematical properties of numerical assignment and distinguishes between various scales on that basis. For example, Stevens lists the statistical procedures that are appropriate to the four scales: nominal, ordinal, interval, and ratio. Another difference between the two views concerns the "scientific dualism" mentioned in the previous chapter. The narrow view is inclined to think of objects "possessing" a certain pre-existing property or characteristic that can be measured. The broad view, mainly the operationists, believe that there are only well-defined operations of measurements and that to attribute pre-existing properties to objects commits one to an untenable metaphysical position.

We believe that there is some merit in both positions. The narrow school's focus on the empirical attributes of measurement emphasizes the restraints given in nature. The broad school's focus on mathematics emphasizes what we can do with the numbers once they have been generated. The "pre-existing property" idea is hard to defend a priori, but once a scale or dimension has been defined, then it is eminently reasonable to speak of objects possessing that property, whether or not it is measured. Thus, there is a pre-existing property of objects, *given* a previously defined scale or dimension. The importance of a well-defined operation can scarcely be overemphasized; but the operation itself does not yield conceptual import.

Two points in the dispute which are not so easily smoothed over concern the nominal scale and the possibility of meaningfully adding the numbers resulting from measurements. The narrow school, as well as the broad school—excepting the nominal scale, agree that some properties or characteristics can be measured and others cannot. All agree that weight and length can be measured but that shape and color cannot. The distinction turns on the ability to rank or order the property. We can say that X is heavier than, or longer than, Y; but we cannot meaningfully say that X is shaper than, or colorer than, Y.

With respect to shape, we may say that things are "identical" or "congruent" but not that they are "equal" or "shaper."[1] One triangle is

1. Whorf argues that this is a restriction on both our thinking and communication that is caused by the structure of our language. See in particular "Thinking in

no more triangular than another triangle; and it is odd to say that a triangle is more triangular than a rectangle. Color is similar, although a little more complex. We can say that an object is redder than another red object, but we cannot meaningfully say that a red object is redder than or less red than a blue or green object. One requirement for a measurement, then, and one on which all writers (excepting the nominal scale) agree, is that the object or event be capable of being ordered or ranked in respect to some property. The explanation for this is, presumably, that we wish to express their relation to one another.

There are, however, many properties by which objects can be ranked which many writers of the narrow school would deny to measurements —for example, hardness, density, sweetness, pitch, etc. For each of these we can meaningfully say that one object is greater than, less than, or equal to, another in respect to the property; and we can assign numbers to represent rank orders. Moh's scale of hardness of minerals provides an example. Mineral X is said to be harder than Y if X scratches Y and Y does not scratch X. Ten minerals of unequal hardness are selected and labeled 1, 2, . . . , 10. A number representing relative hardness can then be assigned to any other mineral by comparing it with this scale.

Many writers (the narrow view) maintain that the above procedure cannot be regarded as measurement for roughly the following reasons. Although X receives the number 1 and Y the number 2, we may not infer from this that Y is *twice* as hard as X. In general, ratio comparisons of this kind are meaningless when numerals are assigned by procedures like that used in Moh's scale. This can be seen from the fact that letters of the alphabet—which have an understood order—could

---

Primitive Communities" for this hypothesis on the comparative aspects of languages.

"We even have to think and boggle over the question for some time, or have it explained to us, before we can see the difference in the relationships . . . whereas the Hopi discriminates these relationships with effortless ease, for the forms of his speech have accustomed him to doing so." (Whorf, p. 85.)

In this paper we take the language as a given constraint, and while we may envy the Hopi his verbal ability to relate, our language requires numbers to make such relationships. Thus, shape is either identical or different, and such either/or concepts are not rankings, although they may be comparisons.

have been used instead of numbers; and from the fact that the choice of numbers for the scale was arbitrary. Instead of 1 through 10, it would have been possible to use prime numbers.

Although we can admit that the lack of ratio comparisons is a serious limitation of Moh's scale, we must also appreciate that an ordinal scale is a useful conception. We will freely admit that a cardinal scale is *more* useful, but to exclude the ordinal scale simply because it is *less* useful seems to be an arbitrary classification of those concepts that can be termed "measurement." A strong argument can be made that one has the right to define any word any way he chooses as long as he makes that definition explicit. That is, the definition of measurement, as Stevens says, is a "matter of taste." On the other hand, this approach is likely to cause serious difficulties in interpersonal communications. If everyone has a unique definition, the convenience of using a single label—word—for a given referent has been lost. In addition, a different referent for the same word is almost certain to cause misunderstanding no matter how explicitly the definitions are made.

It was perhaps arbitrary restrictions of this kind which led Stevens to define measurements as the "assignment of numerals to objects or events according to rule—any rule" (*Definitions*, p. 19). Upon first encountering this definition, one is tempted to present an absurd rule to Stevens and ask if it yields a measurement. This would be of no effect, however, because Stevens lists examples that appear to be absurd. It is quite likely that most people—scientists and non-scientists alike—would agree that it is absurd to call the numbering of football players a measurement. It violates a well-worn, if imprecisely defined, linguistic convention that is common to almost all members of the community. Yet Stevens lists the numbering of football players as a measurement on a nominal scale (*Definitions*, p. 25). Campbell would certainly disagree, since he makes explicit his idea that numbering of houses (street numbers) is not a measurement.

Stevens notes our objection but he implies that it is of no importance.

> The nominal scale is a primitive form, and quite naturally there are many who would urge that it is absurd to attribute to this process of assigning numerals the dignity implied by the term measurement. Certainly there can be no quarrel with this objection, for the naming of things is an arbitrary business. How-

ever we christen it, the use of numerals as names for classes is an example of the "assignment of numerals according to rule." (Stevens, *Handbook,* p. 26, and *Science,* p. 679.)

But the absurdity objection is important. We hesitate to call a nominal scale one of measurement, in either scientific or ordinary parlance, because its values do not represent the order or rank of the objects scaled. To assign numerals to football players is simply to give them convenient names. Surely measuring is to be distinguished from naming. If not, the author is reminded of the comic strip *Peanuts* in which Charlie Brown's new neighbors were named numbers. If Charlie were familiar with Stevens' work, he could say that the mother "measured the children." One child was measured twenty-three, all were measured numbers. The substitution of "named" for "measured" is required before the preceding sentences makes sense. Violations of linguistic conventions of this kind are more apt to cause confusion than to clarify the nature of measurements.

In addition, note that Stevens' definition does not delineate those things that can be measured from those things that cannot. *All* characteristics *can* be assigned numbers, and therefore *everything* can be measured. His definition does not serve as a definition because it does not delimit its applicability.

A more important criticism of Stevens' definition turns on the informational content of assigning numbers according to *any* rule. On the writer's desk are several objects which have just been assigned numbers according to the following rule: Assign the far left object the numeral 1.7, and by adding a positive constant, assign greater numerals to the objects moving from left to right. Now one object is "measured" 3.18 by this procedure, but there is serious doubt that that number has any informational content. Describing it as "an ashtray" carries some information, but describing it as "3.18" carries none. Moreover, if the reader were to follow the rule as stated, it is unlikely that the numerals assigned would be the same, yet there is no question of contradiction or verity involved.

For this reason, Stevens' definition is unacceptable. One needs restrictions upon the kind of rule that can be used. Random number assignment has been excluded: "This is quite different from a 'random' assignment under which no rule would be in force. With no rule in force, the same numeral might be assigned to different classes, and different numerals might be assigned to the same class. A class in this sense may, of course, contain only one member, as when the coach 'numbers' his football players." (Stevens, *Definitions,* pp. 25-26.) Obviously Stevens was thinking of a narrower definition than his "any rule" statement indicates. It may be possible to formulate such restrictions precisely so that "measurements" would be, in fact, defined. As it is now, Stevens' definition is unbearably broad and vague.

For the remainder of our discussion of measurement we will present some propositions of measurement which are germane to this study, but we will attempt to state them in such a way that all metricians would accept them in spirit if not in detail. Metricians who have read this discussion have accepted our propositions as necessary but have criticized the set of propositions as being incomplete. The broad school would consider it incomplete because of the absence of the nominal scale; the narrow school because of the absence of sharp delineation between measurements and nonmeasurements.

GENERAL PROPOSITIONS OF MEASUREMENT

> I often say that when you can measure what you are speaking about and express it in numbers, you know something about it, but when you cannot measure it, your knowledge is of a meager and unsatisfactory kind.—Lord Kelvin

The objective of metrics has been well put by Lord Kelvin. We can all agree that our knowledge is richer, more satisfactory, when we can express it in numbers. Or in terms of the above discussion, our information is more informative if it can be expressed as a measurement. The purpose is clear: measurements make information more informative. But the interesting questions are yet to come. What are the characteristics of measurement that give it this higher status?

Churchman answers this question in one context in terms of "precision." "The contrast between quantitative and nonquantitative seems to imply a contrast between 'precise' and 'vague' information. Precise information is information that enables one to distinguish objects and their properties to some arbitrarily assigned degree of refinement. . . . the reason that precision is useful is that precise information can be used in a wide variety of problems." (Churchman, *Definitions*, pp. 83-84.)

Churchman's concern appears to be with precision. Notice, however, that precision is a concern of the second order. More fundamental is enabling "one to distinguish objects and their properties." Obviously, if there was no need to distinguish, there would be no need to distinguish precisely. Thus, the more fundamental aspect of measurement is its concern with the distinction between properties or characteristics of objects.

In more general terms, measurement is a process of comparison. We say that objects are longer, heavier, more resistant, etc., than other objects. We use the comparative form of the words in order to distinguish certain properties of objects. This basic and simple-minded fact is sometimes overlooked because the results of measurement are ordinarily stated in a positive form of speech. The very fact that we tend to forget that it is a comparison is testimony to its conceptual significance. "Three feet long" brings forth an image that is so definite that we think of it as a positive, black or white, description. Upon reflection, however, it is obvious that the statement is a comparison. It means that this object is longer than all objects that are less than three feet, equal to all objects that are exactly three feet, and shorter than all objects that are greater than three feet. Thus, the fundamental purpose of measurement is to allow us to distinguish or discriminate in respect to some property.

Measurement Proposition 1: The purpose of measurement is to order or compare objects or events to other objects or events.

Comparison of objects can be achieved in many different ways. The examination of any particular object will reveal a multitude of properties or characteristics that can be utilized to discriminate between that object and others. It will have length, volume, color, density, hardness, sweetness, shape, etc., any one or all of which can be utilized to compare. Even the simplest of objects possesses a bewildering array of different characteristics, and the *complete* description of all these characteristics may be well-nigh impossible. An attempt to describe all the characteristics of even the simplest object would require an enormous amount of time and effort, if it were possible at all.

Ordinarily, however, we do not want to know all of the characteristics of any particular object. The comparison is made between only certain selected characteristics of the objects. The purpose of the comparison will determine which characteristics should be measured and which should be ignored. Crusoe's problem (Churchman, *Definitions*, p. 84) of finding a flagstone to fit his hearth specified the characteristics that were relevant. Shape, length, and perhaps smoothness were relevant characteristics. Sweetness, specific gravity, carbon half-life, and perhaps color were not. But, our discussion overlaps. The selection of the characteristic to be measured employs the same relevancy criterion as the selection of the information to be transmitted. The metrician has a problem, and that problem, along with the theory for its solution, specifies which characteristic should be measured.

The primacy of the theory (some say "construct" or "conception") is stated by almost all investigators of the subject of measurement. It becomes even clearer here than in the writings on information. Churchman refers to the efficient use of the information in "any problem-situation"[2] and in another context the generation of "a class of information that will be useful in a wide variety of problems" (*Definitions*, p. 84). Stevens, who seems to disagree with Churchman on several points, is in complete agreement on this point. He puts the question as "What purposes are we trying to serve?"[3] instead of referring to the solution of problems; but the difference is only in the choice of words. The "purpose served" is clearly the solution of a problematic situation even if that problematic situation be entirely theoretical.

But all of this has been said in the chapter on information. The theory provides the criterion of relevance for the metrician in the same

2. "The scaling of a property of an object provides information as to the most efficient use of that property in any problem-situation." (Churchman, "Materialist," p. 490.)

3. "As I see this issue, there can surely be no objection to anyone computing any statistic that suits his fancy, regardless of where the numbers came from in the first place. Our freedom to calculate must remain as firm as our freedom to speak. The only question of substantial interest concerns the use to which the calculated statistic is intended. What purposes are we trying to serve?" (Stevens, *Definitions*, p. 29.)

manner as it did for the transmitter. In addition, however, in measurement theory the theory performs the indispensable service of describing or explaining the dimension (property, characteristic) that is to be measured. As Cassirer puts it, all measurements must be "conceived and sought."[4] That is, we do not discover dimensions; we mentally conceive them and then seek to perform an operation that allows us to express that conception as a measurement.[5] The conception of the dimension is fundamental. One cannot measure an unconceived dimension. The juxtaposition of a meter stick to an object in the absence of a conception of the dimension of length would be pointless. There are philosophical disputes over the existence of a dimension prior to its conception, but this is not germane. It is plain that one cannot seek an expression of something that he has not conceived.

Of course numbers can be generated for a wide variety of things, some of which may be quite abstract and difficult to describe. Length is a conception common to almost everyone, and thus "two yards" brings forth an immediate mental image. Entropy is not so common,

---

4. Caws quotes Cassirer and then presents a cogent argument for the prior conception notion: "This [operationism] is a neat solution to the problem of the identity of the measured and the defined, since the same operation serves for both processes. But it leaves the problem of the nature of what is measured and defined untouched. Suppose we measure a length by the familiar device of putting a standard measuring rod against it, and obtain a numerical result; does this tell us anything about length as such? What it does yield is something that may be called a 'specific length,' by analogy with specific gravity; but when the process is complete we know nothing about length as it applies to the case in question that we did not know about it as it applied to the standard measuring rod that we used. We would know something about length operationally only if the measuring rod itself had no length. . . . one first has a concept of some quality and looks afterwards for quantitative expressions of it." (Caws, p. 8.)

5. Guild refers to a creation of a magnitude instead of a conception: "It is probably usual to regard the experimental processes of determining equality and of adding as something which we have just found to be a convenient method of determining quantitative relations inherent in the nature of the magnitudes, whereas the processes are the necessary connecting links between phenomena and number without which there would be no basis of comparison between the laws of the former and those of the latter. The experimental criteria do not merely enable us to measure a magnitude, they *create* the magnitude by defining the fundamental relations which are to be the basis of the classification." (In Ferguson, p. 298.)

The "definition of the fundamental relation" is a mental conception which must come prior to the operation. "Create" seems to be tantamount to "conceive."

and therefore a measurement of entropy would be totally meaningless to many people. It requires extended explanation of the constructs of physics before measurements of entropy bring forth a meaningful mental image.

Measurement is concerned with a process of comparing or ranking objects in respect to some specific property. Obviously, that property must be amenable to comparison or we cannot measure it. More fundamental is the conception and the definition of the scale or dimension. "Dimension" is a convenient name for the concept of a particular property and the notion of scaling that property.

Measurement Proposition 2: The construction and definition of a dimension is a prerequisite to the operation of measurement.

Given the conceived dimension we can then relate or compare objects to other objects with respect to that dimension. We can align one object to another and discover which is longer without further refinements. This is a crude form of comparison, however, and further, it is only a *specific* relation of one object to another. In order to make the comparison general, we need a unit of measurement; in order to refine the degree of discrimination, we need to make use of numbers.

The operation of measurement involves the comparison of the object with a unit of measure. The purpose is to facilitate the comparison of the object to other objects in the specified dimension. In other words, the use of a unit makes the comparison *general*. By going through the medium of a unit, by expressing the relevant dimension in terms of units, we can relate an object to *all* other objects that have been, or will be, measured. Units allow one to make what appears to be a positive, purely descriptive statement but one which is, in reality, a comparative statement that can be used in a wide variety of circumstances. An ordinal scale of measurement without the units can be established for a class of objects; but this type of scale has the deficiency of the noncomparability of a particular object in one class with an object from another class. For example, we can create an ordinal scale by saying that A is greater than B in some dimension. Likewise, we can say that X is greater than Y in the same dimensions. However, this does not permit the comparison of X to A. We have no idea of the relation of X to A without a further operation. By contrast, if both X and A are described in some kind of units, comparison can be made even though they belong to different classes. Thus, the benefit of utilizing a unit is that it generalizes the results of measurements.

One requirement of a unit is that it "possess" the same dimension as the object. (For example, an inch has the dimension of length, a pound the dimension of weight, etc.) Without this characteristic, it would be impossible to compare the object to the unit. The possession of the dimension, however, implies nothing about the interval of that unit. The original establishment of a unit is quite arbitrary, and no particular unit has any claim to being more proper or correct than any other. The origin of the length unit may have been a King's nose, or a light wave, and although the latter may appear to be more scientific, because it is more esoteric, and the former more humorous, both have equal claim to the title "unit."

Moreover, the different units may be used interchangeably by the process of measuring one in terms of the other. The resulting relationship is called, in metrics theory, a "transformation function."[6] For example, the transformation function of yards to feet is the numeral "three"; from inches to centimeters, "2.54"; etc. It is true that one unit system may be easier to work with, such as metric versus English, but this easiness is due to the decimal base of the number system rather than to a property of the units.

---

6. Suppes distinguishes three separate transformations: "A real-valued function ϕ is a similarity transformation if there is a positive number a such that for every real number x

$$\phi(x) = ax.$$

In transforming from pounds to grams, for instance, the multiplicative factor a is 453.6.

A real-valued function ϕ is a linear transformation if there are numbers a and β with $a > \phi$ such that for every number x

$$\phi(x) = ax + \beta.$$

In transforming from Centigrade to Fahrenheit degrees of temperature, for instance, $a = 9/5$ and $\beta = 32$.

A real-valued function ϕ is a monotone increasing transformation if, for any two numbers x and y, if $x < y$, then $\phi(x) < \phi(y)$.

Such transformations are also called *order-preserving*." (Suppes, *Definitions*, p. 131n.) We utilize the general notion of similarity transformation without distinguishing the different kinds.

Although the origin of a unit is arbitrary, the subsequent selection must be made with some care if the use of the measurement is to be generalized. Wide use of a measurement by different people requires familiarity with the unit in which the measurement is expressed. For example, most English-speaking people use the English system of foot-pound-second. To these people a measurement expressed in meters is meaningless. They must discover the length of a meter before such expressions are meaningful. That is, until they relate meters to something in their own experience (inches or yards), the informational value of the measurement is nil.

The purpose of units is to make the objects comparable to all other objects in the specified dimension, i.e. to make the measurement general. If we want to expand the generality of measurements to different classes of users of the data, the unit selected must be one that is familiar to those users.

Measurement Proposition 3: Units allow a general comparison of objects. A familiar unit allows a general use of measurements by different people.

The comparison of the object to the unit usually results in a statement of numerosity. The reasons for the use of numbers are (1) to gain a greater degree of refinement in discriminating between objects and (2) convenience.

Parts of speech contain only three classifications—positive, comparative, and superlative—which permit only the crudest of comparisons. Using only these classifications we could only positively identify the two extremes. For example, we could point out only the shortest and the longest in a given set of rods. All the others could be described only in the comparative form—longer than the shortest, next to the longest, shorter than the longest—which permits little discrimination and is cumbersome.

By setting up a verbal classification, it is possible to make finer distinctions. The Beaufort scale is an example. "Gentle breeze" is less than "moderate breeze," which is less than "fresh breeze," etc. Such verbal classifications have several unfortunate characteristics.[7] First,

---

7. Other writers describe the advantages of quantitative concepts in more detail. See, e.g., Hempel, pp. 56-57. The Beaufort scale example is from Hempel.

each dimension measured requires the establishment and definition of a new classification. Not only does this require time and effort on the part of the metrician, it also limits the users of the measurements to those who have taken the trouble to learn the classifications. Second, any refinement of the classification scheme requires the introduction of new terms. Very fine gradations become cumbersome. Third, each classification fails to discriminate between items within that classification, although there may be a relatively large deviation, and at the same time it makes very fine distinctions at the boundaries of each classification, often without adequate criteria for making those distinctions.

Numerosity of units does not have such limitations. Only one classification—the unit—is necessary. Beyond that, the general number scheme can be utilized for all units in all dimensions. Thus, one attribute of numerosity is its convenience. Another attribute is the infinitely fine gradation available in the number scheme. Numbers can be fractionalized to any desired degree. If the unit is subject to fractionalization, a measurement expressed in numbers can be carried to any degree of precision. The limitations of precision, when numbers are used, is a result of the limited perception of the metrician and/or the limitation of the instrument; it is not due to any characteristic of numbers.

Measurement Proposition 4: The use of numbers is more convenient and permits a higher degree of precision than a verbal classification scheme.

The operation or procedure of measurement has for its purpose the placement of a given object in a dimensional scale. The *purpose* of the operation has nothing to do with instrumentation, precision, or specification of procedure. There may be a variety of different instruments and procedures available to measure any particular object, but the selection of the instrument is not germane to the purpose. Weight may be measured by the use of several different kinds of instruments each of which require a different procedure. However, in each case the desired end is to *discover*, by *means* of the procedure and instrument, the number of pounds, grams, etc., that the object possesses. Once the numerosity of units has been discovered, the object has then been related to all other objects in this dimensional scale through the medium of the number of units.

This is a fundamental disagreement with the rather common statement that measurement is the *assignment* of numbers to an object. Assignment is much too broad a term in describing operations of measurement. One can assign numbers to objects by means of a table of random numbers. One can mentally project any number to any object in a capricious and arbitrary fashion. Such a projection or assignment cannot be called a measurement, because it does not discriminate among objects in respect to a property. We do not deny that the dimension is a mental conception and that the units are arbitrary. However, once this dimension has been conceived and the units defined, the objects then *possess* a certain number of those dimension units; and the purpose of the operation is to discover that number.

We have a well-defined conception of the dimension of length and several (arbitrary) units of length. Given the conception and the unit, it makes no sense to speak of "assigning" numbers to a rod unless we agree to use the word in a rather peculiar fashion. Discovery is a much more appropriate term, because that is what the operation accomplishes; it discovers, or reveals, the numerosity of the dimension units in that rod. Of course, we could agree to use "assign" in conjunction with the word operation—"assign numbers in accordance with a specified operation"—and this would mean the same thing. For example, we could say "assign the number to this object equal to that number of weights that is required to make this scale balance." However, the purpose of this operation is abundantly clear. It is to discover the number of weights that are required to make the scale balance. The object has the dimension of weight; there is an extant condition of that object; and the operation *reveals* a numerosity of units that allows us to compare it to other objects.

Precisely the same thing is true in an ordinal scale. For example, in Moh's scale of hardness certain minerals have been selected as basic referents and have been assigned numbers. We *assign* numbers to a scale; we *discover* the numerosity of units in an object. These minerals and their corresponding (assigned) numbers constitute a scale of the dimension of hardness. The units in such a scale lack certain attributes that other units possess; but that is not pertinent at the moment. Given the preconceived notion of hardness and the arbitrarily constructed units, the purpose of an operation of a measure of hardness by Moh's test is to discover the proper placement of an object in a preassigned numerical scale. Suppose that objects X and Y have been assigned the numerals 1 and 2 in Moh's scale. If we measure mineral Z by the operation of scratching and find that it scratches X and is scratched by Y, we have discovered its place on Moh's scale: it belongs between 1 and 2. The exact point between 1 and 2 is not known; but the operation *discovered,* albeit imprecisely, the place in the scale where the object belonged.

Of course, one can point out that letters of the alphabet could have been used instead of numbers. Because of that fact some metricians argue that Moh's scale is not properly called a measurement. We will not join in this dispute; our point is much less subtle: given the fact that numbers are used, the operation discovers the particular number (or range of numbers) that describes the object's place in the scale. The object has an existing condition, the operation discovers that condition.

Measurement Proposition 5: The purpose of the operation of measurement is to discover the proper placement of a given object in a given scale. The general statement of placement is in terms of numerosity of units.

SUMMARY

The purpose of measurement is to make information more informative. Given the premise of Criterion I, it follows that, if possible, we should utilize the concept and procedure of measurement in this study. Our basic purpose is to provide information, and measurement provides more information; therefore, we should measure.

The manner in which measurements increase our information is quite different from the relevance criterion. Relevance remains the *sine qua non* of information. An irrelevant measurement is not "information" as we have defined it. We noted that measurements were "conceived and sought"; and the reason they are sought is precisely because they are relevant. Given the requisite of relevance, the question remains: Why are relevant measurements more informative than relevant nonmeasurements?

A review of measurement theory reveals two apparently self-contradictory attributes which make measurements more informative: they are both more general and more precise at the same time—more general because we can relate any object to *all* other objects by utilizing the medium of units; more precise because we can refine our discriminatory powers by expressing the units in degree numerically.

The concept of measurement may be outlined as four temporally ordered steps:

1. The conception of a dimension (because this dimension is relevant to some problematic situation).
2. Definition of the units and scale of the dimension.
3. Agreement to express the units numerically.
4. Description and application of an operation that discovers the numerosity of units in a given object.

The operation of measurement occurs in the reverse order. Two objects, A and B, are not ranked or related when found in experience. The application of the operation discovers the placement of these objects on a scale and expresses that placement in numerosity of units. This expression permits the conceptual ranking of those two objects in the dimension and also, because of the generality of the units and numbers, the potential ranking of those two objects to all other objects. We can now say that A is greater than, less than, or equal to, B in respect to some property which we call a dimension. Also A is greater than, less than, or equal to, C, D, E, . . . , which have been, or will be, expressed in the same units by the same operation. This ranking, presumably, is not an idle exercise; instead it is a deliberate attempt to obtain that information because that dimension is considered to be relevant to some theory and that theory is considered to be applicable to some problematic situation.

Of course, the two objects, A and B, could be ordered one to the other without going through the units. However, if at a later time we wanted to add C to our conceptual order, we would be forced to compare it to both A and B before placing it on the scale. Then if D were added, the same process would be required, and perhaps one of the earlier placements would have to be shifted. In a very short time this would become cumbersome. Thus, the units perform the function of generalizing the relationship of objects to objects. They relate all objects to all other objects with respect to a particular property.

In addition, units generalize the comparison in another direction. To communicate the fact that "A is greater than B" presupposes that the receiver knows the size of B; "A is greater than B and less than C" presupposes that he knows the sizes of both B and C. If the receiver does not know the sizes of the referent objects, there can be no conceptual ordering. The use of a unit permits all receivers who have knowledge of the size of the unit to make the generalized comparison.

The use of numbers is a convenient method of ordering magnitudes that is common to almost all members of the community. Moreover, if the unit is subject to fractionalization, the use of numbers allows us to state the magnitude in a degree of precision that is limited only by our perception or instrumentation. Thus, under ideal conditions of measurement, each object would have a unique place on the scale.

The advantages of expressing income as a measurement are the same as those of any other magnitude: it permits a generalized, precise, convenient, conceptual ordering of a relevant magnitude by all receivers who are familiar with the dimension and unit. The accomplishment of this goal has several prerequisites. We must:

1. Conceive and describe the dimension.
2. Discover a familiar unit.
3. Define an operation that will allow us to discover the numerosity of the units.

These prerequisite tasks are the subject of a subsequent chapter.

VI

MEASUREMENT (Continued)

In the previous chapter we outlined briefly some general propositions of measurement theory. There are several other attributes of measurement that are germane to this study but are rather more specific than the propositions presented above. The purpose of this chapter is to review these characteristics.

CONDITIONS ATTENDING THE OPERATION OF MEASUREMENT

In the previous discussion we referred to the "operation" of measurement. Much of the metrics literature has been devoted to the necessity of carefully defining this operation (procedure), and a major dispute has arisen about the results of such a definition. We do not deny the importance of such a description nor do we wish to join the controversy between the operationalists (often called operationists) and the nonoperationalists. Our point is not that the description of operations is unimportant, but that it is insufficient. Of greater importance are the theory, which calls for an expression of some magnitude, and the problem, which requires that such a theory be used. In view of Stevens' statement about the "purpose served" and of Guild's about the "creation of the magnitude," it appears that we have no fundamental disagreement with these operationalists.

However, Margenau observes that there are other philosophers and scientists who have an oversimplified view of the concept of measurement.

> Most philosophers and many scientists regard measurement as a simple "look-and-see" procedure, requiring at the most a careful description of apparatus and the recording of a number. In doing so, they ignore two things. First, the relevance of the number obtained, its reference to something that is to be measured, and its physical dimension. For the apparatus and the act alone do not tell us that the measured number represents a length, an energy, or a frequency; this identification involves the use of certain rules of correspondence with preformed theoretical constructs which greatly complicates the meaning of measurement. (Margenau, *Definitions*, pp. 164-65.)

Our disagreement is with those people—perhaps they should be called "extreme operationalists"—who seem to think that the description of the apparatus *alone* makes the reported figure meaningful and relevant.

More germane to this study is the following, not atypical, quotation: "To the extent that the figures appearing on the report of earnings and the balance sheet are influenced by such decisions, they can be rendered at all meaningful *only by consistent treatment of like items* and are fully understandable *only if the underlying accounting policies are known.* (Robnett, Hill, and Beckett, p. 511.) The implication is that these figures will be rendered meaningful if the "apparatus" is carefully described and consistently applied. We disagree. Hempel goes through an interesting *reductio ad absurdum* argument in opposition to the operationists position.

> Concepts with empirical import can be readily defined in any number, but most of them will be of no use for systematic purposes. Thus, we might define the hage of a person as the product of his height in millimeters and his age in years. This definition is operationally adequate and the term "hage" thus introduced would have relatively high precision and uniformity of usage; but it lacks theoretical import, for we have no general laws connecting the hage of a person with other characteristics. (Hempel, p. 46.)

No matter how carefully one describes the apparatus of measuring hage, nor how consistently it is applied, the results are not "meaningful." The same is true for figures appearing in accounting reports. The description of the act and apparatus *alone* does not make the figures meaningful or fully understandable.

The overemphasis (or misunderstanding) of the description of the operation should not blind us to its continued importance. Such description may help to clarify and sharpen our conception of the dimension. Children are often taught the conception of length by having them perform the simple operation of juxtaposition of rules. Wooden blocks help in the conception of area and volume. Moreover, the description may render measurements comparable or it may prevent errors. For example, the "C," "F," or "K" that appears in conjunction with temperature measurements is a description of the calibration of the instrument. Given that information, one can adjust centigrade to Kelvin and make the figures comparable. Without that information the figures are either useless or, if one assumes that they are both in the same calibration, productive of errors.

On a more abstract level, the need for the description of the general conditions attending a measure is self-evident: measurements always take place under different conditions. One cannot measure two different objects at the same time, in the same place, with the same instrument. Often these different conditions are of no consequence. The time difference may be so short that it can be ignored; or if the object is temporally invariant in the particular dimension, a large time difference is an "irrelevant" condition. However, the shortness of the time interval or the temporal invariance of the object is an indispensable datum. One cannot legitimately ignore a time difference unless he knows that the distortion caused is negligible. When one ignores in this fashion, he is implicitly making an *adjustment* of the data. It may be a zero adjustment, as in this case, or a similarity transformation (e.g., from centigrade to Fahrenheit), in other cases. In any event the conditions under which the measurement was made must be known before the data can be fully utilized.

There are two ways of making the conditions known:

1. Standardize the conditions and report the standards.
2. Report the conditions with each measurement.

Churchman argues for the first alternative;

> The reason for standardized data is easy enough to give. Without standards, one would have to report all the relevant information about the time, place, persons, etc., in addition to the data report itself. Otherwise, no one would know what values to assign to the variables in the laws that enable one to use the report in other circumstances. But once a standard has been given, then all data reports can be adjusted to the standard, and all that is needed is the data report itself. (Churchman, *Definitions*, p. 91.)

In the terms of a previous chapter, Churchman is concerned with conserving channel capacity. If the standards are reported once and followed consistently, they need not be repeated with each message. In reporting temperature, for example, we could omit the "C," "F," or "K" from each transmission if we standardized the temperature calibration.

We are in complete agreement: Conservation of channel capacity is a commendable goal. However, there is a more fundamental reason for standardizing the conditions. Some measurements are not amenable to adjustment. Some do not have "laws that enable one to use the report in other circumstances." Objects that are not temporally invariant provide an example. There is no known method of weighing a person at birth and adjusting the data so that we know his weight at 21 years of age or his weight today. If the purpose is to relate the weights of people today, then the time of the measurement must be standardized. In such cases the very purpose of the measurement is vitiated if the conditions are not standardized.

Another disadvantage of nonstandard measurements is the time and effort required to make the adjustment. There is a cost attached to adjustment, and therefore adjustments should be minimized.

In summary, we note that the purpose of measurement is to make comparisons. In order for this purpose to be met, the conditions of the measurement must be either standardized or amenable to adjustment. In some cases the former is merely preferable because it (1) conserves channel capacity and (2) minimizes costs. In other cases, standardization is essential because there is no known method of adjusting the data to make it comparable. Thus, there is a need for the standardization of conditions, but this is not possible since no two measurements can be made under precisely the same conditions. For the variation in conditions that cannot be standardized, the only thing that can be done is to *report* the nonstandard conditions so that the user of the data can either make adjustments or estimate the degree of noncomparability.

The notion of standardization is important to this study because of the argument about the uniformity of accounting principles. Critics of the present state of accounting have complained about the wide variations in method that are allowed in the measurement of income. They have urged that the method be standardized in order to make the data comparable. For the opposition, the reply has been that uniformity would make accounting so rigid that experimentation would be prohibited. Experimentation is necessary to progress, and therefore, so the argument goes, uniformity would prohibit progress. In addition, it is thought that a rigid method would not be applicable to all firms, because each firm is different from all others. That is, the differences in the objects to be measured require different methods of measurement. A third school attempts to ameliorate the dispute by allowing different methods but requiring that the method be disclosed in footnotes. Presumably, in this way, the reader can adjust the data to make it comparable.

Since standardization of data is at least a desideratum and may be essential, we applaud the efforts of those who have attempted to make the principles uniform. Accountants have long recognized the necessity of consistency of method within the firm, and interfirm uniformity is simply an extension of that rule. Intrafirm consistency is for the purpose of making the data comparable over time, and interfirm consistency would have the purpose of making it comparable between firms. We fail to see how consistency would inhibit progress. Theoretical advancements could still be made and then consistently implemented. Witness the consistent application of rigid rules by the National Income Bureau, concurrent with theoretical refinements and periodic implementation of those refinements. The implementation of the refinements always causes some disruption and requires adjustments (splicing the series). However, the disruption is the result of the lack of consistency (changing method); and if there were continuous inconsistency, there would be continuous disruption. Inconsistency does not inhibit progress; it causes chaos.

The disclosure argument is similar to the operationists' position and may be criticized on two grounds. First, the adjustments are costly. Fahrenheit requires effort before it can be compared to centigrade; and the continued use of both calibrations demands strong justification. We have not been convinced of the merits of different methods even if they are adjustable. Secondly, and more importantly, a complex method requires a complex adjustment. Most footnotes to financial statements are epigrammatic generalizations about a very complicated method. They permit only the crudest kind of adjustment. For example, lifo cannot be adjusted to fifo—even by an experienced Certified Public Accountant—in the absence of the complete detail of the inventory records. For the average receiver a lifo-fifo comparison is utterly impossible even if he has the detailed inventory account. Thus, in many instances, the data are not adjustable, and standardization is imperative. In all cases standardization is preferable.

Finally, we fail to understand why differences in the objects to be measured require different methods of measurement. The purpose of measurement is to discover differences. If one uses different methods, it is impossible to know whether the different results reflect differences in the objects or differences in the methods. Suppose, for example, that we wanted to measure the resistance of two different metals; but because those metals were used for different purposes—say, one was in a series and the other in a parallel circuit—we decided to use Ohm's method ($R = V \cdot 1/I$) to measure one and Sterling's method ($R = V \cdot 2/I$) to measure the other. The example seems absurd; but compare it to the measurement of first year depreciation, which may be by the straight-line method ($D = C \cdot 1/L$) or the double declining balance method ($D = C \cdot 2/L$). (C is the cost outlay and L is the life.) Both are used in accounting, and the defense is that the objects being measured are different or the circumstances surrounding the objects are different. Note that if the method used is disclosed, even to the extent of precisely specifying the functional form, the figure labeled D is the product of two unknown variables, and therefore it has an infinite number of solutions. Thus, the variables cannot be determined so that they can be recast in the same functional form.

There is no way for the figures to be adjusted by the receiver so that they will be comparable. Exactly what information is being given or what dimension is being measured or what use can be made of the figures in such circumstances is unknown to the author.

For these reasons we are in general agreement with the notion of uniformity of accounting principles. However, even if the principles and methods are uniform, we still have not met Hempel's main objection. Even if hage has "uniformity of usage," it still lacks "theoretical import." In our terms, hage (or values or depreciation) must be relevant; it must reveal a placement of the objects in a dimension that is relevant to some theory. Standardization is a secondary consideration.

THE TEMPORAL CONDITIONS OF THE OPERATION

For some measurements the dimension is conceived as the relation of two other dimensions. These are often called "dependent measurements," because they depend on the measurement of more "fundamental" dimensions. In physics the dimensions of volume, pressure, length, time, force, number, angle, electrical resistance, current, and voltage are classified as fundamental. Temperature, density, magnetic permeability, etc., are "derived" or "dependent" dimensions.[1] Density is often used to illustrate the distinction. The weight and volume of an object is measured and then expressed as a ratio (weight divided by volume). That is, the fundamental dimensions yield the derived dimension.[2] Likewise, temperature is considered derived because it depends on length,[3] and speed because it is dependent on distance (length) and time.

Income falls into the category of a derived dimension because it is change in wealth over a period of *time*. A discussion of wealth is left for a subsequent chapter, but there are several attributes of time that

---

1. This is Campbell's classification. There are others. (Campbell, *Aristotelian*, pp. 126-27.)

2. For further analyses of the dimension density, see, e.g., Campbell, *Physics*, pp. 275-77, 346-48; Cohen and Nagel, pp. 298-301; Pap, pp. 131-35; Bergmann and Spence, p. 108; Guild, in A. Ferguson *et al.*, pp. 298-99.

3. Campbell (*Physics*, pp. 396-402) and Guild (in A. Ferguson *et al.*, pp. 302-05) present lengthy and conflicting analyses of the measurement of temperature.

are general to all measurements. Since income has this vital temporal dimension, we may profit from a general discussion of the relation of time to measurement.

Measurements may be comparisons of two different kinds as they relate to time: instantaneous or intertemporal. One may wish either to compare different objects at a given point in time or to compare the same object at different instants. The former, we define as "instantaneous," the latter as "intertemporal."

Instantaneous measurement has for its purpose the ranking of objects at a specified moment. The operation has for its purpose the discovery of the units contained in an object, and it occurs at a specified moment in time—the present. One cannot perform an operation yesterday or tomorrow; one can only perform an operation now. It is possible to plan to perform an operation in the future, and it is possible to have performed an operation in the past, but the operation is always in fact performed in the present. Of course, one can predict what a future operation will reveal and what a past operation would have revealed; but these are predictions and retrodictions, not measurements. Thus, all measurements—the number resulting from the performance of an operation—are descriptions of the past, because the "present" is just a fleeting moment separating past and future. Thus, one requirement for an instantaneous comparison is that the temporal location of the operation be in the past. More important, however, is the requirement either that the operation on all the objects be performed at the same instant or that the measurement be subject to adjustment. That is, if we wish to compare objects with other objects, the temporal location of the operation must be standardized or there must be a known method for adjusting the data.

A common adjustment for measurements taken at different times is a zero "adjustment." There are many objects that are temporally invariant; and thus the time dimension is said to be irrelevant, i.e. it requires a zero adjustment. The length of a steel rod is an example. Other conditions being equal, the length of one steel rod may be instantaneously compared to the lengths of all other steel rods regardless of when the measurements are made. On the other hand, the lengths of organic objects are not normally temporally invariant; and therefore, unless they are amenable to adjustment, the measurements must be taken at the same time if an instantaneous comparison is desired.

If our purpose is to rank two infants by weight, it would be absurd to weigh one in January and the other in July. The resulting figures would not permit us to rank their weight at any point in time. Since there is no known method of adjustment, the measurements must be taken at approximately the same time. We say "approximately" because the purpose of the measurement may allow for imprecision. For most purposes, we would ignore a difference of one second or one minute. We would probably ignore a difference of one hour, and perhaps even a difference of a week. However, any difference in time results in some degree of noncomparability, and it would be desirable to have the measurements perfectly comparable.

As Pap (p. 128) puts it, such comparisons "must be treated as a triadic relation involving the time variable." Instantaneous comparison of objects A and B could be stated in the following form:

$$[A(t_1) > B(t_1)] \text{ or } [A(t_1) < B(t_1)] \text{ or } [A(t_1) = B(t_1)].$$

The interobject comparison is made with time a constant.

Intertemporal comparisons are in the following form:

$$[A(t_1) > A(t_2)] \text{ or } [A(t_1) < A(t_2)] \text{ or } [A(t_1) = A(t_2)].$$

The purpose here is to rank the object in respect to itself at different points in time. Obviously the time instant could not be standardized, in the sense of holding it constant, because the purpose is to compare over time. If, however, the dimension is additive (discussed *infra*), so that increments can be calculated, then it is desirable to standardize the time interval. In this way we can make the following kind of rankings:

$$[A(t_3) - A(t_2)] > [A(t_2) - A(t_1)].$$

In one sense the standardization of the interval is not required, because various time intervals, being simply different units of the same dimension, are inherently adjustable. Miles per hour is easily adjusted to miles per second, for example. Such adjustments produce quite valuable information in many cases, since they permit projections or dispositional statements. For instance, one can meaningfully say that an object *would have* travelled X miles if it had continued travelling at the measured rate of Y miles per second for Z hours. Likewise one can meaningfully say that an object "travelled at an *average* of X miles per second" after one divides the measured distance it did travel in one hour by 3600. The first statement is not a measurement of the distance that an object travelled during an hour; instead it is a projection of the distance that it would have travelled had it not come to rest. The second statement is not a measurement of the distance travelled in any one second; instead it is an average. If one wishes to compare the actual distance travelled in different time intervals, it is necessary to standardize the intervals.

In summary there are four different kinds of comparisons possible:

1. $A(t_i)$ to $B(t_i)$ to $C(t_i)$ ...
2. $A(t_i)$ to $A(t_{i+1})$ to $A(t_{i+2})$ ...
3. $[A(t_i)$ to $A(t_{i+1})]$ to $[A(t_{i+1})$ to $A(t_{i+2})]$ to $[A(t_{i+2})$ to $A(t_{i+3})]$ ...
4. $[A(t_i)$ to $A(t_{i+1})]$ to $[B(t_i)$ to $B(t_{i+1})]$ to $[C(t_i)$ to $C(t_{i+1})]$ ...

In respect to time, comparison one requires that all objects be measured at the same time; comparison two requires that the same object be measured at different times; comparison three is more general than two, in that the intervals need to be standardized; and comparison four is even more general, in that both the instants and intervals need to be standardized. Comparison four, being an interobject increment comparison, is a combination of comparisons one and three; and the requirements of both one and three must be met.

The standardizations of the instants and intervals refer to the times at which the measurements are made or the operation performed. It is possible to make interobject and increment comparisons when the measurement is made at different times without making adjustments. For example, we could rank the weights of infants at time of birth or at one year of age, or the distance travelled at the time the objects come to rest, etc. Although stated in terms of time, these rankings are actually at an *event,* and the time of the event is irrelevant. "Time of birth" in this instance means "event of birth." Event comparisons are perfectly legitimate; and they are powerful comparisons, since they escape the time boundary altogether. One could compare one's birth weight with that of George Washington or Louis XIV, for example. However, event comparisons are quite different from time comparisons; and the failure to distinguish carefully between the two is productive of error.

This rather lengthy look at temporal conditions of measurement is particularly germane to this study. There are some income metricians who are troubled by the existence of different prices at different times. They claim that prices cannot be utilized in their measurements because of those differences. Yet it is clear that income is an intertemporal comparison, and the measurement is for the purpose of *discovering* the difference in wealth over a period of time. It is also clear that three of the valuation coefficients are prices. If there were no differences in wealth, and one requirement for such a difference is a price change, there would be no point in making the measurement. If wealth is temporally invariant, an intertemporal comparison of wealth is pointless. The claim of these metricians is tantamount to saying that the weight increment of infants is impossible to determine because their weight will change in the future.

The complaint is sometimes stated in terms of prices being only "momentary." However, everything that is temporally variant has "only" a "momentary" number of units. That is the meaning of temporal variance. The specific number of units occurs only at a point in time, and it will change in the future. If the purpose of a measurement is to discover the variation that has occurred during a time interval, it is patently absurd to argue that one should not measure because there *is* a variation.

The school of income measurement that refuses to use prices because they vary and are only momentary does in fact use prices. The only difference is that they use a past instead of a present or future price. Since at one time the past price was both a future and present price, the arguments against using present prices are equally applicable to the past price. That is, if one cannot use a present price because it is only momentary and will vary in the future, then *a fortiori* one cannot use a past price, because it *was* only momentary and *has already varied*. The Accounting Tradition selects a price and decides to hold that price constant over time. Boulding also suggests a constant. But that is a decision, not a reflection of price behavior. By making such decisions one could estimate a future price and hold it constant over time also. In this way one could eliminate recorded variations, if that is what is desired, in the same way that holding a past price constant eliminates recorded variations.

In effect, the Accounting Tradition reverts to an event comparison. Specifically the valuation coefficient selected is the price at the event of purchase. That valuation coefficient is held constant, and no further measurement is made until the event of sale. We could exclude event comparisons from consideration, because we defined income as a wealth change over time, not over events. It is not that simple, however, since the Accounting Tradition measures upon the occurrence of an event, but then sums those event measures for a period of time. Thus, their income measure is the sum of the measures of events that have occurred within a specified time interval.

In one sense the Accounting Tradition avoids the principle problem of this study, viz. valuing under conditions of an incomplete exchange, because it waits until the exchange is complete. But that description is not adequate because the Accounting Tradition does "value" under conditions of an incomplete exchange in the sense that it uses a past transformation coefficient as a present valuation coefficient. It is the question of the informational content of the various valuation coefficients that remains open at this point. Nonetheless, it is clear that the Accounting Tradition is not a temporal measurement. Event comparisons do not permit instantaneous comparisons or intertemporal comparisons or intertemporal increment comparisons.

The distinction can be made clear by considering spatial location and distance travelled. Suppose we have a collection of objects that are in a constant state of motion and they collide with other objects on occasion. If instruments are available, we can measure the location at the event of collision and calculate the distance travelled since the last collision. Under these conditions one can never know the location of the objects relative to one another, since they are colliding at different times. One can never compare the net distance travelled in any particular direction, since the object may have gone off in any direction at its last collision. Thus the net northerly distance travelled may be positive, negative, or zero since its last collision or since its next to the last collision or since its initial collision. If one prepares a report at a point in *time* by reporting the location and distance of the object at its *last collision*, then that report is in error by the amount of the unknown distance and direction travelled between the time of the collision and the report. The temporal measurements are more informative generally, since they permit more comparisons and since the purpose of measurement is to compare or rank objects.

Some income metricians will agree with the example as far as the desirability of making temporal measurements is concerned, but they complain that it is impossible to make such measurements—or, at least, that it is impossible to make them objectively. This is a reasonable position; but it is clear that the trouble lies in our ability to make desired measurements, not in the theory or conception of temporal measurements. It is the author's belief that it is an error to build a theory upon the ability to measure, because that ability can change over time, as the state of the arts changes or the design of the instruments changes. A better procedure is to state the theory and conceive the dimension relevant to that theory, and then to make modifications as necessary to reflect limitations on the ability to measure that dimension.

MEASUREMENTS, PREDICTIONS, AND RETRODICTIONS

We have noted that the operation of measurement is for the purpose of discovering an existing condition. The operation occurs at a given instant and discovers the condition that exists at that instant. The instant in which the operation is performed is always the present. One can *plan* to perform an operation in the future; but one can only perform that operation *now*, in the present, which very soon becomes the past. Thus, all measurements are of past dimensions. This does not mean that the dimension did not exist previously or that it will not exist in the future. However, knowledge of the previous or future existence of a dimension requires an additional step beyond the operation of measurement. The original purpose of making the measurement may be to predict a future condition or retrodict a past condition, but this does not negate the fact that measurement concerns an existing condition and that predictions are of a fundamentally different nature. (See Grünbaum, Chapter 9, for a consideration of retrodictability and predictability.)

For example, Crusoe's search for a flagstone contained a very simple prediction, viz. that the objects would remain spatially and temporally invariant. First, he measured the hearth, and then, in a different time and different place, he measured the flagstone. From this he predicted that the flagstone would fit the hearth. Obviously if the flagstone were temporally or spatially variant, it would not fit the hearth. That is, his prediction would be wrong. Nevertheless, his measurement could have been correct, regardless of the correctness of his predictions.[4] The distinction may blur in practice but conceptually is quite clear.

4. Churchman says that Crusoe "argues" that the hearth will fit the flagstone. We have said above that it requires an adjustment. The distinction between an adjustment and a prediction is basically temporal. A measurement (an expression of an existing property taken under some past conditions) is "adjusted" to make it comparable to a measurement taken under different conditions. The person hypothesizes that if the past conditions had been the same, the measurement would have been some other amount. He says, "If measurement X had been taken under conditions Y, the result would have been Z instead of X." This is a counterfactual-conditional or, if preferred, it is a retrodiction. It states what would have occurred in the past if the conditions had been Y.

A prediction, on the other hand, states what will be in the future. The temporal condition is important because it can be argued that, *cet. par.*, a retrodiction is more probable than a prediction. The argument may be briefly outlined as follows:

First, no "law" that permits either predictions or retrodictions is ever completely verified in the sense that the act has occurred. Goodman uses the simple example of heating some butter.

1. If that butter is heated to 150°F., it will melt.
2. If that butter had been heated to 150°F., it would have melted.

Statement one is a prediction, and statement two is a retrodiction. They both involve the same "law," but that law has not been verified in the sense that all butter has been heated and the reaction observed. If it all had been heated, the "law" would be useless because it would be about a nonexistent thing.

Given the lack of verification of the law, we can argue that the law is "only" a probability statement; it is not *certain* that the butter would have melted or that it will melt every time that it could have been or will be heated. (Cf. Broad.)

Second, there is no unassailable reason to assume that the future will be like the past in all relevant respects. We usually do project the future on the basis of the past, mainly because that is the only evidence we have; but the assumption that the future will be like the past may be unwarranted. Keynes refers to this as the "uniformity of nature" assumption (Keynes, *Probability,* p. 226) and notes the difficult logical problems. Russell's chicken example notes the same problem (*infra,* p. 99). Thus, we can say that a future projection is only a probability statement.

Third, any prediction is a combination of these probabilities. A prediction has

If the dimension is temporally variant, the distinction is thrown in clear relief. At t_1 we could measure the temperature of a given volume of liquid and discover that it was F_1. From our previous experience we can predict that the temperature will vary over time. In fact, under *cet. par.* conditions we can predict with certainty what the temperature will be in the future. A physicist will tell us that the temperature will equal the temperature of its environment at t_n. The experiment has been verified so often that we have a high degree of confidence that the outcome will equal our prediction. It has become a "law" of physics. Note, however, that this law is the result of a functional relationship between measurements. At various times in the past someone has measured the temperatures of the environment and liquid, time, surface exposed to the air, etc., and formally stated the temperature changes as a function of time. The measurements were the original raw data; the law is a method of projecting a future state-of-being. The prediction can be verified by another measurement when the future becomes the present.

Given the lawlike characteristic of this prediction, the fact that it is not a measurement is of little consequence in practical affairs. We would all be willing to act on the basis of this kind of prediction in the same manner as if it were a measurement. Indeed, we could even reverse the variables. By measuring the temperature change we could determine the elapsed time without an independent measurement. By measuring the elapsed time we could obtain the temperature change without a thermometer. Suppose, however, that we remove the *cet. par.* conditions. Assume that we take the liquid out of the laboratory and expose it to the normal atmosphere. This change does not invalidate the law, it simply renders it inoperable for the purpose of predicting a specific future temperature. The temperature of the liquid

---

an understood clause about the future. "If this butter is heated to 150° *and* the world remains unchanged in all relevant respects, this butter will melt." A retrodiction does not need the understood clause, because it concerns the past; and what has been is an empirical question. Since a prediction requires a second connected probability, regardless of how high that probability is, the probability of the successful prediction is less than that of a retrodiction. (See Grünbaum, p. 285, for a different argument which leads to the same conclusion.)

still depends upon the temperature of its environment. If the environment temperature remains stable over sufficiently long periods, the temperature of the liquid will equal it. However, the prediction can no longer be stated as a specific temperature (a number of units) at a given time. It is now stated as a relation: "The temperature of the liquid will tend to equal the temperature of its environment." It will only "tend" because the environment temperature may be quite volatile and may never remain stable long enough for the two to become equal, since the temperature of the liquid may change more slowly. Moreover, the uncertainty about the future temperature of the environment renders the future temperature of the liquid equally uncertain.

One possibility in this situation is to make a conditional statement. That is, we can say:

> If the temperature of the environment remains constant for T time at F temperature, then the temperature of the liquid will equal F at t_n.

Under the present assumption we know that the antecedent is false, and therefore we know that at t_n the temperature will not equal F. In this case we have merely stated the law in a different manner and added the fact that the antecedent is false. In many contexts these statements are useful, and they may be valid. However, it is clear that they are not concerned with an actual state-of-being in either the past, present, or future. They are statements which may have a high degree of probability and perform a valuable function, but they are not measurements.

These points are rather obvious, and we need not belabor them further. The reason for the discussion is that there are income theorists in all four schools that are future oriented. The Fisher Tradition has its very basis in predictions. Its wealth is a report of discounted predictions, and its income is the difference between discounted predictions at two points in time. Clearly the Fisher Tradition is not a measurement of wealth unless one defines wealth as a state of mind.

Accountants are critical of the Fisher Tradition for the reason that it is a prediction. They are fond of pointing out that they are concerned with what is, not with what will be. In view of the uncertainty of predictions we are inclined to agree with them.[5] If there is a choice

5. The view of the future taken here is in agreement with Russell, and it follows

between measurement and prediction we would eschew prediction. However, the accountant often justifies the past (purchase) transformation coefficient on the basis of assuming a "going concern," i.e. assuming that the firm will continue indefinitely in the future. Thus, the accountant avoids the problems of predicting the future by embracing an assumption about the future. This may be likened to a physicist who, knowing the impossibility of predicting the environment temperature, decides to assume an environment temperature. If that assumption is essential to his measurement, it raises some serious doubts about the resulting figures. The accountant uses a past transformation coefficient, but assumes a future for the firm. The relationship between the past (known) state-of-being and an assumed future state-of-being is not clear. Exactly what compels him to justify the past with an assumed future is an enigma. If he is assuming a future in order to justify using a past measurement as a present measurement, the situation is even more confusing. What does the unknown future have to do with a past state-of-being's relationship to a present state-of-being? Edwards and Bell (pp. 9 ff.) allege that this assumption is, in reality, "the stationary state." But whether the state has or has not been stationary is an empirical question. If it has not been stationary, the accountant's "measurement" turns out to be counterfactual conditional. Whether or not it will be stationary in the future is another problem.

Boulding is also concerned with the future, but in a more subtle way. It appears that he arrives at a particular constant by "knowing" a complete pattern of transformation coefficients and then treating each instant in the pattern as if it were the present. Perhaps this is also a counterfactual conditional. "If we knew the future pattern, this constant would be appropriate."

---

from Hume's Skepticism. Russell put the case most strongly in *The Problems of Philosophy* and later amplified it in *Human Knowledge.* In the former he writes: "The mere fact that something has happened a certain number of times causes animals and men to expect that it will happen again. Thus our instincts certainly cause us to believe that the sun will rise to-morrow, but we may be in no better a position than the chicken which unexpectedly has its neck wrung. We have therefore to distinguish the fact that past uniformities *cause* expectations as to the future, from the question whether there is any reasonable ground for giving weight to such expectations after the question of their validity has been raised." (Russell, *Problems,* p. 63.)

Some theorists who argue for present market prices also feel that it is necessary to make some sort of assumption about the future. Edwards and Bell, for example, argue for a present replacement cost (equal to present market prices in our model) and point out that they agree with the going-concern assumption. (Edwards and Bell, pp. 6, 7n.) Moonitz, whose most recent study indicates that present market is acceptable, states: "To make these [value] allocations properly, predictions as to the outcome of the available alternatives are essential." (Moonitz, p. 51.) In another study he states, "The problem of measuring (pricing, valuing) an asset is the problem of measuring future services." He suggests three different methods of valuation which include "a current exchange price" and then concludes: "The proper pricing (valuation) of assets and the allocation of profit to accounting periods are dependent in large part upon estimates of the existence of future benefits, regardless of the bases used to price the assets. The need for estimates is unavoidable and cannot be eliminated by the adoption of any formula as to pricing." (Sprouse and Moonitz, p. 56.) Exactly why one feels that one needs to predict (estimate) the future in order to measure a present state-of-being is not clear. We agree that "valuation" as we define it below is intimately tied to the future, but measurement is a different matter. If one decides to use a present or a past market price as a method of measuring the assets, the problem is to *determine* the present or past market price, not to estimate the future.

In summary, all four schools are deeply concerned about futurity, and yet all claim to "measure income." We do not deny that predictions or reports of the predictions of others are valuable and relevant information. On the contrary, under certain conditions a prediction may be much more useful than a measurement. However, it is important to point out that these predictions are not, in fact, measurements. The phrase "measurement of income" is bandied about quite freely in the literature. In the interest of clarity of exposition the term measurement should not be used to describe a prediction or a retrodiction.

ADDITIVITY

The axiom of additivity is applicable to all the "fundamental" dimensions of physics. The notion is familiar to almost everyone, and it probably is the basis for the ordinary (nonscientific) linguistic usage of the term "measurement." Despite its familiarity the concept is rather elusive when an attempt is made to state it precisely. Examples are abundant, but a concise generalization is difficult to come by.

A most elementary definition might take the following form:

> There is an operation of dimensional addition which corresponds to the operation of arithmetical addition.

There are two distinct operations in this definition. One, the operation of arithmetical addition, which is the familiar notion of combining numerals according to the rules of arithmetic. Two, the operation of dimensional addition, which is the combination of objects. If the sum of the numbers that are discovered by the operation of measurement on the separate objects is equal to the number that is discovered by performing an operation of measurement on the combined objects, the dimension is said to be additive.

For example, the length of two separate rods, A and B, can be measured and discovered to be "2" and "3" feet respectively. By joining these rods end to end and measuring the combination we will discover that it is "5" feet in length. The relation can be symbolized as follows:

$$\mu(A) + \mu(B) = \mu(A \cup B) \qquad (\text{eq. VI-1})$$

Where μ is a measure function on the object A and $\cup$ is the physical joining. Note, however, that in measure theory eq. VI-1 is *assumed*; it is taken as a premise. A and B are assumed to be two sets which are disjoint and do not interact. In measur*ement* theory, by contrast, eq. VI-1 is a contingent proposition. If A and B are taken to be two bodies of liquid, $\cup$ the mixing of those two liquids, and μ the measurement of temperature, then the equality does not hold.

There are many dimensions that are subject to this axiom, and there are many that are not. Length, weight, volume, etc., may be added. Hardness, density, sweetness, and utility are examples of useful concepts that are not additive. We are not claiming that only those dimensions that are additive are measurable, as the narrow view sometimes holds; but we do assert that the additive property makes the measurement *more* useful, more informative, in a wider range of problem-situations by a greater variety of receivers. All writers would agree with this assertion. Stevens' various measurement scales are ranked according to a "crudeness" index, and the least crude scales are those that are additive. He would be the first to agree that the less crude the index, the greater the information.

The paradigm of additive dimensions—length—provides adequate illustration. Length units can be added, subtracted, multiplied, divided, squared, have their roots extracted, etc.; and all of these operations conform exactly to the arithmetical operations of the same name. Temperature does not have this property. If one adds the numbers representing temperatures, the sum is different from the temperature of the combined objects. There are of course laws of temperature that are stated mathematically, but these are not the generalized laws of mathematics.[6]

Bergmann (p. 28) states the advantages as follows: "The essence of measurement is that *some* arithmetical relations among the numbers assigned correspond, by virtue of a shared logical structure, to descriptive relations among the things to which they are assigned. The measurement we prefer to others is so constructed that a *maximum* number of arithmetical relations has such descriptive correlates or, as one also says, empirical meaning." We agree. The greater the arithmetical operations that have descriptive correlates, the greater the informational content of the measurement. Thus, in light of Criterion I, an additive dimension is preferable to a nonadditive dimension. We will be cognizant of this preference when we describe the dimension in a subsequent chapter.[7]

The additive axiom is germane to this study, because there are *two*

---

6. One could quarrel with this view by speculating that the original concept of numbers came from observations of length. Numbers are "squared," for example. This may be true, but is not germane. The body of mathematics extant is a powerful tool regardless of its origin. Thus any dimension that behaves as our mathematics behave has a tremendous advantage over those that do not.

7. The above discussion is only a rough sketch of the additive axiom. A considerable amount of work has been expended in an effort to develop the distinction formally. Explicit presentations of this distinction can be found in Cohen and Nagel, pp. 293-97, and in Bergmann and Spence, pp. 106-07; it is clearly implied in Nagel, "Logic," pp. 18-24, and in Pap, pp. 127-31. In *Measurement*, Campbell

commodities in our model. The heterogeneity of the commodities brings up the comparability problem. We have described above several different kinds of comparisons, and each of them has different requirements with respect to the dimension.

If an intertemporal comparison is desired, there are two alternatives:

1. The commodities must be in the same form at both instants, i.e. they must be intertemporally homogeneous, or
2. There must be a dimension common to both commodities that is at least ordinal and preferably additive.

If the commodities are intertemporally homogeneous, we can discover the number of dollars or the number of bushels at both instants and then determine whether the numerosity at one instant is greater than, equal to, or less than, it was at a previous instant. The requirement that they be in the same form, however, may abrogate the original purpose of the measurement—to provide information at a given point in time regardless of the state of the exchange—and therefore we reject the first alternative.

Given the condition of intertemporal heterogeneity, both commodities must be expressed in a dimension that is at least ordinal. A quantity of money must be related to a quantity of wheat in such a fashion that we can determine an ordinal relationship in the dimension. Temperature provides an example. Certain gases may be transformed into liquids and the temperature of each discovered. We can then ordinally relate the temperature of the heterogeneous objects. The comparison of wheat that has been transformed to money, or vice versa, presents the same problem. The dimension then, must be ordinal for intertemporally heterogeneous commodities. Given the informational attributes of additivity, it would be preferable if the dimension were additive.

If both commodities are held at either instant (if the commodities are instantaneously heterogeneous) and an intertemporal comparison is desired, there are two alternatives:

1. The objects must be combinative in some form that will per-

---

is making the same distinction when he discusses "a-magnitudes" and "b-magnitudes."

Various lists of axioms of measurement have been presented. See, for example, Guilford, p. 11, and Suppes, "Independent Axioms," p. 165, mit an operation of measurement in a dimension that is ordinal, or

2. The dimension must be additive.

The first alternative is the problem of valuing the firm as a whole as opposed to valuing the commodities and summing.

The existence of the first alternative raises some fundamental questions about income measurement which have received too little attention by past investigators. It has been observed that sometimes "the value of the firm" is different from "the sum of the values of the commodities of that firm." Unfortunately the word "value" in the above phrases is left ill-defined, and often it changes meaning from the first phrase to the second. If the observation is true, with the meaning of "value" constant, it means (1) that the dimension of "value" is not additive or (2) that there is an interaction when the commodities are combined or (3) that there is a commodity that is not included in the sum (entrepreneurship or goodwill, perhaps). We will not digress here to examine the issue but will leave the two alternatives open.

Instantaneous comparisons have the same alternatives. The combination of commodities must be measurable in an ordinal dimension, or the dimension must be additive.

If an increment-comparison is desired, the dimension must be additive. Moh's scale provides an example. Suppose that there were two objects, A and B, which changed with respect to hardness over time. Using the scratch test, we could place object A at number "1" on Moh's scale at t_1 and object B at "3" at the same time. At t_2 the numbers "3" and "5" were discovered for A and B respectively. Although both have changed by the same number of units, this does not permit us to say that they have changed equally. In the dimension of hardness, the "degrees" of hardness between "1" and "3" may be greater than, equal to, or less than, the degrees between "3" and "5." That is, the relationship between one increment of "2" and another increment of "2" is indeterminate in an ordinal dimension. Only additive dimensions permit increment-comparisons. A weight increment of one object is comparable to the weight increment of another object. In the case of weight, "2" is known to be equal to "2."

All four schools of income measurement ordinarily take the approach of valuing the commodities and then summing them. By this they must be implicitly claiming that the dimension is additive. This means that all the comparisons can be made.

1. Instantaneous comparison of Firm A to Firm B at both t_1 and t_2.
2. Intertemporal comparison of both firms from t_1 to t_2.
3. Increment-comparison of Firm A to Firm B.

Moreover it means that the arithmetic operations of "+" and "−" on the numerosity of units have "descriptive correlates," that they are meaningful in discriminating the dimension. In more familiar language it means that the wealth of Firm A minus the wealth of Firm B yields a number that is meaningful in the same way that the statement "this rod is longer than that rod by two inches" is meaningful. Likewise, it means that the "income" of the firm has empirical meaning in the same fashion as "this tree has grown five feet."

If the dimension is not additive but the units are added, it is difficult to know what the resultant figure means. Suppose that we sum the figures "2" and "3" on Moh's scale. The figure "5" is easy to come by, but its empirical meaning is nil.

For this study we will follow the general practice of valuing the commodities and summing them. We will utilize the arithmetical operation of "+" by measuring each commodity separately and summing; then we will compare the total to another total. We noted above that we were required to describe a dimension prior to a measurement. In view of the summation approach we must qualify that requirement as an additive dimension.

In light of the enormous increase in information that it provides, there is good reason to have strong preference for an additive dimension; in light of the fact that all four schools utilize summation and the fact that we will follow the same methodology, the property of additivity in a dimension is an abolute requirement.

OBJECTIVE VERSUS SUBJECTIVE MEASUREMENTS

Any comprehensive review of "objectivity" would entail arguments of an epistemological and metaphysical nature that are much beyond the scope of this study. The author wanted to avoid the whole subject, but the literature, particularly the accounting literature, has a plethora of statements about objectivity. Unfortunately most of the statements are in the form of stating objectivity as a criterion without further explanation.

Almost all accounting texts have some phrase about "objective and verifiable evidence." Generally this is given in support of the "cost principle." For example, one modern text states: "There are several reasons for accountants' choice of original costs as the basis of value. The first is *objectivity*. The cost of most assets is contractual and can be verified through business forms. No subjective estimates are required, as would be necessary in the case of direct valuation." (Corbin, p. 230.) The clear implication is that the existence of *business forms* for contractual obligation makes the measurement "objective." Thus, one gets the impression that anyone who can read will come out with an objective valuation.

Another example is in a "comprehensive volume" that is usually used in a course entitled "accounting theory" or "principles of accounting." The following rather lengthy quote is presented because it is the entire discussion of objectivity in a book of 980 pages.

> Accounting seeks to present its findings on a foundation of facts determined objectively and subject to verification. Cash receipts and disbursements can be adequately supported by vouchers, and cash on hand is determined by count; full support and verification for this element and its changes are available. Findings here can be fully objective. Purchases of goods and services as well as sales are also generally well supported by evidence and subject to verification. There are a number of areas in accounting, however, where determinations must be based in part upon judgment, estimate, and other subjective factors. The recognition of depreciation is an example of the latter. But the degree of estimate can be minimized by the attempt to develop evidence that will lend objective support to conclusions. Objective determinations are encouraged as means of closing the doors to possible error, bias, or even intentional fraud, and achieving an accounting that can be accepted with confidence. (Simons and Karrenbrock, p. 48.)

Simons and Karrenbrock feel that cash outlays are completely objective, and perhaps they are, but this avoids the difficult question of whether those outlays should be capitalized or expensed—that is, the question of how the outlay affects the income of the firm. Two accountants could readily agree on the *amount* of an outlay but disagree on the effects of that outlay on income. We can all agree that we should avoid fraud, error, etc., but how does the criterion of objectivity serve this laudable end?

Paton and Littleton (p. 19) present the following definition: "'Objective evidence' therefore is evidence which is impersonal and external to the person most concerned in contrast with that person's unsupported opinion or desire." The referent of "the person concerned" is usually management, and the purpose of the requirement is to prevent fraud or misstatement. The CPA is "independent" of the management, and therefore all measurements would be impersonal and external if he is the metrician. If the sole criterion of objectivity is that it be "impersonal and external," then any person who has no vested interests in the particular measurement would be "objective" and would therefore make objective measurements. Clearly, this is an impoverished criterion of objectivity.

We noted above (p. 7) that Paton "marvels" at accountants who consider cost to be objective. We agree; but we disagree with Paton and Littleton who present the above criterion for objectivity and then conclude that costs or price-aggregates are the "only definite facts available to represent exchange transactions objectively" (p. 7).

The metrics literature also makes wide use of the distinction between "objective" and "subjective" measurements. The discussion is diffused, but the alignment generally follows the distinction between the broad and narrow views. As might be expected since the opposing camps are psychologists and physicists, the quarrel often takes the form of psychological versus physical dimensions. This dimension distinction has wide use and an intuitively compelling character, but unfortunately it is highly confused.

Evidence of the confusion is given by the fact that the dimension distinction is held in two different forms. "Psychological" dimensions of hue, brightness, pitch, etc., are distinguished from "physical" dimensions of length, weight, temperature, etc. Thus, it is thought that there are two different *kinds* of dimensions.[8]

---

8. See Bergmann and Spence; also Campbell, *Aristotelian,* for examples of the distinction held in this form.

A second form of the distinction is given by the differences between apparent (subjective) length and physical (objective?) length. That is, for all the physical dimensions mentioned in the preceding paragraph there is supposed to be a corresponding "psychological" dimension. Physical weight is different from psychological weight, physical temperature is different from psychological warmth, etc.[9]

Many authors attempt to set up a definition to guide us in distinguishing between psychological and physical dimensions. One of the most straightforward definitions is presented by Stevens and Volkmann. They write (p. 329): "Pitch is one of the psychological aspects, or attributes, of tone. It is one of the dimensions in terms of which we are able to distinguish and classify auditory sensations. Pitch differs from frequency in that pitch is determined by the direct response of a human listener to a sound stimulus, whereas frequency is measured with the help of instruments." They apparently employ two distinguishing factors. First, psychological dimensions are concerned with sensations; physical dimensions are concerned with physical entities.[10] Second, psychological dimensions are determined by means of sense perception; physical dimensions by means of instruments.

The first is irrelevant to this essay, and we can pass over it. We stated above that we were here dealing with a firm, and a firm, by definition, has no sensations. Thus, sensation measurements, if they be the correct distinction between subjective and objective measurements, are irrelevant to the discussion at hand.

The second is relevant to our discussion. This criterion seems to assume that verification by sense perception and verification by instruments are opposite, mutually exclusive methods. Thus, unaided sense

9. The following is an example of the second form of the distinction: "Many discriminable characteristics (psychological magnitudes) have known physical correlates. For example, the chief physical correlate of the discriminable characteristics of weight is the 'physical weight,' in fact, the measurements of all physical correlates is a problem for the physicist, but the measurement of the so-called subjective magnitudes is a problem for the psychologist." (Reese, p. 1.)

10. Many other dimensions along with pitch are regarded as purely psychological. For example, brightness and hue are presented in the literature in many instances as psychological dimensions. "It is only in recent years that a fairly clear concept has been gained of the various factors involved in the transition of radiant energy to the *mental* quality 'color.'" (Evans, p. 1.)

perception is "subjective," in contrast to "objective" measurements made with instruments. If this is the distinction between subjective and objective, we are in difficulty. Nevertheless, it is not uncommon to hear that the use of instruments makes the subjective become objective and the vague become precise.[11] Now in some sense of these terms, and to some degree, this claim is probably correct. But it is difficult to see how it could be made, as it often is, with such assurance—almost a priori assurance—except on the hypothesis that its proponent is for the moment overlooking the fact that *someone must read the instrument.* He must be overlooking the fact that the perception of pointers, dials, color changes (as in litmus paper), and other such indicators is subject to most, if not all, of the same errors of perception that plague unaided perception. There are many advantages in the use of instruments in procedures of measurement, but they are not those of a method that does not require perception over one that does.

As Reese has noted, the discriminable characteristic is usually conceived without the aid of an instrument, and the instrument is later invented in order to extend our discriminable powers. That the instrument is a powerful tool as a perception aid is not here disputed. However, the thing that is in dispute is whether an instrument or the lack thereof makes one measurement more or less objective than another measurement. One can state, and one often does, that X is heavier than Y or that X is longer than Y without using an instrument. Can one claim that the above statements are about psy-

---

11. Reese apparently employs this criterion in the following passage (pp. 1-2): "There does seem to be one difference between the procedures adopted by the physicist and that adopted by the psychologist. Having identified a characteristic, the physicist in the interest of consistency and greater discriminatory power, usually abandons it for another characteristic which is correlated with the first one. For example, the characteristic of subjective weight may be identified by a series of operations which involve, among others the operations of hefting. The physicist will find that he is able to construct a magnitude that correlates with the original subjective magnitude but which substitutes operations involving balances for the operation of hefting. Furthermore, the discriminable characteristic is changed from subjective weight to some special characteristic such as the position of a pointer . . . . By this means the physicist is able to extend the scale beyond those limits imposed by the low discriminatory capacity of the observer with respect to the original discriminable characteristic."

chological dimensions, or that they are subjective, and that in order to make them statements about physical dimensions or to make them objective, they would have to be verified by means of an instrument? To say that a dimension changes from a psychological to a physical one because of the operation performed is an odd method of viewing dimensions. The author is quite certain that his desk is longer than the paper on top of that desk. Would that "length" change from a psychological to a physical dimension if we used an instrument? Suppose we used different kinds of instruments. Would the dimensions measured be different? Is the claim that the desk is longer than the paper "subjective," and would it become "objective" if an instrument were used to make the *same* claim?[12]

We should also point out that some "psychological" measurements can be verified by instruments. Unaided sense perceptions of colors, sounds, sweetness, etc., can be verified by instruments. Flicker photometers and colorometers as well as microscopes and telescopes aid in discriminating colors. Amplifiers as well as "visual sounds" aid in discriminating sounds. The use of such instruments increases both observer agreement and precision. We think it is the latter which causes the error of equating instrumentation with objectivity. Precision is desirable; but it is not the same as verity, as we pointed out in Chapter IV, nor does it permit one to distinguish between objectivity and subjectivity.

Some writers seem to believe that a relative magnitude cannot be determined in a procedure of measurement by "direct" perception. One gets this impression from some writers who insist that measurements must be "operationally defined." The notion of an operational definition is a slippery one when held in its extreme form.[13] The extreme form of operationism apparently reverts to the instrumentation view. Its adherents would not permit one to determine that X was

12. Obviously the questions posed are intended to be rhetorical. However, it is only fair to warn the reader that some writers would give an affirmative answer. For example, "In *principle* the operations by which length is measured should be *uniquely* specified. If we have more than one set of operations, we have more than one concept, and strictly there should be a separate name to correspond to each different set of operations." (Bridgman, p. 10.)

13. Bridgman, the chief architect of operationism, retreated from the extreme form by permitting "pencil and paper operations."

heavier than Y by hefting, or that X was warmer than Y by feeling. Now the operationists have a point. They are attempting to avoid incorrigible statements. An incorrigible statement is a first person present tense declaration such as "I see blue dots" or "X feels warmer than Y." Obviously one cannot verify or falsify such reports. Perhaps *we* don't see blue dots, but that has nothing to do with what someone else sees. If we have no reason to doubt the reporter's intentions, then we must accept his report of what *he* sees or feels. Thus, such statements are of little use in science, because the essence of the verification notion is repeatability, i.e. public knowledge.

There are two types of errors in respect to incorrigible statements. One, logical errors; two, errors of perception. By the first—logical errors—we mean that if someone were to describe an object as being both circular and square, we would say that he had made a logical error. We could then criticize his perception as being self-contradictory, and this is what we mean by a logical error. If, however, someone describes an object in a noncontradictory fashion, but it is in disagreement with another person's perception, then we can be certain of only one thing: at least one person is in error. If a person lifts X and says it feels heavier than Y, and we have no reason to doubt his intent, there is no good reason to reject the judgment on grounds of objectivity. If we doubt the person's ability to perceive, we have grounds for rejecting the judgment or at least grounds for making further investigation before we accept it. The criterion, however, is *our judgment* about the person's *ability to perceive,* not subjectivity versus objectivity.

Since we know that errors are made in perception, we need to exercise great caution before we accept or reject perception reports. We need to compare our perceptions to those of other persons, to compare our present perception with the memory of past perceptions, and, if possible, to compare our unaided perception to our perception of a pointer on an instrument. However, the instrument is not the final arbiter. If the butcher's scale reads "10 pounds" when he places one weiner on it, all of us would reject the measurement. We would accept our own "subjective" sense of hefting and complain that the instrument was wrong. If the butcher told us that one weiner weighed "10 pounds" on his scale, we would reject his report, accept our "subjective" judgment, and doubt his perception, if not his honesty.

In the above examples we have accepted our own judgments, "subjective" though they may be, and rejected the "objective" determinations of others. The problem is more complex, however, than the exclusive reliance on our own perception. If we perceive an object as "gray" when everyone else perceives it as "red," we normally accept the majority's perception. The statement "I am color blind" means (1) that my perception is different from others and (2) that, more importantly, I accept others' perceptions as true and reject my own. The principle is clear: observer agreement is both the ordinary and the scientific criterion for accuracy of perception.

In general, the advantage of using instruments is that it increases observer agreement. The purpose of instruments is to make the perception easier, not to avoid perception. If the instrument reduces the discriminable characteristic to a pointer reading, the measurement is easy, and there is apt to be a high degree of interobserver agreement. This is an important advantage, but it has nothing to do with a dichotomized view of measurements as being either "physical or psychological" or "objective or subjective."

Observer agreement is peculiarly amenable to empirical determination. Given the "democratic assumption," errors of perception are subject to test. This is a question of fact. Either one perceives correctly (agrees with the majority), or he does not. Often in the perception of numbers, no single number has a clear majority. In such cases the usual scientific procedure is to change the "democratic assumption" from a mode to a mean. Several readings are taken, and the mean is defined (assumed) to be the true measure. This has troubled some absolutists, and admittedly there are epistemological difficulties. However, in the opinion of the author, the difficulties of using a mean are in essence the same as those of using a mode. The basic question is: How do we know what is correct or true? The usual answer is observer agreement; and the fact that the agreement is expressed as a mean is little different from its expression as a mode.

The reliance on interobserver agreement for "what is" and "what is not" brings us full circle. The notion of "what is" as a simple "look and see" procedure has been subject to a series of experiments that reveal some striking results. The Gestalt psychologists have gone a long way toward proving that the "preformed theoretical construct," or "expectation," greatly influences our perceptions. A classic experiment in visual perception required the subject to wear eyeglasses that reinverted the retinal image. This caused the world to look upside down. The subjects went through three distinct phases:

1. Disorientation and sometimes severe personal crises.
2. Confusion.
3. Assimilation.

After removing the eyeglasses so that they could again perceive things as they "really were," they went through the same disorientation, confusion, and assimilation.

In terms of our earlier discussion they changed "constructs" or "theories"; they assimilated a new method of perceiving the world, and then everything looked normal. Interobserver agreement among the subjects after assimilation would be almost perfect. They would, of course, disagree with all other observers who did not have the same mental constructs as theirs, which were caused by the glasses.

Another example of perception according to a previous construct is provided by Bruner and Postman. They exposed a deck of playing cards to a group of subjects and asked them to identify each card. Most of the cards were normal, but some were not—for example, a red three of spades or a black seven of hearts. The subjects went through an experience similar to that mentioned above. First, on short exposure they nearly always identified the cards, both the normal and the abnormal, with little hesitation and usually correctly, i.e. the normal as they were and the red three of spades as either the three of spades or the three of diamonds. On longer exposure they became confused and anxious and could only say that there was "something wrong." Most, after prolonged exposure, adjusted to the new deck and had no trouble. They identified the anomalous cards correctly, i.e. as a "red three of spades." Their first perceptions were in accordance with the construct of a normal deck of cards. The identifications were made within that construct. After the assimilation of the new construct, the identifications—perceptions—were in accord with it.

There is now quite an accumulation of evidence in psychology that the construct is of primary importance in perception. The old simplistic notions about "reality" are open to serious doubt. "Reality," in some sense which is not yet clear, is a product of a construct. Certainly there is interaction. The construct is also, in some sense, a product of reality; but there is no one-to-one correspondence, nor is there a unilateral chain of evidence. What is "objective," what is perceived to be evidence, is highly influenced by the preformed construct.

Philosophers have also been struggling with this problem for many years. Epistemological theories have necessarily been concerned with "objective" and "subjective," often with surprising results. On occasion the definitions of objective and subjective have been reversed. Some philosophers consider that what goes on in the mind is real, hence objective, and what we perceive is at best a reflection of that reality, and thus subjective. These are the exact opposites of the present dictionary definitions. Lewis has considered such problems in some depth. He writes (p. 435): ". . . the distinction of real from unreal is a classification, and that which is designated as 'unreal' as well as the 'real' is given in experience. Knowledge a priori is knowledge of our own concepts." In another context, when he is trying to describe how we have knowledge of objects, he concludes by saying: "The ascription of this objectivity to the presentation is *the conceptual interpretation of what is presented.*" (Lewis, p. 133.) The point in philosophy is a little more muddled because of internal quarrels and the difficulty of expressing concepts without utilizing a prior concept. However, these very difficulties are important data to the purpose at hand. The existence of such difficulties should prevent the emotive charge that something is "subjective" and therefore unacceptable. The burden of proof should be reversed; if subjective and objective are to be used in a prejudicial manner, the user should be required to define the terms. At the very least this would prevent them from being utilized as a propagandistic smoke screen. Unfortunately the terms are all too often used that way in the present literature.

Perhaps a more important conclusion to be drawn from this discussion is that theoretical arguments are pertinent to empirical disputes. We cited Butterfield above to the effect that it required a different kind of "thinking cap" to change from the geocentric to the heliocentric theory and that observations or empirical evidence were secondary considerations. Kuhn has extended this kind of argument. One example he cites is Dalton's theory of atomic chemistry. "Chemists could not, therefore, simply accept Dalton's theory on the evidence, for much of that was still negative. Instead, even after accepting the theory, they still had to beat nature into line, a process which, in the event, took almost another generation. When it was done, even the percentage composition of well-known compounds was different. The data themselves had changed." (Kuhn, p. 134.) This point ought to have some bearing on the use of such phrases as "actual facts of economic experience" and "transactions are the only objective data." Data is, at least partly, a product of the theory being employed, and therefore theoretical arguments are at least equally as important as "the evidence."

VII

In the preceding chapters we have constantly run up against the need to specify the decision-theory. We found that the criterion of relevance could not be applied in the absence of such a theory. In measurement theory, we found that the dimension must be "conceived" prior to the measurement. Thus, if we are to apply the criteria developed above, we must explicitly consider the theory and the conception of the value dimension. Such a consideration is the purpose of this chapter.

THE VALUE DIMENSION

The word "value" and its derivatives are unfortunate in this discussion because they bring up conjectures of "goodness," and the debate rages. In the sense of "goodness," "value" is quite different from the concept of "measure." Dewey speaks of it as a radical split:

> When one looks at the problem of valuation in this context, one is at once struck by the fact that the sciences of astronomy, physics, chemistry, etc., do not contain expressions that by any

> stretch of the imagination can be regarded as standing for value-facts or conceptions. But, on the other hand, all deliberate, all planned human conduct, personal and collective, seems to be influenced, if not controlled, by estimates of value or worth of ends to be attained. . . . This contrast between natural science and human affairs apparently results in a bifurcation, amounting to a radical split. (Dewey, "Valuation," p. 2.)

An enterprise is obviously deliberate, planned human conduct and thus is influenced by the worth of the end to be obtained. That end, by assumption, is "income."

It is clear that if Dewey is taken literally, the present inquiry would be excluded from science and placed in the discipline of ethics or morals. The valuation coefficient finally selected would fall into a category of "values," which by definition[1] would not be amenable to scientific inquiry. The conclusions reached would be subject to neither validation nor verification and thus "value judgments" or "matters of opinion."

In his analysis of the word "value," Dewey points out that it is used as a noun, an adjective, and a verb. It may have several meanings when used as any one of these parts of speech, but the double usage as a verb is particularly relevant to the subject at hand. He writes: ". . . the words 'valuing' and 'valuation' are verbally employed to designate both *prizing*, in the sense of holding precious . . . and *appraising* in the sense of *putting* a value upon, *assigning* value to." (Dewey, "Valuation," p. 5.) The activity that we are concerned with is obviously the verbal use of value. The trader prizes, or holds dear, his cash and wheat contracts. He also prizes his life, sunsets, art objects, and many other things. He believes these things to be "good" or "beautiful," and therefore he holds them precious. This may be done with a vast array of things without comparisons; one may prize both a sunset and a Picasso without ever bothering to rank them in degree of preciousness.

The second use of the verb "value"—appraise—does imply a comparison, however. By definition, it is "primarily concerned with a re-

---

1. By definition of the logical positivists. There are some who quarrel with the philosophy of logical positivism. For example, Geiger (p. 107) writes, ". . . the dichotomy between ends and means, between morals and technology, is precisely what has been challenged by the very history of the scientific method itself."

lational property of objects." (Dewey, "Valuation," p. 5.) When one "appraises" something, he is ranking it in comparison to another object. This often results in an extremely difficult choice. Many of the interesting and unresolved problems of philosophy are concerned with such choices between two "goods," "beauties," or "values."

The distinction between value as a positive attribution of the good and as the assignation of a degree or rank to that goodness is important to our study. There is considerable debate about the origins of value, i.e. whether good is "intrinsic" or "better than." Mitchell (p. 191) writes: "Though *good* is the central value category it is not necessarily the most fundamental. The question of the logically 'primitive' term is mainly one of system building. Thus Brogan defines good in terms of 'better than' while Felix Cohen defines the latter in terms of the former." We shall not digress here to a discussion of which is more "primitive" or "fundamental." Instead, we will assert that this study is concerned with appraisal, in the "better than," or degrees of goodness, sense, rather than in the sense of the positive attribution of the good. We are thus *assuming* that commodities are good. We attribute goodness to commodities by assumption; and the relevant question is: how does one rank these "goods"?

Once the problem has been stated in this fashion, another fundamental question is raised: *why* should one rank goodness? That is to say, why would one make a decision about the rank of two goods when both are, by definition, "good" and hence desirable? It would obviously be more comfortable to avoid the appraisal and simply prize goodness.

The answer must be concerned with the existence or maintenance of the goods. If all goods were capable of simultaneous existence, any ranking process would be unnecessary. For example, suppose that there is an array of goods, $X_1, X_2, X_3, \ldots, X_n$ (sunsets, food, Bach, etc.). If one could obtain or maintain *all* of these goods at the same time, no ranking would be necessary. Except as an intellectual exercise, there is no reason to say that X_i is better than X_j. However, if X_i obviates the existence of X_j, then a choice is enforced, and the ranking process is necessary.[2]

2. For a full development of this point, see Lamont, pp. 23 ff.

To make the example specific, suppose that one could enjoy a good dinner, with a beautiful view and pleasing background music. Since all three are capable of being simultaneously enjoyed, there is no reason (except as an intellectual exercise) to express a preference. The act of expressing a preference may be distasteful. There are three goods, all desirable; and preference or choice implies the obviation of one or more of these goods. Sacrificing a good is a disagreeable act, and the mental process of choosing which ones to sacrifice may also be disagreeable.

If one posits the example in a different manner, the disagreeableness of choice is made clear. Suppose that the situation is one where restaurant A offers good food and a beautiful view but no music, and restaurant B offers good food and good music but no view. One is *forced* to choose between two goods. "Forced" is an apposite term, because one would not choose if both goods were available. Only when external forces put one in the position of relinquishing one good in order to get another will the disagreeable task of ranking be undertaken.

Valuation, therefore, is intimately related to the concept of sacrifice. There is a sacrifice of one prized good for another prized good. There would be no choice or sacrifice between a good and a bad; no choice is necessary then, because the classificatory procedure has already made the decision. The choice can only arise between two competing goods. In short, the appraisal (comparative, relational judgment) is the expression of a conscious choice between two desired, competing goods or ends and is made—or is useful—only when circumstances force the sacrifice of one for the other.

Valuation Proposition 1: Valuation arises only when we are forced to sacrifice one good in order to obtain or maintain another good.

From this proposition it is clear that a comparative judgment must be made. One must rank the alternatives in order to choose which good is to be sacrificed. An ordinal scale must be created. In terms of the previous example, the person must rank music and view. If he prefers music to view, then he will select restaurant B and sacrifice restaurant A. There are several corollaries to this choice.

(1) The ranking is observable. By his overt act of choosing restau-

rant B over restaurant A, we can infer that the person prefers music to view. That is, if the ordering of the elements yields an ordering of the alternatives, then an ordering of the alternatives yields an ordering of the elements. In this case the alternatives are restaurants A and B, and the elements are food, view, and music.

(2) The final choice conceals a number of previous choices. There were a number of other choices that were eliminated in order to focus on the final alternatives. In the typical situation, a person is not confined to two alternatives; he also has the opportunity (C) to stay home, (D) to go to the theater, etc. Thus, when he focuses on the choice of A or B, he has already ranked both of them higher than C, D, etc. Then the final choice makes B more valuable than A, and A more valuable than C, D, etc.

(3) There is a vital temporal dimension to all valuation. Time is an inherent restraint on the ability to enjoy goods. The sacrifice of one good for another may be temporary, because one can plan to enjoy both. In this case, the valuation process is temporal. One chooses the temporal order of goods, and if the plans work out, both goods will be enjoyed. Thus, one can plan to visit restaurant B today and restaurant A tomorrow. However, the sacrifice is still operating. Since both are "goods," it would be preferable to avoid any sacrifice, but this is impossible. A is sacrificed for B today, and B will be sacrificed for A tomorrow.

Upon first examination, it is tempting to say that B is more valuable than A, because B was chosen first. This may be true in some sense. Perhaps B would always be chosen first if neither B nor A had been visited. But once B has been visited, then the conditions have changed. Now A may be chosen simply for the sake of variety. Regardless of the reason, if when tomorrow arrives, A is chosen and B is sacrificed, A is clearly more valuable at that moment. If not, B would be chosen again. The position of goods in the preference scale may change with the passage of time, and it is therefore imperative to state the time condition when valuations are made.

(4) A further corollary of the time dimension is the impossibility of refusing to value. Any attempt to avoid a valuation will result in the status quo receiving the highest valuation. For example, if the person is at home and procrastinates in the choice between A and B, he is

clearly choosing C (to stay at home—maintain the status quo). One alternative that is often available is the maintenance of the status quo; and the so-called refusal to decide is an overt choice of that alternative. In a most important sense, then, one is forced to evaluate alternatives at all points in time.

Valuation Proposition 2:   Valuation is a continuous activity that is being performed at all instants in time.

This proposition has further conditions. When one is continually choosing among alternatives in a moving temporal dimension, he is necessarily predicting the future. The choice is between competing states-of-being that lie in the future. The choice is not between existing things, but instead between the state-of-being of those things in the future. One may have an existing good and decide to continue holding it, but this decision is about the nonexistent future state of that good, not with its present or past existence. Thus, the sacrifice of A for B *now* is the result of a prediction about the states of A and B in the future.

For example, assume that a person decides to choose restaurant A over restaurant B. At the moment that this decision is made the chooser is anticipating the states-of-being of A and B, and he makes his choice on the basis of this prediction. The sacrificed alternative, B, is an anticipation and not subject to measurement. The chooser ranks A and B, but the ranking is a prognostication of satisfactions. It is not a measurement of an existing state.

A physical analogy may be helpful. Suppose that a person must choose between two objects which, at the present moment, are identical in all respects. The fact that they are substitutable for one another, or that either can be chosen by sacrificing the other, indicates that they are identical at the present moment. Clearly if they are currently identical, the chooser will be indifferent in respect to their present state; and if they are temporally invariant, he will remain indifferent. However, if both are expected to grow in the future, there is a basis for choice. If A is expected to grow at a faster rate than B, then A will be selected. Thus, the "value" of A to the chooser is greater than the value of B, even though the present sizes of both objects are equal. There are two different concepts here: (1) the present size, which is measurable, and (2) the expected size, which may be predicted but not measured.

This leaves us in a quandary since our objective is to select a valuation coefficient that measures the value of commodities. Note however that we can create an ordinal scale of value. Clearly, if A is chosen it has a higher value than B to the chooser. Thus if we can measure B in some acceptable unit, we can then say that A has a greater number of those units. For example, suppose that A and B have five linear feet. A is selected because it is expected to grow at a faster rate. We cannot say that A has more length than B, but we can say that the chooser prizes A more than B. Since the chooser sacrifices B to obtain A, we can measure B and say that A is more valuable than five feet of B. A is equal to B in length, but A is greater than B in preciousness to the chooser. This preciousness obtains at the present moment and may change in the future, but this does not negate the fact that A is more valuable than B at the present moment.

Valuation Proposition 3: The current choice, the selected alternative, is prima facie more valuable to the chooser than all rejected alternatives.

This proposition refers to that moment in time at which the chooser has the opportunity to choose. New knowledge may cause a change in valuations, and there may be a slight time lag before the chooser can act on this new valuation. However, this lag should be quite short, especially in the context of this study, and we will ignore it. This means that if A has been chosen, we will infer that A is more valuable than all other alternatives until such time as A is sacrificed for B; and then we will infer that B is more valuable than all other alternatives.

This is an ordinal scale of value. In such a scale we cannot say anything about the magnitude of interval. This is a serious limitation to measurements, because it does not permit mathematical manipulation. Moh's scale is quite similar to our value scale. We report that mineral X is harder than mineral Y, but we have no well-defined dimension of hardness that permits us the use of an intermediate unit for the comparison. The same is true of the value dimension. We can say that A is more valuable than B, but we cannot say that A has a definite value in the same way that an object has a definite length. This point has troubled economists for a great many years, and more recently the metricians and psychologists have also been concerned.[3]

However, the value can be made a little more precise if the next best alternative can be determined and if the next best alternative is subject to cardinal measurement. For example, if there existed a unit of hardness and we could state mineral X as a specific number of those units, then if Y scratched X, we could infer that Y had more units of hardness than X. In terms of our model we have assumed that the wheat market is the trader's best alternative, and since there are only two alternatives within the wheat market, it is easy to determine the next best alternative. Thus, if A is sacrificed for B, then A is more valuable than B, and B is more valuable than all other alternatives. If B is, say, five bushels of wheat, then A could be said to be more valuable than five bushels of wheat. This permits more comparisons, since the quantity of wheat can be varied.

Valuation Proposition 4: The value of a good may be measured ordinally by comparing it to the measure of the next best alternative.

An ordinal scale is unacceptable in the present study because of the additivity requirement set forth in Chapter VI. We believe that value is inherently limited to an ordinal scale, because it is a personal preference based on personal predictions. Therefore, we must find a substitute or surrogate for value. Sacrifice can be measured cardinally, and such a measure would increase the usefulness of the value measures because of the generality of the sacrifice measure. In addition, as we will argue in the subsequent chapters, the sacrifice measure is relevant to more decision theories than the value measure. For these reasons, we will consider the sacrifice dimension.[4]

For purposes of illustration we have been treating the A and B alternatives as if they were discrete. A more appropriate treatment would be to consider each alternative as a quantity of some particular class

3. See, e.g., Davidson and Marschak, *Definitions,* and the references they cite.

4. As noted in the discussion of measurement, such shifts in consideration are not uncommon in science. This is often the basis for the second form of the physical-psychological dimension distinction. Pitch, for example, is reduced to the "physical" measure of frequency, even though they are not the same things.

of goods. In the market a certain quantity of one class of goods is exchangeable for a certain quantity of another class or classes of goods. Thus, we will say that they are equal in exchangeability.

$$q_1 = q_2 = q_3 = \ldots = q_n \qquad \text{(eq. VII-1)}$$

where q_i is a quantity of the ith class of goods. In any given exchange then the sacrifice may be stated as q_2 *or* q_3 *or* . . . *or* q_n since they are all equal. Equation (VII-1) can be divided by, say, q_1 yielding:

$$1 = \frac{q_2}{q_1} = \frac{q_3}{q_1} = \ldots = \frac{q_n}{q_1} \qquad \text{(eq. VII-2)}$$

For convenience we could let $q_1 = 1$ so that each ratio could be related to unity. Thus, we could say "so many units of class 2 *per* unit of class 1." This of course makes class 1 the "common denominator," and the ratios are the transformation coefficients.

This permits the statement of the sacrifice to be made in general terms. Even though q_2 may be the next best alternative when q_3 is selected, the sacrifice may be stated in terms of class 1, since all classes have been reduced to ratios in respect to class 1. Class 1 could be anything, but we prefer money for the reasons given in Chapter III.

When one holds any good, including money, he is sacrificing a certain quantity of other goods. That is, he has a command over goods which is expressed by equation VII-1; and that command is a general statement of his sacrifice since it relates to *all* other goods. Given that other people operate in the same market, that command over goods is generalized in another direction, since it relates to the command over goods of all other persons or firms.

In a perfect market a combination of goods of two classes yields the same command as the sum of the commands for each class taken individually. Thus, the sacrifice or command-over-goods dimension is additive. Therefore, the sum of the sacrifices for each commodity yields a meaningful total, and that total also yields an ordinal measure of value.

There are several temporal classifications of the sacrifice.

1. The past sacrifice. The good that was originally obviated in order to obtain another good. (The money given up in order to acquire a good.)
2. The present sacrifice. The good that is currently being given

up in order to maintain another good. (The money given up
in order to keep a good.)

3. The *ex ante* sacrifice. The expected size or utility of the
goods that will have to be given up in order to obtain or
maintain another good. (The amount of money that is *expected* to be given up by *not* having acquired a good.)

4. The *ex post* sacrifice. The present size or utility of a good
that was sacrificed in the past in order to obtain or maintain
another good. (The present amount of money that could be
obtained if one had acquired a good but which was given up
by *not* having acquired that good.)

All of these viewpoints may be valuable information. Any one or all
may be relevant to a particular problematic situation. All, save number
four, have been proposed as the proper method of income measurement.

Schindler, in defense of the Accounting Tradition, relies heavily on
the concept of sacrifice and excludes other methods because they are
not sacrifice concepts. He writes (pp. 85-86): "Like the market value
concept, it [the Fisher Tradition] is an economic definition of value in
the sense of the 'worth' at a given time in the light of future expected
advantages, rather than a sacrifice concept. . . . That is, value is concerned with the expectations of advantages to accrue from ownership
or control of a property . . . whereas cost is concerned with the sacrifice
required to obtain the services of the property." Schindler is correct
in one sense, but in another sense the Fisher Tradition is also a sacrifice.
It is true that we normally calculate the "present worth" of the expected
future of two alternatives, but an equivalent procedure is to take the
"future worth" of the alternatives and thereby calculate the *ex ante*
sacrifice. That is, we could calculate the *expected* sacrifice. Viewed in
this way the difference is in the temporal viewpoint, not in the concept
of sacrifice. Both are sacrifices; but one is an expected future sacrifice,
the other a past.

Sometimes writers argue that only one of the above sacrifices is the
"true" one. For example, one may argue that number four is the
"true" sacrifice, because the rejected alternative's *ex post* size is the
amount that was "actually" given up. This is a truism and is relevant
to the verification of the preceding prediction (*ex ante* sacrifice). If
the economy allocates resources to project A and rejects project B, it

is meaningful to say that the conditional *ex post* size of B was the actual sacrifice; i.e., if B had been chosen, X benefits would have resulted, therefore X is the actual sacrifice. However, it is equally meaningful to say that the present good given up is the "true" sacrifice. The good that is currently being sacrificed has some amount of utility associated with it. It is true that the utility is a projection and thus may be in error, but this does not negate the fact that this good is *now* being sacrificed. Both expected and present obviations are sacrifices; it is only the verb tense that distinguishes them. But that is a sufficient distinction.

In short all are "true" sacrifices; and since valuation is intimately tied to sacrifice, they all may be used for valuation. However, the valuation must have the same temporal viewpoint as the sacrifice from which that valuation came. A past sacrifice can yield only a past value, a present sacrifice only a present value, etc. Thus, proposition 5.

Valuation Proposition 5: The temporal modifier of value must coincide with the temporal modifier of the sacrifice.

Thus, we can speak of past values, future expected values, etc.; and the temporal referent of the sacrifice will be understood.

Recall, however, that the act of valuation is concerned with the future state of the object. Valuation, the act of ranking and selecting alternatives, has an inescapable forward-looking attribute. Thus, we can exclude sacrifice concept number four from the valuation process since it is backward-looking. Verification of a prediction is the purpose of concept number four, and verification is always a backward-looking procedure. One can measure the *ex post* sacrifice, but the alternative is no longer available and thus cannot be valued in the relational sense of deciding between alternatives.

Suppose, for example, that there are two alternatives, A and B, that are presently equal in the relevant dimension. A is expected to increase at a faster rate than B. At the present moment, t_1, then A is more valuable (to the chooser) than B, because A is expected to be greater than B in the future, at t_2. Thus, at t_1

A = B in the relevant dimension (say, feet or dollars)

but

$A > B$ in value

because of the prediction that

A will be $> B$ in the relevant dimension at t_2.

Now if at t_2

$A < B$ in the relevant dimension,

i.e. the prediction is wrong, it would be an error to say that B is more valuable than A. It is true that B is larger than A in the relevant dimension, but the process of valuation at t_2 is the same as it was at t_1. That is, we still must choose between A and B by making a prediction about the future state. Such a process would then determine the value at t_2.

What can be said about this example is:

1. A *was* more valuable than B at t_1.
2. At t_1, it *was* predicted that A would be greater than B at t_2 (which is synonymous with the first statement).
3. The prediction was erroneous.

The fact that the prediction was erroneous does not change the valuation or the prediction of t_1. The process at t_2 is a verification. Thus, sacrifice concept number four is a "true" sacrifice and may be valuable information—relevant to a problem—but it has nothing to do with valuation in the sense of making a choice between goods.

Sacrifice concept number three is indispensable to the valuation process. One must project the future size of both A and B in order to choose between them, since they are equal at the time of choosing. If A′ and B′ are the expected future size of A and B, then it is reasonable to say that B′ is the expected sacrifice if A is chosen. This is the *basis* for making the selection; but it is not the present sacrifice; and it may not be the future sacrifice. By the verification procedure (sacrifice concept number four), we will be able to determine what the sacrifice was in fact when the future becomes the present. Until then we only have an expected sacrifice, which may turn out to be right or wrong. Given the difficulties of prediction in matters of commerce, it is almost certain that the expected sacrifice will be wrong to some degree. The only thing that is observable at the time the selection is made is that A is chosen and B is sacrificed; and we infer from this that $A' > B'$; but we cannot observe B' nor can we observe what the actual size will be, since that lies in the future. For this reason we will say that sacrifice concept number three is indispensable to the valuation process, but it is not a measurement;[5] instead it is a prediction. Since we are here concerned with a measurable dimension, concept number three will be excluded.

This leaves only concepts one and two. Both are subject to measurement, and both are or were valuations; the only difference is that one is a past valuation and the other a present valuation. Concept one is a past valuation; it is concerned exclusively with the history of value and is not relevant to the present value. It is concerned exclusively with a past sacrifice (the sacrifice occasioned by acquiring or obtaining a good); and this may be relevant information, but it is clearly historical information that has nothing to do with the current selection of alternatives.

As in the above example, assume that A was expected to be greater than B, and thus it was selected. At t_1 A is more valuable than B. If at t_2 A is selected again (Proposition 2), it is still more valuable than B (Proposition 3). Since value is measured ordinally by measuring the sacrifice (Proposition 4), any time that B changes in size, the value of A changes also. Thus, the value at t_2 can be determined only by measuring B at t_2. The sacrifice at t_1 has no relevance to the value at t_2.

The only difference between these sacrifice concepts is the difference between obtaining and maintaining a good. But this is very little difference. If good A is presently held but good B is more desirable, then A will be sacrificed in order to *obtain* B. If A is more desirable, then it will not be sacrificed; instead B will be sacrificed in order to *maintain* A. The choice is A or B (in the exclusive sense). Therefore: if A, then not-B, and if B, then not-A; and the exclusion or sacrifice of one good is operating all the time, regardless of whether it is operating

5. Even if it were subject to measurement, there are problems of equating the future value with the present or past value. This usually is done by discounting, but the correct discount rate is not clear even under certainty. See "The Fisher Tradition," Chapter IX.

by obtaining or maintaining. There is a sacrifice in both cases; the difference lies in what *form* the sacrifice takes.

Valuation Proposition 6: Current value may be measured ordinally only by measuring current sacrifice.

This proposition is no different from propositions about the current measurement of any dimension. One can state with little fear of disagreement that current length may be measured only by the current juxtaposition of meter sticks or that current hardness may be measured only by the current scratching of minerals, etc. No botanist would claim that he has a current measure of a growing plant if he had not measured that plant since acquisition. No physicist would claim that he knew the current radioactivity of an object that had not been measured since it was bombarded. No physician would claim that he knew the current temperature of his patient if the patient's temperature had not been measured since admission to the hospital. Certainly, we can measure some inert, unchanging object once and then rely on that measurement at other times. But this is a process of *adjusting* the measurement for its temporal invariance. Time is not a relevant variable in some measurements and therefore does not need specification. If time is a relevant variable, then the measurement veritably describes the dimension only at the one instant when that measurement was taken.

The above is truistic and as plain as anything could be. This makes valuations, both past and present, a "pure measurement" problem, i.e. the problems of valuation are the same as those common to all measurements. If there are objections, then, they must be couched in measurement terms. There may be some difficulty in specifying and measuring the dimension of the sacrificed alternative. Since value is ordinally measured by the measurement of the sacrifice, it is clear that any difficulty in the measurement of the sacrifice would cast doubt on the resultant value. However, since the "past" was at one time the "present" and the "present" will soon become the "past," it appears that any difficulties in measuring the sacrifice are equal at all instances in time. If there are problems in measuring the alternative sacrificed, there is no reason to *assume* that these problems are any greater or less at the present instant than they were at some past instant. It may turn out to be true that the problems are greater or less at certain instants, but these are empirical questions; they are questions of fact that must be investigated individually. Until such an investigation is made we will assume that all instants are equally difficult or easy so far as the measurement of the sacrifice is concerned.

This leaves us free to concentrate on the measurement problems of the sacrifice: the dimension, the instrument, the unit, the numbers, etc.—in short, all of the same problems of measurement that all metricians face, including, but not restricted to, those discussed above.

Summary

We have found that valuation—in the appraisal sense of our context —is the expression of a preference from among competing goods. Goods must be sacrificed in order to obtain or maintain another good. The criterion for the selection of a good—and the rejection of all other goods—is the expected future state-of-being of the goods. Goods are ranked in accordance with this expectation, and the value of the selected good may be ordinally measured by measuring the next-best alternative.

Sacrifice may be viewed from several temporal vantage points. All such temporal viewpoints are true sacrifices, but only the present sacrifice is relevant to current valuation. Past sacrifices are past valuations and may have useful historical information, but they are not pertinent to the present valuation. Any difficulties in the measurement of the sacrifice are assumed to be equal for all past and present sacrifices.

Valuation, as we have described it, is a decision process. One must select one good and sacrifice another. Which good to select requires a decision that is similar in structure to all other decisions. In general, the data required for a decision are (1) the available alternatives; (2) the predicted consequences of each alternative; and (3) a preference for certain consequences. The exogenous information relevant to decisions may be classified similarly: (1) information as to which alternatives are available; (2) information necessary for predictions. In matters of economics or commerce the available alternatives are given by the market prices. The sacrifice or command-over-goods dimension is a general expression of the alternatives that are or were available, in addition to being a general expression of the next-best alternative that permits inferences about value or preciousness. Since available alternatives are relevant to all decisions, market prices are relevant to all decisions. Information necessary for predictions is not so easily generalized. The problems faced by various classes of people and their informational needs are the subject of the next section.

THE PROBLEMATIC SITUATION

In the sections on Information and Measurement we noted that the theory was prior to the "fact" or "measure." Considerable emphasis was placed on this methodological order, and two significant conclusions were that the locus of the relevancy criterion is the decision-theory and, further, that the decision-theory was the solution to a particular problem or set of problems. No general criterion of relevancy (or "value") of information or measurements was possible, because relevancy refers to particular decision-theories applicable to particular problems. This section is an attempt to state the principal problematic situations with respect to the Trader Model in a general way.

The general formulation of the receiver's problem is fairly simple. One classification is to state the problems as

1. Information needed by managers relevant to their problems, and
2. Information needed by other interested receivers relevant to their problems.

We are fortunate in that there is a wealth of literature on the first problem. Indeed a large portion of the literature concerning economics and, more recently, managerial economics has been devoted to specifying the information relevant to the goal of maximizing money-profits. We will briefly recapitulate the literature pertinent to this study under the heading of "Decision Theory of the Trader."

Unfortunately the literature on the second problem is both scanty and scattered. For instance, one of the interested receivers is the creditor, and very little has been said about what his problem is and what information he needs.[6] Another interested receiver is the govern-

6. We have excluded debt from our model in order to keep the model simple. However, we will include creditors in this analysis so that our conclusions will be

ment as a taxing authority. There is a large body of literature on Public Finance, but most of it is concerned with equity, welfare functions, etc., not with the specification of information. We will attempt to generalize such problems and the information needed to solve those problems under the heading of "Decision Theory of Other Receivers."

DECISION THEORY OF THE TRADER

Within the restricted model presented above it is clear that the trader has evaluated all previous alternatives and then decided to become a trader. He could have used his funds for consumption or to become a producer or to enter another market or loaned them at interest, etc. He has ranked all of these alternatives and decided that becoming a trader in the wheat market was preferable.

In evaluating the consumption alternative, he has decided that his total utility will be enhanced by entering this market. This may have been done on either of two bases:

1. The usual time-preference analysis, i.e. that his impatience for present consumption is overcome by a prospective larger amount of consumption.
2. Surplus consumable funds, i.e. his utility is increased by delaying consumption due to the declining marginal utility of instantaneous consumption. This is possible even if the prospective future consumption is the same or smaller than the present consumption. A smaller amount of future consumption may yield a larger amount of total utility than a larger amount of present consumption.

Regardless of the reason, he has decided to become a trader instead of a consumer, and he will continually make this decision in this analysis. If at any time he makes another decision, our model will not apply, and we will lose interest in him.

In addition, he has decided that trading in the wheat market is his best alternative from among competing entrepreneurial activities. This may have been done by some formal analysis, by intuition, by default,

---

more general. The addition of creditors to the model changes nothing; it only requires another quadrant in the diagram.

etc.; but for whatever reason, he has evaluated this activity as his "best alternative." This decision must be continued by him for our model to apply; if at any time he changes his mind, the analysis of his activities would go beyond the scope of this study.[7]

With these previous decisions assumed, the problem is considerably simplified. As long as this model is his best alternative, he has only to decide between:

A. Maintaining his present position.
B. Exchanging (transforming) to a new position.

Stated in a slightly different form, he can decide between:

A. Holding wheat.
B. Holding cash.

From what has been said above, it follows that if he holds wheat he values it more than *all other* alternatives—more than consumption, creditor position, etc., and more than cash. Since this market is his best alternative, he values cash more than consumption and other entrepreneurial activities; and thus cash is second only to wheat in his ordinal scale of value if he holds wheat. The same can be said of cash, but need not be, since we have assumed its value to be unity.

Underlying such a valuation is his prediction of the future state-of-being of the alternatives. Making the usual hedonistic assumption, the

---

7. Contrast the going-concern assumption. It is said that the going-concern assumption is necessary to measure income and that true income can be measured only after the firm ceases to be a going concern. This reverts to an event-comparison. The true measurement can be made only at the event of liquidation. Our conception is the exact opposite. We will measure at a point in time and continue to make periodic measurements so long as the firm continues. We make no assumptions about continuity, but we require that the firm continue in order to be able to continue measuring. Once it is liquidated, there is no firm left, and hence no firm income to be measured.

Further we see no reason to *assume* continuity, since to continue or not to continue is a valuation decision that must be made at all points in time (Valuation Proposition 2). Which decision the trader has made and is making at this moment is an empirical question that does not require an assumption. Which decision he may make in the future depends upon his assessment of the alternatives at the time the future becomes the present. One may want to predict what he will decide in the future, but there is little justification for assuming either liquidation or continuity.

alternative with the greatest anticipated increase will be selected.[8] In other words if two alternatives are currently equal in the relevant dimensions, the anticipated increment of both alternatives is the basis for the valuation and the decision.

Cash and wheat are equated in the model by the transformation coefficient. That is, the transformation coefficient permits the addition of units, which permits the equation of two objects. Thus, if the price of wheat is $2 per bushel, then

$$\$2 = 1 \text{ bushel of wheat.}$$

With the two alternatives equated, we can concentrate on the increase and state that the trader:

A. Will value wheat more than cash—hold wheat—if he expects the increase in wheat to be greater than the increase in cash.
B. Will value cash more than wheat—hold cash—if he expects the increase in cash to be greater than the increase in wheat.

Since the value of cash in relation to utility is constant (the stable-price-level assumption), this can be stated more compactly.

Maximization Criterion: Hold wheat only if it is expected that the present price of wheat will increase.[9]

For the decision it is clear that there are only two relevant bits of information:

1. The future expected state-of-being of the good.
2. The present sacrifice.

8. We have neglected a third possibility: selecting a combination of wheat and cash. The trader, because of uncertainty-risk, may decide to hold such a combination. This, in the recent literature, has been termed the "utility problem." (Schlaifer, pp. 31, 32, and *passim.*) In less technical jargon this is the "risk of putting all of your eggs in one basket." This refinement, while important, is not germane to the problem at hand. It would simply add complications that would eventually strengthen the conclusions.

9. In a more realistic situation he would sell short—hold negative wheat—if the wheat was expected to be less than the present transformation coefficient. We have excluded short selling for simplicity's sake. Its inclusion would not alter the results. For the nonce we have neglected any probability distribution in the expectations. It will be included below.

The present price gives the rate at which the trader is required to sacrifice cash for wheat. Thus, the current value of the wheat is the present price. Likewise, the future state-of-being of the wheat is restricted to a change in the price in this model. Thus, in terms of the model these bits of information are equivalent to:

1. The future expected price.
2. The present price.

Nothing else is relevant to the decision. Other information may be relevant to the evaluation of past decisions, but for the decision at hand—the continuing decision—these are the only two information bits that have any value to the trader. All other data is irrelevant and thus has zero informational content for *this problem*. This is incontrovertible regardless of the verity or any other characteristic that other data may possess. Because of the necessity for continually making the decision, these two bits are *always* relevant. They are relevant at all instants in time.

Note that both of the relevant information bits are exogenously determined. The trader has no control over, and no effect on, the present or future transformation coefficient. These are "givens" or "states of nature" to him. The amount of wheat or cash that he can hold is given by the present transformation coefficient. The present sacrifice rate is given by the present transformation coefficient. The prediction of the future transformation coefficient is a composite of predictions about crop yields, weather, etc., none of which are subject to his control. He is completely at the mercy of the market with one single exception: He can control his position on the present transformation line. He cannot control the past positions because they are past, and he cannot control the future position because the alternatives are not yet available. His only decision is his present position on a given line; and once that decision is made, it is forever irrevocable, because that moment will never recur.

In this decision it is important to point out that cash is a "general" alternative—a "general" commodity. Cash is, if wheat is held, the next-best alternative—better than consumption, other entrepreneurial activities, etc. Cash is thus more valuable than, say, consumption; but in order for the trader to know this—to make that decision—he must know the amount of cash that is available to him, because there exist other models for consumption, production, etc., which also have transformation coefficients. That is, the cash available is related to the other alternatives, and in order for this cash to be ranked second, the amount of the sacrifice of the third-ranked alternative must be known. Thus, the prior decision—to enter this market—has four relevant bits of information, the first two of which are:

1. The present price in the wheat market and
2. The present price in the third-ranked alternative.

These present prices may be used to equate the two alternatives, and then we need:

3. The expected future state of the third-ranked alternative and
4. The expected future price in the wheat market.

Comparison of bits 3 and 4 will yield the decision to enter this market. This decision, like the other, must continually be made so that these bits are relevant at all instants in time.

The Trader's Evaluation of Past Decisions

In the above analysis we have been concerned with the trader's *ex ante* decision. The trader may want to evaluate his past decisions in order to check the degree of error in his predictions. It is important to emphasize that such an evaluation is not germane, except indirectly, to his present decision. An evaluation of past decisions—the verification of past predictions—may cause an alteration in the theory utilized to *make the prediction* and thus may indirectly affect his current decision; but this does not alter the information bits for decision-making that were specified above.

The value of verification of this kind lies in checking out the theory used for predictions. The past is evidence that his prediction—and by inference, the theory used for the prediction—was either correct or had some degree of error. The prediction took the following form: At t_1 he predicted—and acted on that prediction—that the transformation coefficient would be P'_2 at t_2. Now the transformation coefficient at t_2 can be observed only at or after t_2. Let P_2 be the observed transformation coefficient, and the error in prediction is

$$P'_2 - P_2 = \text{Error}$$

This is the first step in the alteration of his predictive theory. The error is isolated, and he may now check the theory to see if he can determine what went wrong. The important elements for our purposes are the information bits required for the evaluation. They are:

1. P'_2, the predicted transformation coefficient at t_1.
2. P_2, the actual *(ex post)* transformation coefficient at t_2.

Since this is a continuous decision, there are serious problems in checking the predictive errors. The trader is making a prediction at every instant in time, and presumably this prediction covers an indefinite number of instants in the future. Thus, there will be several, perhaps many, outcomes to compare to each prediction; and the number of predictions on a continuum is infinity. If we follow the $P'_2 - P_2$ approach suggested above, then we will have an infinite number of errors. Obviously this process is too unwieldy to be of practical use. We need some method of weighting the errors to come out with some comprehensible statistical summary.

An additional difficulty in the simple $P'_2 - P_2$ approach is that the trader probably will not have a definite, quantified expectation in mind. Instead he is likely to have some tenuous and tentative notion about the *direction* of the price change. As Keynes puts it:

> An entrepreneur, who has to reach a practical decision as to his scale of production, does not, of course, entertain a single undoubting expectation of what the sale-proceeds of a given output will be, but several hypothetical expectations held with varying degrees of probability and definiteness. By his expectation of proceeds I mean, therefore, that expectation of proceeds which, if it were held with certainty, would lead to the same behavior as does the bundle of vague and more various possibilities which actually makes up his state of expectation when he reaches his decision. (Keynes, *General Theory*, p. 24n.)

This vague bundle can be formalized by assigning subjective probabilities to the various possibilities and calculating a mathematical expectation. Such a formalization may take the form of

$$E = \sum_{i=1}^{n} \theta_i A_i$$

where θ_i is the assigned subjective probability of event i occurring, and A_i is the amount of gain or loss if event i occurs. If E is positive then, the trader has a better-than-even chance of gain. E, however, does not help us in the calculation of the prediction error. It is an abstract number (a mean) the sign of which indicates only the *direction* of the trader's expectation.

We could chop time up into arbitrary periods and take the predicted direction-of-change at the beginning of each period and compare it to the outcome at the end. This would yield the number of "successes" or "failures," but would not solve the problem of weighting. Success and failure are "classifications" in Hempel's terms and are not as useful as metrical concepts. In other words, the trader may "fail," even though his individual "failures" were much fewer than his "successes." One "large" failure (or success) may offset a great many "small" successes (or failures). Thus, we must have some method of weighting.

One method of measuring the prediction method that immediately suggests itself is to take the difference between two completed exchanges. When the trader exchanges, this signals a change in the

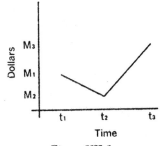

Figure VII-1

direction of the prediction; and this predicted direction remains constant, although the predicted magnitude may vary, until he makes another exchange. When he exchanges cash for wheat, he is predicting a future price of wheat greater than the current price. So long as he holds wheat, he is continuing to predict a future price greater than the current price. When he completes the exchange, he changes his prediction to a future price less than or equal to the current price. He may make several errors before the completion of the exchange, but these will be netted out if the difference is taken between the two exchanges. For example, assume that the trader exchanges for wheat at t_1 and completes the exchange at t_3, with the prices taking the pattern as in Figure VII-1. The trader's prediction is incorrect in direction from t_1 to t_2, but is correct from t_2 to t_3. The monetary amount of his error is M_1 to M_2. The monetary amount of his successful prediction is M_2 to M_3, and the net is M_1 to M_3. If we wanted a longer period to evaluate the prediction error, we could simply extend the above diagram to whatever time was desired. Thus we could have a pattern as in Figure VII-2, and the difference between M_1 and M_j is the net of the prediction error from t_1 to t_j.

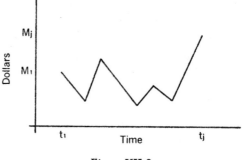

Figure VII-2

Note, however, that the only requirement for the measurement of this error is that the time must have elapsed. That is, we are verifying a prediction, and the only requirement for the verification is that the data become available. If t_j has arrived, the data is available regardless of the state of the exchange. Thus, the prediction error may be measured at t_j, even if the exchange is incomplete. This is permissive; there is no good reason to exclude the price at t_j. But there are powerful reasons to include it. In fact, it makes no sense to speak of measuring the predictive error from t_1 to t_j unless the t_j price is included. One could arbitrarily cut off the time back at, say, t_3; but this is a measurement from t_1 to t_3, *not* from t_1 to t_j. Presumably, one would want to include *all* predictions and verify all of those for which the data was available. Any cutoff prior to t_j arbitrarily excludes the latest predictions. Thus, we can say that the evaluation of a series of decisions requires two bits of information:

1. A past price.
2. The present price.

The evaluation of the next series of decisions must begin with the last price of the last evaluation. If the data is to be linked without gaps, the time periods must be contiguous. This linkage may be accomplished by simply picking up the latest price that was used in the previous evaluation. The two bits may be stated more generally as:

1. The latest price used at the last evaluation.
2. The present price.

So far we have been concerned with the evaluation of the decisions in the case of an incomplete exchange. If the exchange becomes complete in the interim, it requires no more information than that specified. If perchance the exchange is complete at either the beginning or end of the time period under analysis, then the amount of money held is substituted for the pertinent price. It is obvious that these prices, being coefficients, need quantities. We need to know the quantity of both wheat and money at the pertinent instants in order to calculate the total value.

Once the trader has measured and netted his predictive errors in the fashion described, the only additional need is a standard for comparison. There are several conceivable standards:

1. The net result if all predictions had been perfect.
2. The net result of the next-best alternative.
3. The net result of another trader in the same market.

We will not presume to prescribe the standard to be used. However, we will specify the information for all three standards. Standard one requires nothing more than a listing of the peaks and troughs in the above diagram. Standards two and three require the measurement of the net result of either the next-best alternative or the other trader. Note that this is an *instantaneous* comparison and therefore requires that the measurement be made at the same time. This is another compelling reason for using the present price instead of waiting for the completion of the exchange. The next-best alternative standard is a comparison of the accepted alternatives to a rejected alternative; and one cannot complete an exchange that was rejected. The other trader may have completed exchanges, but it would only be in the rarest of circumstances that the completed exchanges of both traders would have occurred at the same point in time.

Summary

We have analyzed three problems of the trader:

      A. The continuing decision to enter and stay in this market.
      B. The continuing decision to hold either cash or wheat.
      C. The evaluation of past decisions.

The purpose of this analysis was to specify the bits of information relevant to these decisions. We found that these were:

      1. The expected future price of wheat.
      2. The expected future price of other alternatives.
      3. The present price of wheat.
      4. The present price of other alternatives.
      5. The price at the last evaluation.
      6. The quantities of wheat and money at the last evaluation.
      7. The present quantities.

Other models exist for the generation of information bits two and four and thus we may exclude them from further consideration. Bit five is a "past present" price that is used as a linkage between two time periods. Bit one is relevant to decisions A and B. Bits three and seven are relevant to all the trader's decisions. Bits six and seven are the multiplicands to get the value of each commodity class.

DECISION THEORY OF OTHER INTERESTED RECEIVERS

We have made a broad classification of two types of receivers—(1) the trader and (2) other interested receivers. The decision theory of the trader was discussed above; and the purpose of this section is to discuss that of the other interested receivers.

The prime distinction between these groups lies in the control that they have over the position on the transformation curve. The trader may decide on a position and then exchange in order to obtain that position. The other interested receivers have no such control; they are observers of the trader's decisions. This is the usual distinction between "management" and "others." Managers have control of the assets of the enterprise. Others observe the results of the manager's decisions.

In a realistic situation, the "others" would include creditors, owners (as opposed to managers), employees, and government. All of these have some degree of authority over the enterprise, but it is of a generalized type that imposes broad constraints instead of specific directives. For example, the creditors may limit expansion or even cause contraction by refusing to lend or by calling in their outstanding loans; owners may replace the managers; employees may stop operations by a strike; government may require payments for the privilege of continuing operations or impose general restraints by law. Such authority may be classified broadly as:

A. Prior restraint. The broad "rules of the game" within which the managers must operate.
B. Decision consequences. The rewards or penalties, usually financial, which are imposed because of the results of the enterprise's activities.

We will take the former as "given" in this study and concentrate solely upon the latter. Every enterprise is subject to certain kinds of control by law, custom, ethics, fear of future reprisal, etc. There are rules governing the relationship to employees, customers, public, etc., which may or may not be formalized. The sanctions imposed may vary widely: penal servitude, economic deprivation, social ostracism, etc. These rules and their enforcement are indispensable to every society, but they come about from a complex set of social mores that are not germane to the study. It is true that the society needs veritable and relevant information to impose and enforce such rules, but the problem of specifying such information is insurmountable without a complete exposition of social, economic, political, etc., constructs and problems of the culture. Obviously, this task is beyond the possibility of any single study. As a result, we assume that such rules are "givens" for the purpose of this study and hope that the conclusions reached will be of some use to the culture at large.

The latter—managerial decision consequences—have a direct bearing on the subject at hand. Certain receivers need information to make immediate and direct decisions affecting the enterprise: The creditor needs information to decide whether or not to grant or extend credit; the taxing authority needs information in order to levy equitable taxes; the employees need information for bargaining purposes, and so forth. This type of decision may be further classified into two broad categories:

1. Those decisions based on the past activity (which determines the present status) of the enterprise.
2. Those decisions based on the expected future of the enterprise.

Examples of receiver interest in the first category are such questions as: ability to pay dividends, to pay off a loan, equitable amount and ability to pay taxes, etc. Examples of interest in the second category are questions about investing for a future return, ability to repay a loan in the future, etc.

Many of these questions are difficult to delineate. For example, the ability to pay dividends is inextricable from the problem of investing, since the absence of disinvestment is, in effect, the same as a positive decision to invest. Nonetheless, we attempt to separate them for the sake of the clarity of presentation.

We classify these receivers as "interested" because they need to make these decisions concerning this enterprise. If at any time they are not required to make decisions about the enterprise, we will classify these as "disinterested" or "receivers with idle curiosity" and abandon them.

Decisions Based on the Expected Future

We saw above that the decision of the trader was a process of ranking alternatives. We first needed to *equate* the alternatives and then to *predict* their future state. The other receivers have the same problem and the same process. They have alternatives that must be equated and then ranked according to prognostications of the future. Thus, the first listing of information is:

1. The present sacrifice. (The equation of the alternatives.)
2. The expected future state of the alternatives.

The difference with these receivers is that they are ranking enterprise versus enterprise—assuming for the nonce, that they have ranked, and rejected, consumption, holding money, etc.—instead of wheat versus money. They have decided to invest their funds[10] in an enterprise rather than to consume or hold them in a riskless state (i.e., cash under conditions of a stable price level). Thus, the choice is between two enterprises, A and B.[11]

The first problem of the receiver is to equate the two enterprises; this will determine his sacrifice. Obviously, the enterprises should be equated at the present moment; the past size of the enterprise is irrelevant to the present equation. There exists some exchange rate—transformation coefficient—that will permit the equation of these two objects by first comparing each to a unit and then comparing the units. This unit, of course, is money, and we can express the sacrifice in dollars as we did above. This is an instantaneous comparison, and therefore the measurements must be made at the same time. Thus, the first bit of information can be stated as:

> The present transformation coefficient
> of enterprise for enterprise.

Underlying this transformation coefficient between enterprises is the transformation coefficient of the elements of the enterprises. That is, suppose the alternatives are A, an enterprise in the wheat market, and B, an enterprise in the corn market. The exchange of enterprise A for enterprise B is essentially an exchange of wheat and/or money for corn and/or money. That is, the "enterprise" is simply a combination of the two commodities at the present moment. Of course the ability of the trader is also a part of the enterprise but is not relevant to the present equation process. We are here concerned with exchanging enterprise for enterprise, so the quantity of the commodities as well as the prices are again relevant. Since the present transformation co-efficient between enterprises is the one in question, it is obvious that

10. In case of the government or public, they have decided to utilize their resources.

11. Of course, the two top alternatives could be assumed to be between enterprise investment and money, as it was with the trader. However, if we did this, we would need to then rank cash with another enterprise to make the point. Since we have already made the case for cash versus wheat above, we are here ranking the enterprises for the purpose of brevity and variety. It will become apparent to the reader that the conclusion would be the same in either case.

the present transformation coefficients of the commodities are appropriate. Thus, the elements of the transformation coefficient between enterprises are:

1. The present prices of the commodities.
2. The quantity of the commodities.

We are here interested in the abstracted transformation coefficient of the enterprises, which is the total of the elements. We can define

Q_{ij} = the quantity of the ith commodity held by firm j. Let money be the mth commodity and $i = 1, 2, \ldots, m$.
P_i = the price of the ith commodity.

Then the value of firm j is defined in equation VII-4.

$$X_j = Q_{mj} + \sum_{i=1}^{m-1} P_i Q_{ij} \qquad (\text{eq. VII-4})$$

Once this has been done, the ratio of the value of one particular firm to another, X_a to X_b, yields the transformation coefficient between the two firms. One can equate the two by adding or subtracting money units. That is, by varying either Q_{ma} or Q_{mb} or both so that equation VII-5 holds.

$$\frac{Q_{ma} + \sum_{i=1}^{m-1} P_i Q_{ia}}{Q_{mb} + \sum_{i=1}^{m-1} P_i Q_{ib}} = 1 \qquad (\text{eq. VII-5})$$

Or if the quantities are not known, by solving Q_m in equation VII-6,

$$\frac{X_a \pm Q_m}{X_b} = 1 \qquad (\text{eq. VII-6})$$

the two enterprises can be equated. The terms of equation VII-5 are the elements of information that go to make up the present transformation coefficients between the enterprises. These elements may be stated more compactly as:

1. The positions of the enterprises.
2. The present prices of the commodities in question.

The "position" refers to the point on the curve from which the quantity of cash and the commodity can be determined.

The second bit of information—the expected future state of the alternative enterprises—is more complicated. The difference between the other receivers and the managers is the control or lack of control that they have over the position of the enterprise. The manager has the ability to control the position of the enterprise; the other receivers have no such control.

The manager is one of the important variables in the other receivers' prognostication of the future state of the enterprise. The success of the enterprise depends upon the manager's decisions; therefore, the other receivers' predictions must be *ad hominem*. This may take two forms:

1. Comparison of predictions. The other receivers may make a prediction (about the price of wheat) and compare their prediction to that of the manager's.
2. Prediction of the manager's success. The other receivers may attempt to make a judgment about the likelihood of the success of the manager.

The former course of action requires a decision model identical to that of the trader. The other receivers can stand in place of the manager and say, in effect, "If I were the manager, I would act in X way, because my prediction is Y." We concluded above that the relevant information for this decision is:

1. The present price.
2. The expected future price.

The only additional bit of information needed for the comparison is the manager's expected future price. They need to make the prediction and then compare it to the manager's prediction; thus, the total information needed is:

1. The present price (applicable to both the manager's and the receivers' predictions).
2. The expected future price of the receivers.
3. The expected future price of the manager.

If there is a variation in the expected prices, the receivers consider theirs to be correct (else they would not hold it) and the manager's to be incorrect. They can weight the variation in some fashion and make the decision about credit-granting, management-replacement, etc.

The difficulties of stating the prediction of the future prices in anything other than direction were noted above. These difficulties are compounded here because of the existence of two predictions, and also because the manager's prediction would have to be communicated. The escape from this dilemma above was to use the *direction* of the predicted movement rather than a quantified magnitude of the movement. For the same reasons we will follow that process here. Thus, the information bits may be restated as:

1. The present price.
2. The direction of the change that the manager expects.
3. The direction of the movement that the other receivers expect.

Note, however, that the direction of the movement expected by the manager is indicated by his present position. If wheat is held, the price is expected to increase, and vice versa. Thus, the same information is given by:

1. The present price.
2. The present position.
3. The direction of the movement that the other receivers expect.

These bits are relevant at all instants in time, because the other receivers' decisions are, like the manager's, continuous.

The second method—prediction of the manager's success—may be selected because the other receivers want to avoid, or feel incapable of, making a prediction about the price movement of the commodity. Or, they may commit their funds for a fixed time period, so that their decision is irrevocable for the stated period in the absence of a secondary market. In either case, these receivers are at the mercy of the manager, and they need a method of comparing their "confidence levels" between managers. That is, they need to predict the ability of the manager to make decisions in the future.

We will assume that this prediction is made on the basis of using the past as evidence for predicting the future. There are several problems in that assumption, however. It may be that receivers actually make this prediction on some other basis—intuition, hearsay, unarticulated hypotheses, astrological signs, etc. Even if they do follow our assumption, there is no way to prove that the "past is evidence of the future" method is superior to, say, astrological signs. As Keynes[12] points out, the future can be projected on the basis of the past only by making an unproved assumption about the "uniformity of nature." Suffice it to say that we *assume* that other receivers make the assumption. If they do, the following is relevant; if not, the other methods require information that is not generated by the model and hence are irrelevant to this study.

The procedure may be broken down into two parts:

1. The gathering of evidence about the past.
2. The projection into the future.

The method used for projection is of no interest to us. The process of gathering the past evidence involves exactly the same problems as those met by the trader in evaluating his past decisions. The other receivers will need some method of measuring the errors of the past decision, a method of summarizing and weighting those errors, and then a standard of comparison. The standard for comparison in this case would be the manager of the next-best alternative enterprise. Thus, the information bits are, as above:

1. The latest price at the time of the last evaluation.

12. "It may be useful to give the reader two examples, more familiar than the Inductive Hypothesis, where, as it appears to me, such knowledge is commonly assumed. The first is that of the casual irrelevance of mere position in time and space, commonly called the Uniformity of Nature. We do believe, and yet have *no adequate inductive reason whatever* for believing, that mere position in time and space cannot make any difference. This belief arises directly, I think, out of our acqaintance with the objects of experience and our understanding of the concepts of 'time' and 'space.'" (Keynes, *Probability*, p. 263, italics added.) The source of this problem is often misunderstood. It is sometimes alleged that one predictive method has been *proven* correct because it has always predicted correctly. But the fact that it *has* always predicted correctly does not provide evidence that it will *continue* to predict correctly. Whether it will or will not continue to predict correctly is a prediction; and there is no "evidence" for that prediction, since it concerns the future and all evidence comes from the past.

2. The present price.
3. The respective positions.

And these bits are needed for both enterprises.

Decisions Based on Past Activity

As we noted above, the distinction between decisions based on the past and on the expected future is difficult to delineate. We have already overlapped by discussing the history of past decisions. The remaining questions fall mainly into the category of "ability to pay" or "liquidity." For example, the receivers may have invested in, or loaned to, or levied a tax on, the enterprise at some time in the past. Their question now is concerned with the enterprise's ability to return their investment or loan or to pay the tax.

This does not involve the question of continuing the investment or loan. There is no difference between continuing an investment or loan and the refusal to withdraw that investment or loan, if that alternative is available. As pointed out above, these decisions are based on the future state-of-being.

If the decisions involve the net results of the activity since the original investment, the evaluation of the trader's past decisions presented above would be appropriate. Thus, the questions must be concerned with the state of the enterprise. That is, these questions are not concerned with the changes in the enterprise over time, but are instead concerned with the state at a given moment in time.

Specifically, the questions are:

1. Is the state of the enterprise such that it can perform X act?
2. Can the enterprise fulfill the obligation that it entered into at some time in the past?

Some of these acts may have specified conditions for them to become applicable. For example, time must have passed for a debt that has a temporal location to become due; income must exist before it can be distributed or taxed; etc. Thus, the first bit of information that is necessary is what the particular factual conditions of the contract or obligation are. We will assume that these conditions have been met. If they have not been met, there is no problem, or the problem is one of predicting what will happen when they are met. Once the problem is stated in this manner, the verb tense implies the answer; the non-predictive state of the enterprise can only be the past or the present.

It seems perfectly clear that the past is irrelevant. Suppose that a debt was contracted at t_1 and became due at t_2. At t_2, then, the interest of the receivers is in their ability to collect the debt. Presumably, it will be collected in money,[13] so the ability of the enterprise to repay the debt is determined by (1) the quantity of money held at t_2 if the exchange is complete or (2) if the exchange is incomplete, the quantity of money that can be obtained by transforming wheat to money. Obviously the relevant price for transforming wheat to money at t_2 is the price at t_2. All past and future prices are not available alternatives. Now assume that the debt was not collected at t_2. There are two possible reasons for its not being collected:

1. The enterprise was unable to pay.
2. There was mutual agreement to postpone.

If the enterprise was unable to pay, the receiver has already received this information at t_2. If he receives it again, say at t_3, it is superfluous; it adds nothing to the information that he already has. Even if by some chance the receiver did not know that the enterprise was unable to pay at t_2, that message may have some useful *historical* information, but it has no relevance to the problem at hand. The problem is to collect the loan, and the price at t_3 is the only relevant price for that problem. If there was a mutual agreement to postpone, this is the same, in effect, as a new loan with a new due date, t_3. The relevant information for a new investment is outlined above; the relevant information at t_3 is the same as at any other due date.

Since the "position" of the trader yields the quantity of both the wheat and money, we list the relevant information as:

1. The position of the trader.
2. The present price.

The Problem of Income Taxation.—The government is currently an interested receiver of information from every enterprise. It requires

---

13. Even if it were paid in wheat, the present price would be relevant. There is no reason to assume that the creditor would take a quantity of wheat smaller than the quantity he could purchase (the present price) if he had been paid in money.

the enterprise to report the results of certain activities; and the quantification of these activities is normally referred to as "taxable income." For the most part, taxable income is defined as the cash difference between completed exchanges. Clearly then the government has different relevant bits of information from those specified above. Thus, a critic may argue that our analysis is incomplete unless we discuss taxable income. For this reason we will digress in an attempt to justify the exclusion of taxable income from our relevant bits.

First, the concept of taxable income has *not* been excluded. In the above analysis we listed as a relevant bit the occurrence of *any* act that places the enterprise in an obligatory position. A completed exchange is one such act that is relevant to a government that levies taxes on that basis. However, this is only *one* of a great many acts that are relevant. Governments also levy taxes on the basis of sales, employees and their earnings, property values defined in a particular fashion, use, possession of certain commodities, being "in business," manufacturing certain commodities, transportation across political boundaries, and so forth. Each of these is a relevant bit to the government, and must be reported. We consider each of these bits to be simply one "factual condition" that is required to be reported and have omitted the impossible task of listing all of them.

Other receivers have similar relevant bits. For example, there are "income bonds" that define income in a certain fashion; some creditors require an accumulation of cash in a trust fund. Most states have a law about dividends being payable from surplus, and then they define surplus (income) by statute or precedent. All of these are relevant bits that we have excluded.

Even if we were to limit the specification of bits to those of taxable income, we would have an impossible task. We made the oversimplification above of equating taxable income to completed exchanges. This is not quite accurate. For example, the exchange of "inventory" for a "marketable security" is a "realization" of "income"; but the exchange of land for cash is not, if the conversion is "involuntary." The exchange of a machine for another like machine cannot be considered a realization; but the exchange of a machine for cash must be in most instances. The exchange of inventory for a 20-year bond is a realization; but the exchange of inventory for an installment note is not, until the cash is collected. Thus, even if we limited the specification of bits to taxable income, it would require the reproduction of the Internal Revenue Code and all related court decisions and interpretations, an obviously impossible task.

Our second reason for excluding taxable income is more fundamental. All of the above factual conditions have one element in common. They are all *definitions,* either statutory, contractual, or precedential. The government, being sovereign, can levy taxes any way it sees fit, i.e. it can define income any way it sees fit and then base the tax on that definition. There is controversy over the manner in which the government *should* define income, but all would agree on the manner in which it *did* define income. It appears that the legislatures accepted the prevailing method of measuring income and codified it. This method, of course, was the Accounting Tradition. Since then the legislatures have been willing to follow the changes in accounting theory. Witness the change to allow Lifo, Nifo (during the Korean War), declining depreciation, and so forth.

Given the fact that the definition of taxable income is subject to alteration because of theoretical refinements, it is clear that the development of our theory should not be prejudiced by the current definition. In addition, one of the alternatives being examined is the Accounting Tradition, and therefore if we allowed our conclusions to be influenced by present tax law—which is based on accounting methodology—our reasoning would be circular.

Finally, we can note that taxation theory falls into two broad (oversimplified) categories: (1) the cynical theory and (2) the equitable theory. The cynical theorists argue that the main business of taxation is to garner revenue for the government and that any tax which performs that function is a good one. Other objectives—e.g., equity, redistribution, ability to pay, fiscal policy—should be subordinated to the main purpose of garnering enough revenue to provide the governmental services. These other objectives, the argument goes, are separate problems and should be treated as such. The equitable theorists argue that taxation is inextricably entwined with the other objectives and that tax policy must be based primarily on "equity" or "justice," coupled with a large dose of fiscal policy.

This distinction is very roughly drawn, of course, and probably no single theorist would fit in either category. However, the distinction is sufficient for our purposes. If one is a cynical theorist, the current definition of taxable income is a good one because it produces revenue. Note, however, that a tax based on the numerosity of windows (as was done in France) would be equally good if it produced revenue. That is, the concept of income is not germane to the cynical theory.

The equity theorists all agree that the current definition is imperfect. Both Haig and Simons went to great pains to prove that the completed transaction method results in inequities. Other theorists have continued this argument up to the present time. There was a panel on "Capital Gains" taxation at the 1963 American Economic Association Meeting which reached the same conclusion as Haig and Simons and also concluded that income should be based on valuation at current market in order to avoid inequities in taxation.

This study has not utilized equity as a criterion, and therefore the analysis is not pertinent. The central point is that since the cynical theorists ignore income as a criterion and the equity theorists want to change the definition, there is no reason from a public finance point of view to pay any particular attention to the current definition.

This rather lengthy digression has had the object of meeting the anticipated criticism that our analysis was incomplete. We have argued that the information bits specified by the current definition of taxable income should not be separately specified for the following reasons:

1. It is only one of a myriad of factual conditions and has no a priori higher status than any of the others. It would be impossible to list them all.
2. The present definition of taxable income springs from a particular theory of income and therefore should not be a factor in a theoretical analysis of various theories of income.
3. The taxation theorists argue that the current definition is either irrelevant or incorrect.

For all these reasons we ignore taxable income in our analysis.

Summary

We have analyzed the problems of the other interested receivers and found them to be similar to those of the trader-manager. The main difference is that the other receivers are at the mercy of the manager, because he has control over the position. There are two lines open to them. They may either

    A. Make predictions continuously and compare their predic-
       tion to the manager's or
    B. Make an *ad hominem* judgment about the manager.

If A is selected, they must make the same type of decision as the manager and need the same bits, viz. present and predicted prices. In addition they need to know the manager's prediction which is given, in direction, by the present position. If B is selected, they need an evaluation of past decisions and some method of projecting the future. The method of projecting the future is not pertinent. The bits needed for the evaluation are the same as those needed by the manager, viz. present prices and position and latest price and position at the last evaluation.

In addition, the other receivers may have some contractual or statutory relationship to the firm. If so, they need to know the factual conditions of that relationship and the ability of the firm to meet its obligation. The bits needed for the latter are the present price and position.

A complete listing of the bits relevant to the decisions of the other receivers are as follows:

    1. The present price.
    2. The present position. (Yields the predicted direction of the
       price movement.)
    3. The latest price at the last evaluation of decisions.
    4. Their own prediction of the future price.
    5. Particular factual conditions.

Information needed from the next-best alternative enterprise would be the same as that listed.

SUMMARY

We have found that the dimension of value—in its verbal sense of valuation—is concerned with the ordering or ranking of goods. The problem arises from the necessity to sacrifice one good for another, and that sacrifice is the basis for the ordinal measurement of value.

The problematic situation that the trader and other interested receivers find themselves in is one of valuation. They need to make a decision that involves the ranking of goods. The ranking process requires a prediction of the future-state-of-being of the competing goods. The choice is simplified if these goods can be equated in the relevant dimension prior to the prediction and if this equation of goods allows a univocal measurement of the sacrifice.

The trader and other receivers may also want to evaluate the past decisions and/or determine the present state of the enterprise. This involves determining the present state of the enterprise at two points in time (or at one point, if the present state is the interest) and using the difference as an estimation of the prediction (decision) error.

One bit of information is relevant to all these decisions: the present price. Other bits that are relevant to one or more, but not all, decisions are:

1. Expected future price direction.
2. Past and present positions.
3. Past prices.
4. Particular factual conditions.

The past prices and positions have a specific temporal location: the latest used at the last evaluation.

The next-ranked alternatives have similar models, and the information needed from them is the same as from this model.

VIII

In the preceding pages we have discussed our problem in relation to measurement and information theory in rather general terms. It is the purpose of this chapter to become rather more specific—to examine the alternative valuation coefficients in light of the conceptions and propositions presented above. We will first try to discover a method of ranking the information in the model, and then we will proceed to an examination of the measurement problems.

INFORMATION IN THE MODEL

In our simplified model there are a limited number of information bits that can be communicated. We will enumerate *all* of the possible bits and then make judgments about which of them *should* be communicated. We will set up a method of valuing information bits according to their relevancy to theories and problems. The assumption that the information is veritable still holds, so that we can concentrate on the relevance.

157

The Communication System[1]

For the purposes of enumerating the bits, we will assume a perfect communication system. There is no noise, loss, or inherent capacity restraint. Our goal, however, is to maximize bits and minimize capacity.

The transmissions will be sent at definite time points, T_i, determined by the desire for information. For reasons presented *supra* (p. 92), time intervals will be assumed to be equal. A series of messages, λ_i, can be visualized as

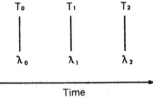

Time

Figure VIII-1

The message will be cumulative in information so that any bits transmitted in message λ_i need not be repeated in message λ_{i+1}. There is no noise; therefore redundancy would not add to the information of the receiver, but it would increase the required capacity. Thus, the last message is concerned only with events since the preceding message Message λ_2 is concerned only with events from T_1 to T_2, since message λ_1 provided information about the previous period.

The interim instants between T_i and T_{i+1} are defined as $t_1, t_2, \ldots, t_n$. The instants between messages are all-inclusive—they include all instants in time—and the first instant, t_1, and the last instant, t_n, correspond to the instants at which successive messages are sent. This may be visualized as

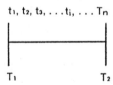

1. The communication system here described is concerned with the problems involved when the transmitter and receiver are different persons. Self-communication is not included in the system.

Message λ_2 contains information about all events from T_1 to T_2. There are an infinite number of instants, t's, between messages, and thus we should select in order to save capacity. This can be done without sacrificing information by transmitting states-of-being with the time specified and then making it known that such a state remains constant unless another bit is transmitted. Thus, a message containing

1. State Z_1 at t_2 and
2. State Z_2 at t_4

would be understood to mean:

State Z_1 came into existence at t_2
and remained in existence until t_4, when
State Z_2 came into existence.

Thus, if the bit

State Z_1 at t_3

were transmitted, it would not add any information, i.e. it would be "superfluous."[2]

Bits in the Model

We will classify the information emanating from the model as (1) Positions and (2) Prices. "Position" refers to the quantities of both wheat, W, and money, M, in bushels and dollars, respectively. Prices, P, refers to the transformation coefficient of money for wheat. Money is the valuing agent, so the price refers only to wheat and the "value" of money is unity. Thus, there are three bits:[3]

1. P, price of wheat.
2. W, quantity of wheat in bushels.
3. M, quantity of money in dollars.

There could be an infinite number of these bits, since they could change at every instant in time. We will denote the jth quantity of

2. We use "superfluous" here to avoid the technical interpretation of "redundant." Redundancy, in information theory, is used to indicate the amount of repetition necessary to overcome noise. Thus, redundancy adds to the information received. We mean by superfluous that it is *unnecessary* repetition.

3. Recall that the valuation coefficients are either past, present, or future expected prices. Hence there is no need to enumerate the valuation coefficients as separate bits.

wheat held at time i by $W_j(t_i)$. All of the t's are in the past, since the present is defined as t_n.

The trader's position—the quantities held—are included in the information enumeration, and thus the direction of the trader's expectations is included. The other receivers' predictions are not relevant to anyone's decisions but their own. Since they are both the sources and receivers of their own predictions, no communication other than self-communication is needed.

A rather detailed example will be helpful in visualizing the bits of information. Assume the following situation:

1. At $T_1 = t_1$ the trader held W_1 bushels and zero money. The price was P_1.
2. At t_2 the trader exchanged W_1 bushels for M_1 dollars at price P_2.
3. At t_3 the price change to P_3.
4. At t_4 the price had remained constant at P_3 and the trader exchanged M_1 dollars for W_2 bushels.
5. At $T_2 = t_n$ the price has changed to P_4.

The times and corresponding events are summarized in Table VIII-1.

Table VIII-1

Messages	λ_1				λ_2
Time	$T_1 = t_1$	t_2	t_3	t_4	$T_2 = t_n$
Quantity of Wheat	W_1	-0-	-0-	W_2	W_2
Price	P_1	P_2	P_3	P_3	P_4
Quantity of Money	-0-	M_1	M_1	-0-	-0-
Value of Money	1	1	1	1	1
Expectations	Up	Down	Down	Up	Up

The requirement of message λ_2 is that it communicate all of the above information—that the receipt of message λ_2 permit the receiver to completely reproduce Table VIII-1. One way of doing this is to transmit all of the above as it appears. However, in order to minimize utilization of the channel, we can "encode" the above in accordance with the assumptions.

The last two rows of Table VIII-1 can be omitted because of the unity assumption and the fact that the expectations are given by the position. The cumulative assumption allows us to omit all of Column 1 since it was reported in message λ_1. The event assumption permits the elimination of all repetitions in the rows and the times in which no event (price change or exchange) occurred.

The final encoded message would contain the ten bits listed in Table VIII-2. Without calculations or further assumptions, these are the minimum number of bits that permit the reproduction of Table VIII-1.

Table VIII-2

Time	Quantity of Money	Quantity of Wheat	Price
t_2	M_2	-0-	P_2
t_4	-0-	W_2	P_3
t_n			P_4

We can generalize the bits as

1. two quantities at every exchange and the time of the exchange;
2. one price at every price change and the time of the price change; and
3. the time of the message.

Defining

m = number of exchanges
n = number of price changes
β = minimum bits per message necessary to reproduce all the events,

then

$$3m + 2n + 1 = \beta.$$

This is a general expression of the number of bits required to reproduce the entire history of the enterprise, its exchanges, positions, price changes, and the expectations of the trader. Any further shortening of the message will have to be done at the expense of some information. If the capacity is not large enough to allow the full message, the problem is one of selecting the bits to be transmitted.

Table VIII-2 reproduces the complete history of this simple enterprise from T_1 to the moment at which the message λ_2 was sent. Since it is likely to require time for the preparation and transmission of the message, the information will be out-of-date by the time the receiver gets it. This is unfortunate, since information has a time value. The argument is often encountered that because the information is out-of-date at the time the receiver gets it, there is no point in bringing the information up-to-date at the time the message is prepared. It is said, for example, that there is no point in reporting prices as of December 31, when the financial statements are prepared, because those prices will be out-of-date when the financial statements are received in March. It is true that the prices will be out-of-date in March, but this merely emphasizes the need for faster preparation and transmission. It does not provide a reason for reporting a price that was in existence *prior* to December 31 and is therefore even *further* out-of-date. This argument is further evidence of the confusion surrounding temporal measurements. The quantities of both wheat and money are also out-of-date in March if the measurement was made on December 31, but no one has suggested that a quantity that was in existence prior to December 31 be reported on the December 31 financial statement. Instead there is a careful cut-off procedure that is followed to ensure that the quantity of cash is stated exactly as of December 31, even though that quantity will become out-of-date very shortly and is only momentary and will vary in the future. Thus, the price P_4 is included in Table VIII-2 because it *was* the present price at t_n in the same way that W_2 was the present quantity at t_n, even though it may have varied since then and is likely to vary in the future.

This argument is not pertinent to Table VIII-2 anyway, since all the prices and quantities up to t_n are presented. Thus, the receiver can value W_2 by P_3 or P_4 or even by P_2, if he wishes. Further, he could use some arbitrarily selected constant, as Boulding suggests, or estimate a future price and discount it by any rate he chooses. The only value not permitted by the table is the discounted expectations of the trader. This would require that the system communicate a specific future price prediction instead of merely indicating the directions of his expectations by his holding. Thus, this communication system does not solve the problem of maximizing the bits of information within a limited channel capacity. Instead it provides only a method of encoding which permits various valuation coefficients to be used. If the capacity of the channel is sufficiently large to permit all of these bits to be transmitted, there is no further problem, and this study could be concluded at this point. It is only when we are constrained that we have to choose; and the question that remains is which of those bits should be omitted if we are so constrained.

Measurement of the Value of the Bits

We have discussed the problems above in terms of the receivers. Since there are common elements to each of the receivers, we may recast these elements under problem categories instead of receiver categories.

Problem I: The problem of choosing between alternatives.

A. The first problem, as we have set it up, is to eliminate lower ranked alternatives. This is done for conceptual convenience, so that we may focus on the last two alternatives. This problem is universal. It is common to all receivers. We conceive all other alternatives as having a model exactly like the one presented.

This is a problem of valuation and requires the projection of the future state-of-being of both alternatives. It also requires the sacrifice of one of the present alternatives. Thus, the present alternatives and the projection are relevant bits of information. Value may be measured ordinally by measuring the sacrifice. Thus, if one selects alternative A (the wheat market or enterprise A), we can say that it is more valuable than alternative B, C, D, etc. The value of A is given by this expression

A > B (B is the next ranked alternative)

The sacrifice required is given by

A = B

It is convenient to have a method of equating the alternatives. This requires a unit; and since money is a general alternative, it was selected. In terms of the models, then, we need the following bits of information:

Alternative A	Alternatives B, C, etc.
1. The present price	1. The present price
2. The present position	2. The present position

 3. The expected future
    price

 3. The expected future
    price

It is important to emphasize that this is a general alternative, and the above bits are relevant to all of the receiver's problems.

The other receivers may have a more abstract price in mind (transformation coefficient of enterprise for enterprise), but the elements of that price are those listed above.

B. Once the general decision is made, we can focus on the alternatives within this firm model. The trader must decide between holding cash and holding wheat. If the other receivers select the comparison-of-predictions method, they also make the same decision. The information bits needed for both are:

 1. The present price
 2. The present position
 3. The expected future price.

Problem II: The problem of evaluating past decisions.

The purpose of the evaluation of past decisions varies with the receiver. The trader may make such an evaluation in order to revise the prediction theory used for selection. The other receivers may make an *ad hominem* prediction and may want a history as evidence for a projection. Although the purposes vary, the problem of both groups is identical. The main difficulty is in summarizing and abstracting the data. We selected a method of measuring the net results of all predictions and then comparing these results to a standard. The information needed follows:

 1. The latest price at the last evaluation
 2. The latest position at the last evaluation
 3. The present price
 4. The present position
 5. The standard.

If the standard is an alternative enterprise or an alternative trader in the same market, the information required for the standard would be the same as that listed above.

Problem III: The problem of fulfilling obligations.

This can be further divided into two parts:
A. Determination of the factual conditions of the obligation.

The question is concerned with whether or not the event has occurred which causes the obligation. This event may be a wide variety of things—as many as the fertile minds of contractors can dream up.
Some examples are
1. the passage of time (creditors);
2. the earning of income* (owners, government);
3. the performance of services (customers);
4. the value of property (property tax).
B. The ability of the firm to meet the obligation.
This is concerned with liquidity, and the relevant information is
1. the present position and
2. the present price.

Finally, we can recast these into bits that are relevant to the problems listed in Table VIII-3.

Table VIII-3

Relevant Bits	Problems				
	I_A	I_B	II	III_A	III_B
1. Present Price	X	X	X		X
2. Present Position	X	X	X		X
3. The latest price at the last evaluation			X		
4. The latest position at the last evaluation			X		
5. Factual Conditions of fulfilling Obligations				X	
6. The traders expectations	X	X			
7. The receiver's expectations	X	X			
8. The Standard for comparison			X		
9. Bits from other Models	X				

Rows 8 and 9 can be eliminated because the information emanates from a different source, and we are here interested in selecting the bits

---

* One may define "income" in any way he chooses. The current method is the net results of the completed exchanges.

that emanate from the trader model. Row 7 is generated by the receiver and is not required to be transmitted, so it can also be eliminated. Row 6 is superfluous, because the direction of the trader's expectations is given by his position.[4] Finally, rows 3 and 4 can be eliminated because of the cumulative nature of the postulated communication system. The present prices and positions will be the latest prices and positions at the time of the next message, and the present prices and positions in the last message are now the latest prices and positions at the last evaluation. Thus, from the problems specified and the specified theories for solution of those problems, we are left with a myriad of particular factual conditions and the present price and position. The latter are relevant to four of the five problems specified and serve as the bit needed in rows 3 and 4 as time passes.

If relevancy to the number of problems is taken as the measure of the value of the bits, we would transmit

1. Present Price and Position and
2. Particular Factual Conditions

in that order. In addition, for the group of receivers that compare their predictions of the price of wheat to the trader's predictions, an array of past prices may be relevant. Such past prices, however, would be selected on the basis of their location in time or their reaction to exogenous events (e.g., drought or crop failure in a competing grain). The prices extant at the time the trader exchanges would not necessarily be included in that array of past prices.

Classification of the Receivers.—There is an undetermined number of receivers who receive messages emanating from the model. We have

4. This elimination applies only to this model. Forecasts and budgets prepared by managements are likely to be equally as valuable to the receiver as the present prices and position if the receiver has confidence in the management and/or does not care to, or is unable to, make his own predictions. Further, the best standard to judge managements by may be their own forecasts. However, in the case at hand the goal (budget) of the trader is likely to be "to earn X per cent rate-of-return" or "make X dollars," and the prediction for each trade is likely to be simply "up" or "down" instead of a specific price. If the trader has some general policy, then that would serve as a substitute for row 6. For example, some traders will trade only if the expected profit is 50% or greater, because of the high risk of loss. If one knew of such a policy, then one could make a rough estimate of the trader's expectations.

above discussed the common problems that they have and also have presented a theory for solution of those problems. There are undoubtedly other receivers who have other theories and other relevant bits. Thus, the problem of different receivers with different theories is met. There is no definitive solution to this problem. However, we can discuss it in general terms.

Suppose that we wish to transmit information so as to satisfy the maximum number of receivers.

Define:

U = universal set of receivers
S_1 = set of receivers who have the problems specified *supra*
S_2 = set of receivers who have other problems

such that

$$S_1 \cup S_2 = U.$$

We have no way of knowing whether or not we are satisfying the receivers in S_2, since we don't even know what their problems are, much less their theory for the solution of those problems. S_2 may be the null set, or it may contain a larger number of elements than S_1, or it may be that they intersect, even to the point where $S_1 \cap S_2 = S_1 = U$. There is no way of knowing without empirical research. However, if the literature can be taken as a guide, then we have specified the common problems. If the receivers have other unknown problems, then there is no way to decide what to transmit until we know those problems.

The second classification required is those receivers who use the decision theories specified above and those who use some other theories.

Let

C_1 = set of receivers who use the theories specified *supra*
C_2 = set of receivers who use other theories

such that

$$C_1 \cup C_2 = S_1$$

It is impossible to determine how many receivers are in subset C_2. To anyone who has ever tried to teach the sunk-cost notion, it is obvious that there are a great many people who cling, with a fierce tenacity, to original cost as the most important datum in decisions. One can only speculate about how much of this is caused by the current method of reporting economic data in terms of original cost. But, for whatever reason, the fact that such a decision theory exists is a serious problem in selecting the information to transmit.

There are other receivers who play numerological and pictorial games with price patterns, e.g. "heads and shoulders," "flags," "pennants," "double bottoms," etc. The author once met a lady who speculated on the sole basis of arthritic pain, and she was quite successful.[5] No doubt there are a great many other theories, too numerous to list. The point is that there are different theories within subset C_2 as well as between C_1 and C_2. Let us further classify the receivers as (1) those with a theory that has original cost as a datum, D_1, and (2) the receivers with other theories, D_2, such that $D_1 \cup D_2 = C_2$.

The task of furnishing information to D_2—everything from astrological signs to "flags"—is overwhelming. There are two reasons for excluding D_2 from further consideration: First, much of the information specified by these other theories does not emanate from the model and therefore would be handled by another communications system. Second, many of the theories are unknown, and we cannot identify the relevant bits without knowledge of the theories.

This leaves us with the receivers in subset D_1. Our task is to rank them in relation to receivers in subset C_1. There is no a priori method of determining the relative number of receivers in each of the sets; therefore the ranking process must be accomplished by other methods. The author's judgment is that the information required by C_1 should have priority for the following reasons:

First, the theory of C_1 is correct and the theory of D_1 is incorrect. The whole of the marginal analysis can be, and has many times been, utilized to prove the theories presented above. It can be, and has been, utilized to prove the complete lack of relevancy of original costs to current decisions. Almost all elementary texts in economics,

---

5. She only speculated on one stock—IBM—and didn't know that she could sell short. It wouldn't be difficult to prove that she could have done better by "investing" rather than "speculating."

accounting, and management go to great pains to prove that erroneous decisions result from the use of original costs.

Second, it is the author's judgment that the use of the right information in the wrong theory would, in this situation, result in less erroneous results. That is, original costs lack any modicum of relevance, and thus the decisions made on the basis of original costs would be correct only by chance. Decisions made on the basis of relevant information, even in a theory that calls for original cost, should have an equal chance of being correct. If chance is the sole determinant of correct decisions, all information is equal. We can now conjecture that relevant information would produce some—however few—correct decisions above chance.

Third, it is likely that the relevant information would have some educational benefits, if for no other reason than that it would force the receivers in D_1 to wonder what to do with the information. The theory that specifies original cost as a datum is unknown to the author.[6] Perhaps the reason why the receivers in D_1 expect original cost and consider it relevant is that they have been conditioned to do so by the previous transmissions. If this is the case, then it is the duty of the transmitters (accountants in this case), not the receivers, to produce that theory and explain it.

Finally, it may be that D_1 contains fewer receivers than C_1. One might think that this is the case, since D_1 is a subset of a subset; but the number of elements in the various subsets is unknown, and thus no ranking can be made. This is another problem which can only be solved by empirical research.

This now leaves us with the set of receivers, C_1, who utilize the theories specified for the problems specified. There are several subsets of C_1:

6. In fact, with the sole exception of the long discredited cost-of-production theory of pricing, the author has never seen a theory for decision-making that specifies original cost as a datum. Decision models often correctly specify the income-tax differentials occasioned by alternative courses of action, and the income tax is based on the difference between receipts and original cost. However, as was pointed out previously, taxes can be based on anything, and therefore original cost is only incidentally relevant. Property-tax differentials are equally as relevant as income-tax differentials; and property taxes may be based on a fixed percentage of present market price or on a past price or some sort of appraisal.

s_1 = subset of those receivers using comparisons of predictions
s_2 = subset of those receivers using a prediction of the trader's success
s_3 = subset of those receivers using factual conditions
s_4 = trader(s) or manager(s)

Since all of these utilize the theories set forth above, if we can determine the number of receivers that need each bit of information, we can rank this information in "value." That is, the receivers are using the same theory, so the number of receivers is the sole determinant of the "value" of information.

We can list the problems, the bits, and the receivers as follows:

PROBLEM	BITS	RECEIVERS
I	Present price	$s_1 \cup s_4$
	Present position	$s_1 \cup s_4$
II	Present price	$s_2 \cup s_4$
	Present position	$s_2 \cup s_4$
	Latest price	$s_2 \cup s_4$
	Latest position	$s_2 \cup s_4$
III	Present price	$s_3 \cup s_4$
	Present position	$s_3 \cup s_4$
	Factual conditions	$s_3 \cup s_4$

We can reclassify these as bits and receivers.

Present Price	$s_1 \cup s_2 \cup s_3 \cup s_4 = s^1$
Present Position	$s_1 \cup s_2 \cup s_3 \cup s_4 = s^1$
Latest Price	$s_2 \cup s_4 \qquad = s^2$
Latest Position	$s_2 \cup s_4 \qquad = s^2$
Factual Conditions	$s_3 \cup s_4 \qquad = s^3$

It appears that $s^1 = C_1$ and thus contains all of the receivers in the set. It is highly probable that $s^1 \supsetneq s^2$ and $s^1 \supsetneq s^3$. For this not to be true, i.e. for $s^1 \supseteq s^2$ or $s^1 \supseteq s^3$, it would require that s_1 and s_2 be empty. Then, we can rank the value of the bits by relevance to numbers of receivers:

1. Present price and present position.
2. Latest price, latest position, and factual conditions.

Note that the factual conditions contain a number of different bits that are relevant to different receivers. Therefore, each element of factual conditions is relevant to a smaller number of receivers than s_3. That is, s_3 is the set of all receivers who need any fact, but any particular fact is relevant to only part of that set. For this reason, we can rank the bits in a finer gradation:

1. Present position, present price.
2. Latest position, latest price.
3. Particular factual conditions.

Thus, from a purely informational point of view, the present price and the present position have the highest priority in a limited channel situation. It would be natural to assume that these would be transmitted, since they have the highest priority; and thus the latest position and the latest price would be superfluous to any subsequent transmission, since they would have been received in a previous message. If there is any idle channel capacity, of course, the other bits—interim price, interim position—could be transmitted, but they would have a lower order of priority.

This ranking, however, is within the subset C_1. We have not satisfied the maximum number of receivers, because we still do not know the relative size of D_1, S_2, and C_1. Empirical research will have to provide the answer to the question of the relative size of the subsets.

There are several corollaries to this problem. We noted previously (p. 52) that feedback was not the solution, because receivers were not likely to ask questions without some prior information. Thus, transmitters can avoid questions about a particular subject by refusing to transmit any information about that subject. The obverse of this situation is that receivers *will* feedback questions about a subject on which they have received information. In a sense, the transmission of information creates a demand for further information on the same or related subjects. One important reason for this is that the receipt of information often reveals the existence of problems that were unknown prior to the receipt of the information. This phenomenon is commonly observed in business when one sets out to gather information on, say, the inventory problem; and that information reveals a problem in, say, production, which requires that more information be gathered; and that information reveals a third problem; and so forth.

Sometimes it is the solution of one of these problems that causes another problem; but often another problem is revealed by simply getting information. This situation is covered by the old adage that "ignorance is bliss." The reason it is blissful is that one is ignorant of the problems. The receipt of some information reveals hitherto unknown problems and requires further information. Thus, information creates its own demand.

A second corollary of the unknown problems of the receivers has more to do with data gathering and storage than with the transmission of information. Given that information (which is relevant to some problems) will reveal other problems and cause feedback requesting other information, the problem of deciding which data to gather (which measurements to make) is complicated further. This requires the transmitter-metrician to anticipate what kinds of problems will be revealed by the information that he gathers and transmits and what kinds of theories will be used to solve those problems. This problem is particularly acute if the measurements are time-dependent. If the metrician does not anticipate correctly and the magnitude is temporally variable, then it will be impossible for the metrician to meet the request for further information, because he cannot go back in time to make the measurement. This situation is commonly experienced and examples of it abound. We presented the example of the Bureau of Labor Statistics above (p. 58). This makes the data gatherer's task an impossible one, since he cannot be expected to anticipate future problems and future theories and he cannot supply the information unless he does anticipate. However, it does emphasize again the fact that the metrician-transmitter cannot be neutral. He must be actively engaged in theory construction in order to know what is relevant to the current theories and anticipate as best he can what will be relevant to the future theories and the problems that will be revealed by the information he transmits.

Thus, the empirical research, which was suggested above, on the number of receivers who have other problems is at best a static answer to a continuing problem. A longer range approach is for the metrician-transmitter to engage in theory construction and use part of his channel capacity for educational purposes.

Summary

We have postulated a perfect communication system and listed all the bits that emanate from the trader model. We have reviewed the problematic situations that are commonly encountered and set forth the theories that are used for the solution of those problems.

Using the relevancy to the number of specified problems and theories to rank the bits, we discovered that the present price and position were ranked first and that particular factual conditions were ranked second. Other bits were excluded as being superfluous.

Using the relevancy to the number of receivers to rank the bits, we discovered that we could not make the ranking without empirical research on the problems encountered and the theories used by the receivers. Nonetheless we classified the receivers into three main categories:

1. Receivers who use the specified theories to solve the specified problems
2. Receivers who have unknown problems and/or unknown theories
3. Receivers whose theory specifies original cost as a datum

Category 2 must be eliminated from consideration until the empirical research is done, because one cannot meet unknown needs. Category 3 should be ranked lower than Category 1, because the theory that specifies original cost is incorrect. Category 1 was broken down into various classes of receivers, and the bits ranked in accordance with number of receivers within that category to whom the bits were relevant:

1. Present price and position
2. Latest price and position at the last evaluation
3. Particular factual conditions
4. Information from other communication systems

Bit 2 was eliminated as being superfluous, and bit 4 as being handled by another system. Ranking category 2 below category 3 then allows the final ranking of the bits as follows:

1. Present price and position
2. Particular factual conditions
3. Past (purchase) prices.

Thus, from both the classification of problems and classification of receivers, the present price and position were found to be ranked first. Given a fixed channel capacity, the bits could be transmitted in accordance with this ranking until the capacity was exhausted.

MEASUREMENT IN THE MODEL

The informational analysis has revealed the bits that are relevant to various theories, and we have set up an order of value of these bits. It is clear that these bits must be capable of measurement—or at least capable of being determined—if they are to be communicated.

We have described the value dimension and the related concept of sacrifice above. We have also accepted money as the proper valuing agent and dollars as the proper unit. Thus, we have gone a long way toward fulfilling the measurement proposition requirements. There are several things that still need to be made explicit, however, and that is the purpose of this section.

There is no measurement problem in determining money. We have assumed that the valuation coefficient of a dollar is unity and that there is no problem in determining quantities. Money can simply be counted and then recorded. The quantity of wheat, likewise by assumption, presents no problem other than counting. The locus of the difficulties, if any, is in the determination of the prices.

We have already pointed out the impossibility of measuring the future. Also we pointed out that measurement requires an act (operation) that can be performed only in the present. Of course one could have measured in the past and recorded that measurement so that the information is still available. Thus, both past and present prices could be measurements. Future prices, on the other hand, cannot be measured. They must be predicted; and then the prediction can be verified when the future becomes the present.

This does not mean that one cannot measure under the Fisher Tradition. Instead it means that what one is measuring is the feelings of the trader or management about the future. There are ways that have developed for measuring feelings of people. One of the most common ways to make such measurements is to observe the actions of individuals in various situations. Often the situation requires that the individual choose between various courses of action; and which course he chooses is what is observed. This is precisely what we are recommending for the problem at hand. The trader has various courses of action open to him; we observe that he chooses the wheat market, and then we observe that he holds either cash or wheat or both. That is, the trader responds to various exogenous stimuli, and we observe those responses. If we are willing to assume that his responses are purposive, then we can infer something about his mental processes (expectations, in this case) from the course of action that he chooses. The weakest link in this procedure is in making the inferences about the mental processes from the observations. Also the information gained about the mental processes is rather sparse, compared to what we would like to know, but it is about the best we can do, given the present state of the arts. Thus, in the case at hand, we observe the position that the trader chooses and infer that he expects the price to go up or down. We would prefer a more precise formulation of his expectations, but that would be difficult to obtain.

The Accounting Tradition utilizes the process described above. Paton and Littleton (p. 22) argue that "the cost of any factor acquired by the enterprise represents, at the outset, the true economic significance of the factor. An assumption of rational business conduct is involved here. . . ." The "rationality" of the action is that the person will not purchase something, hence will not incur the "cost," unless the acquired factor is thought to be worth more than the sacrifice. Then the value of the acquired factor is set equal to the sacrifice, even though it is known that the purchaser expects the value to be greater, else he would not have purchased it. This notion is also in complete harmony with the Fisher Tradition. The capital budgeting model, for example, springs directly from the Fisher Tradition. In essence the capital budgeting model is simply a device for comparing sacrifices and expectations in which the expectations are adjusted for time differences. Thus, all three schools agree with the notion of sacrifice. The difference is that the Fisher Tradition would report the expectation instead of the sacrifice and the Accounting Tradition would report a past sacrifice instead of a present one.

The difference between the author and the Fisher Tradition concerns what ought to be reported. We presented our reasons *supra* for ranking the present price higher than the expected future price, albeit we would transmit both if the capacity was sufficiently large. The difference between the author and the Accounting Tradition is in the measurability of the present price. Often the Accounting Tradition argues that one can determine (measure) the sacrifice for a particular item only when *that particular* item is exchanged. In the case of wheat, one can determine the sacrifice for a particular bushel only when *that* bushel is exchanged. If this were true, it would be impossible for the trader to make his decisions. If the trader holds a particular bushel of wheat, he must continuously make the decision to hold or exchange. Each time he decides to hold he sacrifices a given amount of money that is specified by the price in existence at the time the decision is made. If he cannot determine the present price, he cannot make the decision. Thus, the trader must be able to determine the present price without exchanging. The question, then, is whether or not the accountant can determine that price. The problem, then, is to specify the operation for determining the present price.

First, the price is, per se, a comparison. It is a comparison of objects to units, and its purpose is to facilitate the comparison of objects to objects. One compares the object (wheat) to the unit (dollars), then another object (corn) to the unit, and finally the units to the units, and this permits the object-to-object comparison. This is precisely the way that cotton cords are compared to I-beams in the dimension of length. Note, however, that the procedure is different, and this is where the confusion lies.

If a person had an I-beam he could align it with meter sticks to determine the length. That is, he could perform an *operation* with a *unit object*. The original cause of the length or a possible future change in the length are of no concern to him in this operation; he is simply trying to discover the present length. If he had a number of identical I-beams, he could perform the operation with the unit object on one of those beams and thereby know the length of the others. He doesn't have to measure a particular I-beam to know its length. If you like, this is an inference in which two operations are performed. The first operation is aligning I-beam to unit object to discover the numerosity of units, and the second operation is aligning I-beam to I-beam to discover that they are of the same length (although they may be different in other respects). This permits the inference that the second I-beam has the same number of length units.

Precisely the same thing happens with wheat, but the instrument is rather more complex. The *market* is the instrument that makes the comparisons of objects to units. A person determines that he has wheat that is identical to that traded in the market, and then he "reads the instrument." He "aligns" his wheat with other identical wheat that has been, and is being, measured; and then he can infer that his wheat has the same number of units. The difference is in the complexity of the "instrument," but this shouldn't give us pause; one can prospect for uranium without understanding a Geiger counter if one can count the clicks.

Another difference is in the peculiar nature of the unit object. Dollars are used in the market as a unit *interval*. The unit object (currency) cannot be used to align or balance the wheat or other commodities, but that is not its purpose. The unit object of dollars serves a unique purpose. It is a promise, a tangible indication of a claim, and it cannot be used as an instrument for the measurement of commodities. The unit interval is also rather more complex. One cannot hold up his hands to indicate "this many dollars" as he can indicate "this many meters." The particular unit interval "dollars" is a much more general one. It encompasses all other attributes or characteristics of objects in a general expression of a degree of preciousness or desirability. Thus, the unit interval is quite complex and abstract; but neither should this give us pause. One can become an X-ray technician without a unit object for the rather abstract notion of the unit-interval of a Roengten.

In short, the operation of discovering the present price of wheat is (1) to determine that the wheat is identical to that wheat being traded in the market and (2) to observe the exchanges being made. This permits one to determine the sacrifice that is presently being made by the trader in order to *hold* wheat in exactly the same way that counting the number of dollars paid at purchase permits one to determine the sacrifice required in order to *acquire* wheat.

Of course no two objects are "identical." No I-beam or bushel of wheat is exactly like another, if for no other reason than that they occupy different spatial locations. The differences in this case are irrelevant, or, more accurately, they require a zero adjustment. In other cases they may require a non-zero adjustment. Land, for example, may be identical in all respects except its spatial location, but this difference is likely to cause differences in its desirability, hence differences in price. The problem, and it is a difficult one, is to know what adjustment is required in such cases. However, in the case at hand—a perfect market—no adjustment is required.[7] The "unique good" situation is discussed briefly in Part III. The primary purpose of this discussion is to establish the concept of what ought to be measured. Once this is done, then the problem is reduced to one of the practicalities of making the measurement under difficult conditions. As we noted *supra*, measurements are "conceived and [then] sought."

Additivity Problems

In the previous section on the communication system we presented the information in "bits" in which both the price and quantity were transmitted. Usually only the value—the product of the price and quantity—is transmitted. This may be thought of as further "encoding" of the information. That is, the balance sheet usually contains only "Wheat $100" instead of "Wheat $2 per bushel, 50 bushels," with a saving of one bit. This situation requires that the criterion of additivity be met within the commodity class of wheat. As Hölder and others show, multiplication reduces to addition with respect to measurement theory in the same way that it does in mathematics. Thus, the multiplication of 50 by $2 is the same as summing a column which contains $2 fifty times.

If the commodities held at any point in time are heterogeneous, then they must be additive between commodity classes as well as within the class in order to calculate the total asset figure. Even if they are instantaneously homogeneous, the criterion of additivity must be met if they are intertemporally heterogeneous. In that case, the

---

7. The zero adjustment is because we are trading wheat contracts which are expressed in bushels for convenience. Physical wheat does require an adjustment for grade and location. The contracts traded specify a standard grade delivered at a certain location at a certain time. There are established differentials in price for different grades, and the measurement problem is in grading the wheat. Likewise the differences in price in different markets due to different locations are kept fairly close to transportation costs by arbitraging.

wealth at an earlier point in time needs to be subtracted from the wealth at a later point in time in order to determine the income. Subtraction is merely addition reversed, and it has the same requirements insofar as measurement theory is concerned.

In short, in the measurement of wealth, the values of individual units within a commodity class must be additive in order to get the total value of that class; and the values of commodity classes must be additive in order to get the total value of the firm. In the measurement of income, the values of the firm at different points in time must be additive in order to make the subtractions necessary to get the change. This means that we must be able to demonstrate the empirical meaning of these various sums. The valuation coefficient selected must yield a sum that is empirically meaningful.

We described the sacrifice dimension *supra* and admitted that this dimension does not measure the true degree of preciousness of the held good to the holder. Instead it measures the floor of the preciousness to the holder, because it indicates what he is willing to give up in order to hold that good. Thus, in the case of money there is a series of "or" statements which describes the sacrifice. If one holds money, he is sacrificing a certain quantity of bread, or a certain quantity of theater tickets, or so on indefinitely for all the goods that are offered on the market. The quantity of each of those goods being sacrificed is determined by the present price of each. Thus, the sacrifice may be expressed as a certain command over goods which the holder is foregoing. So long as the command over goods is not large enough to affect the price, the dimension meets the additivity criterion. The empirical meaning of this dimension is the quantity of goods that can be commanded at any point in time.

In one sense, money can be thought of as invariant over time. If a given amount of money is held, the sacrifice is an entire array of goods which produce utility. Under a stable price level, this amount of money would produce the same utility at all points in time. That is the meaning of a "stable price level." However, if we compare the amount of money to any particular good, instead of utility, it is not invariant. A constant quantity of money, then, is a temporally invariant sacrifice for utility, but it is a temporally variant sacrifice for any particular good. Money in relation to a particular good is *always a present* scarifice.

The sacrifice associated with holding wheat is not invariant over time, even with regard to utility, unless the price is constant. Quite the contrary, the change in the price, if wheat is held, *means* a change in the sacrifice of money, and hence of utility. Since wheat can be transformed into money in accordance with the existing price and since money is the general expression of the sacrifice or command of other goods and since the utility varies with that ability to command goods, then the existing price of wheat expresses the existing sacrifice. This means that we can multiply a past quantity of wheat by a past price, add it to a past quantity of money, and then speak meaningfully of the past sacrifice of both utility and goods (if the prices of other goods in the same temporal location are known). We can do the same with present prices and present quantities and then speak meaningfully of the present sacrifice. The sacrifice is additive intertemporally also. We could subtract the past from the present sacrifice and determine the increment.

However, it should be obvious that if we mix the temporal location of the quantities and prices, then they are not additive either instantaneously or intertemporally.

Consider the price of wheat $P(t_1)$ and the quantity of wheat $W(t_2)$ along with the quantity of money $M(t_2)$. The product $P(t_1)W(t_2)$ yields the sacrifice at t_1 if $W(t_1) = W(t_2)$, but it does not yield the sacrifice at t_2 if $P(t_1) \neq P(t_2)$. Moreover, the sum of $P(t_1)W(t_2)$ and $M(t_2)$ does not yield the total sacrifice at t_2 or the command over goods and the accompanying utility.

A physical analogy may be helpful. Assume that a forest ranger has a varying quantity of trees—Q—with an identical amount of board feet per tree—F—but with F varying over time. He can calculate his total board feet—$X(t_1)$—at t_1 as

$$X(t_1) = Q(t_1)F(t_1)$$

and at t_2

$$X(t_2) = Q(t_2)F(t_2)$$

But if he mixes the temporal locations, we have a problem.

$$X^1 = Q(t_1)F(t_2)$$

X^1 can be read as:

> "Total board feet that I would have if I still had the same number of trees that I had at t_1 and if all those trees had grown equal to $F(t_2)$."

This is a counterfactual conditional—a statement in the subjunctive mood. It may be perfectly valid information and relevant to some problems, but it has nothing to do with the discovery of an existing condition—measurement—and little if anything to do with the selection of alternatives.

Now suppose the ranger has another total quantity of board feet, X^2, in another location or in another form.

$$X^3 = X^1 + X^2$$

X^3 is a present existing quantity added to a hypothetical quantity, which makes the entire statement hypothetical. X^3 says nothing about the past, present, or future expected quantity. Its use, if any, is limited to the analysis of hypothetical conditions.

Measurement is concerned with the *discovery* of units in a dimension, not with hypothesizing about what might be. The sum of a measurement—an existing quantity—and a hypothetical quantity can be used only in comparing hypothetical conditions. Since the existing conditions delimit the existing alternatives, X^3 is irrelevant to decision-making. In addition, if X^3 were presented as a measurement of an existing quantity, the information would not only be irrelevant, it would not be veritable.

The conclusion is clear: a mixture of temporal locations is not a measurement of an existing condition.

The point is elementary, but unfortunately the error is often made. Most messages of valuation are derived from a past transformation coefficient multiplied by a present quantity. The result is inevitably a hypothetical situation[8] if measurement of sacrifice is the purpose. The

---

8. The particular hypothetical situation is described as a "static economy assumption" by Edwards and Bell. They argue that only under the conditions of a static economy—in this case the relevant static would be the price—is such a message valid or useful. We argue the same from a different approach below.

usual situation is that only the product and the date of multiplication is presented as a measurement and/or information. In this situation one cannot even guess at the hypothetical conditions, much less at the actual *ex post* quantity.

Suppose one were given X^1 at t_1 and X^2 at t_2. Assume further that we know that $Q(t_1)$ and $Q(t_2)$ were used to calculate X^1 and X^2, respectively, but we have no further information. Now X^1 or X^2 alone is a very interesting statistic. It can be read as

> "This is the total board feet that I would have if I had the quantity (unspecified) of trees that I now have and if the board feet per tree (unspecified) was the same as it had been at a time (unspecified) in the past."

The interesting thing about this statistic is that it is very likely to have negative informational content. At best it is useless and irrelevant, and at worst it is misleading if anyone should attempt to use it.

It may be, and sometimes is, argued that the direction of movement of such a statistic is meaningful, even if the isolated statistic is not. We can calculate the difference

$$X^2 - X^1 = d$$

Assuming d to be positive, what can be said about it? Since both X^1 and X^2 are hypothetical, the most that can be said of d is that it is the difference between hypothetical (unspecified) conditions. We cannot infer anything about the relative size of $X(t_2)$ and $X(t_1)$ or $Q(t_1)$ and $Q(t_2)$ or $F(t_1)$ and $F(t_2)$. The difference could be caused by any one of the following changes:

1. An increase in Q and a decrease in F
2. An increase in Q and an increase in F
3. An increase in Q and a constant F
4. A decrease in Q and an increase in F
5. A constant Q and an increase in F

The magnitude of any of the increases and decreases could be any one of an infinite series of numbers, and the temporal location of F could be any one of an infinite number of instants. Without fear of overstatement, one can say that the results are imprecise. The mind boggles at imagining a possible use for such "information."

The above has been concerned with the intertemporal comparison of board feet. If we have a second ranger and want to make an instantaneous comparison, the mixture of temporal locations results in even more confusion. It is clear that if they both measure at the same time, the results are subject to the additive axiom. Even if they measure at different times, the results may be *adjusted* so that they are additive.[9] However, if the temporal locations of the multiplier and multiplicand are mixed and only the product of each equation is given, the results are completely without meaning.

This can be stated in general terms. Suppose, for example, that we have two objects that are identical in all respects. (We intuit that they are identical.) Thus,

$$Y_1 \equiv Y_2$$

Utilizing Caw's statement (p. 4) that a measurement can be stated as

"2 (length in meters) this rod"

we can measure these objects at the same time and place and then express the relation as follows: (U_1 and U_2 are units.)

$$U_1 \cdot Y_1 = V_1$$
$$U_2 \cdot Y_2 = V_2$$

If

$$U_1 \neq U_2$$

then

$$V_1 \neq V_2$$

Thus we have a contradiction of the worst order. The *sine qua non* of measurement—comparison—has been abrogated. One cannot relate or order Y_1 to Y_2 on the basis of V_1 to V_2 intensively, much less extensively, because of the contradiction. How does one interpret the difference between V_1 and V_2? What does it mean? The only possible interpretation is that it is an error. We know by assumption in this case that Y_1 and Y_2 are identical. Yet the communication of V_1 and V_2 would indicate that they are not identical.

---

9. Of course the specification of the temporal location is essential to the adjustment. In fact one would not know that an adjustment is needed unless he knew that there was a variation in temporal locations.

This rather lengthy analogy is perfectly applicable to the trader's situation. All of this may be more concisely stated:

> Measurements that are invariant as to time conform to the additive axiom only if the temporal locations are homogeneous.

The temporal locations of the prices and quantities that were selected in the information section are homogeneous. The use of a past or future transformation coefficient as the valuation coefficient would yield the same kind of anomalies as the physical analogy. The use of a past (purchase) price for valuing wheat, with the transmission of only "Wheat X^1" and "Wheat X^2" at two different times, would result in a difference that could be caused by any of the five factors listed above. If there are two traders in the market, both of whom hold identical quantities of identical wheat at the same point in time, then the use of different purchase prices will result in the contradiction mentioned above—the values of identical items will be different. The same is true within the commodity class: identical items will be valued at different prices, and the sum of the individual values will have no empirical meaning.

Therefore we conclude that the existing prices and quantities ought to be used at the time the measurement is made in order to calculate the existing value. Since measurements are made in the present, the "existing" price reduces to the "present" price as the preferable valuation coefficient.

Problems of Observation and Instrumentation

As noted above, the present is simply a convenient method of expressing the most recent past. Thus, all of our measurements are in the past, and there is no reason to assume that there is more or less difficulty in observing any particular past instant. In fact, it could be argued a priori that if all past instants are identical, there is good reason to believe that all are equally difficult or easy to observe. We have assumed a perfect market in our model, so the problems of observation have been simplified.

Nevertheless, there are a great many people who argue that the problems of observation are so great that some "critical act" must occur before the measurement can be made. One of the most extreme examples of this was reported recently. An accountant reported (measured?) Canadian dollars at a previous (purchase price) foreign exchange rate.[10] They were then added to American dollars. Presumably the reason for this was because of the difficulty of observing the exchange rate until the exchange was complete. One would think that foreign exchange rates were identical to similarity transformations (like transforming meters to feet) except for their time invariance. Although this case is extreme, there are many others in which the general rule is to continue to report purchase prices until the exchange is complete.[11]

For purposes of discussion, we will grant that certain conditions may make observations more difficult. For example, it is easier to determine the spatial location of a body at rest than that of a body in motion. Thus, Aristotle could contemplate a falling stone and come up with a measurement of the speed of that stone between the times that it was at rest; but he could not measure the speed while it was still in motion. We now know, by use of better instruments, that he was measuring average speed; that the stone accelerates. Aristotle's measurement may be visualized as

$$T_1 \text{--} T_2 \text{ (Time)}$$
$$D_1 \text{--} D_2 \text{ (Space)}$$

with the speed as the quotient

$$\frac{D_2 - D_1}{T_2 - T_1} = S$$

Because of the lack of instruments, Aristotle was forced to wait until the "critical act" of the stone coming to rest before he could measure its spatial location. He could not have measured the distance

10. "On the other hand, perhaps the most extreme adherence to accounting for the historical costs of current assets was recently described by Professor Dixon of the University of Michigan. He discovered an accountant who insisted on disclosing Canadian dollars at par rather than at the current exchange rate of approximately 92 cents. It seems the Canadian dollars were originally acquired dollar for dollar and the accountant was determined to reflect cash at its historical cost." (Sprouse, "Current Assets," p. 694.)

11. There are several other reasons given for following this procedure. They will be presented and criticized in the chapter on the Accounting Tradition.

at, say, t_3 ($T_1 < t_3 < T_2$), but surely he would not report that the spatial location at t_3 was D_1. He might have said that the location at t_3 was "undetermined," even "undeterminable" or simply "in motion," but certainly not D_1.

If he needed to know the spatial location at t_3—if this was relevant information—he would be forced to estimate its location. It is very likely that there would be a considerable lack of interobserver agreement in such an estimation; and this is a serious shortcoming. However, if any observer reported D_1, we would certainly question his perception and perhaps his integrity. Also, we might hesitate to term such an estimation a measurement; but it is at least as much of a measurement as the reporting of D_1.

This example is useful, because it casts the problem in clear relief.

1. The distance travelled at t_3 is relevant. We need to make a decision based on the spatial location at t_3. If that is undeterminable, the decision cannot be made in accordance with the specifications of the decision-theory.

2. D_1 is irrelevant and is not a measurement. We could get unanimous interobserver agreement that the location was *not* D_1 at t_3.

3. An estimation of the distance at t_3 is superior to the complete absence of information. However, estimations suffer from lack of precision and interobserver agreement.

4. A measurement of the distance at t_3 is the desideratum. A measurement is superior to an estimation because it is more precise and there is more interobserver agreement; therefore we have more confidence in the data.

5. Sophisticated instruments and observers are required to make a measurement at t_3. There are two extreme alternatives: (1) we can bewail the lack of instruments and observers and continue to report D_1, or (2) we can try to develop the instruments and observers and utilize the estimation in the interim.

The same is true of difficulties in the measurement of prices. It is true that prices are sometimes difficult to determine in the absence of an exchange. We can all lament this fact, but this does not give us license to report irrelevancies simply because they are easier to determine. The problem is in our observations and instrumentation.

It would appear, then, that the obligation of a metrician is to seek ways to improve his instruments and observations.

In the model we deny that the present price is more difficult to determine than past prices. However, in anticipation of the criticism that this is true only because of the perfect market, it should be pointed out that any measurement benefits derived from a perfect market are equally applicable to all prices. Specifically, the perfect market assumption makes the present price easier to determine, but it also makes the past (purchase) price easier because it avoids all incidental and ancillary costs of purchasing and selling. This, in turn, avoids all the problems of tracing the costs and deciding on the different matching and attaching conventions used in handling ancillary costs. Moreover, it can be argued that in some situations the present price is much easier to determine than the purchase price in either an imperfect or a perfect market. If two bushels of wheat were purchased at different prices and one is sold, it is impossible to know what *the* purchase price of the unsold bushel is. This is evidenced by the existence of the large number of different methods of inventory costing—lifo, fifo, average, etc. One must *assume* which price is the purchase price of the unsold bushel; it is *impossible to determine* that price. For this reason, any difficulties in determination of the present price must be compared to the impossibility of determining *the* purchase price, before a judgment is made. In our judgment the difficulties in determination of the present price are less than those of determining the purchase price.

Summary

We have reviewed the principal problem of this study in light of measurement theory. The requirements of measurement theory were to specify the dimension, units, and operations of a particular system. It has been argued that the use of a present price meets these requirements. The sacrifice dimension was described; and the market is taken as the instrument by which the sacrifice is determined, and this is expressed in the units of dollars. The consideration of the additivity requirements leads to the rejection of past (purchase) and future (sale) prices as valuation coefficients. Both price and quantity need to be temporally homogeneous in order to express an existing, as opposed to a hypothetical, sacrifice. All measurements are made in the present, and this leads to the use of a present price. The difficulties of observing a price in the absence of exchanging the particular good held were considered; and although difficulties do exist, it was argued that those difficulties were less than those encountered in the determination of the past (purchase) price and also less difficult than determining the future (sale) price.

Thus, from a measurement point of view the present price is the appropriate valuation coefficient.

SUMMARY OF PART ONE

In this part we have restricted the discussion to a simplified model of trading in a perfect market. The problem of income determination —under the well-known definitions of income—becomes one of measuring wealth at a point in time. There are four proposals for such a measurement, viz. the Fisher Tradition, the Accounting Tradition, Boulding's Constant, and Present Market.

We selected cash as the proper valuing agent and noted that this reduced the problem to the determination of value under the conditions of an incomplete exchange. A consideration of the timing of the valuation led us to the conclusion that the impetus of the problem was a desire for information at a specified time.

A review of information and measurement theory allowed us to set up some generalized criteria for the selection of the valuation coefficient. An important requirement was the description of the dimension and specification of the problem and the decision theory. The decision theory then allowed us to specify the information relevant to the various problems.

A listing of all the information emanating from the model and an assumed communication system, in relief against the relevant bits, permitted the ordinal measurement of the value of the bits. Certain bits were eliminated because they were exogenous to the model or because they were superfluous. This left us with

1. the present price and position
2. factual conditions

in that order, as the highest-ranked bits to be communicated.

An examination of these bits in light of measurement theory found them acceptable even to the narrow metricians as proper measurements.

Thus, our conclusion is that the present price is the proper and correct valuation coefficient for the measurement of wealth at a point in time. Other prices are irrelevant and/or are not measurements. Income, then, is the difference between the sums of the quantity of money and the quantity of the trading assets times the present price at two points in time, the time being determined by the desire for information.

2

"It is ambition enough to be employed as an under-labourer in clearing the ground a little and removing some of the rubbish that lies in the way of knowledge."

—JOHN LOCKE

"Most philosophers who are engaged in speculative construction employ standards of criticism too loose to detect gross flaws in their own systems, while most philosophers who are engaged in critical analysis do not have the ingenuity to construct any system at all which their own criticism cannot immediately destroy. Neither kind of philosophy has the right to call the other unphilosophical, and neither can stand alone: construction without analysis is irresponsible, analysis without construction is trivial. But although there could never be

a sound defense for a policy of doing only metaphysics, there may sometimes be such a defense for a policy of doing only analysis, namely at times when a great deal of unanalyzed and conflicting metaphysics has been inherited, some of which must be wrong and may be harmful."

—PETER CAWS

IX

BOULDING'S CONSTANT

Boulding's analysis is a masterful one. His model is useful in illuminating several other economic problems in addition to income measurement; his perspicacity and felicitous style allow him to strip away the irrelevant and immediately incise the problem. However, his analysis of the nature and determination of income is imperfect. He states the problem succinctly and, we think, correctly; and he appears to be headed toward an unassailable conclusion, only at the last moment to veer off, sometimes to vacillate and sometimes to err.

Because of his vacillation, it is difficult to present a critique. Some of his statements may be described as misplaced conclusions, most of which are correct; but other statements, which we take to be the final conclusions, are demonstrably wrong. Thus, there is some danger in criticizing him—a danger of misunderstanding what his conclusions are and thus demolishing only a straw man. We will flirt with this danger by taking only Boulding's conclusions that are contrary to ours and discussing them. We will not attempt to cover all of his work. It should be clear that our quarrel finally concerns the brief analysis of income presented in *Reconstruction,* and not all of his writings.

Boulding's conclusion in its most straightforward form is as follows: "All valuation thus seems to possess a certain unavoidable arbitrary element, as long as the asset structure remains heterogeneous." (*Reconstruction,* p. 45.) The word "all," plus the fact that this statement was made after he suggested the constant, indicates that the constant is also arbitrary. In another context, when he does not suggest the constant, he writes: "It must not be thought that the valuation of the 'things' possessed by a society is a simple, easy, or even certain process. There are many undoubtedly valuable things that are not ordinarily valued at all." (*Analysis,* p. 262.) Then under the heading "All Valuations a Matter of Estimate," he continues: "The difficulties of valuation, however, extend far beyond the case of things which are not usually valued. Even those values which normally figure on balance sheets are calculated by a process of estimate according to certain rather arbitrary principles." (*Analysis,* p. 263.) When quarrelling with the profit maximization notion he complains: "The main difficulty is that the quantity which is supposed to be maximized does not really exist! It would be unkind to call it a figment of the accountant's imagination but it is certainly a product of the accountant's rituals." (*Skills,* p. 56.) Presumably the reason for describing these actions as rituals is because they are rites or ceremony over which the accountant has considerable discretion, i.e. they are arbitrary. In another context he defends these rituals: "Ritual is always the proper response when a man *has* to give an answer to a question, the answer to which he cannot really know. Ritual under these circumstances has two functions. It is comforting (and in the face of the great uncertainties of the future, comfort is not to be despised) and it is also *an answer sufficient for action.*" ("Twins," p. 53, italics added.) There are two points here. One, valuation is concerned with the future, and the future is unknown; and two, rituals produce relevant information (answers sufficient for action). Respectively we agree and disagree. Much of Part One of this study was an attempt to prove the validity of the first and the invalidity of the second of these points. Boulding continues:

> It is the sufficient answer rather than the right answer which the accountant really seeks. Under these circumstances, however,

it is important that we should know what the accountant's answer means, which means that we should know what procedure he has employed. The wise businessman will not believe his accountant although he takes what his accountant tells him as important evidence. The quality of that evidence, however, depends in considerable degree on the simplicity of the procedures and the awareness which we have of them. ("Twins," pp. 53-54.)

Two points emerge here also. One, the operation proposition—that the description of the instrument and procedure makes the measurement useful or relevant—and two, that simplicity of procedure produces quality. The first point is common to a goodly number of people from a variety of disciplines.[1] However, as we pointed out above, it will not stand an informational criterion. Hempel's "hage" example (p. 84 *supra*) demolishes it. The second point stands or falls on the first. Of course, the procedure should not be unnecessarily complex, but that judgment depends upon the goal. No one would deny that the procedure should be no more complex than is necessary to furnish the relevant information. However, this statement is truistic and barren of genuine content. Juxtaposition of a meter stick is a very simple procedure, but it hardly produces quality in measuring planetary distances. A cyclotron entails a very complex procedure, but it produces, it does not inhibit, quality in the measurement of the velocity of particles. Quality is an ambiguous term in this context. If it means precision, it is easy to demonstrate that complexity usually varies directly with precision. The more complex the instrument, the more precise the measurement, *cet. par.* It is difficult to see how veritableness would have a relation to simplicity of procedure. Relevance is specified by the decision theory, not the operation. In short, the relation between "quality" and simplicity of procedure escapes us. We agree that simplicity is a desideratum, but it has a very low priority relative to the criteria listed above.

Boulding, however, is so convinced of these points that he is "suspicious of many current efforts to reform accounting in the direc-

---

1. For example, from physics Bridgman argues that a nonoperationally defined construct is "a Platonic view of the world diametrically opposed to the whole operational approach." His book is in large part an attempt to prove the primacy of operations. The quotation is from Caws, *Definitions*, p. 15.

tion of making it more 'accurate.'" ("Twins," p. 54.) This suspicion does not follow from the operational viewpoint—operationalists are continually seeking improvements in instrumentation and accuracy. Instead, it is the restatement of his unwavering belief that all valuations are arbitrary.

With such a belief as a starting point, it is not difficult to understand how he reaches his conclusion. All valuations are arbitrary; a constant is no more arbitrary than other valuation coefficients; a constant is simple; therefore, a constant is the preferable valuation coefficient. Our basic disagreement is with his belief that all valuation coefficients are arbitrary. The superficial disagreement is with his proposal that a constant is the preferable valuation coefficient. To put it otherwise—if we agreed with the arbitrary proposition, then the selection of a valuation coefficient would turn on the relative simplicity of the alternatives, and we would select the constant as the simplest.

Webster's dictionary defines "arbitrary" as "arising from unrestrained exercise of the will, caprice or personal preference . . . based on random or convenient selection or choice rather than on reason or nature. . . ." In short, arbitrary implies that there is no rational method of selection. Obviously we disagree. This entire study is an attempt to make a selection based on rational criteria. We set forth our criteria in Part One; and thus if one is willing to call our criteria "rational," the selection is not arbitrary. Boulding gives every indication that he would accept our criteria, if not our analysis. He shows great respect for "information," noting that it is perhaps the chief contribution of operations research. (*Trends*, p. 12.) In another context he echoes the complaint of this study:

> My plea for naïveté, or at least for simplicity in accounting practice, does not preclude the hope that one day we may be able to set the whole information-collecting and processing operation of an organization on a somewhat more rational basis than now exists. At present one suspects that a great deal of information is collected and processed which actually is irrelevant to the making of decisions or the taking of any kind of action. The collection of such information is pure waste from the point of view of the organization even though it may have certain scientific value. ("Twins," p. 55.)

And finally he succinctly sets forth the criteria: "Nobody, to my mind, has yet developed an adequate theory of information collection and processing from the point of view of the decision-making process." ("Twins," p. 55.) Such a development, in a very narrow context, is the central purpose of this study. Thus, it seems eminently reasonable to assume that if Boulding accepted our analysis he would abandon his "arbitrary selection" position, and there would be no fundamental disagreement.

In fact on one occasion he implies that profit is measurable under perfect market conditions. He writes: "This is to say that the theory of profit maximization is only applicable to the case in which all markets are perfect, where there is no difficulty in transforming any asset into any other, and where the *form* of the asset structure is unimportant." (*Skills*, p. 59.) Since he previously complains about the lack of existence of the maximand and uses this as a reason for arguing against the notion of profit maximization, but then states here that profit maximization is applicable to perfect markets, we may conclude that he thinks that the maximand does exist in perfect markets. Nevertheless, in *Reconstruction* he uses a perfect-market model and concludes that this existing maximand—profit—is arbitrarily determined. Because of this inconsistency, it is not clear how we stand in relation to Boulding. On the one hand there appears to be complete agreement, especially in view of our perfect market assumption; but on the other hand his perfect market analysis conclusions are diametrically opposed to ours. For this reason we feel obliged to discuss the analysis that leads to the conclusion of a constant. The conclusion and analysis are presented in *Reconstruction,* and the following is from that source.

First, Boulding's fear that a particular valuation coefficient would indicate that profit comes about only from a price change is fallacious. It is clear that both a price change and an exchange are necessary for income. The trader must put himself in the position to profit from the price change; if he holds the riskless asset (money with a stable price level) without exchanging, it is clear that he can never increase his utility. Yet he can exchange all he wants in a constant price market and never change his stock of money. There are two variables to the income process:

1. Position—which is achieved only by exchange.
2. Price change.

Both are prerequisites to income. Income cannot be garnered without both variables being present. Since both are indispensable, one cannot say that either one is more important than the other.

Of course Boulding does not say this, but what he does say is that the selection of a particular valuation coefficient necessitates the proposition that income arises solely from one variable. The complete quote is:

> If we follow the rule of equating the valuation coefficient with the transformation coefficient, i.e. if we value our wheat stocks at the market price of wheat, we run into several difficulties. This assumption, as we have seen, necessitates the proposition that no values are created and no profits made in the pure act of exchange, but that profits and losses come only when stocks are revalued because of a change in price. (*Reconstruction,* p. 43.)

We agree with the first part of the proposition—that no profits arise from the *pure* act of exchange—but we fail to see how any of the proposition follows from the selection of a particular valuation coefficient.

Both an exchange and a price change are necessary, indispensable prerequisites to income, and thus we would never recognize income on one alone. However, when both are *present*, we see no reason not to recognize income. Boulding's problem may be in imputing causality to the temporal location of a variable. The temporal order of the prerequisites is first, position and second, price change. One cannot obtain the position after the price change, because that alternative no longer exists; and thus the temporal order is specified by the process.

The same is true in many physical processes. For example, one must plant (position) a tree first, and then it must rain. If it rains without planting there is no growth, and vice versa. If it rains first and then the tree is planted, there is no growth without further rain. The alternative of planting before rain is no longer available. Thus, the analogy contains the essential elements.

1. Two variables, both indispensable.
2. Temporal order specified by the process.

3. Nonrecurring opportunities.

If we measured the growth of the trees after the rain, no one would suggest that the rain was the sole cause of the growth. By the same token, there is no reason to impute single causality to a price change simply because the measurement is made after the change occurs. The proposition does not follow. In fact one could push the analogy further by assuming that the volume of growth was equal to the volume of water. Under this assumption, one can determine the growth by measuring the rain as it occurs, without necessitating any propositions about "pure act of planting" or "pure act of raining." The growth is the conjunction of two variables, temporally ordered, and the last variable indicates nothing about causality, even if it is used as a measuring rod.

There is one important distinction between the variables however. The trader (planter) has *control over his position,* but no control over the price change (rain). Clearly though, the endogenous or exogenous nature of the variable has little if anything to do with measurement or valuation, and nothing to do with causality.

Boulding slips at another point by vacillating on the valuing agent. He points out that net worth could be stated in either money or wheat and then: "A 'rise' in the dollar value, or 'price,' of wheat is the same thing as a fall in the wheat value of dollars; . . . This results in a rise in the net worth measured in dollars, and a fall in the net worth measured in bushels. We shall see later that this apparent paradox leads to some serious difficulties in the interpretation of accounting procedures." (*Reconstruction*, p. 41.) There is no paradox, either apparent or real. It simply is the result of shifting valuing agents—measuring units—and it should not come as a surprise that the results of using different units are different magnitudes. Surely no one would be surprised if a measurement of an object in feet was different from the measurement in inches or pounds.

This unfortunately is an all-too-common error. Many writers argue about whether one should "keep physical capital intact" or "keep money capital intact." Then they get confused by the "apparent paradox" of the conflicting results. For example, assume the following facts:

$100 cash upon entering the market.
Purchase of 100 bushels of wheat at $1.00 per bushel.
Sale of 100 bushels at $2.00 per bushel.
The present price—replacement price—is $2.00 per bushel.

The argument then runs that if we view the series of transactions from "keeping money capital intact," we have made $100; but if we view it from "keeping physical capital intact," we are no better off than before. That is, we started with 100 bushels, and if we now replaced this *physical* capital, we would be able to purchase only 100 bushels; ergo, there is no income.

This argument is valid if wheat is used as the valuing agent. One can interchange the words "wheat" and "money" in the assumed facts and using money as a valuing agent, conclude that there was no income. Assume the facts to be as follows:

100 bushels upon entering the market.
Purchase of 100 dollars at 1 bushel per dollar.
Sale of 100 dollars at 2 bushels per dollar.
The present price—replacement price—is 2 bushels per dollar.

The trader started with 100 bushels, ended with 200; and thus there is a 100 bushel income. However, there is no change in the amount of money available to him, and thus a zero dollar income.

Both statements are valid. The problem is simply one of valuing agent selection and consistent use of that valuing agent. We selected money as the appropriate valuing agent above and gave our reasons for doing so.

There is one further point in the apparent paradox. Boulding's statement is true only for a special case, and the specification of the conditions of that case further clarify the paradox. If the trader holds *all* wheat—the position is the intercept of the x-axis—the rise in price does not result in a fall in the net worth measured in bushels. The net worth in bushels remains constant. If the trader holds all money, the rise in price does not affect his net worth in money, but it does decrease his net worth in bushels. Boulding's paradox of opposite movements in net worth occurs only when the trader's position is somewhere between the two axes—when he holds *both* commodities. However, a moment's reflection on the two extreme cases will dispel the paradox. The decrease in bushel net worth, under conditions of holding money when prices are rising, is a direct measurement of the opportunity of gaining that the trader has lost. The trader was in the wrong position for a price increase, and he lost an opportunity to gain. This opportunity to gain may be measured by calculating the increase in money net worth if he had been in the right position, or by valuing the decrease in bushel net worth by the present price. When all money is held, there is no question that a rise in price results in an opportunity loss from being in the wrong position. When the trader is between the axes, the paradox is the result of the same phenomena. The trader holds a portion of his assets in money, and the rise in price results in an opportunity loss for that portion. There are degrees of wrongness in position, and the trader will always suffer some opportunity loss when he is in the wrong position.

Essentially the same type of error is made when he speaks of "apparent losses."

> The revaluation (fall in price) at the beginning of the next day lowers the net worth, however, to $0M_2$; there is an apparent loss of M_1M_2. Nevertheless it is upon the foundation of this apparent loss that subsequent profits are made, for if it were not for the *changes* in price the net worth could never be increased through exchange: moving to P_3, to be able to take advantage of the subsequent rise in price, brings the net worth on the fourth day to M_3. (*Reconstruction,* p. 45.)

The apparent loss is a real loss, because the trader failed to take advantage of his opportunity to change his position. The trader held wheat, and the price fell. That is a real loss, because the trader was in the wrong position—making the wrong prediction—when the price changed; and no future price change will obviate *that* loss for that time period. If the trader had exchanged at the higher price before the price fell, he would clearly have a larger amount of net worth.

The error in the analysis seems to be in Boulding's assumption about the pattern of the price changes. The next line reads: "So the process goes on, with an apparent alternation of losses and profits, decreases and increases in net worth, even though the general process is clearly a profit-making one." (*Reconstruction,* p. 45.) The process is profit making only after-the-fact. *Ex ante,* it could just as clearly be a loss-making one. It could be that "it is upon the foundation of this apparent *loss* that subsequent *losses* are made." Boulding has assumed a pattern of price changes and positions which yields a *final profit.* Then he has taken a point in the middle of this pattern and said that this is only an "apparent loss," because the final outcome is profit. If, however, we do not know what the final outcome will be, i.e. if we are measuring at the instant of the fall in price, then the general process is uncertain and the foundation may be for either profits or losses. Facing such a situation, there is no reason to modify loss with "apparent," and there is good reason to exclude the modifier since the final outcome could make the loss "real."

Both the "apparent paradox" and the "apparent loss" are products of uncertainty. Both would disappear if the future were certain.

Under certainty, the trader would always be at the intercept of one of the axes. He would never hold both wheat and cash at the same time, because he would know the direction of the next price movement and would be unwilling to suffer the opportunity loss of holding cash when the price is going to rise. Thus, his position would be perfect.

However, since the trader does in fact continually face uncertainty, he is subject to both the paradox and the loss. A metrician facing the same uncertainty would not be troubled, because he would not shift units and he would eschew predictions. If he called the loss "apparent," he would be predicting an uncertain future instead of measuring an existing condition.

There is, however, one important difference between the paradox and the loss. The paradox is the result of the lack of one of the variables, and hence we called it an "opportunity loss." The trader held a portion of his assets in cash when the price rose. For that portion of his assets, the position variable was absent; hence it was impossible for him to either gain or lose. That portion of his assets was riskless, because it was held in cash under conditions of a stable price level. The reverse is true for the "apparent loss." He held his assets in wheat and thus had a chance for either a gain or a loss. The position variable was present, and then when the price change occurred, both variables were present.

This is an important distinction, because it is often argued that both are counterfactual conditionals; that both are equally hypothetical.[2]

The argument runs along the following lines:
Assume:

Condition A: Cash is held, and the price of wheat rises.
Condition B: Wheat is held, and the price of wheat declines.

The statements can take the following form:

A. If I had held wheat, I would have gained.
B. If I had held cash, I would not have lost.

It may be argued that the word "lost" in B grants the point, so let us restate them in more general form.

A. If I had been in position X, my net worth would be Y.
B. If I had been in position W, my net worth would be Z.

The antecedents of both are false; the second clause of both is a retrodiction, and the statements as they stand are perfectly identical. Thus, the argument seems credible. Upon closer inspection, however, the difference becomes clear.

Statement A, to be complete, requires an additional clause. It runs:

A. 1. If I had been in position X at t_1
   2. and then the price had risen,
   3. my net worth would be Y.

Clause one is false; he was not in position X at t_i. Clause two is an empirical question concerning the past, which is, in this case, true.

Statement B does not require the additional clause.

B. 1. If I had been in position W (if I had accepted an available alternative),
   2. my net worth would be Z (regardless of the events which later occurred).

Clause one is false; he did not accept his available alternative. The existence of that alternative is an empirical question, which, in this case, is true.

2. Boulding does not make the argument, and the author suspects he would not. However, the word "apparent" suggests a hypothetical situation, and the distinction is important.

The distinction is now clear:

1. Statement A requires two conditions, statement B requires only one, for the retrodiction to be true.
2. Statement A requires a temporal order of the conditions; statement B has no such order.
3. Statement A is applicable to the entire universe; statement B to a specific alternative.
4. Statement A refers to a hypothetical value; statement B to the *form* of an existing value.

To reduce it to the absurd, suppose we said, "If I had bought Manhattan Island in 1775, I would be a billionaire today." That statement is quite different from "If I had sold Manhattan Island (implying that we had the alternative) last week, I would now have a billion one dollar bills." The only quarrel that could arise about the latter statement is an empirical one; there may be some lack of agreement about the selling price. However, no one could deny that these two statements are significantly different.

The reason for this rather long digression has been simply to point up the difference between hypothetical situations. To show that some situations are "more hypothetical" than others—that some are closer to reality than others. Some opponents of this view argue that all hypothetical — counterfactual — situations are essentially the same. Moreover, they utilize what Sidney Hook calls the "slippery slope" argument—that once one accepts any hypothetical statement, then *all* such statements are acceptable and we are doomed to slide all the way down. As Hook points out in other contexts, and as we have demonstrated here, this is simply not true. There is a meaningful distinction between types of foregone alternatives. There is a vital difference between a "loss" occasioned by *failure to risk* and a "loss" *caused by risking*. The former we have called an "opportunity loss," and the latter a "loss" sans modifier.

Measurement by a Constant

The use of a constant suggests that there is a "similarity transformation," of bushels to dollars. There is such a similarity transformation of miles to yards, meters to feet, pounds to grams, etc. One can measure an object in one unit and transform it to another by multiplying by a constant. We have a similar situation here. One can measure the wheat in, say, bushels, and then, it is suggested, transform it into dollars by multiplying by a constant. Note, however, that the prerequisite for this process is that the units be temporally invariant— that there exist an unchanging ratio between the units. If this is not true, then no similarity transformation can be performed.

The question of invariance between units is one of definition and experimentation. There exists a definition of a "foot" and a "yard," and one can, by experimentation, discover the constant that will transform one into the other. The invariance of this constant is suggested by the fact that we often define one by the other. Thus, "3 feet = 1 yard" is both a "definition" and a "similarity transformation." The statement "20 yards = 3(20 feet)" indicates that the number 3 is the (constant) similarity transformation of feet to yards. In pounds to grams it is 453.6, etc. However, there exists no such constant to transform, say, pounds to feet. In the statement "40 feet = X pounds," X can be discovered only by a separate measurement. Certainly X would be different for I-beams and cotton cord. The search for a general constant that would allow one to transform feet to pounds is futile.

Precisely the same is true for the search for a constant to transform bushels to dollars. There is no ratio that is invariant; in fact, the *raison d'être* of the measurement is to find the magnitude of the variation. Thus, a search for a constant is not only futile, but it also violates the purpose of the measurement. Moreover, if such a constant could be discovered, the transformation process is not a measurement. The measurement would occur in the determination of the quantity of bushels, and the multiplication by the constant would be a restatement of the magnitude in different units, not an independent measurement.

Boulding is searching for a constant that shows a continued growth in net worth—one that avoids the "apparent alternation of losses and profits." The full quote is:

> A possible method of escape from this dilemma is to perform all valuations at a constant valuation ratio, independent of the market price. This is shown in Fig. 19. P_0, P_1, P_2, P_3, are successive positions of the balance sheet. If now the valuation of wheat is performed always at a constant valuation coefficient

("price") equal to the slope of the parallel lines P_0M_0, P_1M_1, P_2M_2, etc., the net worth will rise continually through OM_0, OM_1, OM_2, etc. Unfortunately, however, the mere procedure of valuation at a constant valuation coefficient is not sufficient to insure a steady rise in net worth. Thus we see that if a smaller valuation coefficient is selected, equal to the slope of the parallel lines P_0N_0, P_1N_1, P_2N_2, etc., the net worth again exhibits a back-and-forth movement, ON_0, ON_1, ON_2, etc. There is clearly a range of constant valuation coefficients within which the net worth grows steadily without any ups and downs, and there seems to be no particular principle by which we can select any one of these valuation coefficients within the range as better than any other. All valuation thus seems to possess a certain unavoidable arbitrary element, as long as the asset structure remains heterogeneous. Only in processes which begin and end with a homogeneous quantity of some single asset, e.g. money, can the amount of profit be measured unequivocally. (*Reconstruction*, p. 45.)

If one is faced with uncertainty at any of the intermediate points, there is no good reason to find a constant that will allow net worth to increase without ups and downs. If we do not know the final outcome (and we will never know the *final* outcome until the trader leaves the market), there is an equally good—or bad—reason to search for a constant that shows a continual decrease.

Since Boulding states that the general process is clearly a profit-making one, we may interpret his constant as an *ex post* valuation of *past* positions. That is, he knows that the difference between the first and last position yields a profit, so he wants all intermediate positions to also yield a profit. Thus, the valuation of past "intermediate" positions is a kind of average between the first and last position. If this interpretation is taken, there are three points that may be raised.

One, how does Boulding know that the difference between the first and last position yields a profit? Obviously he must value the first and last position in order to know this. How does he value the first and last position? If he does it at a constant, he is thereby insuring that the general process is clearly a profit-making one (as long as the quantities are greater), and then, of course, the "average" is determined. It seems to the author that the way Boulding "knows" there is a profit is to tacitly use the present price to value the first and last position. Whether or not this is the case, our second point is—why average? We noted in Part One that a possible reason for averaging was the check on the trader's predictions. But this could not be the case here, since the trader is predicting a price and the constant has nothing to do with price.

Three, if one wants an average of intermediate points we might note Boulding's plea for simplicity and suggest that either of the following is simpler than the suggested constant.

1. Average increase in price per exchange or per time period.
2. Average increase in net worth per exchange or per time period.

In summary, we can find no reason to search for a constant for either the valuation of the present position or to average past "intermediate" positions. If there were such a search, we are convinced that it would be futile.

Informational Content of a Constant

In the various problems and decision theories set forth in Part One, we failed to find any to which a constant was relevant. All of the receivers were in a decision situation in which existing alternatives were relevant. The constant has nothing to do with alternatives—past, present, or future. Thus, the "measure" by a constant has no economic significance or relevance to a problem. A constant having to do with temperature would be equally significant to the decision of the traders.

A constant has no self-information, because it is meaningless. To prove the point we can take the opposite and prove that it is absurd. Suppose the trader thought that a constant was meaningful to him personally. Thus, he could value his wheat at the constant, irrespective of the market activities. This puts the trader in the enviable position of having possible gains, but no possible losses. Any time the price was below the constant, he could purchase and immediately profit. That profit would be maintained regardless of any further price fluctuations. The price of wheat could go to zero without affecting his valuation of wheat. Obviously this valuation cannot be used to choose between alternatives. Anyone who presently thinks of himself as a millionaire—especially if he acts as if he were a millionaire—because he holds Confederate money or South Sea Island Co. stock is very likely to find himself incarcerated.

We know of no case in which a constant would be meaningful— have informational content—to any receiver, with any problem, with any decision theory.

SUMMARY

Our basic disagreement is with Boulding's assertion that all valuation coefficients are arbitrary. The purpose of this study has been to present criteria for the selection of a valuation coefficient on a rational basis. Boulding could now charge that our criteria were arbitrary and thus conclude that the valuation coefficient selected was arbitrary because of the nature of the criteria. From his other writings, however, it is evident that he would accept our informational criterion. Thus, there appears to be no fundamental disagreement.

Whether or not Boulding would accept our measurement criterion is not clear. From the absence of a discussion of measurement in his writings, we could conjecture that he does not think measurement theory is pertinent to the problem. From his insistence that an unequivocal profit can be determined only "when the process begins and ends with a single asset, e.g. money," we could conjecture that he does not think that a value-sacrifice dimension is appropriate.

Regardless of the validity of these conjectures, it is important to point out that the absence of measurement concepts weakens Boulding's analysis. The "apparent paradox" of a fall in wheat net worth accompanied by an increase in money net worth would not arise if the valuation process were considered a measurement in consistent units. There are many other writers (both in Accounting Tradition and Present Market) who have been seduced by this apparent paradox. The argument over "replacement costs" is but a restatement of this paradox. Given the conception of a dimension, given the prior selection of units, the problem solves itself.

Measurements exist for the purpose of comparing different (heterogeneous) objects. For this reason, we disagree with Boulding's assertion that the objects must be in the same form (homogeneous) before they can be compared. It seems that at the very least we could make an unequivocal comparison by stating a counterfactual condition: "If I sold this wheat now, I would receive X dollars."

"X dollars" could then be compared to the "Y dollars" held previously and also compared to the future expectations. Thus, the statement provides an "answer sufficient for action" which is neither arbitrary nor ritualistic. A constant, on the contrary, is arbitrary. More importantly, the constant does *not* provide an answer sufficient for action.

This last point is our major reason for rejecting the constant: it is not relevant to any problem that we know of. Given the lack of relevancy, we can say that a constant is not information, and therefore it is not appropriate for the measurement of income.

X

THE FISHER TRADITION

As we previously pointed out, Fisher disqualifies himself from the consideration of Enterprise Income. His concern is with personal income that involves a psychic satisfaction. Wealth increments of an enterprise are but intermediate steps toward that goal, and if they were called income, there would be double counting. If we may reformulate Fisher's basic notion as "all productive activity is for the ultimate purpose of human enjoyment,"[1] then we agree. There is no disagreement with the notion that the ultimate resting place of income is with humans as opposed to land, capital, or enterprises.

Fisher is also concerned with wealth changes and the valuation of capital, but he insists that the changes should not be called income. Fisher's disciples, particularly Lindahl, disagree with him on this point. They argue that the wealth increments, calculated by Fisher's method, should be included in income. Except for this semantic disagreement, the difference between Fisher and his disciples is negligi-

---

1. He implies this in several places, e.g. on p. 164 of *Capital*.

211

ble. The differences among the disciples are also negligible; they quarrel, but over technical points, not with the fundamental notion of valuation. For this reason, we can present one theory of valuation and say that it is "The Fisher Tradition." Our basic source is Fisher's *The Nature of Capital and Income.*

The Fisher theory of value (and valuation) is elegant in its stark simplicity and logical rigor. An epitome of that theory follows.

First argument:

1. The motivation of humans is satisfaction. (*Capital,* Chapter III.)
2. Goods are nothing more than vehicles for the production of that satisfaction. (*Capital,* p. 151 *et passim.*)
3. Therefore, the only reason for prizing a good is the satisfaction that it yields.[2]

Second argument:

1. Present satisfaction is preferable to future satisfaction.[3]
2. Goods yield only future satisfaction.[4]
3. Therefore, goods are prized less, are less valuable, than an equivalent amount of present satisfaction. (*Capital,* p. 227.)

Third argument:

1. Satisfactions equal income. (*Capital,* Chapter X.)
2. Interest is a method of quantifying the preference for present income over future income. (*Ibid.,* Chapter XII.)
3. Therefore, the value of goods can be ascertained by discounting the income.[5]

Classification:[6]

1. Subjective-income is the final psychic satisfaction received by a person from the goods.

2. Commodities are not income, only services. *Ibid.,* see especially Chapter VI, Section 5.

3. *Ibid., passim.* Cf. also Fisher, *Interest,* for a complete statement of the impatience notion.

4. *Capital,* p. 165, where objective income leads to subjective income, i.e. goods lead to future satisfaction.

5. *Ibid.,* Chapter XIII. Here is the presentation of the value of capital. Fisher does not discount "objective income," presumably because it is so near in time to subjective income.

6. *Ibid.,* p. 178. This is Fisher's famous three-fold classification of income.

2. Objective-income is the actual goods which may be used to furnish the satisfaction.
3. Money-income is the amount of money actually received which may be used to purchase the goods to obtain the satisfaction.

Final conclusion:

The value of goods may be determined by discounting the future money-income.[7]

From this incomplete outline, it is easy to see why Fisher insisted that value increments were not income. Value increments are *caused by anticipations of income,* and surely there is a difference between income and anticipation of income. If we accept Fisher's definitions, it is plain that income does not arise from value increments. Just the reverse, value increments arise from anticipated income.

The causal direction is of supreme importance in the Fisher analysis. Indeed, it would not be far wrong to sum up the purpose of *The Nature of Capital and Income* as an attempt to prove the causal relationship of income *to* capital. The causal order in its simplest form may be outlined as two corollary arguments:

Corollary A	Corollary B
1. Man seeks satisfactions.	1. Present satisfactions are preferable to future satisfactions.
2. Goods yield satisfactions; thus man seeks goods.	2. Present goods are preferable to future goods.
3. Money obtains goods; thus man seeks money.	3. Present money is preferable to future money.
4. Capital goods yield money; thus man prizes capital goods.	4. Capital goods that yield money sooner are preferable to those that yield it later.
5. The value of capital is caused by its yield.	5. Discounting is a method of equating monies at different temporal locations.

6. The value of capital goods may be ascertained by discounting the future receipts of money.

Obviously the receipt of money is different from the nonreceipt of money. The receipt of money is income (money-income); the non-

7. He spells this out in more detail in *Interest.*

receipt of money is not income. An increase in anticipated receipts will increase the value of the capital goods; but this increase is not to be included in income. Fisher makes this abundantly clear:

> That "saving" or increase of capital is *not* income coordinately with ordinary income is evident from the fact that this item is never discounted in making up capital-value. As we have seen, one of the fundamental characteristics of income is that it is the desirable event which occurs by means of wealth, and for the sake of which, consequently, that wealth is valued. This definition implies that every item of income is discounted in order to obtain its contribution to capital-value. The mere increase or decrease of capital-value, on the other hand, is never thus discounted. Suppose, for instance, with interest at 4 per cent, that a man buys an annuity of $4 a year, which does not begin at once but is deferred one year. Since this annuity will be worth $100 one year hence, its present value will be about $96, which, during the ensuing year, will gradually increase to $100. If this increase of value of (about) $4 is itself to be called income, it should be treated like every other item of income, and should be discounted. But this is absurd. The discounted value of $4 would be $3.85, which, if added to the $96, would require that the entire value of the property today should be $99.85, or practically the same as a year later instead of $4 less as is actually the case. In other words, the hypothesis which counts an increase of value as income is self-destructive; for if the increment *is* income, it must be discounted, but, if discounted, it is practically abolished. Clearly, then, increase of capital is not income in the sense that it can be discounted in addition to other items of income. If it is income at all, it is income in a very peculiar sense, and nothing but confusion can result from having to consider two kinds of income so widely divergent that whereas one is discounted to obtain capital-value, the other is not. (*Capital*, pp. 248-49.)

Fisher's disciples disagree only on this last point. They argue that the change in the present worth (discounted value) of the future cash receipts plus withdrawals should be termed "income."

A good summary of the Fisher Tradition was recently presented by Hansen. He clarifies the issue by presenting profit (income) as a pure valuation problem. He writes:

> As appears from the previous discussion, the profit of a period

will generally be in conformity with the equation:
$$P = W + E_u - E_p$$
where

P = the profit of the period,

W = the realized income (consumption) of the owner(s), which can be positive or negative—the amounts actually withdrawn,

E_u = the equity at the end (ultimo) of the period,

E_p = the equity at the beginning (primo) of the period.

In this equation E is quite clearly defined as the discounted value (the present value) of future withdrawals, while W equals the withdrawals in the period in question (the owner's consumption). (Hansen, *Profit*, pp. 39-40.)

This definition of income is identical to Fisher's "earnings." Fisher would call W the "realized income," i.e. the receipt of money by the owner is the "money income," and the change in E would be termed "appreciation" or "depreciation." The sum of the two is earnings. "Expressed in a single sentence, the general principle connecting realized and earned income is that they differ by the appreciation or depreciation of capital. It is thus possible to describe earned income as realized income less depreciation of capital, or else as realized income plus appreciation of capital." (*Capital*, p. 238.)

Because of this equivalence, we have classified the disagreement between Fisher and his disciples as "semantic." It has been argued that the disciples are missing Fisher's fundamental point; but it is clear that if they were willing to call their concept "earnings," there would be no disagreement.

There is one point of difference between Hansen and Fisher that is puzzling. Hansen makes it clear that the receipt of money by the owner must pass on to the subjective stage of income. The withdrawals are *consumed*. This appears to be in complete harmony with Fisher's general notion of the final residence of income. However, Fisher never states that the money income must be consumed if it is to be properly considered "income." He speaks of his concept *including* money-income and of *measuring* income, and he says that any of the three types of income (subjective, objective, money) may be considered separately. At the same time he goes to great pains to prove that the residue is *only* the subjective income. Thus, it is not clear whether or not Fisher would agree with Hansen that the withdrawals must be consumed in order to be part of this income.

This point offers no difficulties if one is willing to take E, in Hansen's equation, as the *total* equity of the *individual*, including unconsumed commodities and money. However, this interpretation means that we are taking *to be* income things that are *only capable of becoming income*. In other words, if income is, after all, only consumption, then money is only an intermediate step *toward* income. But then so are capital goods an intermediate step, albeit one step further from the goal. Neither Fisher nor any of his disciples ever reconciles this point.

To put the question in its most elementary form: Why is money-income income? Is it because money is on the way toward consumption? But this is a question of fact. The receipt of money from a capital good may be used to purchase another capital good. Hence, we have money-income that is equivalent to an appreciation of capital, but capital appreciation is not income at all. Functionally, however, there is no difference between reinvested money-income and appreciation of capital.

One way to answer the question is to note that money-income is immediately transferrable to subjective-income. But then we are measuring what is capable of becoming income or available to become income, not "income" per se. Yet this seems to be the only rational explanation of Fisher's distinction between earnings and income. The total earnings are not available for consumption; only that portion of earnings—realized income, money—that is available for consumption is income. However, if we follow this criterion—wealth *available* for consumption—we reach a much broader concept of income. That is, money is available for consumption by exchange, but then so is a capital good. Thus, is everything that can be exchanged for consumption income? But clearly the total value of a capital good is not income; income could only be the increment in value. But this is the appreciation, which is part of earnings but not income. Still, in a market economy that appreciation is just as available for consumption as the money-income.

Fisher's disciples recognize this, but their valuation procedure does not follow from the premise. The implied premise is "The incremental amount available for consumption plus that amount consumed is income." The "availability" is given by the market prices. We agree that the market prices are caused by the future expectations of consumption, but the cause of the availability is not part of the premise. If it is desired, this income may be classified:

1. Subjective-income—the amount consumed.
2. Objective-income—the incremental commodities on hand that are immediately available for consumption.
3. Money-income—the incremental money on hand that is immediately available to acquire objective-income.
4. Appreciation-income—the incremental capital on hand that is immediately available to acquire money-income.

The sum of these four categories, under the implied premise, is income; and each has equal status. The transfer of one for the other, moving from 4 to 1, is determined by the present market price, not by any individual's expectations.

The reader may think that the author is reading-in the implied premise and that it is not actually there. The author's impression of Fisher and his disciples is that the premise exists, albeit tacitly. Whether the premise is there or not, there are other problems in the Fisher Tradition which yield sufficient reason to reject it. As a decision-making tool we have great respect for the Fisher notion,[8] but we disagree with those who would use it for measuring changes in wealth.

Since many writers leave the impression that all problems in the Fisher Tradition would be solved under certainty and since Fisher makes most of his analyses with perfect foreknowledge, we will begin our critique with a certainty model.

DISCOUNTING UNDER CONDITIONS OF CERTAINTY

Our model is one of discrete movements of prices at a point in time. The price changes at a given instant in time, and the trader exchanges to a position that allows him to take advantage of this movement. Under certainty there can be no losses, and the amount of the gain is known beforehand.

It is important to remember that this is the trader's best alternative.

---

8 Much of "modern" decision theory is nothing more than a restatement of Fisher, coupled with an awakened realization that bygones are really bygones.

He has no opportunity to gain more satisfaction by consumption or to gain more command-over-goods by other entrepreneurial activities. In this case there is no reason to leave the funds idle if there is a possibility of gain. Thus, the trader will hold wheat anytime that the price is going to rise, no matter how small that rise, because there is no better alternative. If there were a better alternative, this model would no longer be applicable.

We are now in a situation where the trader has an existing price and perfect knowledge of the future price. To make the example explicit, assume that the present price is P_1 at T_1 and the future price is P_2 at T_2. Assume further that P_2 is greater than P_1, so that the trader exchanges to a position of holding wheat.

No one in the Fisher Tradition suggests that the value is P_2 at T_1. Presumably this is because P_2 is in the future and because, even though it be certain, the time-preference concept precludes it from being a present value. Instead, they suggest that P_2 be discounted to obtain the present value. Discounting involves a rate and a time period, the selection of which causes some difficulties.

Rate Selection

We will begin by neglecting the time period problem, and we will arbitrarily assume that the time is one year. Thus, in Fisher's usage, we have a "premium" rate of interest.

> This also may be readily shown by an example. If \$100 will buy \$4 a year forever, the first \$4 being due one year hence, the buyer of such an annuity at the end of one year may, immediately upon the receipt of his first \$4, sell out his rights. By hypothesis they will bring \$100. Consequently, he receives \$104 in all for his \$100 a year ago. He has thus virtually exchanged \$100 one year for \$104 the year after. That is, the *premium* rate of interest for this year is also 4 per cent. (*Capital*, pp. 197-98.)

Fisher continues to show the equivalence of the premium concept to various other concepts. These are sufficiently well known for us to omit them here, and we can generalize the above statement as follows:

$$\frac{P_2Q_1 - P_1Q_1}{P_1Q_1} = r \qquad \text{(eq. X-1)}$$

Which is equivalent to

$$\frac{P_2 - P_1}{P_1} = r \qquad \text{(eq. X-2)}$$

Solving for P_1 yields the discounting equation.[9]

$$P_1 = \frac{P_2}{1 + r} \qquad \text{(eq. X-3)}$$

Fisher does not consider an alternative rate and we see no reason to use any other.[10] Note, however, that this is circular and that the discounting equation will always result in valuing the wheat at P_1 at T_1. Thus, the value of the wheat at entry is the market price at the time of entry. Thus, under conditions of certainty, the initial value is the present market price, which is the same as the initial value under both the Accounting Tradition and Present Market.

The problems arise if we want to make an interim valuation. We define the interim instants at $t_1 = T_1$ and $t_n = T_2$. Now if we want to make a valuation at, say, t_3, there are two different possibilities:

1. The exchange opportunities are available only at T_1 and T_2.
2. The exchange opportunities are available at interim instants.

The Locked-in Case.—If the trader purchases wheat at T_1 and there are no further exchange opportunities available until T_2, we say that he is "locked in" the market. This may be Fisher's assumption. The above quote indicates that he considers the bond-holder to be locked-in for the year; i.e., although he can exchange at the end of each year, there are no exchange opportunities during the year. In other connections the locked-in interpretation seems plausible also.

> We have then two methods of defining interest. In both of them the time element is prominent. Before passing on we should here remark that the *time* element enters not only as referring

9. "In other words, the rate of interest is, briefly stated, the ratio between income and capital." (*Capital*, p. 191.) Here Fisher calls this the "realized rate."

10. For different purposes there may be different rates. For example, a pure rate of interest might be applied in order to distinguish pure profits from return on capital. However, the purpose is to analyze (separate) the income, not to determine the total.

to the times of payment but also to the time of contract. A rate of interest implies not only the *two points of time* between which the goods *for exchange are available,* but also the *point at which the decision to exchange them is made.* (*Capital,* p. 196, italics added.)

Although Fisher's later examples do not completely confirm the locked-in assumption, the gist of the presentation indicates it. However, it makes no difference whether this is or is not Fisher's assumption. We will consider the case as one of the two possibilities that need analysis. It is clear that he would value the wheat contract by using the discount rate in equation X-2. That is, he would discount P_2 for the period t_3 to T_2 at r.

The result would be a value increment which Fisher denies to be income. This is perfectly consistent with his other positions.[11] Note that if he were to contend that the value increment was income, this would put him in the rather peculiar position of saying that changes in the temporal location produce income. The trader has no alternative at t_3; there is no price at that time, therefore there is no available consumption. Likewise, there is no available money nor any command over goods. In fact the trader's position at t_3 is *worse* than at T_1. At T_1 he had money and all the alternatives consequent on holding money; but he has had an "outgo" which obviates those alternatives until T_2.

Under such conditions it is easy to see why Fisher would argue that a value increment is not income. The trader has nothing at t_3, and nothing is clearly not income. But if we take this line of argument, it also leads to *zero value* at t_3. The trader has nothing, and nothing is clearly not value.

It may be argued that the trader does have something at t_3, viz. a certain future income and value. But how does one measure the future? How does one value a *single* "alternative?" We have pointed out that the future cannot be measured and, further, that the valuation was a decision, a selection from *among* alternatives. This trader has no alternatives to choose between; he has only one certain outcome.

11. This includes his notion that the "return of principal" is no different from other receipts and that therefore the principal becomes "income" when it is received.

Still, Fisher's answer is to discount P_2 for the period t_3 to T_2. In order to make his position clear, we present the following:

> We may, if we choose, trace the history of the value of a security from the time immediately before its purchase, and consider the purchase price itself as an outgo. If this price is exactly equal to the discounted value of the succeeding income, it is evident that the value immediately before its purchase must be exactly zero. Thus in Figure 6 let OM be the purchase price, and equal to OA, which is the capital-value immediately after purchase. The capital-value immediately *before* purchase is, therefore, zero, and the entire capital curve is the line OABCDEFH, which starts at zero, and ends at zero, but is above the zero line at all intermediate intervals (*Capital,* p. 219-20.)

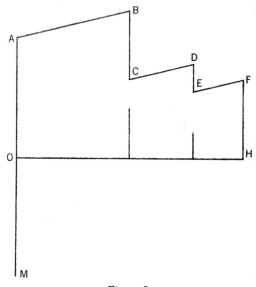

Figure 6

We can abstract from Fisher's Figure 6 and use his reasoning on our locked-in assumption. The value at t_3 is the distance from t_3 to J (Fig. X-1). Note however that this *assumes* that value accrues or accumulates in the indicated pattern over the period; and there is no evidence for that assumption. On the contrary, there is evidence that value *occurs precisely* at T_2. It must be granted that at T_1 the trader valued this contract more than money. Further, we can measure the sacrifice, OM, and then ordinally measure the value as OA. However, this *was* the valuation at T_1. There is no valuation at t_3 in the sense of sacrificing alternatives. Thus, it is just as reasonable to say that the value at t_3 is zero and will remain zero until T_2.

One may argue that the value is not zero at t_3, because the trader receives feelings of security, pleasure, etc., from contemplating his

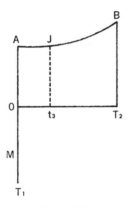

Figure X-1

future. In other words, he receives satisfactions from his position at t_3. But satisfaction, in Fisher's terminology, is income! It is not value.

Thus, if one measured the satisfactions of the trader, he would get income; if one measured the sacrifice, he would get zero. The only way to get value equal to t_3J is to make it so by definition. However, if we allow this, it is easy enough to define any other curve and get any other value.

Thus, the locked-in case, even under certainty, does not yield an unassailable rate nor a univocal value. Let us relax the locked-in assumption and see if a continuous alternative yields a satisfactory rate.

The Assumption of Continuous Exchange Opportunities.—We will continue the same assumptions as above—perfect foreknowledge and a discrete move in price to P_2 at T_2—except that the trader will be allowed to exchange at any of the interim instants. We can still figure the rate as the difference between P_2 and P_1, divided by P_1. There is the problem, however, of adjusting the rate for the time that the trader holds the wheat. If the trader exchanges at T_1, the rate will be "per year." The trader could exchange, under the assumptions, at any of the interim instants from t_1 to t_{n-1} and gain the difference between P_2 and P_1. The quotient of equation X-2—r—will remain constant for all the instants; but when r is adjusted for time—put on a comparable temporal basis—it will vary widely between an exchange at t_1 and t_{n-1}. Thus, even for the purposes of analysis, such a rate is useless. That is, if some rate is selected—e.g., time preference, reservation rate, pure interest, rates of alternatives—for analysis, the surplus, economic rent, pure profits, etc., would vary greatly, depending upon the timing of the exchange. There is no reason for the trader to exchange before t_{n-1} and have a large surplus. On the other hand, there is no reason for him not to exchange before t_{n-1} (this is his best alternative) and have a small surplus. The rate and the surplus depend upon the whim of the trader.

An opponent may reply that this is a misuse of the rate, that the rate is for the total gain over the entire period. We cannot object to this conception of the rate; but it is clear that this is an *ex post* concept from T_2 and is not useful in interim valuations. If the trader does not exchange until t_{n-1}, he holds money at all other interim points. If we want to value at t_3, then, and use the implied rate, we are in the incongruous position of valuing money at more than unity. Surely no one would maintain that the valuing agent, the *unit* of value, was more valuable than unity. This would be tantamount to claiming that a meter had more length than a meter. We repeat, however, that if someone wants to *view the past events from T_2* and express the change as a rate, there is no objection. Indeed such a rate may be quite useful in adjusting data for comparisons, but it is not useful for measuring value at t_3.

The same reasoning can be applied to a series of discrete price movements of different magnitudes. One can take an *ex post* view at any of the instants and calculate the *average* rate from some previous instant. This can be done whether there has been one price change or many, whether there has been one exchange or many, and the average *ex post* rate may be used for making the data comparable. However, each of these price changes and exchanges will have interim instants identical to those analyzed above; and the conclusion holds.

The reader may complain that the above assumptions are unrealistic. Seldom, if ever, is one locked in a market. "Secondary" markets exist for almost everything.[12] Likewise, a discrete price movement under certainty has an unreal sound. A more realistic situation would be for the price to be "continuously" bid up as time passed.[13]

All of the traders would bid on the wheat until the rate was equal to the marginal trader's next-best alternative. As time passed, the price would increase from P_1 to P_2 in interim steps, p_1 to p_n, corresponding to the interim instants. This may be visualized in Figure X-2.

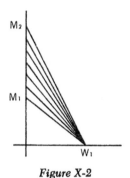

Figure X-2

This situation may be more realistic. It is tantamount to a government bond market with a pegged interest rate. If the rate is better than the trader's next-best alternative, including being high enough to overcome his impatience, he will hold wheat. Again there may be reason to analyze his income into various parts. He may have a reservation rate below the market rate and thus receive a surplus of the

12. Even trust funds have developed a secondary market. One can now sell the rights to a future receipt in direct abrogation of the intent of the trust.

13. It is difficult to conceive of a continuous price increase because our money is not infinitely divisible. A more accurate description would be "very small discrete price movements over very short time periods." For brevity we call this "continuous." However, the lack of continuity does bring up some accrual problems which we will consider below.

difference. However, if our purpose is to measure the total value, such an analysis is not relevant.

The alternatives are relevant, and these are expressed as prices at some temporal location. The rate is nothing more than a convenient means of calculating the prices at different instants. If the market price is being continuously bid up as time passes, the discounted value of P_2 is *always* equal to the present price. Thus, under these assumptions, where the rate seems to be most relevant, the truth of the matter is that it is unnecessary. The present price yields the correct "Fisher value" without bothering to utilize the Fisher valuation method.

One further variation on the assumption will complete the certainty case. It may be assumed that some traders have foreknowledge that is superior to that which other traders have. In other words, there are some traders operating under conditions of certainty and others having some degree of uncertainty. If our trader be one of the latter, the analysis presented below, when we relax the certainty assumption, will be pertinent. Thus, for purposes of this analysis, we will assume that our trader is omniscient in a market where others are uncertain.

For example, assume that the trader knows the complete pattern of prices from T_1 to T_2. However, because of the uncertainty of the other traders, the price between T_1 and T_2 does not follow the discount path. The price moves sporadically and irregularly from P_1 to P_2 over the time T_1 to T_2. Now it may be argued that since the trader is certain of the final outcome, P_2, the correct valuation at the interim instants is P_2, discounted by the implied rate. The argument will not stand, however, because this situation reverts to the locked-in case.

Note first that if the interim prices moved up and down, the trader could gain more than the difference between P_2 and P_1 by making interim exchanges. Thus, the implied rate is not applicable. A rate can be determined by calculating the gain from each individual exchange and then averaging. Or the quantity of money after the "final" exchange at T_2 can be figured *ex ante* and then a rate figured as

$$\frac{M(T_2) - M(T_1)}{M(T_1)} = r_1 \qquad \text{(eq. X-4)}$$

But clearly this is an *average* of all the interim exchanges and is subject to the same criticism of averages that was presented above. The trader may be holding money because he knows the price is going to fall. Application of the average rate will result in valuing money at more than unity.

Since he knows that he is moving inexorably toward $M(T_2)$, it may be that he *feels* that his money should be valued at more than unity. Note, however, that the excess above unity is locked in the market and is subject to the criticism presented above. At other times the discounted value of $M(T_2)$ will be less than the money held. Is it possible to contend that the trader *feels* that his real value is less than the money held?

This example is, of course, caged so that it violates the assumption of unequivocal measure of income under conditions of a completed exchange. We may alter the conditions so that the exchange is not completed until T_2, however, and get similar results.

If the price movements are all upward, there is no reason to complete the exchange. Let us make that assumption and further assume that the discounted value of P_2 at t_3 is p_3, but that the price at t_3 is p_2. If we value at t_3, should we select the discounted value, p_3, or the price, p_2?

It has been noted that p_3 is an average over an arbitrary time period that has nothing to do with alternatives. On the other hand, p_2 is an alternative relevant to the continuing decision and is the current sacrifice. It is true that P_2 is certain to be eventually realized, and it may even be granted that it is reasonable to assume a pattern that yields p_3 at t_3. However, P_2 is locked in the future, and thus the difference between p_3 and p_2—d—is locked in the market. In order to garner d, the trader has *no alternative* except to stay in the market until T_2. Thus, the valuation of d reverts to the locked-in case. As we saw above, valuation in the locked-in case requires an assumption about the pattern of value accumulation. Further, we assume that from a sacrifice or decision viewpoint the most reasonable assumption is a zero valuation if we are truly locked-in. The same reasoning applies here: d does not become a value until T_2; it does not accrue over time, it occurs at an instant.

Moreover, d's existence depends upon an arbitrary time period selection. We averaged the rate of return from T_1 to T_2 to find p_3, which was used to find d. The time period T_1 to T_2 is a reasonable one if there are no other alternatives during the period. In this case, however, there are other alternatives. The trader may discover a better opportunity in another market at t_3 and exercise his alternative by exiting from the market. Thus, d would never become a value, and it would make more sense to average (if there is a compulsion to average) from T_1 to t_3. Of course, if this were done, d would not exist at t_3. Likewise, other traders would enter the market at t_3. Their average rate would be for the period t_3 to T_2, and d would be zero at t_3. Because of the existence of these continuous alternatives, the time period over which the average is calculated is completely arbitrary. Since the time period determines the rate and the rate, in turn, determines d, we may conclude that d is completely arbitrary also.

The results of arbitrary valuation are almost certain to vary. Traders entering and leaving the market at different times are almost certain to average over different time periods. Even those entering at the same time are very likely to use different periods for their average. The result is that identical objects in identical spatio-temporal relations receive different "measurements." One wonders just what kind of comparisons can be made under such circumstances.

Under the assumption of discrete price movements, we described a locked-in case and concluded the most reasonable value was zero. Under the assumption of continuous alternatives, we have described a quasi locked-in case—a case in which a portion, d, of an average certain future is locked-in. For the reasons presented, it seems that this portion should also be valued at zero. With d equal to zero, the value left is the present price.

Summary

We have taken a rather detailed excursion into the problems of valuation by discounting under conditions of certainty. Several variations on the assumptions have been explored, and the conclusions for each have essentially been the same. These conclusions may be outlined as follows:

1. The rate selected should be the one implied by the prices at different dates. Other rates have no bearing on the problem of valuation.

2. The rate has a time dimension. Prices occur at a point in time, and different periods of time yield different rates and different interim values.
3. To calculate the present value, the present instant should be selected as a starting point for discounting. This always yields the present price; and thus the rate of calculation is superfluous for valuation purposes.
4. If other arbitrary time periods are used, one is in effect assuming a pattern of value accumulation that has no relation to alternatives, decisions, or sacrifices. The difference between the assumed pattern and the actual alternative is locked in the market. (Including the complete locked-in case in which there are no alternatives; when the sacrifice is zero at interim instants.) The amount that is locked-in should be valued at zero; thus the value reverts to the present price.

In short, even under conditions of certainty, even on Fisher's own ground, we find that for purposes of valuation, the discounting process is, at best, superfluous—yields identical results to other more direct methods—and, at worst, demonstrably wrong.

Little use has been made in this section of the more generalized information-measurement criteria. We could object that the Fisher Tradition is a prediction instead of a measurement; but under certainty, the results are identical. Thus, any such objection would be more on grounds of technicalities than substance; and therefore we have not raised it.

Likewise, it is difficult to conceive of "information" when everyone is certain of the future. With perfect foreknowledge, the only thing needed is a timepiece in order to know what has happened. In the case of the one omniscient trader, it is not likely that he would let us in on his secret; and thus we could not transmit information about the future with certainty. If by some chance he was willing to share his foreknowledge, this would be the most valuable information conceivable and would take priority. This also is unrealistic. The more realistic situation is uncertainty; and that is our next subject.

VALUATION UNDER UNCERTAINTY

In the above analysis we assumed that the trader had perfect foreknowledge of the prices. Thus, we could focus upon a single outcome and discuss the problems of discounting that outcome. Under the more realistic conditions of uncertainty there is a range of possible outcomes, and we will be forced to select a single number from this range before we can discount. That is, we must decide what the future value is before we can obtain the present value. The future value must be known in order to discount it at a given rate to obtain the present value. But the rate also must be determined, and as we indicated above, we need to know both the present value and the future value in order to determine the correct rate.

Fisher attempts to divide the issue into two separate problems: (1) uncertainty in the rate and (2) uncertainty in the final outcome. He does this by using the "present rate of interest" to make the initial valuation and then by adjusting the value as the "present rate" changes in the future. Only after the discussion of the rate does he venture into the problem of determining the final outcome, and he never attempts to combine the two.

Unfortunately, only the last chapter of the fundamental work—*The Nature of Capital and Income*—is devoted to uncertainty.[14] Furthermore, much of this chapter is concerned with insurance vice valuation. Because of the minute portion of analysis devoted to valuation under conditions of uncertainty, it is difficult to know precisely what Fisher thought. He begins the chapter by relaxing the certainty assumption and presenting a few general remarks on chance:

> Throughout the three previous chapters, we have assumed the existence of artificially simple conditions. We have assumed that the entire future history of the capital in question is definitely known in advance; in other words, we have ignored *chance*. The factory which was taken for illustration was supposed to yield definite future income which could be counted upon as a bondholder counts upon his interest. (*Capital*, p. 265.)

The previous chapter's valuation method under certainty is presented as: "A merchant's balance sheet is a statement of the prospects of his business. Each item in it represents the discounted value of items [receipts of cash] which he may expect [be certain of] later to enter in

---

14. Fisher, *Capital*, Chapter XVI; "The Risk Element," pp. 265-300. This is the last chapter of analysis. There are succeeding chapters, but they are summaries of the previous analyses.

his income account." (*Capital,* p. 264.) Presumably the rate of interest used in this discounting process is not arbitrarily selected, but
Fisher never clarifies its origin. He says only, "supposing the rate of
interest to be 5 per cent" (*Capital,* p. 256), and then proceeds to use 5
per cent throughout without further discussion. However, since he is
never bothered with adjustments to the capital account, the rate must
be equal to the "realized rate." Under uncertainty, however, the
realized rate could be determined only *ex post.* Whether or not he
calculates the rate in this fashion is not known, but any other rate would
require adjustments; therefore it is reasonable to assume that the way
he gets the 5 per cent is by an *ex post* calculation.[15] It is quite a different matter to get an *ex ante* rate under uncertainty, and therefore one
would hope for a rather complete explanation. Unfortunately, anyone
who has such hopes is due for a disappointment.

Fisher sets the stage by noting that chance brings about "even more
important changes in capital-value" than the changes met when the
future is certain. The price changes (equal to capital value?) are due
"chiefly . . . [to] changing estimates of futurity, due to what is called
chance, rather than of a record of the foreknown approach and detach-
ment of income." (*Capital,* p. 265.)

After a few pages of discussion of the concept of chance and probability, he divides the problem: "In order to apply this theory of
chance to the valuation of capital, we observe that both the future rate

---

15. The above appears to be a vicious circle that is much too obvious for a
man of Fisher's ability to fall into. We hope we are not doing him an injustice,
but there seems to be no other way to get the rate. We could assume that the 5
per cent was a pure time-preference or reservation rate, but the existence of
different preferences would yield surpluses to all except the marginal investor.
Likewise, we could assume perfect competition, but the rate of all except the
marginal producer would yield surpluses also. Assuming that the rate is determined in a separate market—the money market—does not help either. The rate
paid in the money market has to be high enough to overcome the consumer's impatience, but it has to be lower than, or equal to, the return on the capital into which
it is invested. But the calculation of the "return on the capital" requires both the
present and the future value.

We repeat: for decision-making purposes the discounting procedure is useful
and valid. We can discount (by a reservation rate) a future sum and make comparisons, or we can calculate the rate on two alternatives (by using the present and
future values) and make a decision. However, we do not understand how Fisher
arrives at a rate that does not require capital adjustment.

of interest and the future items of income are uncertain." (*Capital,* p. 271.) However, he then denies that the future rate of interest is a problem: "In the problem of capital-valuation, however, the uncertainty in the rate of interest does not always enter, for only present and not future rates are employed at the time at which the valuation of capital is made." (*Capital,* p. 271.) But how do we get the "present" rate of interest? A rate, by definition, covers a time period. It is not an instantaneous amount. Is it the rate that was earned on the last trade? Is it an average from some previous time? Is it a reservation rate? Fisher says it is the rate that applies to the present contract. But to know the rate that applies to the present contract requires that we know the future outcome of that contract, and this contradicts the assumption of uncertainty. The full quote follows:

> When we call a rate a "present" rate we mean, of course, that the contract or estimate to which it relates is a present contract or estimate. The very fact of valuation implies a known rate or rates at which the valuer is contrasting present and future goods. There may be several "present" rates. . . . [Examples of different rates for different length contracts are presented.] All of these rates are fixed and known and hold true in the year 1906 [the present], but they do not determine the rates which will hold true for the contracts or estimates of 1907 or 1914. (*Capital,* p. 271.)

It seems clear that Fisher is implying an exogenous rate here that is "known and holds true." That is, there is a rate that is given to us from an outside source, and that rate is the proper one to use for valuation. He seems to indicate this in other places, when he speaks of the "ordinary rate" and "earnings above the rate." Apropos of our study he writes: "Those who believe that wheat or any other article is likely to rise in value and hence yield more than the 'rate of interest,' will hold it. . . ." (*Capital,* p. 298.) The quotation marks are extremely puzzling. If it is an exogenous rate, then there is a chance to earn more than the rate of interest and there is no need to add the quotes. Another way of interpreting the quote, however, is that he is calculating the rate as in equation X-2 and thus indicating by quotation marks that the exogenous rate is not the "real" rate. We are confused.

Fisher continues with an example in which the interest changes in the interim. In order to discuss the problem in Fisher's own terms, we present this rather lengthy quote:

> Let us suppose that in Figure 10 the income AB is due at the end of the time FA, and that the rate of interest is such as to produce the discount curve BE. Then the present value of AB is FE. But the future valuations of AB may not follow the line EB as they would were the rate of interest unchanged. Thus, at a midway point of time, G, the valuation of AB may be only GD, found by means of a higher rate of interest involving the steeper discount curve DB. The history of the value of the property, namely, the right to AB, therefore follows the broken line ECDB, abruptly changing from GC to GD, if we suppose G to be the point at which the rate of interest changes unexpectedly from one level to the other. Had the owner of the property foreseen at the start that when the point G was reached the rate of interest would be higher, he would have

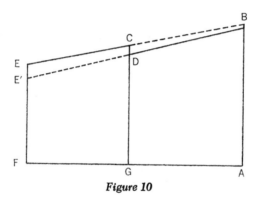

Figure 10

taken this fact into account in valuing the property at the moment F, and the value would have been FE', found by using the discount curve BDE'. This curve has a slight angle at D, being composed of the curve BD, constructed according to the high rate of interest prevailing at the time G, and the curve DE', constructed according to the lower rate of interest which applies to the period FG and which was employed in the curve EC. The essential fact, therefore, is that because of the failure to foresee the future rise in the rate of interest, the value of the property is FE, instead of FE', and that the value of the capital will fall, as at CD, or it may be rise, in accordance with successive future adjustments in the rate of interest. Since these readjustments are usually small and gradual, fluctuations in the capital-value will not ordinarily be as great or as abrupt as here represented, but the principle involved will still hold true. We see, therefore, a new cause for the fluctuations in capital-value, namely, unforeseen changes in the rate of interest. (*Capital*, pp. 271-73.)

Suppose that we expect to receive $110 (AB) one year from today. The exogenous rate (however determined) is 5 per cent. Thus, the present value is $104.76 (FE). If the market price at F is $104.76, there is no problem. The exogenous rate is equal to the implied rate. However, if we paid $100 for the contract at F, several questions arise.

The value of the consumption sacrificed is $100. We have $100 from some previous source that is immediately available for conversion into enjoyable capital and then into satisfactions. (Compare Figure 27, p. 315, for Fisher's saw-tooth changes in money which change enjoyable capital by *the same amount*, i.e. they are *of equal value*.) Thus, we have $100 of value at F; but when the contract is purchased, the value increases to $104.76. From whence comes the $4.76? After the exchange is completed, the trader has $110 of value. Thus there is a value increment of $10—an increment in money which is equal to the increment in enjoyable capital, $10 of separated, "realized income." Yet only $5.24 is accounted for by the exogenous rate. The realized rate is 10 per cent, but this can be determined only *ex post* under uncertainty. In short, the exogenous rate does not exhaust the amount which Fisher terms "income." Thus an adjustment would be required.

Fisher's disciples make it clear that they are using an exogenous rate, viz. the "subjective" rate. They also recognize the problems of adjustment that arise under conditions of uncertainty and spend a considerable amount of effort on these adjustments. However, the analysis of adjustments is invariably presented as a result of changes in expectations, not as a result of the subjective rate differing from the realized rate. Hansen briefly mentions the problem in a summary: "Furthermore, it should be pointed out that throughout the previous discussion *complete identity has been assumed to exist between the anticipated and the 'realized' subjective rate of interest*. At this point discrepancies may also occur, which may cause the described ideal and ex-ante concepts to take on a different content to that found during our discussion." (Hansen, p. 38, italics added.) Hansen recognizes the problem but there is no further mention of it beyond this brief passage.[16]

If we interpret Fisher's Figure 10 in Hansen's terms, it does not make sense. Evidently the "subjective rate" has to do with the trader's personal, internal, psychic "feelings." The trader's feelings at F were, say, 5 per cent. (Assuming that a trader can "feel 5 per cent.") He expects AB at instant A, and he discounts by 5 per cent to obtain FE. At instant G he changes his feelings to, say, 7 per cent and discounts AB at that rate for the remaining time, which results in the lower value of GD. Note that two things remain constant during this entire exercise, viz. the expectation (AB) and the entry price (unspecified).

The trader's feeling about interest is the *only* variable in the entire process. Normally we would think that if the expectations changed, there would be a change in the rate. We could then understand a change in prediction of the final outcome and would have no objection to that change being expressed as a rate. But a change in feelings about a rate is rather puzzling. Clearly such feelings have nothing to do with Fisher's explicit assumptions of economic motivation, because they have nothing to do with consumption, enjoyable capital, money, or any other economic concept. They could be nothing more than a psychological curiosity which would have relevance only to the trader's analyst.

For the reasons presented it is reasonable to assume that Fisher was not speaking of a subjective rate.

After he gets into the problem of changing expectations of final outcomes, he defines three linked rates—(1) riskless, (2) mathematical, and (3) commercial. He then selects the commercial rate.

> The question sometimes arises, where the element of risk thus raises the basis on which the bond is sold, whether the 6 per cent [commercial rate] is a true "rate of interest." The question is purely one of definition. Were it possible, it would be simpler to confine the application of the phrase "rate of interest" to an

16. Note that this is not purely a problem of uncertainty. A "subjective" rate could be used that is different from the certain-to-be-realized rate, and the adjustment would still be required.

exchange between present and future riskless income. (*Capital,* p. 279, italics added.)

Note that the calculation of such an *exchange* is determined by equation X-2. Thus, it is not exogenous but is the quotient of an equation in which both the present and future values are known or are estimated. He continues: "But in this case, it is always exceedingly difficult to state what the riskless rate of interest is, since some slight risk attaches to almost every investment. Accordingly it is usual to regard the commercial rate as a true 'rate of interest.'" (*Capital,* pp. 279–80.)

From the rest of his discussion it is clear that the chief use of the commercial rate is to determine what the contract *ought* to sell for. That is, given the elements of risk and time-preference, an individual could calculate the *maximum* that he, personally, would be willing to pay by discounting at the commercial rate. But if anyone buys at less than this maximum, an adjustment is required. Everyone in the market except the marginal trader will purchase at less than the maximum, and thus an adjustment will be required for all traders, save one.

In the case of "surplus consumable funds" the reservation rate is zero. Any time that there is *any* positive rate, the trader will exchange in order to gain something instead of nothing. Thus, an adjustment is required for the entire amount of the gain.[17]

We feel that all of these difficulties with the rate make it incumbent upon Fisher's disciples to explain their valuation suggestions in some detail. The author cannot solve the problems; and therefore we will leave the question of rates and turn to Fisher's second point.

Determination of the Final Outcome

The main application of risk to capital valuation is, however, not to the rate of interest, but to the income items themselves. To this application we now address ourselves. (*Capital,* p. 275.)

Following Fisher, we will now address ourselves to these items of

---

17. This case is not as far-fetched as it may appear. Certainly in the extreme example of a Rockefeller, who has the chore of consuming sixty-five million dollars, there would be surplus consumable funds. These funds would be employed in the best alternative, with a zero reservation rate.

income (or, in our terminology, the determination of the future prices) and neglect the problem of rate determination.

Fisher begins by explaining the concept of "mathematical expectation," E, which he calls the "mathematical value." As we explained above, the trader facing uncertainty is likely to perceive a range of various outcomes and have some notion of the probability of those outcomes. The mathematical expectation is a formalization of the range and the probabilities.

We will posit that the decision method used in this model is based upon an E calculation. This is a legitimate assumption for rational decision making, and we are quick to give Fisher credit for presenting it as early as 1906. E serves as a signal for action: if it is positive, hold wheat; if negative, hold cash.

A Risk Model.—The variables will be easier to handle if we assume a gambling-type model, e.g., like rolling dice or flipping coins. The characteristics of such a model allow us to list all the possibilities and assign a priori probabilities.

This assumption is unrealistic of course. When one is dealing with prices there are an infinite number of possibilities and no a priori probabilities. Nonetheless, we will make the assumption in order to clarify the valuation problems under the simplest of conditions. If the problem can be solved in this case, it should point the way in a more realistic case; if it can not be solved in a simple case, there is no reason to expect that the addition of complexities will make it more amenable to solution.

In addition, we use this model because Fisher's analysis is exclusively under conditions of risk—as opposed to uncertainty—although he never names the assumption. Thus, our criticism will be directly relevant to Fisher's valuation suggestions. He begins by assuming a magnitude that is certain to occur, but is uncertain with regard to the recipient of that magnitude, i.e. a lottery. He then multiplies the certain magnitude by the probability of receiving that amount and terms the product the "mathematical value." After further adjustments for "caution"—which we neglect—he obtains the commercial value which is the correct valuation for balance sheet purposes.

Later he presents a case that is more relevant to our problem. "In the general case we have to do not simply with the risk of falling below a specified income, nor with the chance of rising above a specified income, but with both." (*Capital,* p. 281.) "Income" here is "realized-income" or receipts of cash. His example is on the basis of a stock that pays cash dividends: "For instance, in the case of stock which has yielded, in successive years, the following percentages: 5, 5, 6, 5, 5, 4, 5, 7, 5, 3, 4, 5, we may for convenience take 5 per cent to serve for a basis of computation." (*Capital,* p. 281.) Here is the rate problem again. "Yielded" implies a base which, when divided into the cash dividend, gives the percentage (rate). The purpose of the discussion is to *discover* the correct base; therefore it is impossible to state the example in terms of a rate (yield) prior to the discovery. But the base is determined by using a rate which insures that the yield will be equal to that rate. Let us neglect the rate problem and follow along with Fisher's discussion.

> Thus, the "riskless" value, in this case, signifies that value which the stock would have if it were *certain* to yield the (arbitrarily assumed) 5 per cent forever—never more and never less. The riskless value is therefore simply the capitalized value of a perpetual annuity of $5 per share of $100 face value. If the rate of interest is 4 per cent, the result is $5 divided by 4 per cent, or $125. (*Capital,* pp. 281-82.)

The assumption of perpetuity is important here. It seems to imply the locked-in case again, because if there was any chance that the principal would be returned and the dividend stream discontinued, the present worth would be vastly different.

Fisher continues in a rather roundabout fashion to calculate the mathematical value.

> To obtain the "mathematical" value we simply add to the riskless value the value of the chance of getting more, and subtract that of the chance of getting less. The chance of getting an additional $1 a year is found by experience, as set forth above, to be two in twelve, or 1/6 each year. The present value of the right to this chance has therefore a mathematical value 1/6 as great as though the $1 increment were a certainty. But the certainty of $1 a year would be worth $25. Hence a chance of 1 in 6 of getting $1 a year would be worth mathematically 1/6 of $25, or $4.16 2/3. In like manner the chance of a second additional dollar is one in twelve and is worth (mathematically)

1/12 of $25, or $2.08 1/3. These two terms, $4.16 2/3 and $2.08 1/3, are the additive terms sought. The subtractive terms are the mathematical value of the chance of getting $1 less than the $5, and of getting still another $1 less. These chances, being 3 in 12 and 1 in 12 respectively, are worth 3/12 of $25 and 1/12 of $25 respectively, or $6.25 and $2.08 1/3. The whole mathematical value is therefore $125 + ($4.16 2/3 + $2.08 1/3) − ($6.25 + $2.08 1/3), or $122.91 2/3. (*Capital*, pp. 281-82.)

This is equivalent to capitalizing E by 4 per cent. The general form of E is

$$E = \sum_{i=1}^{n} \theta_i A_i$$

where

θ_i = probability of A_i occurring,
A_i = amount gained or lost when event A_i occurs.

In this case

$$E = 3(1/12) + 4(2/12) + 5(7/12) + 6(1/12) + 7(1/12)$$
$$E = 4.91 \ 2/3$$

Then E capitalized by 4 per cent is

$$\frac{4.91 \ 2/3}{.04} = 122.91 \ 2/3.$$

Thus, approximately $123 is the amount that a person should pay for the right to obtain this income.[18]

Fisher sets up sawtoothed curves which show the value gradually accruing as the dividend payment date is approached and then abruptly falling off when the payment is detached. The rate of accrual in this example is 4 per cent; thus the capital value would follow the pattern in Figure X-3, rising from $123 to approximately $128 ($123 plus 4 per cent of $123) and then falling back to $123. The fall in the capital value is, in all Fisher's diagrams, *equal* to the

---

18. Again we neglect the further discounting by the coefficient of caution. If we included it, the amount paid would be lowered further and the discrepancy would widen.

income. The magnitude of the receipt is also equal to the income. In this case the fall in capital value is always $4.92 but the receipt is *never* $4.92. The receipt can be only 3, 4, 5, 6, or 7 dollars by the terms of his own example. There is a contradiction here.

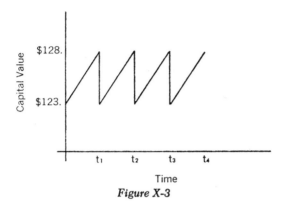

Figure X-3

Assume, for example, that the first dividend was $3. The capital at the time of receipt, t_2, is $127.92; and the fall of $3 leaves a capital value of $124.92. But the capitalization of E at t_2 remains at $123.[19] The $1.92 discrepancy is never mentioned by Fisher. He points out that there will be disruptions in the capital-value curve because of changing estimates of the future (p. 320); but in this case our estimate of the future has remained constant, and we have an unexplained disruption.

All of the above only serves to emphasize that E is an average value. It is a value that is expected to occur only after an infinite number of trials. The difficulty of discounting an average is that the *pattern* of receipts is an important factor in the determination of a present value. Lassiter has proved that changes in skewness and kurtosis of

---

19. Assuming independence, the fact that one event has occurred does not change the probabilities of future events. The number of times that a coin has turned up heads does not change our estimation of the probability for future flips. If we use the relative frequency as an estimation of probability, the occurrence of an event will change the probability of future events. If that is the case here, the probability of the dividend being $3 is now 2/13 (0.1538) which lowers E and consequently lowers the capitalized value below $123.

a receipt curve will markedly change the yield. Reversing Lassiter's procedure, it is obvious that a constant rate applied to various receipt curves will markedly change the present value. Thus, it is not only the magnitude of E which influences the present value, it is also the *pattern* over which receipts come in. But even under the simple conditions of risk, we do not know the pattern, and therefore we cannot determine the present value.

Moreover, the difference between E and any particular receipt is locked in the market. The average of the receipts will equal E only after an infinite number of trials, and therefore the cumulative deviation will remain locked-in until an infinite number of trials has occurred. An infinite number of trials will take an infinite amount of time—in this case an infinite number of years. Any magnitude discounted by *any* rate approaches zero as a limit if the time period is infinitely long. Thus, regardless of rate selection problems, the deviation has a present value of zero.

When we take these factors into account, we are required to focus on discounting the *next* receipt in order to avoid giving a positive value to the deviation. That is, the deviation has a zero present value; but if we discount any magnitude other than that of the next receipt, we will be giving the deviation a present value other than zero. There is the rub; we do not know what the next receipt is, or even the pattern of receipts; we only know the average after an infinite number of trials. Therefore, we may conclude that E is not useful for valuation purposes.

If we attempt to utilize E in our trader model, the situation becomes absurd. In order for E to be applicable, there would have to be an infinite number of exchanges of exactly the same magnitude; and the time interval between each of the exchanges would have to be foreknown. There would have to be exchanges in order to detach the income. If there were only growth with no detachments, the discount period would be infinity, resulting in a zero present value. Thus, there must be exchanges. Each exchange (purchase) must be of exactly the same amount; otherwise the compounding process would require perfect foreknowledge of the exact pattern of the prices.

Suppose, for example, that the trader wishes to withdraw, or detach, $5 per year and an E calculation indicates that on the average he can do this. His rate is (arbitrarily assumed) 5 per cent, and thus he is willing to pay $100 for the initial contract. Since E is an average, it is almost certain that the completion of the first exchange will yield something different from $105. Let us assume that the first exchange yields $155, of which he withdraws $5. Nothing has changed, neither E nor the rate, so he is still willing to pay $100 for a contract, and the present value of that contract is still $100. But what about the other $50? It is not a future receipt and it has no future yield, so it need not be discounted. Its value is $50, and it is also money-income. Surely the trader is better off now than before, but the value of the future income is still only $100.

The trader may be required to keep the $50 in "reserve" against the day when a particular exchange will lose. If this is the case, he is investing $150 to insure a continuation of a $5 income. But he is unwilling to do that, since his rate is 5 per cent. E would have to be $7.50 in order to induce the trader to stay in this market. Therefore, the trader either gets out of the market, or he lowers his rate.

It may be argued that the reason for this paradox is that we have misstated E in the example. Perhaps it should be stated that "E is equal to $5 per $100 invested." In this case the trader's rate will remain the same; and if he starts with only $100, presumably he can withdraw $5 per year. This also leads to absurdity, because we have reversed the valuation order. "An investment of $100 yields $5 per year" is different from "$5 per year is worth $100 at 5 per cent." That is, the value becomes the determinant of the income instead of the causal direction being income to capital. There can be no rate other than 5 per cent. If the trader values $5 per year at 4 per cent he is willing to pay $125. But this amount, under the assumption, will yield him $6.25, i.e. 5 per cent instead of 4.

It would be tedious to continue this analysis in detail. In the author's opinion, enough has been said to cause us to reject the discounted value of E as a method of valuation. There are plenty of additional problems, e.g. time-interval equivalence, continuous alternative E calculation from the present price, being forced out of the market by losing all on the first trade even though E was positive, etc. We will leave the details of these and other problems to the interested reader's imagination.

The Risk Assumption Relaxed.—Under the assumptions set forth above, the enterprise was insurable. Under the more realistic assumption of uncertainty—vice risk, using Knight's distinction—we could not insure, because we could not list all the possibilities and, more importantly, because the assignation of probabilities is little more than a guess. There are no a priori probabilities, and there is no reason to assume that relative frequencies are applicable. The probabilities are those that result from someone's feelings. Thus, E is nothing more than a quantification of someone's feelings about the future.

We concluded above that E was not useful for valuation under conditions of risk, and we may conclude here that the added complexities of uncertainty add weight to the prior conclusion.

VALUATION DISSONANCE

Another difficulty that arises in the Fisher Tradition is the dissonance of valuation among valuers. That is, assuming away the problems presented above, the difference in expectations and rates between traders would result in identical objects having different values.

If every trader's expectations and rate were exactly the same, the market price would move to equal that expectation, and the only gain possible would be pure interest. Obviously this is not the case. Consequently we can say that two traders in a given market at a given time will have different expectations. Hence, if the Fisher Tradition is used under uncertainty, the value of identical objects in the same spatio-temporal relation will be different.

Moreover, in the commodity market every "long" would be offset by a "short" with exactly *opposite* expectations. If we valued each contract by the discounted expectation, we would be in the incongruous position of applying opposite algebraic signs to one object. At interim instants both would show an increase in value—income— when it is *certain* that one must suffer a loss.

The same is true for trading markets that do not have short contracts. The demand curve describes the range of the purchaser's expectations of a price increase. The supply curve describes the seller's expectations of a decrease in price.[20] Thus for every dollar in the market with a positive expectation there is a dollar with a negative expectation. One expectation must be wrong.

It is difficult to know just what kind of comparison can result when identical objects receive different values at the same time. The comparison cannot be of objects; it must be of valuers. But one cannot compare valuers unless one knows about the objects that they are valuing. Suppose trader A and trader B held identical objects, which they valued as $10 and $20 respectively. If the bit

$$A = \$10 \text{ worth of wheat}$$
$$B = \$20 \text{ worth of wheat}$$

is reported, there is not even the possibility of comparing valuers, because we do not know that the quantity of the objects held is identical. Trader A may be an optimist with a small quantity, and B may be a pessimist with a larger quantity. Thus, unless there is some method of reporting that the objects are identical, the reporting of different values does not even allow a comparison of valuers. We cannot say that such a message quantifies the trader's expectation, because a discount rate is also involved. Two traders with identical expectations could have different rates and, hence, different values. We fail to understand how any meaningful instantaneous comparison can be made under the Fisher Tradition.

If we desire to make intertemporal comparisons of the same trader, we run into similar difficulties. The three variables—expectations, rate, and quantity—are still present; and any intertemporal change in value may be caused by any one, or any combination, of the three. That is, if we report an increase in the value of wheat, there is no way for the receiver to know what caused the change in value. It may be nothing more than that the trader now "feels like 1 per cent" instead of "feeling like 10 per cent."

Equally as much information about expectations is given if we simply report that the trader holds wheat. His position indicates the direction, from the present price, of his expectations. The value under

20. Or at least it describes a lower expectation than some other alternative. Only when this is the trader's best-alternative does a sale indicate the expectation of a decline.

the Fisher method indicates little more than the direction, because of the rate variable. Thus, the Fisher Tradition, which is based solely on expectation, yields little more information about expectations than the simple report that "wheat is held."

If the receivers wish to compare the trader's predictions with theirs, another indispensable datum must be transmitted, viz. the present price. The Fisher value does not indicate the present price, yet the other receivers must know its magnitude before they can make their own predictions and then compare them to the trader's predictions.

SUMMARY

Fisher's work, in the opinion of the author, is primarily directed toward proving that value is caused by income; it was not intended as a method of *reporting* general values. Fisher notes that market value is determined by the activities of humans and that the motive force of humans is want satisfaction. With this we have no quarrel. Our first disagreement with Fisher is over his equation of satisfaction with consumption. Satisfaction can arise from sources other than direct consumption. Further, we object to equating consumption to income. He relents somewhat on this point by allowing money and goods to also be called income. This seems to imply that things that are capable of becoming satisfactions by consumption are properly part of income. If we allow this "command-over-satisfaction" notion to enter, we reach a broader concept which could easily include the market value of capital goods.

On a more technical level, there are grave problems in the Fisher Tradition. First, it is not clear which of several rates should be selected. If any rate other than the one implied by the market is used, there are problems of adjusting the value to equal the money received. If the rate implied by the market is used, the discounted value is always equal to the current market price. Second, the time period over which the discount should be made is ambiguous, even under certainty. The rate will vary with the time period used, unless the rate and time are the ones implied by the market. Again, if the rate and time period implied by the market are used, the value reverts to the present market price. Third, the determination of the final outcome, even under the simplified assumption of risk, does not yield a figure which can logically be discounted. Different patterns of receipts yield widely different discounted values. Moreover, the discounting of a mathematical expectation results in a value change that is almost certain to be different from the cash received. A strong argument can be made that the difference should be discounted over an infinite number of time periods and thus valued at zero. If this is accepted, the value obtained is again equal to the present market price. Finally, when the simplifying assumptions are relaxed, there are even more problems to contend with.

The Fisher Tradition, in the sense of projecting a future value, is relevant to almost all the decisions of almost all the receivers. However, the expectations and the reservation rate are very likely to be different for each. Thus, it is more appropriate for each receiver to make his own personal estimations of the Fisher value instead of using it as a method for reporting value. For these reasons we reject the Fisher Tradition as a method of measuring income.

XI

THE ACCOUNTING TRADITION

To analyze "The Accounting Tradition" is much more difficult than it appears. There are a variety of different valuation methods in present-day accounting practice and a variety of reasons given in justification of each method. In addition, there are academic accountants who propose valuation methods that are not accepted in practice.

It would be a happy situation if we could equate "The Accounting Tradition" to the purchase-price valuation coefficient and then proceed directly to a discussion of the theory justifying purchase prices. Unfortunately, this is impossible. It is said that the valuation basis used in the accounting tradition is "historical cost," which seems to be an intuitively simple concept. That it is not simple is indicated by the vast literature on the subject, most of which is devoted to explaining how one arrives at a historical cost figure in a given situation. Much more space is devoted to explaining how one calculates the figures than is devoted to explaining why one should calculate the figures or what they mean once they are calculated.

Much of the accounting literature is concerned with valuation of specific assets instead of a general theory of valuation. Most textbooks consider the assets seriatim and often insulate the discussion. The result is different valuation methods for different assets. We could find the same author proposing the following:

1. Undiscounted future receipts (Accounts and Notes Receivable).
2. Discounted future receipts (Bonds Receivable).
3. Current market price (Agricultural Commodities).
4. Lower of cost or market (Inventories).
5. Unamortized purchase price (Organizational Expenses, Land).
6. Amortized purchase price (Equipment).
7. Market price at date of gift (Donated Assets).
8. Market price at date of legal action (Some or all of the assets at time of quasi-reorganization or partnership formation).
9. Zero (Advertising and Research Costs).
10. Constant (Exchange rate applied to Foreign Subsidiary assets).

All of these are acceptable accounting valuation methods. To value a gift, as in method seven, at its market price, or to revalue held assets at market price, as in methods four and eight, and describe that valuation as "historical cost" is a contradiction of the intuitive meaning of those terms. Likewise, valuations by methods one and two are not "costs" in the sense of purchase prices or acquisition sacrifices.

Since our model is concerned with a specific asset, it may be thought that we could confine the description of the Accounting Tradition to that asset. We don't do this for two reasons: First, and most importantly, the valuation of any particular asset in accounting is thought to be subsumed under a general method of valuation. Justification for the valuation method is sometimes subsumed in the same fashion, i.e. the justification for valuing a particular asset in a particular way is given by noting that it is consistent with the general method of valuation. Thus, it is necessary to examine the general method prior to examining the application of that method in a specific case. Second, there is no single method of valuing a particular asset in the Accounting Tradition. Instead, there are several different methods which are used under different conditions. Therefore, it is impossible to discuss *the* valuation method applicable to a given asset, because there are several methods applicable to that asset.

The second point needs some elaboration. One example should suffice. Since there is little literature devoted to commodity contracts, let us consider the various valuation methods of the closest substitute. Stocks and/or bonds that are traded in an almost perfect market may be classified in a variety of ways under different criteria. For example:

Criterion	*Classification*
1. Managerial intent about length of time to be held.	(a) Current or (b) fixed.
2. Contractual Agreement with Trustee.	(a) Asset or (b) offset to liability.
3. Kind of security held.	(a) Asset or (b) offset to liability.
4. Type of firm.	(a) Marketable security or (b) inventory or (c) earning asset.
5. Amount held or effective control that the owner corporation has over the owned corporation.	(a) Offset against the net worth of the owned corporation and the "real" assets summed or (b) shown separately as an investment.

Any particular criterion-classification combination may have alternative valuation methods. For example: criterion four, classification b, may be valued at (1) cost, (2) market, (3) lower of cost or market; criterion four, classification a, is said to be shown "at cost" but this usually means lower of cost or market; criterion four, classification c, is also said to be shown at cost (because market is irrelevant since it is intended to be held instead of sold), but it will be shown at market if the difference is "significant" and will be "permanent"; criterion three, classification a, is valued at cost on which dividends are not permitted to be accrued if it is a stock but interest is required to be accrued if it is a bond, and there are alternative procedures for calculating the accrual; criterion five, classification a, may be shown on the "cost" or the "equity" basis, both of which have alternative subprocedures; criterion five, classification b, is not permitted to be valued on the equity basis.

As this scant analysis shows, it would be tedious to consider all the valuation methods and subprocedures resulting from the combinations on this list. However, for the reader who is relatively unfamiliar with the literature, it would be illuminating to detail one classification. Let us restrict our discussion to the valuation variations of "inventory" items.

Inventory items may be valued on the basis of market prices existing at (1) the date of purchase or (2) the date of any financial statement subsequent to purchase if the price on that date is lower than the purchase price ("market value" *becomes* "cost" when written down by this procedure) or lower than a previous price that was lower than the purchase price and therefore used on a previous financial statement. Thus, there is some ambiguity as to the temporal location of the market price being used as a valuation coefficient.

Certain ancillary outlays and amortizations are added to the purchase price to get the "cost" of the items. Other ancillary outlays and amortizations are not added to the purchase price. Some ambiguity exists as to just what the cutoff point should be, and different accountants will include and exclude different things.

If the items are sold piecemeal, the residual cost value may be calculated by several acceptable conventions:

1. Lifo
2. Fifo
3. Average
4. Specific Identification

Each of these conventions may result in wide variations in the cost value. Then under each convention there are different subprocedures. There are several methods of calculating the average, for example, and lifo is subject to a "periodic" or "perpetual" subprocedure. Each of these subprocedures may result in wide variations in the cost value.

In application of the lower-of-cost-or-market rule, discussed above, we noted that it was necessary to compare "the purchase price" with market prices existing at subsequent reporting dates. It is now clear that this statement was an oversimplification, because the various conventions, procedures, and subprocedures make it impossible to define *the* purchase price. Instead there are a large number of different purchase prices that may have been recorded. This recorded purchase price must be compared to the market price at each reporting date in order to apply the rule. Unfortunately, "market" is also subject to several interpretations:

1. Replacement cost. (Current purchase price of the item or current purchase price of the factors necessary to replace the item.)
2. Net proceeds if sold.
3. Net proceeds if sold less "normal profits."

The question then arises as to whether the "market" should be applied to individual items or classes of like items or to the entire inventory, and, of course, differences in application result in different values. Some authors suggest that minor variations in market should be excluded and only marked depreciation should occasion a change in value. Others differentiate temporary and permanent changes in market price and argue that only the permanent type is sufficient reason for a value change.[1]

In addition to these variations in valuation methods there is disagreement over the effect of a value change on income. In writing down an inventory from cost to market, some accountants would report the decrement on the income statement, thereby decreasing the reported income for the current period, while others would deduct it from retained income, thereby decreasing the reported income since the inception of the firm without decreasing the reported income of any particular period. Still others would argue that the value change is not realized or crystallized and therefore should not affect reported income at all, that instead the decrement should be deducted from total net worth and kept in suspense until it is realized. Those who posit the realization test are usually arguing that the value decrements should be treated in the same way as value increments. On the few occasions when value increments are recorded, the increment is considered to be "unrealized"; and therefore it does not affect either current or retained income. Only when the item is sold, in the case

---

1. Bulletin 43 (p. 23) applies these criteria and uses the terms "substantial amount" and "temporary conditions" to describe them in respect to marketable securities. In order to know that a change is permanent or temporary requires that one know the future. This is a common situation in accounting. It is said to be "historical," but the kind of history being recorded in accounting requires that one know the future.

of inventory, is the increment considered to be realized and reported as income. In fact it is possible for a recorded value increment to have the effect of a net decrease in reported income. The appreciation may be recorded as a permanent net-worth subdivision other than retained income, e.g. appraisal surplus. Then the appreciation is charged piecemeal to expense, thereby reducing reported income without ever having increased reported income and without ever incurring a "cost." An alternative is to realize the appreciation in retained income, thereby reducing the current reported income by the same amount as retained income is increased.

This example, although not as detailed as it could be, should be sufficient to make our point: There is no single valuation method, even for a specific asset, which we can call "The Accounting Tradition." Instead, there is a variety of valuation methods in accounting, and there is a variety of reasons for the variations. The valuation method will vary from asset to asset, from condition to condition, from criterion to criterion, from firm to firm, from practitioner to practitioner, from author to author, and in a kaleidoscopic combination of these factors. In addition, as we reviewed the literature, we were struck by the lack of any genuine theoretical analysis of valuation. We join Spacek in his lament: "Instead of standards of measurement, attention is focused on techniques. Most documents are overburdened with procedural comment on how to handle certain transactions, but little is said about the effect sought, and still more important—why." (Spacek, "Court," p. 369.) Often the reasons given in justification of a proposed valuation method are cursory and cryptic, with the majority of the space and effort devoted to lengthy descriptions of technique.

We think that such a condition has a very simple explanation: There is no adequate, explicit accounting theory in existence. The valuation variations per se are evidence for this thesis; the dearth of theoretical analysis is further evidence. As might be expected, we have been unable to locate any single theory of accounting that synthesizes all these views into one tradition.

For this reason, we must alter our methodology at this point. In the last two chapters, we outlined and discussed a personified theory from essentially a single source. Here, we are without a universally accepted spokesman and, therefore, cannot follow that methodology. We have two lines open to us:

1. A seriatim examination of selected theories and theorists.
2. A presentation of our own hypothesis about the Accounting Tradition.

Both are fraught with difficulties. Because of space limitations, we would be forced to select from a multitude of theorists if we followed the first line. This would leave us open to the charge of omitting someone's favorite theorist and/or theory. In addition, because of the literature's emphasis on technique at the expense of theory, we would be forced to hypothesize about each author. Their epigrammatic statements are not amenable to analysis in their present form, and thus we would have to present several alternative interpretations prior to analysis. If we follow the second line, we are in the peculiar position of being both the originator and the critic of a line of thought. We would be forced to abstract a theory from a number of diverse theorists. Like all generalizations, such an abstraction would be false. The degree of falseness would vary from theorist to theorist, but no theorist would be described with complete accuracy. We will compromise by following a combination of the two lines.

First, we will abstract what we consider to be the de facto principles of accounting. We will set forth a generalized description of what we perceive to be the underlying operative theory of accounting. Then we will criticize the Accounting Tradition as described. This procedure is subject to several types of errors: (1) Given the diversity of accounting, there is some doubt that any single generalization can be adequate in its description; (2) our perception of accounting may be faulty, and therefore our generalization may be in error; (3) a system of logic may be formulated in different ways so that the axioms or principles of one formulation are the theorems of the other, and vice versa, thus our formulation is only one of several possible formulations; (4) there are different levels of formulation, and our principles may be theorems of higher principles.[2] Any or all of these

2. The existence of higher principles is particularly important to this study. In our view, the highest and first principle of accounting has always been an ethical one, or "fairness" as Spacek terms it. We think that conservatism came from ethical

may invalidate our criticism. We may be criticizing our own misconceptions or misstatements. For this reason, we will turn to the second type of analysis.

Second, we will critically examine some specific rules of valuation and the justifications presented by selected accounting theorists. We will argue that the specific rules and justifications must originate in higher principles, since they cannot stand alone.

Our fundamental thesis is that accounting theory has been an amalgamation of cognitively insulated rules of valuation. Ladd (p. 160) speaks of it as expedients: "The development and regulation of accounting theory and practice is basically the result of *ad hoc* expedients, largely dictated by the very corporations whose affairs are being accounted for." We will attempt to explain the result of these expedients and the tenuous thread that links them.

Such a hypothesis necessarily involves some conjecture. An abstraction of this kind is not subject to conclusive proof, instead it is the result of fragmentary evidence coupled with an intuitive leap. Also, it will not serve as a complete explanation of every author or every valuation method. It is intended to be an explanation of the *mainstream* of accounting thought and the *de facto* practice of accounting. Thus, it will exclude people who call themselves accountants, but who, from our point of view, are either on the fringes or in another tradition.

Another reason for excluding the fringe group is their lack of impact on the practice of accounting and the textbook literature. Canning, for example, has had some influence; but we would classify him mainly in the Fisher Tradition. MacNeal plumps for current market values and has been ignored. Sprouse and Moonitz are more difficult to classify; and since their most revolutionary work is very recent, its impact is unknown. We exclude these people and others like them from what we consider to be the Accounting Tradition.

The "mainstream of thought" is usually rather accurately mirrored

---

considerations, and the cost rule came from conservatism. The difficulty is that these theorems have been transformed into principles, and thus have become ingrained habits of thought that are not subject to examination. With liturgical regularity the cost principle is invoked to defend or condemn something, without regard to the higher principle from whence the cost rule springs.

by textbooks. In addition, the impact of a successful text is probably greater than an academic treatise, if for no other reason than that it is read by more people. Thus, much of our evidence is taken from textbooks.

CONSERVATISM: THE FUNDAMENTAL PRINCIPLE OF VALUATION*

Accounting has always been a highly practical discipline. Accountants have been faced with the problem of making immediate decisions in order to meet the exigencies of practice. They have not had the luxury of extensive reflection before taking a position. In addition, they were not much more than specialized craftsmen when an almost overwhelming responsibility was rather suddenly thrust upon them. They were asked to become the stewards of the community's wealth. They were required to make public what had previously been jealously guarded private information. They were asked to make independent judgments about the affairs of persons who had previously directed their activities. They were asked to provide information via a device that had sometimes been used to misinform or conceal. They were required to have integrity when deceit was not uncommon.

As a consequence of these factors, there were twin developments: (1) problems were solved in isolation; and (2) the solutions became accepted and rather rigid. The accountants met a problem and solved it on the basis of their best judgment about the particulars of that specific problem. Very likely the cognition was completely insulated from a similar problem that they had previously solved. The resulting inconsistencies probably did not bother the accountant, because his main concern was with the ethical effects of that particular decision. Meanwhile, another practitioner in another firm was solving a problem that was only slightly different and often coming up with a vastly different answer. Thus, there developed intra- and inter-practitioner inconsistencies. At the same time, the accountant needed a strong defense against the often optimistic, sometimes dishonest, financiers and entrepreneurs. He was placed in the precarious position of being

* Much of the following material appeared as "Conservatism: The Fundamental Principle of Valuation in Traditional Accounting" in *Abacus*, III (December 1967), 109-32.

subject to the pecuniary discretion of the person he was obliged to keep honest. In the absence of a cohesive theory, in the absence of police power, in the presence of ignorance and apathy of the community, his only defense was precedent and persuasion. Precedent soon became rule, and the rigid application of rules was his primary weapon. It is easier to accuse someone of breaking a rule than to accuse him of not telling the truth.

The accountant passed through the era of swashbuckling manipulation; the era of watered stock and financial bubbles; in short, the era of chicanery by financial overstatement. In addition, he has always been faced with the effervescent optimism of the entrepreneur. The entrepreneur is naturally optimistic about his project. If he were not, he would not be engaged in it. This optimism was exhibited by a tendency to overvalue the enterprise. Faced with the universal tendency to overstate, the accountant conceived his role to be one of temperance. As a steward, he needed to be the ultimate in solidarity and stability. He wanted to insure that the value was *at least* the amount he reported. Often, to combat overstatement, he proposed understatement, perhaps with the hope of striking a balance.[3]

Thus, the most ancient and probably the most pervasive rule of valuation is "conservatism." Recently this rule has come under attack. Many people have pointed out that deliberate understatement is equivalent to deliberate misrepresentation and have urged that the accountant's function was "to tell the truth."

We recognize that conservatism has lost favor in accounting circles, that it is not applied in practice as much as it once was, and that the academics challenge it. Nevertheless, the author considers conservatism to be the most influential principle of valuation in accounting. Other principles, e.g. cost, consistency, realization, going concern, etc., are often given higher (never less than equal) status. We regard such lists as erroneous and consider conservatism to be a much more fundamental and pervasive principle than the others usually listed.

Evidence for this assertion comes more from the accountant's deeds than his words. Accountants violate the historical cost principle when

---

3. It is interesting that one of the consequences of the Federal Income Tax has been a tendency to reverse the roles. The accountant has had to resist the entrepreneur's desire to avoid taxes by financial understatement.

they value at the *lower* of cost or market. The realization convention is violated in the case of installment sales and the write-down of obsolete inventory, both of which result in *lower* value for assets and current income. The going-concern assumption is abrogated when it results in a value greater than market. (See Finney and Miller, *Intermediate*, p. 120.) If the consistent application of a valuation rule becomes unconservative, accountants usually become inconsistent. The basic "benefit theory" is violated in favor of conservatism in several instances, e.g. advertising and research expenditures.

In addition to these examples, evidence comes from justifications presented in the literature. Many authors take a "moderately conservative" or even "anticonservative" position when they are writing under the head of "Principles." However, when they are discussing the valuation of a specific asset, the recurrent phrase that something "is or is not conservative" is almost inevitable.

For example, Johnson and Kreigman take an "anti-ultraconservative" view in their chapter on "Accounting Theory."

> Misrepresentation was often injected in the balance sheets of businesses by policies involving the deliberate understatement of asset values in order to achieve so-called "conservative" values for these assets. . . . By these practices, "conservative" values became "ultra-conservative" values *not* fairly presenting the net income and financial position of a given business. (Johnson and Kriegman, p. 740.)

The tone is clearly anti-ultraconservative. Perhaps it is anticonservative when we juxtapose a statement from an earlier discussion of principles. "The statement of income and the balance sheet, therefore, must be built upon the cornerstone of *truth*." (Johnson and Kriegman, p. 5.) Yet when they discuss the valuation of stocks, they write:

> The valuation at current market of stocks and bonds held for short-term investment purposes, when market is higher than cost, is a practice not generally approved by accountants. This disapproval rests on the fact that the practice not only involves a departure from original cost as the time-honored yardstick of accounting valuation but also involves accounting recognition of appreciated values. *The practice is obviously not conservative*; and accountants generally have been loathe to place an unrealized surplus account on the balance sheet. What support

has been given the practice has been defended on the grounds
of showing the financial position of the business on a realistic
basis. (Johnson and Kriegman, p. 129, italics added.)

It is not clear whether these are the authors' arguments or whether
they are reporting the predominant view of the profession. Either
case supports our point.

The above quotation sets out two conflicting concepts: Conservatism
versus realism. Without further argument, the above quote is the
entire discussion of the pros and cons of market valuation of securities;
they draw a conclusion. They point out that valuation at market "is
not generally approved" by the accounting profession, and then they
support a cost valuation: "The authors believe that profits and losses
on marketable securities should be recognized *only* at the date of their
sale. On the balance sheet, marketable securities should be valued at
cost." (Johnson and Kriegman, p. 129.) We suspect that the authors
would abandon their strict cost position if the price were to decline
substantially. Moreover, they state explicitly the connection of the
realization convention to conservatism: "Today, the doctrine of conservatism is essentially a policy of caution. Revenue, for example, will
receive accounting recognition only after it has been realized." (Johnson and Kriegman, p. 740.) That is, the realization convention has its
roots in the principle of conservatism. Therefore, we may infer that
their argument for cost valuation is based on conservatism.

Another widely used text supports this thesis:

> The doctrine of conservatism is illustrated in the application of
> practices such as the following: increases in the values of assets
> and anticipated gains are normally ignored until realized by
> means of sale; declines in asset values and anticipated losses,
> however, are normally recognized . . . certain expenditures are
> charged in full against current revenue despite the possibility
> of future benefits. (Simons and Karrenbrock, p. 49.)

This text then takes a moderately conservative position: "A conservative approach in the measurement process is desirable." (Simons
and Karrenbrock, p. 49.)

Later, the arguments for valuation at market are briefly surveyed
and then rejected. The reasons for the rejection in their entirety follow: "Little tendency to accept valuation at market has been shown

by the accounting profession. Such procedure has been challenged chiefly on the grounds that it represents a departure from the cost concept and would *violate accounting conservatism.*" (Simons and Karrenbrock, p. 248, italics added.) In view of their previous statement, which justifies departure from the cost concept in favor of conservatism, we could infer that the violation of accounting conservatism is the fundamental argument against valuation at market.

One additional reason for the thesis—conservatism is the fundamental principle—is the odd character of the attacks on it. Much of the literature opposes conservatism because it is not conservative! A common argument against conservatism in one period is that it produces unconservative values in another period. The Patons argue that "cost or market is not truly conservative" because "A low inventory at the end of one year is reflected in the cost of sales of the ensuing period, and as a result the income of the second period is increased (or the loss reduced) by precisely the amount by which the opening inventory was reduced through the operation of the 'conservative' rule." (Paton and Paton, p. 84.) That is, intertemporally an apparently conservative procedure is not "truly conservative."

A variation on this argument is presented in an official pronouncement of the AICPA:

> The argument advanced in favor of immediately writing off discount was that it extinguished an asset that was only nominal in character and that it resulted in a conservative balance sheet. The weight attached to this argument has steadily diminished, and increasing weight has been given to the arguments that all such charges should be reflected under the proper head in the income account, *and that conservatism in the balance sheet is of dubious value if attained at the expense of a lack of conservatism in the income account, which is far more significant.* (Bulletin 43, p. 129, italics added.)

That is, the fundamental principle is conservatism, and therefore a conservative value on the more important statement is more desirable than a conservative value on the less important statement.

In sum, our primary hypothesis is:

> Conservatism is the fundamental principle of valuation in the Accounting Tradition.

The reasons for this thesis are:

1. The development of accounting has a natural tendency toward conservatism.
2. There are many instances when other principles are violated in favor of conservatism.
3. Many accountants who deny conservatism continue to use it as a justification for specific practices.
4. One argument against conservatism is that it is not conservative.

Our secondary hypothesis is:

Conservatism is the premise, often tacit, from which other rules of valuation are derived.

There is some support for our secondary hypothesis in the accounting literature. We indicated some examples above. Some authors freely admit that certain valuation rules are applications of the conservative principle. Other authors, the most conservative, in fact, if not in statement, strain to justify valuation rules on grounds other than conservatism. We think that such straining and the resulting invalidity of the arguments is evidence of their tacit premise of conservatism. An examination of representative arguments of this type is the task of the next chapter.

We should not leave this section without indicating that we think there are principles of accounting other than conservatism which affect valuation, viz. convenience and causality.

Briefly, the notion of convenience is that throughout the history of accounting there has been an unyielding pressure to get *some* statistic out in the shortest possible time, at the lowest possible cost, with the least chance of being challenged. This has resulted in valuation rules which are convenient. For example, purchase price is a readily available statistic; realization at point of sale is a fairly clean-cut, easy-to-apply rule; materiality is a justification for breaking the rules if it is too troublesome to trace the causes and if the amount is relatively insignificant.

The third principle—causality—is a relatively recent addition coming from academics who attempted to apply causal reasoning to the existing accounting practices. Cost accountants were in the forefront of this process, arguing that cost should be attached to the unit that caused the cost to be incurred. They became involved in long arguments over the allocation of overhead, culminating in the recent controversy over "direct costing," i.e. charging to units only the incremental costs that were caused by the incremental units. Other examples are the "benefit theory," which charges costs to the period which they benefit, i.e. periods in which those costs cause revenue. The whole of the "matching" and "attaching" concepts spring directly from causality arguments.

We think that these three principles, singularly or in mixed weight combinations, serve to explain almost all that accountants do and most of what they say. However, the last two principles are more concerned with the manipulation of the values than with the derivation of the valuation rules. For this reason, the principle of conservatism is more germane to this study.

THE FUNDAMENTAL RULE OF VALUATION

In the previous section we put forth the hypothesis that "conservatism" is the fundamental principle of valuation in the Accounting Tradition. The most widely accepted rule of valuation is said to be "historical cost." As we have previously pointed out, "cost" has many variations in application; and thus it is difficult to analyze the rule in the abstract.

We think that the explanation for the variations is contained in our hypothesis. Cost is not a fundamental tenet of accounting: instead it is a derivative of the principle of conservatism. First, and most importantly, the rule almost always yields a conservative value. Cost, particularly in assets that have been amortized, i.e. valued below purchase price, is likely to be below market price. If not, it is written down; i.e., when the cost rule is not conservative, it is violated. Second, cost figures are usually far more convenient to obtain than any other value. Ordinarily there is easy access to documents—invoices, checks—which yield a figure. Occasionally, there is some difficulty in obtaining the cost figures, and the accountant reverts to conservatism by making a rather low estimate or, if the amount is "immaterial," by assigning a zero value. Third, costs are attached to products or periods by some causally derived rules. Some costs "benefit future periods"—cause revenue in the future—and the value is maintained on the books. Other costs have "benefited past periods"— caused past revenue—and are valued at zero. If a cost produces a product that is "expected to benefit future periods," the cost attaches to the product until it is sold (causes revenue). If the product "loses utility" (loses part of its capability to cause revenue), there is a reversion to conservatism as it is written down. Of course, values other than cost could "attach," so the cost rule does not follow from the causality principle.

In short, cost is both conservative and convenient, and thus it fits our general hypothesis. Our secondary hypothesis—that cost is a derivative of the general principle of conservatism—is supported by the fact that when cost and conservatism conflict, conservatism prevails.

Additional evidence, albeit indirect, for both hypotheses is the manifestly specious character of the arguments for the cost rule when removed from the context of conservatism. Several arguments will be presented below and shown to be invalid. We think that the explanation for this is that the arguments are essentially apologetics for accounting practice. The practice is governed by conservatism, but the authors deny the principle of conservatism and thus are left in the untenable position of defending what they deny. As a consequence, the arguments become strained in attempting to defend the rule.

The Cost Rule

There is some disagreement on the proper term to be applied to the cost rule. Some authors refer to it as a "convention," others as a "concept," and still others as a "principle."

Tunick and Saxe, in a chapter entitled "An Integrated Summary of Accounting Theory," break "principles" down into three categories:

> . . . "principles" is in reality a combination of the following related elements: (1) accounting *conventions*, or postulated basic conditions and assumptions, accepted as such by common consent; (2) accounting *standards*, or systematic and impartial measures, based on observable objective conditions, against which conduct and practice must be squared, not as absolute measures, but rather as a safeguard against irresponsible ac-

tion; and (3) *doctrines* concerning the proper reporting of accounting data, which have received general acceptance. (Tunick and Saxe, pp. 618-19.)

Then in a "brief, formal restatement" of the principles under the heading of "Accounting Conventions" and the subheading of "The Valuation Convention," they write: "Money is accepted as a stable measuring unit, and original recorded cost as the quantitative basis for accounting valuations. . . . Thus far, the valuation convention has been reiterated as a guiding principle by all professional agencies which have re-examined it. . . ." (Tunick and Saxe, p. 620.) On the following page they list "cost" as the first subheading under "Accounting Standards." For these authors it appears that "cost" is a "principle," "convention," and "standard," all at the same time.

Paton and Littleton (pp. 11-13) distinguish between "concepts" and "standards." In a discussion of the former, they employ the term "price-aggregates" as a substitute for "cost" and state that it is one of the basic "concepts" of accounting. Later they devote an entire chapter to the "concept" of "cost" (p. 24).

Finney and Miller refer to "The Cost Principle" and say that it "may be stated as follows: Subject to generally recognized exceptions, cost is the proper basis of accounting for assets and expenses, and accounting records should reflect acquisition costs and the transformation, flow, and expiration of these costs." (Finney and Miller, *Intermediate*, p. 120.) Apart from any difficulties in classification, these examples give ample evidence of the importance and pervasiveness of the cost rule in the Accounting Tradition.

Stated in its simplest form, the cost rule is:

> Assets are to be valued at the same magnitude as the assets that were sacrificed in order to obtain them.

This is an exchange rule which makes the implicit assumption that the sacrificed asset is valued correctly. It also assumes that the exchange is an even transaction with neither gain nor loss in value. This presents no problem if one recognizes that accountants are normally thinking of *cash* as the sacrificed asset.

> In cash transactions cost is measured by the amount of the immediate *cash consideration;* in credit transactions cost is the

> amount of *money* which would be required to effect immediate settlement of the obligation incurred. If the consideration is in the form of property or securities of uncertain value, the basis of measurement is the estimated *cash equivalent* of the medium employed." (Paton and Littleton, p. 24, italics added.)

That is, the value received is equal to the value (of cash) sacrificed. The difficulty with such an equation is that it does not allow for value changes. The strict application of such a rule would maintain a *constant total value* regardless of the form of the asset or the number of exchanges. If one valued the assets only at the event of exchange and set the value of the acquired asset equal to the value of the sacrificed asset, then there would never be any recorded gain or loss in value.

Recognizing the need for changes in total value, accountants have adopted rules which permit exceptions to the strict interpretation of the cost rule. One of these rules is classified as a separate "principle," "convention," or "concept," viz. realization or recognition of revenues. This rule provides a means for breaking out of the cost equation by valuing the received asset independently of the previously recorded value of the sacrificed asset. The conception of this rule is also in terms of cash exchanges:

> Revenue is the product of the enterprise, measured by the amount of new assets received from customers; . . . revenue is *realized* by conversion of product into *cash* or other valid assets . . . for most enterprises the value of sales furnishes the most satisfactory measure of realized revenue . . . with sale, product is converted into new, measurable assets, *cash* or receivables ("cash in process"). (Paton and Littleton, p. 46, italics added.)

Thus, there are two elements in "the cost rule":

1. Non-cash assets are originally valued at the cash sacrificed in exchange.
2. Cash and near-cash are valued at unity.

These are usually considered to be two separate one-way rules. "Cost" is the rule for "purchases," and "realization" is the rule for "sales." However, the distinction between a purchase and a sale is simply the direction of cash flow. Thus, the rules are identical in that cash is valued independently in both cases and the offset to cash—asset or revenue—is set equal. Given this, one might say that the accountant never values non-cash assets. Instead he values only the cash and infers or imputes that value to the item sacrificed or received in exchange for cash.

Reflection on the cost-realization rule yields two basic elements of valuation in the Accounting Tradition:

1. Valuation occurs at the *event of exchange.*
2. The magnitude of the valuation is determined by the *cash* exchanged.

The first violates the informational purpose of valuation. It denies the problem of this study by reverting to the completed exchange method of valuation. Only if no information is desired prior to the completion of the exchange is this method of valuation acceptable.[4]

---

4. It often appears that the exchange element is more basic to the tradition than cash. Several years ago a debate occurred which evidences the oneness of the rule. Some accountants interpreted "original" in "original cost" as "aboriginal." They questioned the propriety of valuing assets at the amount of cash given in exchange, because this cash had been received from sales, and thus, was more than the aboriginal cost.
For example.
1. Start with $10.00.
2. Buy merchandise for $10 and value it at $10.
3. Sell merchandise for $15.
4. Use the $15 to buy equipment.
If the equipment is valued at $15, the cost rule is violated, because the aboriginal cost was $10. Finney and Miller refer to this problem when they note that cash and receivables are not valued at cost. (*Intermediate*, p. 120.)
The proponents lost, but vestiges of this argument still creep in when there are trade-ins. Some still argue that an asset acquired on a trade-in should be valued at the original unexpired cost of the asset given up. However, most accountants now agree that the "fair market value" of the asset is the proper basis for valuation. Some still quarrel over whether the fair market value should be of the received asset or the one given up.
The cash-basis of valuation has been violated in this specific instance, and market price became the final arbiter. However, the exchange requirement is still stubbornly defended. A gain on this type of exchange is considered income, even though the assets are in the same form; but increments in market value without an exchange are seldom recorded, and if they are recorded, they are not considered income.
A violation of both the cash and exchange requirements occurs when an asset is

The second element is a reversion to the much maligned "cash basis of accounting." If the rule were strictly applied, income would simply be the difference between the receipts and disbursements of cash. It is not strictly applied, however, and the result is the celebrated "accrual-basis of accounting."

Generally speaking, the accrual-basis provides for specified exceptions to the cash-basis. The exceptions are:

1. Value increments may be recorded by the receipt of near-cash or occasionally by cash-equivalents of one of the assets involved in the exchange.
2. Value decrements may be recorded by adherence to individually specified conservative, causal, and convenient rules.

As we see it, this is but one minuscule step removed from the cash-basis. Certainly value increments are very close to the cash-basis. Value seldom "accrues" (accumulates) in accounting; it almost always "occurs" by the receipt of cash or contractual obligations for cash. On the decrement side, there are methods of amortization (averaging the cash outlay over time or events) but it seems odd to speak of "decrements accumulating." Thus, we think "accrual-basis" is misleading. Perhaps "modified cash-basis" or "exchange-amortization-basis" would be more descriptive.

Whatever the title, we have described the fundamental rule of valuation by combining several lesser rules and their exceptions. Applying it to our model the single rule is:[5]

> The value of wheat shall be set equal to the amount of cash given in exchange. Cash shall be valued at unity.

There are several difficulties with this rule when compared to the information-measurement criteria. First, the rule does not supply in-

---

donated or when there is "discovery (of minerals) value." Without the exchange, however, the value increment is not considered to be income. Therefore, it appears that the exchange requirement is the more fundamental one in valuation for income purposes.

5. We simplify by neglecting to state the variations, such as market when lower than cost, or the problems of allocation when a portion is sold. These problems are discussed *infra*.

formation at a point in time. If the trader holds all wheat which cost him $X, then each message (report) will contain "Wheat $X." The most information that is given by the repeated transmission of this message is that no further exchanges have been made. Thus, we would call all such transmissions, save the first, "superfluous." Also this reverts to the completed exchange basis of measurement. We postulated that the reason for the measurement and transmissions was that information was desired at a point in time, regardless of the state of the exchange. This rule avoids the measurement problem by waiting until the exchange is complete, but it does so at the expense of not providing information at the desired point in time. Second, this is an event measurement, and therefore it prevents temporal comparisons. We argued that income was a concept bounded by time, not events, and therefore the event measurement avoids the income question. We agreed that event comparisons were useful in many circumstances, but in the case at hand we think they are apt to be more misleading than useful. Note that one cannot make any of the four comparisons listed above (p. 92), and therefore the informational content due to the greater number of comparisons is missing.[6] Third, one wonders what dimension is being measured here, especially in reference to the problem of additivity. Suppose at t_1 the trader held M_1 amount of money and purchased W_1 quantity of wheat for ΔM. Then his balance

---

6. The last point is supported by many accountants. They often complain that the "true" income and wealth of a firm can be measured only after the firm is liquidated, i.e. only after all of the assets are converted into cash. This means, in our terms, only when all exchanges are complete (and no further exchanges will be made) and when all of the assets are homogeneous in the form of cash. This means that all of the assets had to be homogeneous in the form of cash at the inception in order to take the difference. That is, the firm must start with all cash in order to be able to measure its income at liquidation. This excludes the possibility of measuring the true income for all those partnerships in which the assets are required to be valued at "fair market" upon formation. But it also means that one cannot compare two firms until *both* have been liquidated. That is, under the Accounting Tradition the conditions necessary to compare the wealth of a given firm at two points in time (and therefore measure its income) or compare the wealth and/or income of two different firms is that the assets be homogeneous in the form of cash—that is, that the firms be liquidated. After the firm has been liquidated, no decisions about that firm are required, because it no longer exists. Thus, the only comparisons permitted by the Accounting Tradition are ones that are not needed.

sheet would show "Cash $M_1 - \Delta M$," "Wheat ΔM," and "Total Assets $M_1 - \Delta M + \Delta M$." The money held has a clear empirical meaning. By reference to current prices one can calculate his command over goods. The valuation of the wheat may also be explained empirically as the money sacrificed in order to obtain wheat; i.e., it is sound history. However, the best that can be said about the total asset figure is that it is the amount of money that the trader would have had if he had not purchased the wheat. Exactly what relevance that figure has to any problematic situation or what alternatives it delineates or what dimension it measures is not known to the author. Fourth, the historical cost "dimension" is not familiar to the general population. Accounting textbooks point out that people often think of balance sheets as statements of value instead of unexpired costs. In cases where accounting reports are subject to "dangerous misinterpretation," as Butters (p. 136) has explained, "the alternatives are to change present accounting practices or to change the public . . . ." We think that the former is infinitely more feasible than the latter.

Further Problems of the Cost-Realization Rule

The above description of the cost rule is incomplete. In most cases "assets" are purchased as a whole, but they are sold or written off in pieces. These pieces are referred to as "service potentials" or "units of capacity" or "benefits." Thus, each asset is thought to be composed of a certain *quantity* of some more elementary unit. This quantity is the basic unit of account. As already explained, the event of valuation is the *exchange* in which one quantity is received and another sacrificed. Thus, two quantities with opposite signs may be said to be *related* by exchange.

$$\Delta^+ q_{ij} \;\circledR\; \Delta^- q_{kj} \qquad\qquad (\text{eq. XI-1})$$

where Δq_{ij} is the change in the ith quantity class at time j.

One of these quantities is independently valued, and the valuation coefficient for the other quantity is calculated.

$$p_{ij} = \frac{-\Delta^- q_{kj}}{\Delta^+ q_{ij}} \qquad\qquad (\text{eq. XI-2})$$

where p_{ij} is the valuation coefficient that is "attached" to each unit of the ith quantity and the kth quantity is independently valued at unity. This then is the cost rule, because the acquired quantity's value is set equal to the independently determined value of the sacrificed quantity.

$$p_{ij}\Delta^+q_{ij} + \Delta^-q_{kj} = 0 \qquad\qquad (\text{eq. XI-3})$$

The realization rule is simply equation XI-3, with the signs reversed. In that case a quantity of the kth class is received, and a quantity of the ith class is sacrificed. The receipt is called "revenues," and the problem is to "match" the previously incurred cost against those revenues. Thus,

$$\Delta^+q_{km} + p_{ij}\Delta^-q_{im} = \pi \qquad\qquad (\text{eq. XI-4})$$

where Δ^-q_{im} is the quantity sacrificed, Δ^+q_{km} is the quantity received *for* Δ^-q_{im}, and π is the gain or loss on the exchange.

In concept this is quite simple. It may be alternatively formulated as follows: Let p be the purchase price, p′ be sales price, and q be the quantity sold. Then p′q is the revenues—cash or near-cash acquired—and pq is the expense—cash or near-cash previously sacrificed—and p is "matched" against p′ by noting the occurrence of q in both expressions, i.e. one can factor out the q and restate the equation as $(p'-p)q = \pi$. The sale of q *caused* the revenues p′q; and p was previously "attached" to q, so that the cost to be matched is pq. Any quantity that remains unsold is expected to cause future revenues, and thus the *quantity* unsold (or otherwise undisposed of) is classified as an asset and valued with the same previously attached p.

This process is repeated for all other quantities. The only variant is in the *kind* of quantities. For example, for some depreciable assets the quantity is "years of service life," and the passing of one year results in that quantity being matched against the revenues of that year, and the matched quantity is valued on the basis of a previously attached valuation coefficient calculated as in equation XI-2. Other depreciable assets are conceived of as a certain quantity of outputs; and as the outputs occur, the cost is matched. Sometimes sacrifices are made for which there is no discernible physical quantity, and the general conception of "future benefits" is utilized as the quantity in order to match the costs and revenues.

The causality basis of the matching process is indicated by the language used. Costs are said to "produce" or "generate" revenues, for example. The distinction between "expenses" and "assets" is that expenses are costs that have produced revenues; and assets are costs that are expected to produce revenues. "Losses" are costs that have not caused revenues and that are not expected to cause revenues.

The above generalization of the valuation procedure used in accounting permits us to focus on the empirical operations and decisions of the accountant.

1. The determination of which quantities are related.
2. The decision as to which kind of quantity each asset is composed of.
3. The decision as to which quantity is to be valued independently.
4. The determination of the numerosity of the quantity in any particular asset.

Each of these presents some difficulty. The decision as to which kind of quantity is important because interpractitioner differences in selection are likely to result in differences in cost values assigned to otherwise identical assets. Depreciation based on output or service life is an example of using two different kinds of quantities for the same asset and getting different cost values as a result. In the trader model this is unimportant, because we have postulated the kind of quantities to be used.

The decision as to which quantity is to be valued independently is also solved in the trader model. However, it is not always clear in the Accounting Tradition. Lifo proponents often argue that the value of the dollars received depends upon the inventory units that those dollars can purchase. This is the same confusion as Boulding's apparent paradox discussed *supra* (p. 199).

A consideration of the problems presented by decision three is illuminating, although not directly relevant to the trader model. Note that in a complex firm there are a large number of different accounts or quantity classes. It may be observed that the accountant has different preferences in valuing these quantity classes independently. Cash is clearly at the top of this preference list. Accounts Receivable is also high on the list, but it is dominated by cash in the sense that Accounts Receivable is valued independently at the event of the exchange of inventory for the receivable; but cash is valued independently at the event of the exchange of cash for the receivable (collection). That is, cash is valued independently at the collection regardless of the previous valuation of the receivable. In fact, the account receivable is merely counterfactual cash (that is, the amount of cash that would have been received if the sale had been for cash), or, as Paton and Littleton say, it is the "cash-equivalent." In general, "monetary" assets and liabilities are valued independently if the exchange is between a monetary and a nonmonetary account class.[7] But there are further subdivisions within both the monetary and nonmonetary classes.

Thus, we perceive that there is a tacit valuation preference array that the accountant uses to make the decision as to which quantity is to be valued independently. This array probably follows very closely the liquidity or the nearness-to-cash of the assets or liabilities, which is roughly the way that the accounts are arranged on the balance sheet. The distinction between a "purchase" and a "sale," then, is the relative placement of the quantity classes on the preference array. This distinction is important because, as we noted above, income is recognized at sale but not at purchase.

That this rule is not completely unambiguous is evidenced by the conflicting analyses of barter transactions. Paton and Littleton (pp. 27-28) set forth the rule that the sacrificed item is to be valued independently in such cases, but they provide for valuing the acquired item independently when it is too difficult to value the sacrificed one. Simons and Karrenbrock (p. 443 in the 1958 edition), on the other hand, state that the acquired asset should be recorded at its market value. Bulletin 43 (p. 38) supports our valuation preference array hypothesis by allowing for the valuation of whichever item "is the more clearly evident." Moonitz and Jordan (p. 361) note that there are arguments against valuing *either* independently. This procedure would assign a value to the acquired item equal to the value of the sacrificed item; and the value of the sacrificed item would have been previously valued, presumably when cash was sacrificed for it. They

7. When bonds are issued for cash, the Bonds Payable account is set equal to the net cash proceeds; but when bonds are issued for real property, the value of the real property is set equal to the independently determined value of the bonds.

reject this argument and propose that the barter transaction be treated as if a sale for cash had been made and then the cash had been used to purchase the new item.

Although the question of *which* item is to be independently valued is important, it is more germane to this study to note that it is now generally agreed that an independent valuation *is* to be made.

The accounting literature supports the idea that an independent valuation should be made at the event of a barter exchange, and the author has made a study which indicates that practitioners do in fact make such independent valuations. In that study a hypothetical problem was presented in which one firm exchanged cash for marketable securities and another firm exchanged cash for land. Then the two firms exchanged the marketable securities for the land after the market price of both had appreciated considerably. All respondents ($n=53$), save one, realized income on the exchange in *both* firms. The amounts varied, because some used the closing price of the security and others used the appraisal value of the land (which was less than the price of the securities). This does not square with our valuation preference array hypothesis, because marketable securities are surely more liquid than land. Also it does not square with our purchase-sale distinction, because income was recorded on the books of both firms and thus the transaction was viewed by the accountants as a sale (because income is realized only at sale) by both firms.

The important point is that the accountants refused to revalue the assets in question prior to the exchange. Reasons given were lack of objectivity, that the revenue was not realized, the historical cost rule, that market prices were not trustworthy in the absence of a transaction, and so forth. At the event of exchange, *all* of these objections were overcome, and the assets were valued at some version of present market price. Exactly how this barter exchange made the market prices trustworthy, objective, etc., is not clear to the author. Regardless of those considerations, we can conclude that the exchange element of valuation is a very important one. It is important enough to overcome the accountant's reluctance to independently value non-cash assets and important enough to at least partially overcome his conservatism.

We disagree with the exchange rule. We do not know why one

should value *only* at the event of an exchange or why an exchange, particularly barter, should be considered a "separation of income from capital" or a "realization of income" or "objective and verifiable," when an increment in market price is not considered to have any of these attributes. In a barter exchange, the only change is in the particular firm that holds the assets; and if the previous holder could not use current prices for all those reasons, then the present holder could not use current prices for the same reasons.

The empirical determination of which quantities are related presents some insuperable problems. In an imperfect market there are certain ancillary costs which are supposed to be attached to the quantities acquired, and the causal tracing of all those costs is impossible. Tracing is usually cut off on the basis of convenience. Many cost attachments are joint—either joint product or joint facility—and it is impossible in principle to make the causal tracings. More pertinent to the trader model is the matching problem—the determination of which quantities caused the revenue. Suppose that the trader purchased W_1 bushels at t_1 for price p_1 and W_2 bushels at t_2 for price p_2 ($p_1 \neq p_2$) and sold W_3 bushels ($W_3 < W_1$, $W_3 < W_2$) at t_3 for price p'. The revenue (cash acquired) is easily determined ($p'W_3$), but the cost is not. The observable phenomenon is that W_3 bushels have been sold, but it is impossible to determine which valuation coefficient should be attached to W_3. Some income possibilities are:

$$(p'W_3) - (p_2W_3) = \pi_1 \quad \text{(lifo)}$$
$$(p'W_3) - (p_1W_3) = \pi_2 \quad \text{(fifo)}$$
$$(p'W_3) - \frac{p_1W_1 + p_2W_2}{W_1 + W_2} W_3 = \pi_3 \quad \text{(weighted average)}$$

The problem of relation is important, because $\pi_1 \neq \pi_2$, $\pi_1 \neq \pi_3$, and $\pi_2 \neq \pi_3$. Since all three methods are acceptable, three different accountants might use different methods in accounting for the trader; and therefore there could be different values describing the same phenomenon. Thus, it is possible for the different values to reflect differences in the activities of the firm *or* different methods of measurement or both. This ambiguity renders the figures useless.[8]

8. We have not included the specific identification method in the possibilities. Some accountants argue that the above problem occurs only when the goods are

We raised the problem of additivity among commodity classes above, and this ambiguity intensifies that problem, as well as creating problems of additivity within the commodity class.

Manipulation of the numbers representing bushels is an intuitively obvious example of a case where additivity has empirical meaning. $W_1+W_2-W_3$ would yield a result that we would be so confident of that if the empirical count were different, we would look for pilferage, leakage, or errors in computation. It is impossible to prove that the summation of different valuation coefficients weighted by those bushels is completely devoid of empirical meaning. The author views this procedure in the same light as the forest ranger example presented in chapter 8 (pp. 181-82). The valuation coefficients are market prices at different past dates, which are multiplied by a present quantity. Thus, the requirement of temporal homogeneity is not met, and the resulting sum is an enigma. Accountants sometimes argue that the figures should be adjusted by price indices, because the "dollars are of different values" and therefore not additive. Theirs is the price-level problem; but we have assumed a stable price-level and are still puzzled by the empirical meaning of the described sum.

We granted above that the money sacrificed for a given quantity of wheat was sound history. Once apportioned, however, we have mixed the history of sacrifices with the history of the particular method selected by the accountant. The resulting record is equally as much a history of the accountant's selection process as it is a history of money sacrificed. We have postulated that our receivers are sometimes interested in the history of the firm, but not in the history of

---

fungible, because otherwise one can determine the "actual" cost by specifically identifying which units were sold. Three things may be said in reply:

1. The number of possible values increases with specific identification. In this case the possible values are p_2W_3, $p_1 + p_2(W_3-1)$, $2p_1 + p_2(W_3-2)$, $3p_1 + p_2(W_3-3)$, . . . , $p_1(W_3-3) + 3p_2$, $p_1(W_3-2) + 2p_2$, $p_1(W_3-1) + p_2$, $p_1 W_3$.

2. Which units are sold, and therefore which of the possible values in the preceding paragraph, may be determined by the whim of the selector, by random selection, or by deliberately establishing a pattern.

3. It doesn't make any difference which units are sold. The alternatives, decisions, and position of the trader are the same regardless of whether all were sold from W_1 or W_2.

accounting; and therefore we would classify the mixed history as irrelevant.

We granted above that the total asset figure could be characterized as the amount of money that the trader would have had if he had not purchased wheat. Now that the wheat value has been apportioned, we cannot describe the total asset figure at all.

Since such sums have been reported for many years, we would assume that they have meaning to those people who receive them and to those people who report them. We cannot prove that they are devoid of meaning. However, we can report that we have searched diligently for that meaning and have failed to find it.

The last problem—determining the numerosity of the quantity—is more acute in cases of depreciable or intangible assets where the quantity lies in the future. In the trader model we have assumed away the difficulties of determining the quantity of bushels and dollars. In the Accounting Tradition, however, there is a more fundamental quantity, viz. service potentials or future benefits, and the unit "bushel" may be thought of as a collection of those fundamental units.

Paton and Littleton, Vatter, and others have emphasized the significance of these fundamental units and pointed out that money and prices are only convenient means of expressing those units. Exactly what the units are or how they are determined is not specified. We suspect that those units are ultimately nothing more than the ability to produce revenue or to produce a good that can be used to produce revenue. It is easy to conceive of a painting containing service potential or potential utility and to conceive of a person garnering those services or utils by viewing the painting. For a firm, however, it is more likely that the purpose of the objects is to produce revenues. That is to say, to command money which can be used to command other goods. Bulletin 43 (pp. 30-31) explains that a departure from cost is required when the utility of the goods held in inventory has diminished and that "the measurement of such losses is accomplished by applying the rule of pricing inventories at *cost or market, whichever is lower*." Since inventories are held for sale, it would appear that the utility of inventories is simply their ability to command money. There is further evidence of this view when Bulletin 43 (p. 32) says,

"When no loss of income [revenue?] is expected to take place as a result of a reduction of cost prices," then no adjustment is required. Obviously the authors of Bulletin 43 were thinking of prospective revenue or income, but preferred to call it "utility."

Some accountants argue that losses must be "realized" in the same way that revenues are realized—only at the event of sale.[9] However, this view has not been generally accepted, and we suspect that the proponents would abandon the view if the goods were worthless, i.e. had a zero current price. In that case there is no possibility of a sale and therefore no possibility of "realizing" the loss. Thus, one would be forced to carry worthless assets on his books forever—which consequent is absurd.

We agree with the lower-of-cost-or-market rule. We agree that the realization requirement results in absurdity when the market is below cost, but we consider it *in pari delicto* when the market is above cost.

SUMMARY

Accounting is a discipline without any cohesive, unified theory of valuation. The existing valuation methods vary widely for a wide variety of reasons. The method used is generally called "historical cost," which implies that if A is sacrificed for B, then the value of A is determined and the value of B is set equal and held constant. However, this is an inadequate explication because the items acquired are usually conceived of as being separable quantities. The total quantity is set equal to the independently valued monetary sacrifice, and a per-unit valuation coefficient is calculated. It is the valuation coefficient that is held constant, and the total value of the item varies as the quantity varies. That is, cost-value is a product of a valuation coefficient and a quantity. The valuation coefficient is a constant, and the quantity is a variable. The valuation coefficient is said to "attach" to each unit and to remain an "asset" or "unexpired cost" so long as the unit remains in existence. The valuation coefficient is said to be "matched" against revenues (independently valued monetary acquisition) whenever the unit is sacrificed or otherwise goes out of existence. This procedure is subject to several lines of criticism.

9. For an excellent discussion of this point, see Devine.

First, there is the question of the relevance of the figures generated by this procedure. In our review of the problematic situations and the decision theories applicable to those situations we failed to come across a single instance where the historical cost figures were specified by an explicit decision theory. Thus, until the decision theory which specifies historical cost is made known to us, we must conclude that historical costs are irrelevant and therefore not informative.

Second, although we were able to describe the method of calculation in rather general terms, we failed to find any empirical meaning for the described sums and differences. Of course one is free to calculate any statistic that he desires, and we must presume that the historical-cost figures have empirical meaning to those who calculate them. Our failure to find the empirical meaning is not proof that it does not exist, but it does indicate that if accountants are attempting to communicate information, then it is their duty to explain the empirical meaning of their figures.

Third, accounting reports are issued periodically, and therefore we would assume that accountants agree that income and wealth should be measured at a point in time. Yet they in fact measure at the event of exchange. We argued that periodic reports of event measurements were in error by the change, if any, that has occurred between the time of the event and the time of the report.

Fourth, it is difficult to know exactly what attribute the Accounting Tradition is attempting to measure. The fundamental unit of measure is variously described as "future benefits," "service potentials," and "utility." In respect to inventories this fundamental unit seems to reduce to dollars that will be received when the inventory items are sold, i.e. a future sales price. Yet they use a past purchase price to value the inventory items unless the present price is less than the past price. Neither the logical nor the empirical connection of a past price to a future price is clear to us, especially when the past price is used to calculate a cost-value which is reported on a current or present financial statement.

Fifth, there are serious operational difficulties in making the desired measurements. This is due in part to the fact that the fundamental unit to be measured has not been precisely defined. If one does not have a precise conception of a service potential, it is difficult to prescribe an operation which will allow it to be measured. If the conception reduces to a future sales price, or even future benefits, then one must predict that magnitude; it is impossible in principle to measure a magnitude that lies in the future. An additional operational difficulty stems from the necessity to determine which particular quantities are related. We examined the relational problem in respect to inventories and found several different inventory conventions that are in general use. The existence of the different conventions indicates that the Accounting Tradition has been unable to solve the problem of determining which quantities are related. We believe that this problem reduces to a joint cost allocation and therefore is in principle unresolvable.

Sixth, the existence of the different conventions for relating the quantities raises some questions about the meaning of the resultant figures. Since any of these conventions may be used, there are several different figures which may be generated to describe the same phenomena. In such cases it is impossible for the receiver to know whether the differences in the figures are a result of differences in the conventions used or differences in the underlying phenomena or both. It is impossible to adjust the figures to the same convention from the information given. This unadjustable ambiguity renders the figures useless for discriminating changes in the underlying phenomena.

Seventh, the unexpired cost dimension is not familiar to the receivers of the reports. That accountants are aware of this fact is indicated by their complaint that the receivers erroneously think of the balance sheet as a statement of values. When such differences exist between the transmitter and receiver, the transmitter must choose between educating the receiver and changing his transmissions. In the case at hand we believe that the latter is both preferable and more feasible.

Finally, the method of valuation used in the Accounting Tradition can be criticized on grounds of verity. Previously we described a cost-value as the product of a valuation coefficient and a quantity, and we said that the cost-value varies as the quantity varies and that the valuation coefficient is held constant. This is not quite accurate. Two qualifications are needed: (1) Cost-values decrease with quantity decrements but do not normally increase with quantity increments. (2) The valuation coefficient can be recalculated or restated at a lower value but it cannot normally be recalculated or restated at a higher value. In general the effect of these two qualifications is to permit decrements and prohibit increments in cost-values. We believe that this asymmetrical rule of valuation is evidence for our hypothesis that the underlying rationale is the principle of conservatism.

Criticism of conservatism as a principle tends to take on a moral tone. Conservative accountants consider it a virtue; anticonservatives consider it unethical. We would like to avoid moral controversies. Perhaps Hill and Gordon (p. 170) hit on the explanation when they described conservatism as an "inborn tendency." We were not born with the tendency and, therefore, find ourselves in sharp disagreement with the principle.

In terms of measurement-information criteria it is clear that deliberate understatements are not veritable. This fact is indicated by the language used by those who have extolled the "conservative virtue" of creating "secret reserves." The process of concealing or secreting is antithetical to the notion of informing. Since conservatism conceals or secretes, it ought to be clear that a conservative measure yields at best imprecise information and at worst misinformation.

There is another interpretation of conservatism that has more justification than the one given above. If one is uncertain of the true measure but knows the range within which the true measure lies, then under some conditions it would be appropriate to report the lower end of that range. This seems to be the interpretation of those who say that the accountant is conservative because he wants to ensure that the true value is at least the amount he reports. This interpretation is difficult to assess, because there seems to be a shift in the conception of the *attribute* to be measured when this statement is made. On most occasions it is said that the objective of the Accounting Tradition is to measure "costs" not "values." That is, costs are contrasted with values, and the attribute sought is the cost. But whenever one wants to ensure that the true value is no less than the reported figure, then the attribute sought is the "value," not the "cost." That is, one must know the range within which the true value falls before he can know that any particular figure is no greater than the true value. Now if one is uncertain of the true value and wants to report the lower end of the possible range of *values*, or if one is uncertain of the true cost and wants to report the lower end of the possible range of *costs,* then we can see some justification; but to report the lower of cost or value is a mixture of two different kinds of attributes, and we see no justification for that procedure.

This shift and the ambiguity is illustrated by the discussion of the lower-of-cost-or-market rule: "Although the cost basis ordinarily achieves the objective of a proper matching of costs and revenues, under certain circumstances cost may not be the amount properly chargeable against the revenues of future periods." (Bulletin 43, p. 30.) We fail to understand how anything other than cost can be appropriate to the *objective* of properly matching *costs* and revenues. Thus, the fundamental attribute that is being sought is not cost. Instead it is some sort of value measure. Yet when that value measure is found to be above cost, then cost is reported; and when it is found to be below cost, then the value measure is reported. This is not a process of reporting the lower end of a range when one is uncertain of the true measure. Instead it is a process of creating a secret reserve when the value is *known* to be greater than the cost.

Given the development of accounting, it is easy to understand how the conservatism principle came into being. As we view it, the ethical considerations of the accountant led to a conservative stance and thence to the cost rule. However, the cost rule and its variants have now become ingrained habits of thought, and we have lost sight of the ethical considerations which gave birth to the rule. We believe that the cost rule is justified if and only if conservatism is justified. We have argued that the principle of conservatism violates the criterion of verity and therefore that the cost rule is not justified.

Several people have attempted to justify the cost rule without reference to conservatism. Those justifications will be examined in the next chapter.

XII

THE ACCOUNTING TRADITION (Continued)

In the previous chapter we formulated the principles and rules of valuation in the Accounting Tradition as we perceive them and critically examined our own formulation. Since there is a possibility of error in our perception and formulation, we now turn to a critical examination of selected arguments that have been advanced in support of the cost-realization rule. The bases for selection are two: (1) Since we have considered conservatism above, we have excluded arguments which are explicitly grounded on conservatism. (2) We have attempted to select arguments that have influenced accounting thought and practice, as is indicated either by the reputation of the authors and their works or by the pervasiveness of certain concepts which are not associated with any particular author or work.

ARGUMENTS FOR THE COST RULE

For our purposes it will be convenient to distinguish two broad categories of arguments for the cost rule. The distinguishing factor is the temporal location of the valuation; valuations are made at

1. the time of acquisition (initial valuation) and
2. times subsequent to acquisition (subsequent valuation).

Initial valuation is accomplished by setting the acquired asset equal to the cash (or cash equivalent) sacrificed, and with this we have no quarrel. We usually find ourselves in disagreement with the arguments; but since the conclusions are identical, we omit the criticism.[1]

Our quarrel is with subsequent valuation. Subsequent valuation at historical cost is a measure of a past sacrifice, which we think is irrelevant to the present valuation. We will analyze only those arguments that are most pertinent to this quarrel.

Finney's Argument

Finney begins his argument with reference to marketable securities and specifically raises the question of subsequent valuation in terms of "revenue realization." Essentially the question is "Should securities be valued at original cost or at present market price?" There are some accountants who would value at present market price but would not allow the value increment to affect income. Finney does not make the distinction. He is concerned with both valuation and income at the same time.

His argument has appeared in texts and learned journals. For ease of reference, we present it in its entirety with marginal indications of the progress of the argument.

(Question) Is unrealized appreciation revenue? Let us consider this question first with respect to marketable securities, as to which it is possible to make the strongest case for an affirmative answer.

(Example) If marketable securities were purchased for $50,000, were worth $60,000 at the end of the year of purchase, and were sold for $70,000 in the following year, was there a $20,000 profit in the second year or a $10,000 profit in each year? While it possibly may be said that $10,000 of the profit accrued each year, and while it certainly can be said that a $10,000 profit could have been realized the first year, it nevertheless is true that realization did not occur until the second year,

---

1. For a striking exception, cf. Bowers.

(Principle,   The requirements of the accounting principle relative to
  Premise)   revenue realization were not met during the first year
                  because, when the management elected not to sell at the
                  end of the first year but preferred to take the hazards of
(Conclu-   market fluctuation, there was no realization of profit nor
  sion)   any reasonable assurance that a profit would be realized.

                  If readily marketable securities cannot properly be valued
                  at a price in excess of cost, although a profit could be
                  immediately realized by a sale at the market price, the
                  valuation of inventories at market prices in excess of
(General-   cost is, under ordinary conditions, even less proper.
  ization)   (Finney, "Principles," pp. 365-66. The argument has
                  also been reprinted with minor changes in the texts.
                  See Finney and Miller, *Intermediate*, 5th ed., p. 176.)

In order to understand the argument we must reproduce the principle: "The governing accounting principle is: *Revenue* should not be regarded as *earned* until an asset increment has been *realized* or until its realization is reasonably assured." (Finney, "Principles," p. 364, italics added.)

Before we can utilize the principle, we need definitions for revenue, earned and realized. "*Revenue* consists of an *inflow of assets,* in the form of cash, receivables, or other property, *from customers and clients,* and is related to the *disposal of product* in the form of goods or to the *rendering of services.*" (Finney, "Principles," p. 363, italics added.) "Consists" and "related to" are not sharp words, but the meaning is clear:

Definition 1: Revenue is the receipt of cash or near-cash from sales.

"Realized," in the Fisher Tradition, is unequivocally the receipt of cash. However, when the cash basis of accounting was modified, the terms were retained and some confusion resulted. Finney says:

Realization of revenue does not necessarily require a collection in cash, since a valid receivable from a solvent debtor is an asset in as good standing as cash. The point of sale, therefore, is the step in the series of activities at which the revenue generally is regarded as realized. This point has been generally adopted because (1) it is the point at which a conversion takes place—an exchange of one asset for another—and conversion is regarded as evidence of realization; and (2) it is the point at which the amount of the revenue is objectively determinable from the sale price acceptable to both parties. (Finney, "Principles," p. 363.)

Realization is concerned with the occurrence of an act—a sale—and with the form of assets—cash or near-cash—that can be included as "realized." It is a trifle obscure in light of the phrase about "conversion *being evidence* of realization," because realization is defined as occurring at conversion. Nevertheless, in view of the rest of the literature and Finney's other works,[2] we can define it explicitly:

Definition 2. Realization occurs when cash or near-cash is received from sales.

"Earned" is simply a synonym for "realized." "As used in accounting, however, 'earned' and 'realized' are generally regarded as synonymous." (Finney, "Principles," p. 363.) Again, "generally regarded" prohibits sharpness, but in light of the above quotation the definition is clear:

Definition 3. "Earned" equals "realized."

Since one cannot have receipts from sales without the occurrence of a sale, it appears that revenue is the more general term. Substitution of "revenue" for "realization" in Definition 2 does not distort the meaning:

Definition 2: [Revenue] occurs when cash or near-cash is received from sales.

Revenue is defined as receipts-from-sales; therefore, revenue occurs when the sale is made. There can be no lapse of time as there might be on a cash basis, because receivables are included in the "realization." Thus, "revenue" and "realization" are synonyms, and "realized revenue" is redundant. Receipts-from-sales is the basic concept. At

2. The latest edition of the Finney and Miller introductory book answers the question in slightly more direct fashion: "When is revenue earned? Revenue is earned when goods are disposed of or when services are rendered. A transfer or exchange occurs. The business gives up goods or renders services and acquires other assets in exchange. There is a performance accompanied by a concurrent acquisition of an asset." (Finney and Miller, *Introductory*, 6th ed, p. 241.) As we note in the text, Finney equates earnings with realization.

the very most, the distinction is that realization refers to the *timing* of the receipt, while revenue refers to the receipt (inflow) per se. With very little, if any, distortion, the general definition may be stated as:

> Receipts-from-sales = revenue
> = realization
> = earnings
> = realized revenue
> = earned revenue

By making the substitutions in brackets we can now restate and understand the governing principle:

> [Receipts-from-sales] should not be regarded as [receipts-from-sales] until an asset increment has been [received-from-sales] or until its [receipt-from-sales] is reasonably assured.

A "principle" of this kind needs no commentary. We can now restate Finney's argument.

(Question) Is [not-receipts-from-sales] [receipts-from-sales]? . . .

(Example) . . . While it possibly may be said that $10,000 of the profit accrued each year, and while it certainly can be said that a $10,000 profit could have been [received-from-sales] the first year, it nevertheless is true that [receipts-from-sales] did not occur until the second year.

(Principle, Premise) The requirements of the accounting principle relative to [receipts-from-sales] [receipts-from-sales] were not met during the first year because, when the management elected not to sell at the end of the first year but preferred to take the hazards of market fluctuation, there (Conclusion) was no [receipts-from-sales] nor any reasonable assurance that a profit would be [received-from-sales]. . . .

No one would deny that "realization did not occur." By assumption, no sale was made and by definition, realization occurs at sale. His conclusion is of the same order. In effect he says "when management elected not to sell there was no sale," i.e. "when there was no sale there was no sale." A more exquisite example of *petitio principii* is impossible to imagine. Finney made many important contributions to accounting. In this case, however, it appears that he was seduced by his own words.

Two minor points remain. First, the tense of the last statement is important. It is said there was no "reasonable assurance that a profit *would be* realized." Finney is concerned with the future, with the ultimate profit to be realized from sale, not with the measurement of past events. He says "it certainly can be said that a $10,000 profit *could have been* realized." He does not deny that he could measure the amount that could have been realized, but he refuses to do so because that may not be the amount that will ultimately be realized. That is, the fact that the future price is unknown leads him to reject a known present price. We do not follow this reasoning, and in addition we do not understand how it leads to the acceptance of a past price.

Second, the word "certainly" implies *sureness of the amount* that "could have been realized." Could this be interpreted as admission of an objective measurement prior to sale? His second justification of realization is that the sale "is the point at which the amount . . . *is* objectively determinable . . . ," not that it is *more* objective; yet he seems to imply that there may be other points when the amount is objective. Both of these points will come up again in the subsequent sections of this chapter.

Finney's argument must be rejected as circular, repetitious, and ambiguous. Many explanations for this circularity could be advanced, but in light of the report that over a million copies of his work have been sold to a rather conservative audience, we prefer the hypothesis of a tacit assumption of conservatism.

May's Assumption and Argument

May's argument is presented in an AICPA research study, because it is "pertinent for the light it throws on the reasoning behind this guide [realization convention]." (Sprouse and Moonitz, p. 13.) We consider it for the same reason.

> Manifestly, when a laborious process of manufacture and sale culminates in the delivery of the product at a profit, that profit is not attributable, except conventionally, to the moment when the sale or delivery occurred. The accounting convention which makes such an attribution is justified only by its demonstrated practical utility.

It is instructive to consider how it happens that a rule which is violative of fact produces results that are practically useful and reliable. The explanation is that in the normal business there are at any one moment transactions at every stage of the production of profit, from beginning to end. *If the distribution* were exactly uniform, an allocation of income according to the proportion of completion of each unit would *produce the same result* as the attribution of the entire profit to a single stage. (May, p. 30, italics added.)

The general thesis is correct, under the assumption given. If a firm engages in a repetitive process of purchasing and selling at constant prices in constant quantities with constant time lapses, the recognition of income at sale will yield a valid figure. More precisely, it will yield a constant income figure for all temporal instants except the first and the last.

If we take May's assumption of exact uniformity and assign t_0 to the instant of the first purchase (at the inception of the business), which is to be sold at t_1, and another purchase at t_1, to be sold at t_2, etc., and the last sale (at the cessation of the business), at t_n, we can represent the transactions in full as in Figure XII-1. At t_0 a product is acquired which cost, say, \$100; and it is sold for, say, \$125 at t_1. Another product is purchased at t_1 for \$100 and sold at t_2 for \$125; and so on, until the firm makes its final sale at t_n and closes down.

The accounting rules require that the cost of the merchandise be deferred until sold, at which time the cost expires and is matched against the revenue. There is an asset of \$100 from t_0 to t_n. The first revenue occurs at t_1 and the asset acquired at t_0 then becomes an expense. Revenue remains constant from t_1 to t_n at \$125, and expenses remain constant at \$100, and thus there is a profit of \$25 per instant. In short, the accountant shifts the purchase curve one instant to the right and changes its name.

Under these assumptions, the virtues ascribed to the rule are perfectly correct. As May pointed out, the rule would produce the same result as an allocation according to the "proportion of completion." We agree. Our criticism is that he did not go far enough. Precisely the same result would be achieved by recognizing income on the cash basis, the sale basis, the purchase basis, or more simply by recognizing it on Tuesdays, equinoxes, or phases of the moon. Except for the first and last instants, *any* temporally uniform basis would produce the same result if the distribution were exactly uniform. Thus, we could ask what is special about the sale basis that would cause us to select it as the only point for revaluations. Unfortunately, May does

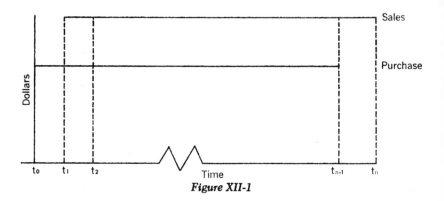

Figure XII-1

not address this question. His argument for a sale basis of recognition is equally applicable to all other temporally uniform bases.

May goes on to say that the realization convention should be violated when the stable-firm assumptions are not met, and he gives construction contracts as an example. With this we can agree, but note that the assumption requires constant prices and constant quantities at all instants in time. Since these requirements are seldom, if ever,

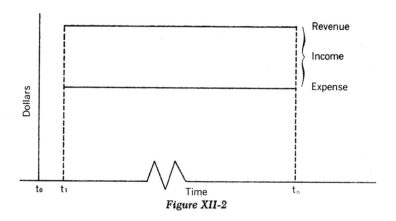

Figure XII-2

met, we could conclude that the realization convention should be violated in almost all valuation situations.

May's argument is enlightening, because the assumptions are made explicit. As far as we know, this is the only place where an accountant has explicitly stated these assumptions in defense of the cost-realization rule, although other authors have claimed that the stationary state is a necessary condition for validity. It is tempting to speculate about the relationship of the notions of the stable firm and the stationary state to the notion of the going concern. Some of the arguments for going-concern values seem implicitly to assume the stable firm, and it may be that the two assumptions are identical. In addition, the argument is enlightening because it requires a future. The purchased good has a value because it *will* be *sold* in the succeeding time period. However, the fact that the good has a value does not necessarily lead to a cost valuation. Instead, the argument seems to turn on convenience and conservatism. It is likely that the convenient-conservative practice existed and that May hit upon the stable-firm assumption as a means of justifying the practice. Other observations by May lend some credence to this view; for example, "To me, conservatism is still the first virtue of accounting. . . ." (May, p. 44.)

Paton and Littleton

About thirty years ago the American Accounting Association became increasingly disturbed about the lack of theory in accounting. It formed committees and study groups in order to remedy the deficiency and "to bring order out of this chaos of conflicting ideas and practices." (Paton and Littleton, p. vi.) The result of this concern was the publication of *An Introduction to Corporate Accounting Standards*, which, it was hoped, "would be one of the really significant contributions to accounting literature" (p. vi). If acceptance, use, and citation are the criteria, their hopes were realized. *Standards* has had a tremendous influence on accounting thought and has since become a classic. It has been accurately described as the "accountants' theoretical bible." For this reason, we feel obliged to analyze the authors' argument for the cost rule.

Our consideration of *Standards* is much more difficult than that of either Finney or May, because we are unable to locate a concise valuation argument that we could analyze. The discussion is somewhat diffuse, and the reader will have to depend upon our outline of the argument instead of a complete direct quotation. That is the source of our first criticism. One would hope that such a basic treatise would present a rather full argument for the endorsed valuation method. Unfortunately this is not the case; its lack is a major defect in an otherwise noble effort.

Paton and Littleton's approach is to derive "standards" (norms for behavior)[3] from "concepts."

> The circumstances surrounding the use of accounting clearly indicate the need for accounting standards. But such standards cannot be determined by an appeal to authority or to common opinion. The doctrines supported by writers and the practices accepted by professional accountants need to be subjected to analysis and coordination, with a consequent sifting out of inconsistencies and unessentials and an integration of essentials. The approach to standards should be by way of the broad function of accounting so that the standards formulated may be relevant thereto, and by way of the *basic concepts or assumptions* underlying accounting so that the standards formulated may be well grounded. To be relevant, a standard needs to be clearly related to the essential purposes of accounting; to be well grounded, a standard needs to be recognized as resting upon known and accepted assumptions.
>
> The *basic concepts, or assumptions,* here summarized constitute a suitable foundation for the discussion of accounting standards which follows. (Paton and Littleton, p. 7, italics added.)

Thus, the behavioral norms (standards) spring directly from the *assumptions.* There are several headings in the chapter, which presumably are a list of these basic assumptions. Under each of the headings there is some statement about cost, with no consideration of any competing method of valuation.

Under the caption "The Business Entity," they write: "With the entity concept as a basis, there is no difficulty in accepting the proposition that all costs legitimately incurred by the enterprise are properly

---

3. "Accounting standards therefore become responsible for furnishing guideposts to fair dealing in the midst of flexible rules and techniques" (p. 2).

included, in the first instance, in the total of assets. Thus organization expenditures, costs of raising capital, and related charges are elements of enterprise assets and capital." (Paton and Littleton, p. 9.) Their analysis is concerned with the segregation of business from personal affairs and with the *items* that can be properly included as assets. After they justify the inclusion of certain items, the term "cost" is used as a general description. They do not give reasons for their selection of cost as opposed to another value.

Under the caption "Continuity of Activity," they write:

> To the courts, concerned with the problem of determining immediate equities and restoring rights if damage has been suffered, assumptions with respect to future activity seem largely irrelevant. Hence the stress on "values" and "valuations" rather than on costs and the processes of accounting for costs. *The accountant,* on the other hand, deals primarily with the administration of the affairs of the continuing business institution and *accordingly emphasizes* the flow of costs and the interpretation of assets as balances of unamortized costs. (Paton and Littleton, pp. 10-11, italics added.)

They never say *why* the accountant "accordingly emphasizes the flow of *costs,*" simply that he does emphasize it. In fact, they say that "earning power—not price . . . is the significant basis of enterprise value." But they then switch to a discussion of income statements, and they define income as the resultant of the proper matching of *costs* and revenues.

Under the caption "Measured Consideration," they introduce the term "price-aggregate"; and then in the summary they conclude that "price-aggregates involved in the exchanges . . . constitute the basic subject matter of accounting." The word "consideration" is being used here in the same way as it is used in the law of contracts, i.e. it means the amount given in exchange. Thus "consideration" appears to be both one of the basic assumptions of accounting and "the basic subject matter of accounting." The next assumption is that "*costs* attach." Then, "*costs are considered* as measuring effort," under the caption "Efforts and Accomplishments." Under the caption "Verifiable, Objective Evidence," they *never mention* price-aggregates or cost (except the cost of obtaining evidence); yet in the summary, the reasons given for costs being the basic data is that they are "objective."

The full statement in the summary is: "In general the only definite facts available to represent exchange transactions objectively and to express them homogeneously are the price-aggregates involved in the exchanges; hence such data constitute the basic subject matter of accounting." (Paton and Littleton, p. 7.) Their concern is only with exchange transactions; purchase prices are proper for the valuation at time of exchange. But they do not say why they are proper for *subsequent* valuations. One could speculate about the reasons for their conclusions, but it would be preferable if they had stated them.

Perhaps the explanation for the use of cost without justification lies under the last heading. Under the caption "Assumptions," they write: "The fundamental concepts or propositions of accounting, like those of other fields, are in themselves assumptions in considerable measure or are predicated upon assumptions which are not subject to conclusive demonstration or proof." (Paton and Littleton, p. 21.) It appears that cost is one of the basic assumptions that is not subject to proof. Upon this basic assumption they build their superstructure of concepts.

Stout evidence that they assume the cost rule comes from the peculiar character of their methodology. Their approach is tersely stated in the preface. "We have attempted to *weave together* the fundamental ideas of accounting rather than to state standards as such." (Paton and Littleton, p. ix, italics added.) That is, they have taken the fundamental ideas that they have found in practice and woven them together.[4] One idea that they found was cost. "The assumption that recorded dollar cost continues to represent actual cost permeates accounting thought and practice, as it does the law." (Paton and Littleton, p. 23.) Upon finding this permeation, and without explicit critical analysis of the effects of using cost, they wove cost in as a basic assumption. It is hardly surprising, therefore, that the final chapter of *Standards* concludes that cost is the proper value for use in accounting.

It would be unfair to accuse them of circular reasoning. Their arguments turn out to be circular, but this is because of their methodology. They conceive their role to be one of rationalizing (making

4. In a later work, Littleton makes the process more explicit. He devotes an entire chapter to "Inductively Derived Principles," i.e. principles derived from observing the practices of accountants. (Littleton, *Structure*.)

rational) the existing practice of accounting. Thus, they are not guilty of circular reasoning, because they do not attempt to reason from premise *to* conclusion. They take the existing ideas and try to connect them; they are apologists in the strict sense of the term. As it turns out, they are apologists for a practice that is conservative.

The Liquidity Argument

A number of authors have argued that income should not be recognized until the asset that it represents is in liquid form, a form that is distributable, available to pay dividends. The most readily available (liquid) asset is cash, and this may be one of the reasons underlying the preoccupation with exchanges and money.

We do not know exactly why this position is taken. There has been little analysis in the literature since the *Eisner* v. *Macomber* case. The profession seems to have believed that the court settled the "separation" issue and that nothing was left to be said. Bowers has pointed out that this is based upon a misunderstanding of the court's decision.

> This decision seems to have been misunderstood by many practitioners and textbook writers. The court did not hold, as is often supposed, that a stock dividend in the same class of stock is not income. The earlier Macomber decision had merely denied that the receipt of common stock constituted effective realization if received as a dividend on common stock, that is, if it were merely capitalized surplus which was already a common stock equity. (Bowers, pp. 90-91.)

The court held that the receipt of stock did not effectively change the position of the recipient, since it was simply a different form of the equity that he had previously owned. Thus, it could be interpreted to mean that the "income" arose *before* the issuance of the stock dividend.

Because of this misunderstanding, the separation notion seems to be an *assumption* of accountants. This hypothesis is strengthened by the absence of analysis and the occasional explicit statement that it is an assumption. For example, Bowers discards the economic power theory on measurement grounds and then *assumes* availability: "If the economic-power theory has any conceptual superiority the possibility of applying new measuring devices should be studied more carefully. In the remainder of this article it will be *assumed* that the efficacy of any realization criterion lies in two essential attributes, first, measurability, and second, *availability."* (Bowers, pp. 91-92, italics added.)

The reason behind the assumption is that income is not available to pay dividends until it is in liquid form. Accountants "help" management by restricting income (receipts) to assets that are in distributable form. From this they assume that income cannot arise until the availabiliity criterion is met. The argument is confused and unsound.

First, there is the possibility of paying dividends in kind. This has been done, particularly during the Great Depression, but it is cumbersome. It is more convenient to pay cash dividends and, of course, this requires possession of cash before they can be paid. Usually a corporation has several sources of cash. It could, for example, pledge a non-liquid asset on a loan and obtain sufficient cash to pay a dividend.

Second and more important, however, is the confusion of two separate concepts. The possession of cash is a question of fact about the *form* of the assets at a given *moment in time*. The income question is concerned with *changes* in wealth *over time*. If the ability to pay cash dividends is the sole criterion, the income question becomes the ultimate in simplicity. Either the company has cash or it does not, and that is the end of the problem.

In their writings on earned surplus and retained income, accountants not only recognize, they emphasize, the difference between the two questions. They lament the confusion resulting from the equation of retained income to "ability to pay dividends." In an effort to prevent this confusion, they carefully point out that the final determinant of dividend payments is the *availability of cash,* not income.

Hill and Gordon (p. 51) present a fairly typical statement: "This order gives recognition to the fact that dividends are legally paid out of accumulated, rather than current, earnings. In this connection, it should be noted that while dividends are decalred 'out of earnings,' they are paid 'out of cash.' Consequently, insofar as past retained earnings have been invested in productive assets, they are not available for distribution." That is, dividends are distributions of income, but a *separate requirement* is that the assets must be in distributable form.

When the increment in assets that represents income is reinvested in productive facilities, it is no longer in distributable form, and this is exactly what has happened in the majority of corporations in America. It is very common to find the retained earnings figure to be several times the amount of cash, and it is not uncommon for it to be larger than total current assets. It is clear that such a situation prohibits the immediate payment of cash dividends equal to the retained income, and it is clear that accountants recognize this. Their cognizance somehow leads them to the conclusion that liquidity should be the deciding factor in the recognition of current income.

A consistent application of the liquidity argument would require that income could never be more than cash on hand. Thus, even if income were realized upon receipt, it would have to be "disrealized" upon the transformation of cash to a nonliquid asset. Since most corporations have an aversion to holding idle cash, income would be realized only momentarily.

For example, suppose that a trader started with $100 cash at t_1 and had $150 at t_2. This meets the distribution requirement, and the unequivocal amount of income is $50. If one instant later he makes a purchase, the distribution requirement is not met. Should we disrealize the income? If so, has he suffered a loss? Of course the accountant would not disrealize the income. He would value the purchased asset at $150 (cost), and the difference ($50) would remain in the retained income account.

If the price of this latter asset rose between the date of purchase and a reporting date, t_3, the report at t_3 will show a current income of zero, regardless of how high the price has gone, because the amount of the rise in price is not in distributable form. However, the t_3 report will show $50 of retained income which also is not in distributable form. The only difference between current and retained income is the period of time that is covered. Retained income includes all income from t_1 to t_3, and current income is only that income from t_2 to t_3. Thus, the inclusive income concept, the longer period income, does not meet the distribution requirement; but the requirement must be met before the income of the shorter period can be realized. Something is not quite right here.

If Devine's notion of administering working capital is taken literally, we can be more insistent that income be disrealized. He writes (p. 163, italics added): "For our present purposes the important aspect of income realization is that accountants usually *insist on helping* management administer its working capital by *recognizing income only when working capital is available to permit withdrawal* (if desired) without impairing the current position of the firm." The accountant restricts the amount of legally payable dividends by not recognizing income until it is liquid. Leaving aside the ethical question of the accountant taking it upon himself to do this, it is clear that the accountant could be of even more "help" if he disrealized income when there was no cash available. If he thinks that management needs help on such matters, it would be eminently reasonable to reduce income at least to the cash on hand; and perhaps he should even deduct planned disbursements.

We are not seriously suggesting such a procedure. Instead we are trying to emphasize that the problems should be separated by showing that the connection leads to absurdity. We think that the liquidity argument is nothing more than conservatism in evidence again.

The Going-Concern Concept

The going-concern assumption is common to almost all accountants. Textbooks seldom fail to list it as a "standard," "convention," etc. The following is fairly representative:

> When the future is unpredictable, one can only assume a continuity of existence and a business environment to follow that is similar to that in which the enterprise finds itself currently. The business unit, thus, is viewed as a "going concern" in the absence of evidence to the contrary. The continuity assumption is support for the preparation of a balance sheet that reports costs that are assignable to future activities rather than realizable values that would attach to properties in the event of voluntary liquidation or forced sale. (Simons and Karrenbrock, p. 48.)

The assertion that one "can *only* assume a continuity of existence" is absurd. One *can* assume anything he pleases about the future. There is a continuing philosophical debate about what one should (logically) assume, but we have found no philosopher who prescribes one assumption. Even the most future-minded of the philosophers insist on an evidentially (historically) based *projection*, not an assumption. The high rate of business failures would make it difficult to build an evidential case for a projection of continuity. No business has ever continued "indefinitely" into the future. All businesses, except those presently in existence, have ceased operations. Thus, it would seem more reasonable to assume cessation instead of continuity.

A case could be built for a mean life-expectancy of businesses, and this, like other statistical generalizations, would have some conceptual use. However, the generalization is about a universe, and to apply it blindly to any particular element in that universe would be a gross misuse of statistical projection. Surely no one would *assume* that a leukemia patient is expected to reach the mean life-expectancy of the population.

It is difficult to come to grips with this assumption. There seems to be little reasoning behind it and even less evidence. Another investigator had similar difficulties:

> *The continuity (or permanence) of the business enterprise.* Relatively little can be found explaining this concept other than (a) the postulate itself—that in the absence of actual evidence to the contrary, the prospective life of the enterprise may be deemed to be indefinitely long, and (2) [sic] the statement that it is an accepted postulate because continuity is typical of all entities. (Arthur Andersen & Co., p. 18.)

Our reading leads us to the same conclusion. We think that the reason why relatively little is said about it is because there is relatively little that can be said about it. We have a propensity to be suspicious of bald assertions, and therefore we reject postulate "a." A perusal of *Dun's Quarterly Failure Report* leads us to deny that "continuity is typical."

For purposes of discussion, however, let us make the continuity assumption and examine the valuation consequences.

Futurity is an overriding concern of the accountants. For example, we found it in both Finney and May, *supra*. This is apparently contradictory, because accounting is generally thought to be purely historical. Further, most accountants think of themselves as recorders of past facts. Yet the benefit theory, the matching process, attaching notions, etc., are clearly futurity concepts. A typical statement of the criterion for distinguishing between a positive and a zero carrying value follows:

> (1) . . . any acquisition cost or portion thereof which is productive of *current period revenue* is an *expense* [zero value], and
>
> (2) . . . any acquisition cost or portion thereof which is to be productive of *future revenue* is an *asset* [positive value]. (Hill and Gordon, p. 168.)

To follow these rules, the accountant assumes the continuity of the firm and then *projects* the benefits from each individual expenditure.

From this, he reasons that the proper value of these projected benefits is always equal to the historical cost. This reasoning normally takes the form of concentrating on the intended use and disallowing alternatives and/or sacrifices. The following is typical:

> Even when a disparity exists between old costs shown in the balance sheet and current values, the usefulness of the balance sheet is not destroyed, because in most cases the assets in question will have been acquired to be used and not to be resold. In such cases current values often are of slight significance to a "going concern" (an established business which is being conducted with the expectation of continuing indefinitely), because in most cases, assets with current values differing materially from cost would be such things as buildings, machinery, and equipment that were acquired to be used and not to be resold. (Finney and Miller, *Introductory*, p. 10.)

We fail to follow the reasoning that connects intended use and value. We can understand how the expected net revenue from an intended use affects the valuation decision of a given entrepreneur, but since those expectations are certain to change over time, the value would also change. Only if one assumed that the expectations remained constant could the intended use have a one-to-one relationship with value. If one takes this view, the intended use notion is additional evidence for the existence of the "stable-firm, stable-economy" assumption.

Moonitz and Jordan (I, 168) explicitly deny the stable economy assumption by introducing uncertainty, and they defend the use of cost as an initial value: "The choice of cost as the basis of *initial* valuation is, in most cases, reasonable." However, in a refreshingly candid statement, they point out that cost is a conservative value, initially, and, further, that the subsequent valuation at cost is solely on the basis of conservatism.

> In terms of the basic accounting problem, the cost rule is apparently conservative. Initial entry at cost results in no change in the difference between assets and liabilities; the acquisition of merchandise or of a fixed asset is treated as a "dead-level" transaction without effect on profits or proprietorship . . . . At dates subsequent to purchase, the reasons for adherence to cost differ. Here the *rationale is frankly on conservative grounds.* (Moonitz and Jordan, I, 168-69, italics added.)

We are in complete agreement with this assessment. Note, however, that their justifications of the cost rule are based on futurity considerations. The theoretical framework is very close to that of Fisher, although the conclusions vary.

Moonitz and Jordan's notion of value is grounded firmly in expected future receipts of *cash.* They make this explicit in several places: ". . . for only through a carefully prepared projection of *estimated* cash receipts and cash disbursements, based on past experience corrected for anticipated variations, can the value amounts assignable to any of the items that become reflected in the financial picture of an enterprise be even approximately determined." (Moonitz and Jordan, I, 126.) Moreover, and this is crucial, these cash receipts must come from the intended use of the assets. In neither of the cases— complete certainty and complete uncertainty—do they ever consider any alternative use of the assets; presumably because they think that only the intended use is relevant to valuation problems. But under complete uncertainty the cash receipts from the intended use are unknown, and therefore no valuation can be made.

> When the future is presumed to be completely unknown, our accounting must deal entirely with the past. We can prepare, for example, a schedule of cash received to date and from whom, and of cash paid out to date and for what. But we cannot prepare a balance sheet, because each asset in a balance sheet *represents something applicable to the future,* and each liability likewise indicates a commitment to do something in the future. (Moonitz and Jordan, I, 127, italics added.)

The underlying assumption must be of the "locked-in" variety, i.e. the firm is locked in the market with no alternatives. Otherwise the receipts from an immediate *sale* of the asset would yield some recordable value. We can think of no justification for the intended use valuation other than the locked-in assumption. If this be the authors' assumption, we are basically in agreement with the conclusions, i.e. zero value. However, we do not see why the locked-in assumption should be made. (See pp. 219-22 *supra* for a discussion of the locked-in assumption.)

Because of this futurity notion, most accountants claim that income cannot be measured until the enterprise ceases operations. Robnett, Hill, and Beckett describe this as an "inherent limitation" in accounting.

> *Business earnings are fundamentally indeterminate short of the total life of the business venture.* Any interim calculation of earnings is, therefore, an estimate. . . . In the first place, potential difficulty stems from the necessity, noted earlier in this chapter, for forecasting the future in order to interpret the past. *Underlying all interim valuation estimates is the general assumption that the business unit will continue as a going concern,* i.e., that it will function in the future in much the same manner as it has in the past. (Robnett, Hill, and Beckett, pp. 509-10.)

Note the odd twist in the juxtaposition of the emphasized statements. All valuations, at all instants in time, are made on the basis of the going-concern assumption. This would include the "last" valuation, when the business has ceased operations. Thus, the earnings are *always* indeterminate. Of course this is not their intent. They mean that income is indeterminate until all assets are converted into cash. At that time one can take the difference in the beginning and ending cash magnitudes and determine the income finally and unequivocally.

This again points up the accountant's preoccupation with cash. He conceives income almost exclusively in terms of cash receipts and disbursements, but facing uncertainty, he cannot forecast the cash movements and, therefore, denies his ability to measure income. This is an uncomfortable position. He claims to measure income on the accrual basis, but conceives of it on the cash basis, and then denies that he can measure it. It is patently impossible to *measure* the future, and we could sympathize with the accountant's dilemma if it were not for the fact that it is self-imposed.

We do not understand the going-concern assumption. First, we do not know why the assumption is made, and second, we do not understand how it leads to the cost rule. The assumption seems to have sprung from Dicksee's consideration of parliamentary companies (public utilities) which were *required* to continue operations. Thus, the intended use of the asset was the only source of receipts, and price fluctuations were irrelevant except at replacement. However, Dicksee did not apply it to private enterprises; instead he suggested a net worth accretion measurement. Perhaps the reason why the specific has become general is that in the periods of rising prices, the net worth accretion rule was unconservative.

This is a point of fundamental disagreement with the Accounting Tradition. We believe that income ought to be *measured* and that measurement is the operation of discovering the numerosity of units descriptive of an *existing condition*, not a prognostication of the future.

Objectivity

The assertion that cost is objective is probably used more often to defend the cost rule than any other single argument. There are several lines of reply, any one of which is sufficient grounds for rejecting this argument.

First, the construct criticism. What is or is not objective depends to some degree upon the perceiver's preformed theoretical construct.[5] One cannot get intersubjective agreement from those whose constructs vary. Thus, if the question is on ontological reality, we must first have some method of choosing from among the competing constructs. Perception of reality is an epistemological question of vast consequences. Accountants have been extremely cavalier in their treatment of the problem. Usually they do no more than make an unsupported assertion that cost is objective and that other values are not. We consider

5. Chambers (p. 270) implicitly uses the construct criticism when he writes: "It is no defense to argue that all accountants or auditors would agree that the method of accounting and reporting used is a method acceptable to them. This would be equivalent to asking the flat-earthists whether the earth is flat."

that assertion unwarranted and have presented some evidence in support of our view above.

Second, the defensive criticism. We agree that cash receipts and disbursements are convenient and univocal. However, that is not the question. Every basic text lists widely varying alternatives for the *initial* recording of cash outflows. The problem of determining which cash outlays should be treated as "capital" in nature and which as expenses is one of the most difficult problems in accounting. The continuing valuation problems are subject to even wider deviations. Lifo and depreciation disputes are well known, but the myriad of lesser attaching alternatives are relatively unfamiliar. The author once amazed himself by setting up a game tree which revealed over a thousand valuation alternatives in a very simple enterprise. The degree of divergence is astounding. A glance at the literature discloses that the most discussed and hotly debated issue is the lack of uniformity in valuation concepts, in theory as well as practice. For the accountant to reject present values because they are "subjective" is an example of the pot calling the kettle black. Like the Patons (Paton and Paton, p. 54), we "marvel" at accountants who consider cost to be objective. We suspect, but cannot prove, that the present-price method would produce less variation in value than the historical-cost method, and thus it would be more objective in the inter-observer agreement sense.

Third, the conservative argument. This has been detailed above. The telling point is that accountants are always willing to record a "subjective" (other than cost) value if it is *lower* than the "objective" (cash cost) value. No asset on the balance sheet is valued at its cash cost, with perhaps the single exception of land, and land is likely to be valued at cost only if the market price is above or equal to the cost. Almost all assets are valued at less than their cost, because they have been subjected to amortization, allowances, lower of cost or market, or some other procedure which results in lowering the value. The result is that the assets are valued at something other than their "objective" cost; they are almost all valued "subjectively."

The Study Group on Business Income, in understatement more characteristic of the British, has written: "Those who have favored adherence to present practice have commonly talked in terms of 'factual' and 'objective' determinations and 'uniformity.' They perhaps have not given adequate recognition to the extent to which accounting is necessarily characterized by 'postulates,' 'estimates,' 'subjective choice of method,' and 'variety in methods.' " (Report of Study Group on Business Income, p. 50.) This may be true. Perhaps accountants, although they work with the materials daily, have not given adequate recognition to their own subjectivity. We think that a more reasonable hypothesis might be that they resist change, which is simply another aspect of conservatism.

Fourth, the information criticism. The final point is the strongest; yet it is most often misunderstood. Many writers outside the field of accounting continually refer to the precision and objectivity of accounting data. They lament the lack of theoretical validity, but excuse it on practical grounds. We believe that the cost figures are neither precise nor objective. However, even if they were, they are irrelevant.

We have set forth the problems and decision theories that we are aware of above and specified the data that is relevant. There was a noticeable absence of historical cost data on those lists. A guess at a relevant figure is infinitely more valuable than a precise and objective irrelevancy. If one's decision theory prescribes that length is relevant and radioactivity is not, then radioactivity has zero value regardless of its precision or objectivity. A rough estimate of length has at least some value, no matter how imprecise or unobjective.

Methodology

Although the accountants' methodological statements are not per se arguments for the cost rule, they are often used as ancillary support for that rule. Thus, it is incumbent upon us to examine their methodology. A complete survey of methodology would be a study in itself, but the differences between the author and the Accounting Tradition are so basic that a few comments must be made before we proceed.

Goldberg has reviewed the accounting literature and has classified the "theories" as "gerundive" and "substantive." The former—gerundive—are described as "rationalizations" of the existing practice of bookkeeping. The latter is theory in the more ordinary usage. Theory in the gerundive sense, what we have previously called apologetics, has been documented by several writers; and the profession has often bewailed the fact that this was the only kind of theory in existence. Greer, in the preface to *Standards,* indicated that this was the prime reason that the committee commissioned Paton and Littleton to write their treatise. He noted that the texts on theory "concentrated on the facts of existing practice," and that Paton and Littleton were to "make order of the chaos" by presenting "a coherent, coordinated, consistent body of doctrine."

Note, however, that the result was another gerundive theory. Paton and Littleton took the existing fundamental ideas and wove them together. This is still apologetics or rationalization. Later, Littleton wrote his treatise on methodology, which is an explanation and justification of that method.

Littleton points out that accounting theory has developed out of practice and that its character is gerundive—apologetic.

> We know that accounting practices were developed and in use
> before theories appeared explaining the things done. . . .
> Methods devised by many different people were used . . . [and
> became] generally accepted practices. Teachers of bookkeeping
> and later accounting and auditing found it necessary to supple-
> ment the accumulated rules and descriptions of procedure by
> explanations and justifications. This was done in order that
> study should be something more than the memorizing of rules.
> Hence it is appropriate to say that both the methods of practice
> and the explanations of theory were inductively derived out
> of experience. (Littleton, *Structure,* p. 185.)

Thus, theories are explanations of things done by accountants. They were derived to justify and explain what was in fact being done. This notion pervades the entire treatise. In another chapter he sets up a heading entitled "Theory as Explanation" and writes (p. 132): "Evidently accounting theory, far from being an exercise in abstract hairsplitting, is simply thinking that is focused upon doing. Practice is fact and action; theory consists of explanations and reasons." He proceeds to explain that in accounting there are no "immutable laws" and that it is not "scientific"; yet there are "relationships."

> These relationships are not so precise and measurable as to
> produce laws and formulas. But there are truths in accountancy,
> truths that rest upon such factors as carefully *defined classifica-
> tions,* closely *drawn distinctions,* clearly *perceived objectives,* a

strong sense of relevance among data. When these truths, these significant relationships, are formulated in careful phrasing, we may find that principles of accounting are emerging. (Littleton, *Structure,* p. 135, italics added.)

This seems clear enough, but how does one define classifications, draw distinctions, perceive objectives, sense relevance? In short, how does one come upon principles or truths? For Littleton, the proper procedure is induction.

He says (p. 186) that "the object of this chapter" is "to show . . . that accounting principles can be derived inductively out of accounting actions." Yet earlier (p. 175) he says that viewed broadly, "theory can properly be called a body of doctrine. It is an area of beliefs, explanations, and justifications related to an area of practice."

We disagree with this approach. We think that "inductively" derived theories of accounting commit the fallacy of getting *ought* from *is.* One may describe the activities of people; one may get insights about the underlying motives by observing them; this is acceptable methodology in Anthropology and Sociology. But how does one get from there to standards (norms of behavior)? How does one get to beliefs about what they ought to do from observations of what they in fact do? Just the opposite has occurred. Anthropology has described behavior but has been very careful to avoid value judgments or to attempt to prescribe general laws of behavior.

Littleton is the foremost proponent of this methodology, and we agree with Goldberg when he says that Littleton "got somewhat out of his depth or on the wrong track" in his discussion of the nature of theory. "His 'theory' is too obviously and too directly geared to the providing of rules of action; one gets the impression that the theory he proposes or rather his 'theoretical' propositions are rationalisations of practice, whether present or prospective." (Goldberg, p. 462.) We agree.

It is, of course, possible to maintain that theories are or ought to be inductively derived. There are conflicting speculations about the origins of geometry, for example. Some writers present persuasive speculations about someone laying three sticks together and discovering the theorem that is incorrectly credited to Pythagoras. The regular flooding of the Nile necessitated establishing property boundaries, and thus "geo-metry" was developed to meet that practical problem. Later, it is argued, the theorists rationalized that geometry by merely abstracting the general principles and formalizing them. To some degree such stories are probably true. But even if we accept this account, we must distinguish several things.

First, the geometry theorists were concerned with rationalizing geometry, not with rationalizing the activities of geometricians. In accounting, it sometimes appears that the attempt is to rationalize the activities of accountants instead of accounting. Diverse and conflicting practices are included in the theory of accounting because they are practiced by accountants. The reasoning behind this is obscure, but we think it is an *ad hominem* judgment. Accountants are presumed to have integrity, to exercise their best professional judgment, to tell the truth, etc. Therefore, their practices must have the same attributes. The result is a theory about the motivations of accountants instead of about income and wealth.

The second distinction is related to the first. The geometry theorists at some point began to observe the earth instead of the geometricians. They may have gotten their original notions about geometry from observations of geometricians, but in order to distinguish the correct from the incorrect practices, they began to observe the relationship of the geometricians' figures to independent observations of the earth. Insofar as we know, this has never been done in accounting. In fact we do not know how it could be done. One can take conflicting formulations of the method of calculating the length of a hypotenuse and test them by an independent measurement. We do not know how one could test alternative methods of calculating the historical cost of an inventory. This may be the essence of the claim that such procedures lack empirical meaning. Auditors are said to independently verify historical costs, but note that the procedure followed is not an independent measurement. Their method of verification is similar to the one available to historians. A historian may check the records of the measurements made in the past, and he may discover *calculation* errors, but he cannot repeat the measurement.

Third, at some stage geometry became a deductive or mental activity. When this happened and whether or not it was originally inductive will not be disputed. Our only claim is that Euclidean geometry exists and that it concerns itself with dimensionless points, unidimensional lines of infinite length, and other purely mental constructs. There have been attempts to formalize accounting in the same way that geometry was formalized, e.g. the works of Sprouse and Moonitz, but such efforts have been rejected. Accountants tend to be "practically" oriented and suspicious of mere "theories." Thus, the last step in the evolution of geometry is not acceptable to accountants.

Marple, for example, makes the distinction between the practical-useful and the theoretical-logical in a critique of Moonitz and Sprouse.[6] The distinction between the practical and the theoretical is a valid and useful one, but it has a tendency to be overdrawn, especially by accountants. The practical man must work with real points, not conceptions. The theorist can use "π" or "$\sqrt{-1}$" in his conceptions, but the practical man must use numerical values instead of symbols representing conceptions. To decide exactly where to round off π depends on practical considerations, i.e. the specific use of the calculation. To measure length on the rough and wrinkled curved surface of the earth instead of on a plane is a difficult practical problem. Yet what could be more practical than Euclid's principles? Every surveyor, construction engineer, forest ranger, navigator, etc. uses those

---

6. Marple's article is a delight. His writing pulsates with emotion and is a welcome relief from the arid, lifeless, restrained writing one usually finds in journals. He describes theorists as being "nurtured in the academic atmosphere which stresses theories and logic" and suffering from "overexposure to economic theory." This author pleads guilty. He even impugns our motives and questions our altruism by noting that theorists "write for publication because it improves their academic standings." We knew that there was *some* reason for writing this book.

In addition, the article is delightful because it succinctly presents almost all of those arguments for historical cost that we considered above. For example, he presents the liquidity argument (p. 479b); the argument that a fall in price makes previous price increases invalid or unreal (p. 480a); the argument that income cannot be measured at a point in time (p. 480b), instead one must wait until the "*whole* process is complete" (p. 480b); the argument that one ought not report profits that "will never be realized" (p. 481a), which requires that he know the future in order to make the statement, even though he conceives of his measure as entirely historical (pp. 480-81); and so forth.

In short, Marple's piece is an excellent collection of blunt and brief invalidities and absurdities. Of course, that cannot be taken as a criticism of Marple, because he disavows logic and is concerned only with truth, not logical validity. Exactly how he arrives at truth is not revealed, however.

principles. Practical men are also theoretical. Consider May's conception of the firm, discussed *supra*. His conception is quite "abstract" and "unrealistic," yet May was a practicing accountant. We did not object to the process of conceiving and reasoning that May used, indeed we think it is indispensable; we simply disagreed with that *particular* conception and the extent to which the deductive reasoning was carried. The practicing accountant must also apply some theory. Surely it is not instinct which leads him to value a quantity of wheat by multiplying it by a purchase price instead of by the square root of his belt size. Thus, the question is not theoretical versus practical or deductive versus inductive. Instead the question is *which* theory one should choose and how one goes about checking his deductions against his inductive observations.

Fourth, there is some question about the very possibility of inductively deriving theories. We alluded to this problem above in connection with the section on objectivity of measurements. N. R. Hanson and others argue that perceptions are "theory-laden." *What* one sees when one looks at something depends to a large extent upon what Margenau has called the perceiver's preformed theoretical construct. Hanson presents several line drawings which illustrate the problem. At first glance the lines "clearly" and "obviously" represent X, but to another perceiver they "clearly" and "obviously" represent Y. Thus, two different perceivers would report contradictory perceptions. More revealing is that once the possibility of another perception is made known, then the perceiver may stare and boggle for a long time until he finally "sees" the other possibility. But once he has seen it, then it is "clear" and "obvious" in the same way that the original perception was clear and obvious. The perceiver's world has now changed, and he is no longer able to look at that drawing without recognizing that it represents *two* different things.

Hanson presents these perceptions as a way of suggesting what happens in scientific observations. In the case of geometry we are probably all Euclideans, because we observe the world from a Euclidean construct. But Einstein comes along and presents an alternative view. His language is suggestive of the phenomenon described above when he says, e.g., ". . . we have not been accustomed to regard the world in this sense. . . ." (Einstein, p. 56.) We then ponder and boggle at Einstein's outlandish suggestions. But once we have "seen" the world in the way Einstein suggests, then it seems clear and obvious, and we can never again see the world in quite the same way as before.

This point is of supreme importance to the Accounting Tradition. In our review of the literature we were struck by the recurring claims that only "actual occurrences," "facts of economic experience," "objective events," or "actual costs" were to enter the books of account. Paton and Littleton point to "the only definite facts available." We think that such phrases reveal more about the accountant's preformed theoretical construct than they reveal about the world. This makes the accountant's induction self-supporting. He chooses to regard the world in a certain fashion, and this dictates not only what he considers to be facts, but also influences what he in fact perceives.

This, of course, is not unique to accounting. A considerable amount of evidence has been gathered in support of the proposition that changes in preformed theoretical constructs are the causes of scientific revolutions. It is not the case that a theory is overthrown by disconfirming empirical evidence. The Copernican Revolution has been heavily investigated on this point, because it was so dramatic and important and also because it seems quite clear that all observers were observing the same thing, but that different observers perceived different things. We noted above that all of us are probably Euclideans; but Aristotle had regarded Euclidean space as "unthinkable" and "absurd," and therefore he could not possibly "see" motion in the same way that Galileo saw it. Butterfield writes of this change and notes that the conflicting theories "were based on the ordinary observation of the data available to common sense" and that it was "supremely difficult to escape from the Aristotelian doctrine by merely observing things more closely." He contrasts present-day schoolboys, who "start off on the right foot" and *therefore* find it easy to understand the modern law of inertia, with the greatest intellects of the past, who could not understand *because* they "had already started off on the wrong foot and were hampered beforehand with the whole system of interlocking Aristotelian ideas." He notes that the change requires "a different kind of thinking-cap" and says, "In the long run, therefore, we have to recognize that here was a problem of a fundamental nature, and it could not be solved by close observation within the framework of the older system of ideas—it required a transposition in the mind . . . of the scientist himself." (Butterfield, pp. 14-17.) The same situation is true in accounting. The inductive method will not produce a revolution. Perhaps a revolution is not needed or desirable; but that judgment cannot be made by appealing to the "actual facts," because those facts are dictated by the existing theory. Instead it will require a theoretical argument about which way we ought to regard the world.

We are cognizant of the possibility of a retort of the *tu quoque* type. We, too, have a preformed theoretical construct which affects our perceptions about income and wealth. The discerning reader will have also noted that our notion of a preformed theoretical construct may spring from a preformed theoretical construct about constructs; and thus the evidence presented above in support of our position may be dictated by our metaconstruct. Thus, the metaconstruct is subject to the same kind of analysis. We offer no defense against such retorts. Our purpose here is to try to convince the inductivists that there are alternative ways of viewing the world and to detail our reasons for selecting the view we prefer.

SUMMARY AND CONCLUSION TO PART TWO

Present market price was selected as the proper valuation coefficient for the reasons given in Part I. The other suggested valuation coefficients were rejected for the reasons given in this Part.

Boulding's argument for the use of a constant seems to depend upon his belief that all valuation coefficients are arbitrary and that present market prices cause meaningless fluctuations in value. We believe that such fluctuations are quite meaningful. They reflect the changes in the command over goods that have in fact occurred. The error seems to lie in the characterization of some losses as only "apparent"; but in order to know that a loss is apparent, as opposed to real, requires that we know that the downward fluctuation will be offset by a future upward fluctuation. Since we do not know the future course of prices, we cannot determine whether the loss will be offset or not. Instead we can only measure what has occurred.

Boulding also errs by vacillating on the valuing agent. This leads him to set forth an apparent paradox which is the result of using different units to measure the same thing. The apparent paradox arises only when the trader is in the wrong position to take advantage of a price fluctuation; and it is in fact nothing more than a measure of the opportunity to gain, which the trader lost by being in the wrong position.

For these reasons we reject Boulding's argument for the use of a constant as a valuation coefficient. In other places he has asked for an application of information criteria to such problems, which we have tried to supply in this limited case; and he has agreed that present market price was appropriate in perfect markets, which is our assumption; therefore, we suspect that our disagreement with Boulding is superficial.

The Fisher Tradition has supplied a useful and valid decision tool. It correctly concentrates on the comparison of the present sacrifice to the future expected result. Our disagreement with it is with its use of the future expected result as a valuation coefficient. The future expected result is a prediction made by a particular person instead of a measurement of an existing condition. It is likely that in matters of commerce such predictions are rather vaguely formulated and that the present position would give equally as much information, since it indicates the direction of the expectations.

There are several anomalies in the Fisher Tradition. In commodity markets, for every long there is a short and therefore directly opposite expectations as to the direction of price movements. Valuation on the basis of expectations will show a profit for both, when it is certain that at least one of the expectations will not be realized. A careful analysis of the rate to be used for discounting, even under conditions of certainty, reveals that in order to account for all the income (exhaust the profit) the future price must be known. By knowing the future price and the date at which that price will exist, one can calculate a rate that will allow the value to gradually increase from the present price to the future price. However, the discounted future price will either revert to the present price, and therefore the discounting procedure is unnecessary, or a continuous adjustment would be required. Under conditions of uncertainty the problems with the rate are even greater. We believe that a reservation rate or cost-of-capital rate is appropriate to compare alternatives and make decisions, but such a rate is not appropriate for valuation. We do not know of a rate that is appropriate for valuation.

The Accounting Tradition is based on a set of loosely related rules that have been derived by practitioners to meet specific problems and have later been rationalized by academics. Thus, there is no "theory" of accounting in the ordinary sense of that term. We hypothesized that conservatism was the tenuous thread that connected the valuation rules and that this conservatism was originally derived from ethical considerations. We believe that conservatism violates the notion of verity, that a deliberate understatement is a misrepresentation equally as bad as a deliberate overstatement.

We set forth our perception of the structure of accounting and noted that (1) cash or near-cash was valued at unity; (2) the offset to the cash or near-cash was set equal to the value of cash; (3) the value was averaged over a quantity; and (4) the quantities were causally matched with their attached average.

Although we were able to describe accounting in rather general terms, we were unable to discover the relevance of the figures generated. Accountants often speak of the usefulness of accounting data, but we were unable to find any specific examples of where the cost-value figures were useful. In addition, we were unable to discover the empirical meaning of sums of the described figures. For this reason, we concluded that historical costs were without theoretical import.

There are no criticisms of present market value that we consider warranted. On the matter of objectivity, we would appeal to inter-observer agreement, and we are confident that there would be greater agreement on present market value than on discounted expectations or historical costs. Obviously the expectations would be different, else there would be no market. Historical costs require a matching which is in essence a joint cost allocation, and there are a large number of alternative ways to allocate joint costs. Thus, we claim that present market values are "objective" and that the other methods are "subjective," in the sense described. We would have to agree that price increments are not "realized" or "separated," since those terms require the receipt of value in a different form. However, we do not understand the import of that requirement. In the liquidity argument we showed that confusion of the form of wealth with the question of income led to absurdity. Since our institutions normally lend on the basis of present market price, any price increment could be partially and indirectly converted to a liquid form by obtaining a loan, and then dividends or taxes could be paid. It has been argued with respect to taxes that this would create a hardship because the price might decline, and therefore a loss would be suffered on which taxes had previously been paid. This is a genuine problem, but it is a problem in the equity of tax collection, not in income measurement. It is no worse than the current situation in which realized income may be taxed, and then that realized income reinvested and lost. Loss carry-forwards and carry-backs would restore equally as much equity under the proposed income tax scheme as under the current scheme. In addition, it would prevent the kind of income manipulation now possible; and it would make our taxes more progressive, by levying a tax on all the "unrealized appreciation" that only the very wealthy can afford to let remain unrealized and then pass on to their heirs in an unrealized and partially untaxed state. These are problems in public finance which we have not fully investigated and which are beyond the scope of this study. However, we can report that both Simons and Haig investigated the income taxation problem from an equity viewpoint and came to the same conclusions on income that we arrived at from an information-measurement viewpoint.

It would be tedious to continue to refute the other criticisms that have been leveled at present market value. Instead, let us suggest that comparisons be made. That is, if some standard is used to criticize present market values, then let that same standard be applied with equal force to the other valuation methods. We think that on balance the present market method of valuation can better withstand criticism than the other methods.

From the positive side, present market value meets all the established criteria. The present price of a held good defines *all* of the alternatives that are available to the trader. It is indispensable, because it delineates what courses of action are available and it is necessary to know them before one can project the outcomes of the various courses of action. Present prices in a perfect market are additive, and they permit all the comparisons—instantaneous interfirm, intertemporal for the same firm, increment for the same firm, and interfirm increments.

The final and telling point in favor of using present market value involves a conjecture about the decision theories of the receivers. The wealth and income figures go to a very large heterogeneous audience. A transmitter must make a judgment about how those receivers think. The question in its simplest form is "Do they think in terms of (a) unexpired costs, (b) constants, (c) discounted expectations, or (d) present market prices?"

In a market economy the answer should be obvious. Every housewife knows the price of potatoes and bread. She also knows her cash-on-hand and realizes, although she may never express it, that the purchase of some potatoes precludes the purchase of some bread. She knows that the family automobile is "worth more" to her than its current sale price but that the sale price is available to meet emergencies. She also knows that the sale price of the automobile could be used to purchase that coveted fur coat; but in order to know this she must know the present, not the past or future, price of both the coat and automobile. On the other hand, the notions of unexpired costs are arcane, even to the businessman who has incurred those costs. The author has never met a businessman who fully understood or accepted the accountant's methodology. Experts on investment—financial analysts—have come to favor cash-flows over income calculated by the historical cost method. To anyone who has ever taught the subject, it is obvious that the concept of discounting is foreign to all but a few students. Thus, we believe that present market value is a much more familiar and understandable method of valuation than the others suggested.

The editors of one of the most popular magazines in America have made a similar judgment.

> The accounting firm retained by the President said, in explaining how they arrived at their low $3.5 million estimate: "The investments . . . [are] carried at cost, less allowance for depreciation or improvements. . . . The amounts at which [they] are carried are not intended to indicate the values that might be realized if the investments were sold." LIFE considers it more

> realistic to give the amounts these properties would bring in a sale today rather than what they originally cost. (*Life,* September 18, 1964, p. 32.)

They might have said that present market is not only "realistic" but is also the way that their readers think about wealth. When people ask such questions they want to know what a person is "worth" today, not what his property cost him at various unspecified times in the past. The cost figures in the above quotation do not permit a meaningful comparison of the wealth of the candidates at the *time* of voting, because the measurements were made at the *event* of purchase; they do not permit a meaningful calculation of any candidate's wealth-increments from some previous *time* to the *time* of voting, for the same reason; they do not permit a meaningful comparison of the wealth-increments among candidates for a *time* period, because the wealth-increments are calculated at the *event* of sale.

The irony of this is that the journalist—a confessed novice in matters of income and wealth—was forced to supply the desired, realistic information, because the accountant—the expert on income and wealth—was unwilling or (if we are to believe his protestations) unable to do so. Sometimes the accountant argues that historical cost is the proper or correct valuation method and laments the fact that the receivers do not understand that method. We have argued that historical cost is not appropriate, and therefore we think that the attempts to educate the receivers in that method are dysfunctional. At other times the accountant argues that he cannot supply the desired information because it is too difficult to determine or because it is not objective. We feel that the accountant is much better qualified than the journalist, and we agree with Devine (p. 171) when he says, "It is high time that this nonsense of denying any ability as an expert in materials or values be stopped."

At the level of sophistication of the general public—the readers of *Life*—as well as at the level of academic abstraction, the decision theories of the receivers specify that present market be reported. This alone is a prima facie case for present market. Relevance is the overriding criterion without which all else is nought. Present market, however, has the additional virtue of meeting all the established criteria including the additive axiom, which makes it acceptable even to the narrowest of metricians. There is nothing on the negative side and everything on the positive side.

Our models and assumptions have served the purpose of narrowing the subject to the point where our thoroughness bordered on tedium. Many of our readers would have granted the conclusion a priori, but we felt it necessary to go through the detail in order to lay a firm foundation for the models which are to follow. However, because of this detail in the analysis of the trader model, we are confident of our conclusion. At the risk of being proven wrong, as Mill was eventually proven wrong, we echo his famous conclusion (p. 436):

> Happily there is nothing in the laws of value which remains for the present or any future writer to clear up; the theory of the subject is complete: the only difficulty to be overcome is that of so stating it so as to solve by anticipation the chief perplexities which occur in applying it.

That is, given a perfect market with a stable price level and only trading activities, the theory of which valuation coefficient is appropriate is complete. The perplexities of applying it are the subject for the next part.

3

"As organisms become . . . related to a more complex
environment, the importance of a particular act in
establishing conditions favorable to subsequent acts . . .
becomes at once more difficult and more imperative. . . .
Conditions of the environment become more ambivalent; it
is more uncertain what sort of actions they call for . . ."

—JOHN DEWEY

We might add that the information necessary to act
becomes more difficult to obtain and we are less confident
in the information that we can obtain.

XIII

THE ASSUMPTIONS RELAXED

There are two assumptions—perfect market and stable prices—which we will relax in order to make our model more general as well as more realistic. We will maintain the other basic assumptions—the maximands—because they come closer to describing reality than any other generalizations that we are aware of. Also we will maintain the assumption of trading, as opposed to merchandising or producing, since those activities require a different model and a different analysis.

PERFECT MARKET

There is no denying that the degree of difficulty in the determination of the present price varies in the same direction, and probably more than proportionately, with the imperfections in the market. Unique goods present perplexing problems; fungible goods have a curvilinear transformation function when one potential buyer or seller has a relatively large effective demand or supply of the commodity. Even in the face of these hardships we argue that the present price is the correct selection. Our reasons are:

1. The positive-relevance argument. A guess at the relevant figure is infinitely more valuable than an easily obtained irrelevancy. However, we think that when the problem is viewed in the proper light, the difficulties are essentially the same as those of sampling.
2. The negative-comparative argument. We need to compare what is now being done to the proposed method.

The first argument may be stated as a conditional. If rational decisions are to be made, then the relevant figures must be furnished. The force of the prescription—the "must"—depends upon the force of the antecedent. In our view the antecedent is compelling, and therefore the prescription is irrefutable. The relevant figures *must* be furnished.

The decision requires a selection among alternatives. The total money that could be garnered by the sale of the commodity is the figure that relates these alternatives. The total money is the present sacrifice which the entrepreneur makes in order to obtain or maintain another good. Likewise, the sacrifice is relevant to all other receivers for both their instantaneous and intertemporal comparisons. Thus, the present market must be determined before rational decisions can be made. Relevance is a compelling criterion which forces us to reject the previous rationalizations and to begin the task of overcoming the vast difficulties of determining current prices.

From the viewpoint of metrics theory the problem is one of instrumentation and observation. We need to develop better instruments and to train better observers. Stating the problem in these terms is not an attempt to gloss it over with verbiage. Instead it is an attempt to point the direction of progress. We cannot be certain of success in the attempt, but we can be certain that the refusal to try will produce nothing. Mourning over the problems and rationalizing the existing practices simply entrenches the problem without contributing anything toward its solution. Most of the effort expended is now in the direction of rationalization. Little if anything is done in the direction of a solution.

There is now a considerable body of literature on appraisal techniques. Unfortunately, there is a considerable lack of precision, and interobserver agreement is at a low level. The techniques must be refined, and the standards of observation must be improved. In the meantime, the instruments at hand, imperfect though they may be, must be used for the compelling reason that no other instruments are available.

The conditions of such a measurement must be explicitly stated. The temporal element is central to the purpose of this measurement, and the resulting figure will be meaningless if it is not stated. Likewise, place utility and transportation costs require that the spatial condition be stated. Thus, the measurement statement would come out something like the following:

> (In our best judgment the figure) X (is the total amount of cash that could have been received if this asset had been sold) at time t_1 in location S_1.

The understood clauses are in parentheses. Omitting them, the message reads:

> $X at t_1 at S_1.

The figure $X will be imprecise, and there will be disagreement about it. Note, however, that the same situation plagues the "exact" sciences. There have been sufficient experiments to demonstrate conclusively that the simplest of operations result in different magnitudes even when performed by highly qualified scientists with elaborate instruments.[1] This had led most metricians to the notion that measurements are probability functions and that perhaps the mean of several observations is closest to the "true" figure. Quite naturally, then, there has been an increasing use of dispersion measures and confidence levels in the "exact" sciences.

There is no reason why such techniques could not be extended, *mutatis mutandis*, to the determination of market prices. Of course, it would be a greatly preferable situation if there was a perfect market and thus an unequivocable, univocal figure. But in the absence of this ideal, some estimate of the dispersion could be made. The size of the deviation would vary directly with the degree of market imperfection and the quantity held relative to the total supply. If the trader holds

1. For a reference to these experiments see Churchman, "Materialist," pp. 485-86.

a relatively small quantity of a fungible commodity, the deviation should be quite small, even if the market is highly imperfect. As the trader holds relatively larger quantities, so that his exchanges directly cause wide price fluctuations, the accuracy of the measurement depends upon the accuracy of the estimate of the demand schedule. In all likelihood this will result in greater divergence in observations and larger deviations.

Most of the past criticism of such measurements has been caused by confusion over the temporal location. Measurements of this kind are conditionals in which the antecedent is false. The antecedent will forever remain false, because it specifies an immediate past instant which will never recur. "If I had sold at time t_1" can never be verified *by sale,* because the sale did not occur at t_1. If the sale had occurred, the conditional would be pointless. Sales at other temporal locations have no bearing on the verification of that statement, because they are at different times. To state that a sale at t_2 *proved* the appraisal wrong, as is often done, is an error. The appraisal was concerned with t_1, not t_2, and a sale at t_2 does not prove anything about the statement. Subsequent sales are not pertinent.[2]

The only means of verifying such a conditional is by setting standards for observers and observations and then checking on the divergence among observers. We can have "absolute" confidence in some conditionals and less confidence in others. A glance at the newspaper would give the author absolute confidence that he could have sold wheat for exactly $2.13⅞ at yesterday's closing bell. On the other hand, the confidence that one would have in the appraisal of a house (a unique commodity in a highly imperfect market) would be much lower. It would depend in part on the confidence that one has in the appraiser. No one would expect that an appraisal of $20,000 would

---

2. This problem has been particularly acute in accounting circles since the Great Depression. One hears about the write-ups made during the 1920's and the subsequent write-downs of the 1930's. The implication is that the prices existing in the 1930's proved the prices existing in the 1920's to be wrong. (Cf. Marple, p. 480.) Our view is that the prices were simply different in the same way that any temporally variant magnitude is *expected to be different* after a time lapse. Also note, e.g., Finney's statements (*supra*, p. 286) about the present price not being the price that *will be* realized. Such a situation is to be expected.

yield *exactly* $20,000. However, one could be almost certain that the final figure would have been say, $20,000 ± 3($1,500).

The absence of verification by sale has caused, and probably will continue to cause, a number of people to reject the procedure. Some people seem to be uncomfortable with conditionals and to yearn for absolutes. It may be some comfort to point out that there are many procedures where verification by performing the relevant act is impossible. In quality control, verification by testing sometimes destroys the product (flash bulbs for example), and quite often 100 per cent testing is too expensive. Sampling and statistical projection has been the answer. That is, we assume that if a particular flash bulb had been tested it would have lit. If it doesn't light 10 years later, that might be a result of deterioration instead of an incorrect statement. In quantum mechanics, there is observer-observation interaction which destroys the state that one is trying to measure. Projection from the observable to the unobservable is the only data available. No one would deny that we could be more certain of our figures if these conditions were not in the nature of things. However, to pretest all flash bulbs would be absurd, and to wait until they had all been used would be irrelevant to the decision. The only solution is to use the best device currently available and continue to try to refine it.

On a more abstract level it is difficult to conceive of a world without probabilities. All conditionals have only a degree of probability, and all of them presently in existence have not been completely verified in the sense of the consequent having occurred. For them to have been verified, in that sense, we would have a world in which all conceivable actions had already occurred. Thus, we must operate at all levels "only" on the basis of probabilities, not certainties. This is likely to be slight comfort for the absolutists who will reject our procedure as "unobjective" and "unverifiable." We are sorry about this; but from our viewpoint that is the way of the world, and there is nothing to be done about it.

The second argument is a comparison of the proposed method to the existing method of calculating income. More specifically the function of the auditor is called into question.

Every year the enterprise is obliged to call in an independent auditor to express his opinion on the fairness of the financial statements. The auditor arrives at his opinion by applying what the textbooks call "professional judgment." The term is left undefined and unbearably vague. The author has had the privilege of observing several of the largest and most respected auditing firms in the country. They invite academics to participant-observer summer programs, and we were privileged to attend some. This "practical" experience, coupled with the textbook ambiguities, has led us to the conclusion that auditing historical costs is much more difficult than verifying market prices.

For example, on one occasion we participated in the audit of a corporation that had a large inventory of reusable containers. They were charged to "inventory" when bought and to "expense" on a lifo basis upon initial use. The containers that had been used at least once outnumbered the new ones by about 10 to 1 on an equivalent unit basis. The auditors were very careful to verify the "inventory" (the unused containers). They spent a considerable amount of time observing the firm's count and making spot-checks by counting certain sections themselves. Then they made sample tracings of the original cash outlays that had gone into and out of the inventory account. They never bothered to do anything about the used inventory "because the costs had already expired." Yet the used inventory had an intended-use value, as well as a market value, several times the value of the unused. Since they were on lifo and were an expanding company, all of the costs in the inventory account were at least four years old and most were older. Thus, the market value of the unused was several times the reported value. The result was that the company reported about one tenth of the quantity of their inventory and valued it at rather ancient costs. The auditors spent a great deal of time checking on this inventory before they were willing to express an opinion that the figure did in fact "present fairly the financial position." When queried, the auditors replied that their only function was to ensure that the company had followed its self-established procedures and that all their efforts were toward that end. Further, they admitted that the company could have originally established different procedures which would have resulted in quantity variations of about 10q and a price variation of about 10p, thus a cost variation of about 100pq. This figure also would have "presented fairly" in their opinion. If they had found even the grossest error—a doubling or halving of the "correct" figure—it would have still been smaller than the *acceptable* variation.

On another occasion the auditors discovered an error in the sale of a parcel of land. The bookkeeper had erroneously charged off the cost of an unsold parcel and left the cost of the sold parcel in the asset account. The junior auditor had discovered the error in a routine check of the account. He had traced back several incidental costs to ensure that they were properly capitalizable and had found, of course, that the tax-minded management had expensed most of the costs. In tracing the credits, he found that the description of the sale did not agree with the book entry and thus discovered the error. The notation of the error on the worksheet occasioned several conferences; between the junior and his immediate supervisor, between the supervisor and the auditor-in-charge, between the auditor-in-charge and the head bookkeeper, at which time the correction was made.

This transaction had a fascinating history. A very brief summary should be enlightening. Several acres had been purchased for a lump sum over 20 years earlier. Only a small portion was put into use by the business. Another portion was contiguous to a rail spur and was sold shortly after the purchase. The major portion of the purchase price was allocated to the section sold. The remaining land was made up of some "worthless" sand dunes and the site of the business. Over the years there were several cash outlays in connection with the land. Some of these were capitalized, but most were expensed. One outlay was a relatively recent tax assessment, the magnitude of which was greater than the original purchase price of all the land. Several additional parcels were sold sporadically. The original purchase price and the subsequent capitalized costs were apportioned to the parcels, as they were sold, on two different bases—square footage for the earlier, and market value for the later, sales.

Several years earlier it had become apparent that the worthless sand dunes were becoming very valuable for use as beach front resorts. Accordingly, the management had the land platted, and the accountants allocated the unexpired costs between the industrial site and the remaining beach front on the basis of the then existing market prices. They added the cost of platting to the costs previously allocated to the beach front, and then apportioned the costs to each individual parcel on the basis of the then existing market. The management held the land for about five years and watched its value grow as the houses and motels built up along the beach.

When they started selling it, the bookkeeper erred by expensing a parcel that had not been sold. She charged off a parcel "costing" $1,700, instead of the correct one which "cost" $1,100. However, the acceptable range of cost was from about $400 to $5,300, had different allocation procedures been selected.

After the ensuing conferences, the auditor commented that the amount was "immaterial" anyway. We agree, but in a different sense of materiality. The $600 deviation could have been occasioned by almost any of the previous allocations or capitalizations. If they had been, they would have been acceptable to the auditor. Thus, the auditor spent many man-hours "correcting" an "error" that was much smaller than the *acceptable* deviations.

Examples of this type could be related at length. The vast divergence in historical cost resulting from different accounting methods is well known. We think that this is evidence for the fact that there is no way of verifying, in any reasonable sense of that term, historical costs. How does one verify the decision to allocate total inventory costs on a lifo instead of fifo basis? How does one verify the decision to include only unused containers in the inventory? How does one verify the expense versus capital decision and the subsequent allocations in connection with the land? These problems are not subject to empirical test and are in principle unresolvable.

This is the negative argument. We believe that the standards applied to the alternative valuation methods should be on a comparative basis. In an imperfect market the determination of present prices would be difficult, but less difficult than a meaningful allocation of joint costs. The estimates of present price would vary from observer to observer, but it is doubtful that they would vary more than historical costs vary among accountants. To revalue at present prices would be expensive, yet the audit fees are now rather large. The thing that must be compared is the results gained from the expenditure. What do we gain when the auditor seeks out "errors" of less magnitude than the acceptable variation? Couldn't his time, energy, and talents be devoted to more fruitful inquiries at about the same cost?

Which Present Price?

In an imperfect market there are at least two prices: entry and exit. Even in our perfect market the trader buys at the present price *plus* commissions, but sells at the present price *less* commissions. In other situations there is the piecemeal selling price of the normal stock-in-trade through normal channels, and the sum is different from the selling price of the entire stock. A firm buys its capital goods through an established distribution channel; but it sells them in an unfamiliar setting, sometimes as scrap and sometimes in an ill-defined second-hand market. The question arises as to which of these is the appropriate present price.

We will restrict the discussion to the trader. First, it should be obvious from our previous discussion on the sacrifice dimension that we favor the present exit or sale price. Adding commissions and then allocating them to units is a joint-cost problem that we would like to avoid. More important, the trader's alternatives are defined by what he can sell for, not what he could purchase for. Thus, we would value the wheat at present market less commissions. This means that at the time of the first valuation we show two commissions as a loss: the purchase price plus commission, less the sale price minus commission, results in a loss of two commissions, even if the price has remained constant. Such commissions are a sunk cost and therefore have no relevance to any decision.

Also we would value the wheat at the exit price of the total stock for the same reason. It is true that piecemeal selling stretched out over time would often yield higher receipts. However, in order for the trader to make the decision to sell piecemeal in the future, he must compare those estimated future receipts to the present exit value of the total stock. Thus, the present exit value must be determined if rational decisions are to be made; and since we have defined income as a quantum bounded by time, we would naturally conclude that the time must be the present.

We must admit that we would allow for some ambiguity in the temporal location. Even in the case of the almost perfect market for wheat, there are times when the market is closed. If a report was to be prepared when the market was closed, we would be forced to use the price at the last time the market was open. This is the same problem as comparing the weights of infants, which was discussed above. We would prefer that the measurement be made at exactly the same temporal location; but we would be perfectly willing to ignore a difference of one minute and reluctantly willing to ignore a difference of two weeks if no better figures were available.

The admission of temporal ambiguity would also extend to the future in complex situations, despite our reluctance to use predictions as values. Some writers speak of "forced liquidation prices" and consider it absurd to use them when the "true value" is so much greater. We do not know what "true value" they have in mind. There are several different values that may be characterized as "true." "Forced-liquidation value" is also ill defined, but it sometimes seems to mean the price that could be obtained by selling to the first man on the street that one happened to meet. If this is the meaning, then we agree that it would be absurd to report such values. A less radical notion of immediate exit price is obviously called for. We must admit to ambiguity in the complex situations, but we believe that it is possible to use terms like "liquidation in the normal course of events" to describe a more reasonable procedure. This dictates the market in which the goods would be sold and indicates that some relatively short period of time would be necessary to effect the sale. Although this redefines the problem of determination instead of solving it, these are in fact the values needed by managements and entrepreneurs in order to decide whether to continue or liquidate. The reasonable alternatives are between normal liquidation and continuation, not between forced liquidation (by definition, when one is forced to do something, he has no alternative) and continuation. In the case of wheat (physical) in an imperfect market, this is quite clear. The trader may liquidate his stock through normal channels in the wheat market, or he may hold his stock if he expects a more favorable future price. He could of course sell it in another market for lesser amounts, but the best and next-best alternatives are an immediate sale in the wheat market and a future sale in the wheat market.

Edwards and Bell also build a case for exit prices, but then reject them in favor of entry prices. We were not convinced by their reasons for rejecting exit values, and we particularly disagree with the idea that exit values would be less useful to external users of the data. They note that their reasoning is based on the assumption that "current reported profits can be projected into the future" (pp. 103[n] ff.) and conclude that current cost income is a better method of measuring current income, because it is a better indicator of future income. We believe that they have mixed two problems. Figures that are used to indicate the future are usually adjusted to eliminate the effect of factors that existed in the past but that are not expected to exist in the future and to add the effect of factors that are expected to exist in the future but that did not exist in the past. A measurement that describes an existing condition can be adjusted in this fashion. However, we know of no reason to assume that entry price income requires less adjustment than exit price income. Entry prices for the inputs may be expected to rise or fall; substitutes for the output may be expected to come on the market or not; competitors may enter or not; technological change may make the current production process obsolete or more useful; etc. All of these factors would affect future income, regardless of whether entry or exit prices were used.

Sometimes we "smooth" or "adjust" past measures in order to extrapolate the trend and thereby predict the future. This is a method of eliminating extraneous or unwanted factors (e.g., seasonally adjusted data), but the raw measures show what did happen and *then* the adjustments are made. Both entry and exit price income could be subjected to this procedure, and there is no reason to suspect that entry price income would yield a better trend line than exit price income.

More important is the distinction between predictors and measures. One can measure wind velocity and consider the measurement to be veritable and relevant, irrespective of whether or not it yields a trend line that predicts future wind velocities. In point of fact, wind velocities go up and down, and thus there is no trend line. Income can also go up and down and fail to yield a trend line. To smooth or adjust or "average out" income so that the data yields a trend line is an error. It is an error because the smoothed income does not *reveal* what one set out to measure and because the smoothing of future income ensures that the trend line is a good predictor. That is, smoothing of this kind is a self-fulfilling prophecy. Worse, what it prophesies is that the metrician will smooth in the future. It says little about the activities of the firm.

To continue the analogy, note that changes in atmospheric pressure presage storms, and one of the defining characteristics of "storms" is relatively high wind velocity. Thus, a present measurement is used to predict a future measurement. It would be an error to adjust wind velocity measurements for the sole purpose of making barometer readings a good predictor or to claim that barometer readings are a better measure of something just because they predict something else. In physics such distinctions are fairly easy, but in the social sciences they are more difficult. Nonetheless the distinction can be made, at least conceptually. Thus, we think that selecting a method of measuring profits on the basis of how well that measure predicts future profits is an error.

Of course, Edwards and Bell present other reasons for selecting the entry price method of measuring income, and they do not explicitly consider the relative predictive powers of the two measures. It seems instead that they assumed a going concern in which productive assets would be replaced, and thus the cost of replacement was a better measure of income. We disagree with the *assumption* of a going concern and think that one ought to predict the future of the firm. Even if one predicts a long term existence of the firm, we are not convinced that *present* replacement prices of assets that are expected to be replaced in the *future* are the best measure of current income. In short, we think that Edwards and Bell built a sound case for exit prices and then erred by rejecting them in favor of entry prices.

We agree that a case can be made for entry prices when one considers a productive process that is expected to continue. However, we think a better case can be made for exit prices. In any event, the productive process is not pertinent to this study. For the trading firm it makes little sense to speak of costs savings or to distinguish between operating and holding gains, since all gains are holding gains. Therefore, we select exit prices as the appropriate valuation coefficient for the trader model.

Summary

The figures that are currently reported as "income" are irrelevant,

The relevant figures are more difficult to come by, but they are infinitely more valuable. The difficulties increase as the market becomes more imperfect, and they result in more chance of error and less observer agreement. However, once the conceptual confusion about the temporal location of the measurement is cleared up, the problem becomes one of instrumentation and observation; i.e., it is exactly like other problems in metrics.

Recognizing the similarity in problems, we can borrow from the metricians and make the measurement. The dispersion can be estimated and reported. Perhaps the dispersion can be narrowed as experience is gained and new techniques are devised.

This will be an expensive and difficult process. However, the current method of measuring income is equally difficult and expensive. The effort now being expended could be redirected toward the determination of the relevant figure with little, if any, additional costs and with fewer conceptual and observational problems.

The question of which present price was examined, and we argued that the current exit or selling price of the entire lot of wheat was the figure relevant to the decision and that the argument for entry prices confused the problem of measurement with the problem of prediction. In complex cases an extension of the temporal location from a point to a relatively short period is required.

STABLE PRICE LEVEL

One of the most ancient and perplexing problems in economics is caused by what Simons (p. 55) has called the "patent instability of the monetary *numeraire.*" Most economists have discussed it at one time or another, and the concept was cleared up long ago. Mill (p. 439) drew the basic distinction as early as 1849: "There is such a thing as a general rise of price. All commodities may rise in their money price. But there cannot be a general rise of values. It is a contradiction in terms. A can rise in value by exchanging for a greater quantity of B and C; in which case these must exchange for a small quantity of A. All things cannot rise relatively to one another." This distinction is still valid. It is the difference between a change in the ratio of exchange and a change in the numeraire. In concept it is the epitome of simplicity, but in application there are a number of grave problems.

The problem in its simplest terms is one of pure metrics. At any given moment in time there exists a ratio at which goods are exchanged. For convenience, all these goods are stated as a specific number of units of the monetary numeraire. By this relation to units, all the goods are related one to another. This is an instantaneous comparison which we have previously referred to as a transformation coefficient and which is commonly known as a price. By means of these prices a person can exchange until his utility is at a maximum, or a firm can exchange until its monetary expectations are at a maximum.

At a different moment in time there is another series of prices which permits the same process. If the price level has been stable, i.e. if the same magnitude of money yields the same utility, the two moments are comparable and the measurements are additive. That is, the difference between the wealth—with the commodities valued at the present prices and money at unity—will yield a meaningful difference between the level of satisfaction that is available at the two instants. However, if this relationship of money to utility changes over time, i.e. if the same magnitude of money yields a different amount of utility at two instants, the moments are not comparable and the price level is said to be unstable.

Proportional Price Changes

The simplest case is one where the ratios remain constant but the price level changes. In other words, where all the price changes are proportional in the same direction. In this situation wealth will not change when goods are held, but there will be a wealth change if cash is held.

For example, suppose that there is a simple economy with only three goods. At t_1 the prices of these goods are

$1 per X
$2 per Y
$3 per Z

At t_2 the prices are doubled.

$2 per X
$4 per Y
$6 per Z

The ratio of dollars to goods has changed, but the ratio of goods to goods has remained constant. At both instants the ratio of goods to goods is

$$2X = Y$$
$$3X = Z$$
$$1\tfrac{1}{2}Y = Z$$

The only thing that has changed is the "size" of the unit. A similarity transformation is needed in order to make the instants comparable in dollars. That is, we need to discover a constant coefficient that will equate the two units. This is precisely the same problem in concept as changing, say, feet to yards or pounds to tons.

In any similarity transformation there must be some basic factor that is invariant before the coefficient of transformation can be discovered. For length this is relatively easy. The French government maintains a physical representation of an arbitrarily defined "meter" —a platinum bar with two marks on it. It is assumed that this physical representation is invariant over time.[3]

3. We say "assumed" to be invariant because there is no way of verifying by comparison that the physical representation has not changed. The previous moment is gone, and one can never *directly compare* the state of anything with its state in the past. That is, one cannot align the "standard meter at t_1" with the "standard meter at t_2," because the two moments are mutually exclusive.

Of course, the French government maintains the standard meter under carefully controlled conditions. They *assume* that the conditions are constant and therefore strengthen their conclusion that the meter is constant. But note the assertion that, say, the temperature is constant is not verifiable by direct comparison, because the two moments are mutually exclusive.

This is an infinite regression that again leads back to one's conception of the universe. It is an epistemological question that depends on the construct. We are not seriously suggesting that the meter varies over time and that all other lengths vary proportionately with it. The only purpose of this note is to point out the impossibility of verification by *direct* intertemporal comparisons. For this reason, one can only assume that the basic unit is temporally invariant.

The problem is pertinent to our suggestion that verification is a function of observer agreement rather than of direct comparison. The insistence on verification by conversion is similar. The requirement that a commodity be sold before its value can be verified is an unbearably narrow interpretation of the concept of verification.

If the length of a meter changed over time, however, there would have to be some third unit (which was temporally invariant) that could be used as the basic unit of comparison. That is the situation with dollars, since they vary over time in relation to goods. In order to discover the similarity transformation a third unit, which does not vary, must be discovered. In the simplest case—proportional changes —the price relative of any particular good may be used. The ratio of goods to goods has remained constant, and therefore we could use goods as the unit assumed to be temporally invariant.

The operation is fairly straightforward.

1. Make the measurement in the existing units at both instants.
2. Discover a unit that is temporally invariant.
3. Compare the existing units at both instants to the invariant unit and express them as a ratio. This ratio is the similarity transformation.
4. Select one of the instants as a base.
5. Multiply the measurement taken at the other (non-base) instant by the similarity transformation.

This operation is general.[4] It is applicable to all similarity transformations.

---

4. For example, if the meter stick varied over time, then the same object measured at two times would not be comparable.

Length of Object A $= X_1$ meters at t_1.
Length of Object A $= X_2$ meters at t_2.
$X_2 - X_1 =$ Change in length of Object A $+$ change in length of the meter stick from t_1 to t_2.

Thus, one does not know how much of the difference between X_1 and X_2 is attributable to the change in the object and how much is attributable to the change in the meter stick.

Now if one had an invariant unit—call it a Seter—then one could make the following measurements and calculations.

Length of meter at $t_1 = Y_1$ Seters.
Length of meter at $t_2 = Y_2$ Seters.

Then

$X_2 - X_1(Y_2/Y_1) =$ Change in length of Object A in meters of t_2.

or

$X_2(Y_1/Y_2) - X_1 =$ Change in length of Object A in meters of t_1.

One can say that although the measurements are stated in meter units, the basic unit is a Seter. The problem is to discover or select that basic unit. In the measurement of wealth and income, any randomly selected good or set of goods could

In this case the prices have doubled, and the similarity transformation is obvious. It is 2, if we select t_1 as the base, and ½ if t_2 is selected. The value of X is either $1 or $2 at *both* instants, depending upon the base. The value of X is constant and will remain constant so long as the price changes are proportional. Thus, there can be no gain or loss, no income, when goods are held. The change is only in the "size" of the unit.

However, if one *holds the units*—dollars—over this period, there is a change in wealth or command over goods or utility. One dollar at t_1 is exchangeable for one X, and consequently one dollar is equal to whatever utility is associated with one X. At t_2 one dollar will yield only one-half X, and there is a consequent reduction in utility. The command over goods has been halved and the utility reduced.

Note that the effect of proportional price changes is to reverse the roles of money and commodities. Money is now risky, and commodities are riskless. The trader can ensure a constant amount of wealth by holding wheat, but the holding of money subjects him to risk. Under the assumption of a stable price level, it is the change in *ratios* of goods which causes risk and permits gains or losses. Under the proportional price change assumption, the change in the "size" of the unit causes the risk, and only by holding money can there be a gain or loss.

Nonproportional Price Level Changes

The serious problems arise in the more complex case of changes in both the ratio of goods to goods and the level of prices. It is still relatively easy in concept; but because of the errors in the literature, we need to be precise in the formulation of that concept.

---

serve. For example, one could use wheat without committing any technical error. However, from a higher criterion the use of wheat as the basic unit leads to absurdity. If one holds a certain quantity of wheat and continues to adjust the value of that wheat by the price relative of wheat, then the value differences are always zero. That is

$$p_1W_1 - p_2W_1(p_1/p_2) = p_1W_1 - p_1W_1 = 0.$$

or

$$p_1W_1(p_2/p_1) - p_2W_1 = p_2W_1 - p_2W_1 = 0.$$

In terms of our previous discussion the valuing agent is wheat when this procedure is selected, and we gave our reasons for preferring money as the valuing agent.

The difficulties lie in the determination of the similarity transformation. Just what the invariant unit is, or should be, is not apparent. Suppose that in the three-commodity economy the prices at t_1 were

> $1 per X
> $2 per Y
> $3 per Z

and at t_2 the prices were

> $3 per X
> $4 per Y
> $5 per Z.

The total dollars required to purchase one unit of *all three* commodities has doubled. However, this does not mean that the proper similarity transformation is 2 or ½. It is true that $6 will buy one half of each good at t_2, but a similarity transformation of ½ tacitly assumes that each commodity should be weighted equally. There is no a priori reason to weight the commodities in that fashion, and there are strong reasons for not doing it. Suppose, for example, that one was interested only in the commodity X. One dollar at t_1 is exchangeable for one X, but only for one-third X at t_2. Thus, in terms of X alone, there is a similarity transformation of 3, or ⅓, if cash is held.

The situation is even more muddled if a commodity is held over the period. If the trader starts with one X at t_1 and still holds it at t_2, he is in exactly the same position in terms of X. He started with one X and ended with one X, and if X is used as the invariant unit, no change has occurred. However, in relation to Y and/or Z he is better off, because of the ratio change, i.e. the price relatives of Y and Z are less than that of X. At t_1 one X was exchangeable for ½Y; at t_2 it is exchangeable for ¾Y. Thus, in terms of Y, he is 50 per cent better off. In terms of Z, he is 80 per cent better off. In terms of X and Y equally weighted, he is 65 per cent better off. In terms of all three weighted equally, he is about 30 per cent better off. Here are five different figures representing the degree of "better-offness," each depending upon the particular good or combination that was selected for comparison. If unequal weights were used, there would be an infinite number of measures of better-offness, since there is an infinite number of possible weights.

One possible escape from the dilemma is to project a pattern of purchases and to use the goods in that pattern as the invariant unit. In terms of the example, we could project that the trader will purchase commodity X; and therefore X is the pertinent invariant. This has been suggested in the literature. The arguments for "specific price indices" are, in effect, this proposal. That is, the prices of the goods that a firm has been, and is expected to continue, purchasing are used to calculate the index.

In the trader model the "specific price index" turns out to be the price relative of wheat. Under this assumption, it is impossible to make gains or losses from holding the commodity. The relative of the prices at two instants is used as the similarity transformation, and then one of the prices is either deflated or inflated. The difference between the values is always equal to zero, and thus there is no possibility of either gain or loss.

For example, suppose that the price of wheat was $1 per bushel at t_1 and $2 per bushel at t_2. The specific price index is either 2 or ½, and the difference in the adjusted values is always zero. Moreover, note that it is true in more complex cases. No matter how many goods are held, a *perfect* specific price index will always yield a difference of precisely zero. This basic fact apparently has been overlooked by the people who have suggested the use of specific price indices for adjusting the asset values of a firm.

The "keeping physical capital intact" notion seems to be the basic assumption of those who have made the suggestion. We have previously pointed out that this assumption has the effect of shifting units in the measurement. It is equally true in the case of specific price indices. That is, the specific good that the enterprise holds becomes the unit of measurement if specific indices are used.

This view has been supported by appealing to the "entity concept." Some writers argue that an enterprise is a separate and distinct "entity" and that the relation to the owners, managers, and creditors is secondary. As we have previously emphasized, this is not our view. It seems self-evident that the enterprise exists only because people have created it and that the motivation of humans is the motive force of the enterprise. We view "enterprise" as nothing more than a convenient name for the vehicle that humans establish to maximize (or satisfice) their utility.

For this reason, utility must be the basic referent—the invariant unit—that is used to calculate the similarity transformation. We have previously argued that under conditions of stable prices, money is the proper valuing agent (unit of measurement), because it relates to all goods and therefore is an expression, albeit an imperfect one, of utility. Under unstable prices, the unit of money is no longer invariant, and therefore we must revert to the more primitive concept of utility.

The use of utility as the temporally invariant unit makes the price-index notion abundantly clear. By use of the indifference analysis, one can plot the ratio of goods to goods on a utility map and observe the highest possible level of satisfaction. The same procedure can be followed for different instants, and then the two amounts of money necessary to yield a constant level of satisfaction can be expressed as a ratio. This ratio is the perfect price index; i.e., it can be used as a similarity transformation to equate the money at both instants.[5]

Unhappily, however, there are two major obstacles in the utility analysis. First, it is not subject to empirical determination. The unit has been named (utils), and there have been scattered experiments in which attempts have been made to measure it. "Satisfactions" are in the realm of the psyche, however, and we have been singularly unsuccessful in attempts to measure such things. There has been some success in measuring a particular individual's sensations, but these only point up the second obstacle. Second, utility is highly personal. It varies from individual to individual, and thus any index derived directly from the utility analysis would be peculiar to a single person. As a general measure it would be useless. It would have no relevance to a heterogeneous group of receivers.

Both problems are well known, but the first receives more attention in the literature than the second. However, the second is more pertinent to this study and deserves emphasis. A perfect price index is a purely personal concept and is applicable only to that person. Thus, changes in wealth, under conditions of unstable prices, are purely personal measurements; and any attempt to generalize is prone to a wide margin of error.

5. For a more complete description, see almost any basic economics text. For a nontechnical discussion directed toward a lay audience, see Greenwald.

Statisticians have attempted to overcome the first problem by postulating patterns of purchases ("market baskets") as a substitute for the undeterminable utility. They have noted the second problem and have warned against the indiscriminate use of the indices. All indices that are now constructed are weighted means of an assumed market basket of goods. Some are more complex than others, e.g. geometric vice arithmetic mean, and some have special features, e.g. reversibility, that others do not. Still they are basically the same: The weighted mean of the prices of selected goods. Obviously, the meaningfulness of any index varies inversely with the degree of deviation from the assumed pattern of purchases. The pattern is unlikely to fit any particular person perfectly, and it may vary widely. The consumer price index includes meat and milk which have little relevance to a vegetarian or to a playboy who consumes wine, women, and song.

The personal nature of these measurements, both from the utility and the pattern-of-purchases point of view, must mitigate any appeal for the use of indices. One could argue, with some merit, that each man should be his own metrician. Each man should construct his own index and make his own calculation of wealth changes. For the contrary, one could argue that few people are likely to have the past records, knowledge, time, and facilities necessary to make the calculation.

One conclusion, however, is inescapable. The current market price is the only number that relates all the extant alternatives. Any tinkering with that price will destroy that relationship. The present price is an instantaneous measure of goods in their relation to other goods. The attempt to make an intertemporal comparison should not be done at the expense of destroying the present instantaneous comparison. Further, it is almost axiomatic that people have a wider range of knowledge about present prices than they do about past prices. If they need to know the price of a particular alternative, the present price is usually much easier to obtain than the past price. For these reasons, the adjustment should be made on past valuations (based on the then present prices), and the present valuations (based on the now present prices) should be reported unadjusted.

Any attempt, therefore, to make the dollars intertemporally comparable must utilize the present as the base and inflate or deflate the previous valuations. With this primary conclusion understood, we will argue that index numbers should be constructed. Our reasons follow.

First, it is unlikely that the receivers will construct their own personal index, and thus the choice is between an imperfect general index and no index. In the absence of any index, the units are clearly not comparable; they are not additive, and thus the difference in wealth is erroneous. Use of a general index will not eliminate these errors, but the degree of error should be lessened.

Second, the adjustment of past valuations means that the present valuations will be reported at each information date. Hence, both time series—the adjusted and the unadjusted—will have been presented to the receivers. Each receiver can then calculate his own index, if that is what is desired. Regardless of the individual index, the presentation of both series has more informational content than either alone.

Third, our institutional structure makes certain obligations dependent upon income. If the wealth change is due solely to inflation in some cases and not in other cases, unadjusted figures will cause inequities. An imperfect index will reduce these inequities, even if it does not eliminate them.

Fourth, the index is a useful conceptual tool. It is a generalization that admittedly does not fit any specific case, but it, like other generalizations, organizes the data in a comprehensible fashion. The individual prices are too complex to be comprehended in the absence of an index.

For these reasons we conclude that the data should be adjusted. In view of the second point, it does not appear that it could do any harm; it has no negative aspects; and there are several sound reasons in its favor.

The only problem left is the selection of the index. In view of the motivation of the enterprise, it should be obvious that we think the Consumer Price Index is most appropriate. It is the closest substitute for a utility measurement that is currently available. In addition, it is a more general concept of purchasing power than any of the competing indices. We say "more general" because the Consumer Price Index includes only final goods. The other indices which are often described as general, e.g. the implicit GNP deflator, include intermediate goods. Intermediate goods should be excluded from the purchasing power concept, because they are only indirectly productive of utility. That is, they produce utility by producing the final goods or by being exchanged for consumer goods. The only direct connection with utility is their sale price at the present moment which yields a command over goods. However, this command over goods is given by the present market price at each instant; the *ultimate* purpose of an intermediate good is to garner command over *final* goods, and thus only final goods should be used in the construction of the index.[6]

Application of the index is not difficult. The previous valuation(s) should be multiplied by the index number either singularly by commodity or in toto. The previous valuation(s) is (are) readily available from the last report, and the Consumer Price Index is regularly published. Thus, there are no practical problems of application. In order to be perfectly clear on the meaning of the figures, we will state the ideas symbolically and give an example.

The wealth of the trader at time t_i is given by the sum of the quantity of money held, $M(t_i)$, and the quantity of wheat, $W(t_i)$, multiplied by the price of wheat $P_w(t_i)$, as follows.

$$V(t_i) = M(t_i) + P_w(t_i)W(t_i) \qquad (\text{eq. XIII-1})$$

The significance of $V(t_i)$ is that it can command a certain quantity of goods at time t_i. Let P_j be the price and Q_j be the quantity of the jth good. Then $V(t_i)$ can be stated as an equation.

$$V(t_i) = \sum_{j=1}^{n} P_j(t_i)Q_j(t_i) \qquad (\text{eq. XIII-2})$$

6. This point has been given rather short shrift here because it is so well understood in the economics literature. Smith's famous statement that "consumption is the sole end and purpose of production" (*Wealth of Nations*, p. 625) set the stage. Mill's distinction between price and value is cut from the same cloth. Walras touches on it (*Elements*, p. 317). Marshall, as usual the synthesizer and clarifier, leaves no room for doubt. "The general purchasing power of money should properly be measured by reference to the retail prices paid by the ultimate consumers of finished goods." (Marshall, *Money, Credit and Commerce*, p. 30).

Later, Keynes wrote the following: "We mean by the Purchasing Power of Money the power of money to buy the goods and services on the purchase of which for purposes of consumption a given community of individuals expend their money income." (*Money*, I, 54.) After the syntax is straightened out, one finds that Keynes was saying the same thing.

This equation should be understood to mean that given the market prices in existence at t_i and the quantities of money and wheat held by the trader, then one can calculate the quantities of all other goods that the trader can command. One can solve for any particular Q_j in equation XIII-2 or for any combination of Q_j's. Of course, there are an infinite number of Q_j's that will satisfy the equation.

Now the increase in wealth (income), Y, measured in dollars for the period t_i to t_{i+1} is simply

$$V(t_{i+1}) - V(t_i) = Y \qquad\qquad (\text{eq. XIII-3})$$

One could select any good as his unit of measurement and state his increase in wealth in terms of that good. For example,

$$V(t_i) = P_1(t_i)Q_1(t_i)$$
$$V(t_{i+1}) = P_1(t_{i+1})Q_1(t_{i+1})$$

and

$$Q_1(t_{i+1}) - Q_1(t_i) = \text{income for the period expressed in units of good number one.}$$

If good number one is potatoes measured in pounds, then the income for the period is the increase in pounds of potatoes that the trader could command.

For reasons given in Chapter III, we think that the selection of the valuing agent or unit of measure is important and that the selection should be based on the maximand (utility) of the trader. For reasons given immediately above, we consider the Consumer Price Index to be the best measure of utility. The set of consumer goods is a proper subset of all the goods offered in the market. We denoted all goods above as Q_j ($j = 1,2,...,n$) and will denote consumer goods as Q_j ($j = 1,2,...,m$) where $m < n$. Let K_j be the constant weights assigned to consumer goods, and we can define a consumer price index as follows.

$$I = \frac{\displaystyle\sum_{j=1}^{m} P_j(t_{i+1})K_j}{\displaystyle\sum_{j=1}^{m} P_j(t_i)K_j} \qquad\qquad (\text{eq. XIII-4})$$

In equation XIII-4 we have held the quantities constant, and we determine the prices by reference to the market. We adjust $V(t_i)$ as follows

$$IV(t_i) = V'(t_i) \qquad \text{(eq. XIII-5)}$$

and $V'(t_i)$ is interpreted as the command over a quantity of consumer goods that the trader had at t_i stated in t_{i+1} prices. Now the unadjusted $V(t_{i+1})$ also gives a command over consumer goods in t_{i+1} prices.

$$V(t_{i+1}) - V'(t_i) = Y' \qquad \text{(eq. XIII-6)}$$

Thus, Y' is a measure of the change in the *quantity* of consumer goods that the trader can command. The basic measurement unit has been shifted from a quantity of dollars to a quantity of consumer goods. Since consumer goods yield utility, this then is a measure, albeit imperfect, of the change in utility of the trader.

An example of a one commodity index—the simplest case—may help to clarify the point. Assume that the trader holds 100 bushels of wheat at t_i, when the price is $2 per bushel. As a result of several exchanges (unspecified) he holds 200 bushels at t_{i+1}, when the price is $1.50 per bushel. Thus, his total asset value in current prices is $200 at t_i and $450 at t_{i+1}.

Also assume that the consumer price index contains only one commodity, say potatoes, which are priced at $.50 per pound at t_i and at $.75 per pound at t_{i+1}. Thus, the price index is $.75/.50 = 1.5$. The respective balance sheets would appear as follows:

	t_i Unadjusted	t_i Adjusted	t_{i+1} Unadjusted
Wheat	$200	$300	$450
Total Assets	$200	$300	$450
Net Worth	$200	$300	$300
Income for the Period			150
Total Equities	$200	$300	$450

The figures have a clear empirical meaning. At t_i the trader could have purchased $200/.50 = 400$ pounds of potatoes. At t_{i+1} he could purchase $450/.75 = 600$ pounds of potatoes. Thus, his income stated in pounds of potatoes is 200, a 50% increase. The adjusted figures have the same meaning. His adjusted value is $300, which when divided by the price of potatoes at t_{i+1}, yields a command of 400 pounds. The income for the period is 150% of the adjusted previous value, and it is also an income of 200 (150/.75) when reconverted to pounds of potatoes. Thus, the basic measuring unit is pounds of potatoes in this simple example. Assuming that the trader's utility varies with his command over potatoes, then we have measured his increase in utility.

Of course, when one uses a weighted average of several consumer goods, the above calculations cannot be made. But the *concept* is the same. The difference in the respective market values adjusted for changes in the consumer price index yields a difference in the quantity of consumer goods that can be commanded. We have shifted the basic unit of measure from money to quantities of goods, and we assume that utility varies with those quantities.

Other Valuation Methods

Relaxing the stable price level assumption strengthens the case against the other methods of valuation. Under the Fisher Tradition, one would need to project the future price index as well as the future revenue in order to discount comparable figures. This is an even more herculean task than the original. Boulding's Constant is by definition not concerned with the present price of the particular commodity, and thus it is reasonable to assume that it would not be concerned with the price changes of other commodities, i.e. the price index.

The amount of accounting literature devoted to the price index problem is second only to that devoted to uniformity of principles. There is a plethora of argument and analysis, but unfortunately it is concerned almost exclusively with adjusting historical costs. No attempt will be made at a comprehensive review. Instead, we will classify the arguments and briefly discuss them. (These classifications are not necessarily mutually exclusive and are certainly not exhaustive.)[7]

---

7. See Littleton (*Structure*, pp. 214 ff.) for an argument that unadjusted historical costs are appropriate and no change is needed. The accounting literature on the problem is vast and conflicting. One recurrent error in the literature is the confusion of price-level adjusted historical costs with valuations based on current prices. Some consider price-level adjustments of historical costs to be a means of

1. Those opposed to the adjustments for two reasons.
    a. Income is now being properly measured in historical costs and therefore, no adjustment is called for.
    b. The price indices are too crude and arbitrary to be used.
2. Those in favor of price level adjustments, but who differ as to
    a. Selection of the kind of index, i.e. general or specific.
    b. Method of application of the index.

We have previously concluded that income was not properly measured in the Accounting Tradition and therefore reject reason 1a. Although we can sympathize with the crudeness argument, 1b, we also reject it on the grounds presented above.

Most accountants now have recanted on the specific index proposal, presumably because they have discovered that the *most specific* index is a price relative that leads them to current prices.[8] The original

---

getting to current values; and then this set is divided into those who oppose this because it is a departure from historical costs and those who favor it for the same reason. Some think that valuations based on current prices would make the adjustments unnecessary.

Paton states the problem of deciding between index numbers as follows: "... the basic question of index numbers. There are two main possibilities (and a host of minor variations). One approach is that of replacement costs or values as related to the affairs of the particular concern. . . .

"The second main possibility is the use of index numbers designed to reflect the change in the general level of prices for the whole economy and hence the change in the value of the monetary unit itself. This approach has an especial appeal in that it is fundamentally consistent with the strict cost basis of accounting. This approach doesn't actually abandon recorded costs; instead it modifies such costs. . . ." (Paton, "Inflation," pp. 542-43.)

The solution as we see it is to use values based on the prices existing at two points in time in order to take account of the price *ratio* change *and* then to adjust those values by an index to take account of the price *level* change. It is an error to think that either procedure alone will suffice or that one is a substitute for the other.

8. "Its [general index] weakness is in the fact that the over-all purchasing power of the dollar is not a meaningful concept to most individuals or business firms. . . . The price of any commodity or the average of the prices of any group of commodities may move at a markedly different rate, or even in a different direction, from the average of all prices. . . . However, if we think of adjusting historical costs for changes in the purchasing power of money *as measured between prices specific to the operations of the individual firm,* we find that we have again entered the realm of current cost, but by a new avenue." (Hill and Gordon, pp. 238-39.)

suggestions were for the adjustments to be made without recognizing the change as income. The problem was stated as one of matching current costs against current revenue. The results should be obvious: no income would ever be recognized. That is, the inflation of the historical costs by the price relative yields the same magnitude as the sales price. When they are matched, the difference (income) is always zero. This again is a switch in the valuing agent from cash to the commodity. It usually goes under the heading of "keeping physical capital intact" versus "keeping monetary capital intact." By keeping physical capital intact, the command over goods can go to infinity without any income ever being recognized.[9]

The more recent work has recommended that a general price index be applied to the historical cost figures. Both the American Accounting Association and the AICPA have made studies that reach this conclusion. For example, in adjusting the land account, Mason (p. 20) writes: "*Land.*—The land was acquired in 1932 when the price-level index was 58.4 or the purchasing power 1.954 times that of December, 1952. In order to express its cost in terms of the December, 1952 dollars, this calculation is made: $12,000 × 1.954 = $23,400." More recently the Research Staff of the AICPA has recommended the same procedure. They write:

> At this point a summary statement is given to provide prospective. With respect to "invested costs" or "nonmonetary items" (e.g., assets that are not in the form of money or claims to money), and with all technical details aside, the dollar amounts ascribed to the item at one point of time may be restated in terms of the dollar at any other point of time . . . . (ARS 6, p. 10.)

Their example is provided by "land, at cost of $1,000," held through

9. This is true only in trading enterprises. In the case of producer goods or commodities bought and sold in different markets, the recommended adjustments would serve to lessen reported income (in periods of inflation), but not necessarily reduce it to zero. Paton succinctly describes this method. In essence, one records the appreciation in the asset, but does not classify that appreciation as income. Then the amount of the expense to be matched against revenue is based on the appreciated figure. The net effect in a period of inflation is to lessen net income; and Paton says that this procedure "might be called the compromise (have-your-cake-and-eat-it-too) approach." (Paton, "Inflation," p. 24.)

a period when the "general price-level index rises from 100 to 200." The land is then stated in end-of-period prices, by multiplying $1,000 by two and valuing it on the balance sheet at $2,000.

Thus, in both cases a past (purchase) price is multiplied by a weighted average of price changes in other commodities. The resulting figure of $23,400 or $2,000 is an enigma. It is difficult to state exactly what it means. For example, does the $2,000 represent the amount of goods (or dollars) that would have to be sacrificed now in order to obtain the land? No, not unless the price changes were proportional. Does the $2,000 represent the amount that could be received if the land is sold? No, not unless the changes were proportional. Does it represent the discounted expected receipts? Clearly not.

The figure, at best, represents the present quantity of goods that would have to be sacrificed in order to acquire the asset at a *previous* exchange ratio that has now changed. That is, there is an implicit denial of the importance of price ratio changes, but a **recognition of** the need to adjust for price *level* changes. The resulting figure has the same effect as the proportional price change assumption. The assumption is not made, but the results are recognized. "The result is consistent with a common sense interpretation—an invested cost of 1,000 'date-of-acquisition' dollars is restated as the equivalent of 2,000 'end-of-period' dollars, with *no gain or loss* recorded, while *cash* held through a doubling of the price level *loses half its* value, or $1,000, measured in 'end-of-period' dollars." (ARS 6, p. 12, italics added.) Cash has become the risky asset, with the loss being recorded because cash was held; but the land has simply been "restated," and that "restatement" is not a gain or loss, hence it has become riskless. Of course, if the land were now sold it would be sold for $2,000 if the price changes were proportional, and we could agree that there was no gain or loss. If the price changes were not proportional, then the land would be sold for something different from $2,000; and the gain or loss would be "realized."

To make our disagreement with the procedure of adjusting historical costs explicit, let us consider it in respect to the trading firm. Assume that the trader purchases $W(t_i)$ bushels at a price of $P_w(t_i)$. Thus, $P_w(t_i)W(t_i)$ is the historical cost of the wheat. To "restate" those costs, there are two proposed procedures: a specific and a general price index adjustment.

The specific price index is simply the price relative at two points in time, i.e. $\dfrac{P_w(t_{i+1})}{P_w(t_i)}$, and therefore the "adjustment" always results in the current price.

$$\frac{P_w(t_{i+1})}{P_w(t_i)} P_w(t_i)W(t_i) = P_w(t_{i+1})W(t_i)$$

Thus, if one restates the historical cost of wheat (and the capital account), then one is simply valuing the wheat at current prices. The difficulty arises because this revaluation is not classified as income. Thus, if the wheat were sold at t_{i+1}, the revenue would be $P_w(t_{i+1})W(t_i)$ and the adjusted cost of goods sold (or replacement cost) would also be $P_w(t_{i+1})W(t_i)$ and of course the difference (income) would be zero.[10]

The second procedure is to restate the historical cost by use of a general price index. To continue the simple example presented above, assume that the consumer goods market basket consists only of potatoes, which have increased in price from $.50 to $.75 per pound from t_i to t_{i+1}. Also assume that the trader purchased 100 bushels of wheat at t_i, when the price was $2.00 per bushel, and holds 100 bushels at t_{i+1}, when the price is $1.50 per bushel. The historical cost balance sheets follow:

	t_i Unadjusted	t_{i+1} Unadjusted	t_{i+1} Adjusted
Wheat	$200	$200	$300
Total Assets	$200	$200	$300
Net Worth	$200	$200	$300
Income	-0-	-0-	-0-
Total Equities	$200	$200	$300

10. This is because, as we have repeatedly emphasized, this shifts the measuring unit to bushels of wheat. One could never profit by holding wheat in this situation, because regardless of what one sold his wheat for, the replacement cost would be equal. One could profit by holding money while the price of wheat was declining, or lose by holding money while the price of wheat was rising—the exact opposite of our ordinary conception.

The t_i unadjusted balance sheet has the same empirical meaning as in the previous example—the trader could have purchased 400 pounds of potatoes if he had desired to do so. However, the t_{i+1} balance sheets do not have the same meaning. The $300 figure represents the equivalent pounds of potatoes that he did sacrifice at t_i—400 = 300/.75—but that information was given in the t_i report and is therefore superfluous. The $300 does not represent the pounds that he is currently sacrificing nor the dollars that he could currently command. The $300 would represent the current sacrifice or command if, and only if, the price change of wheat was proportional with the price change of potatoes.

The anomaly in the above arises if there were cash on the balance sheet. The cash represents a current value or command, and if it were added to a past command, the sum is inexplicable. This is easily illustrated by assuming that the wheat was sold at t_{i+1}. The cash received would be $150, which can command only 200 pounds of potatoes as opposed to the original 400 pounds sacrificed.

The example is caged, of course, because we have assumed a price decline. If the price had risen, the accountant would argue that the profit was "unrealized" but that a price decline would be "realized" under the lower of cost or market rule. That is, price ratio changes are taken into account when they result in losses, but not when they result in gains. Also note that the monetary assets would be adjusted to show the *loss* in purchasing power (ARS 6, p. 11). For these reasons, the recommended price level adjustments seem to be extensions of the principle of conservatism and lend further support to our hypothesis that conservatism is the fundamental principle of valuation in the Accounting Tradition.

We disagree with the principle of conservatism. We see no valid reason for adjusting for price level changes without also adjusting for price ratio changes regardless of the direction of the change. There are *two* significant factors that need to be taken into account when the price changes are nonproportional. Taking account of only one of those factors, or taking account of changes in only one direction of those factors, does not solve the problem.

Summary

Instability of the price level is defined as a change in the size of the unit. In order to determine the magnitude of the similarity transformation for the units, there must be an invariant referent. Such a referent is found in the concept of utility. Thus, the similarity transformation—the price index—is the ratio of two amounts of money that will yield the same utility.

The concept is clear. The basic purpose is to discover how much "better off" a person is who holds money or monetary claims at two points in time. It is an intertemporal problem of the change in wealth, and as such it is vital to the concept of income.

In application of the concept, there are two main problems. First, utility is not subject to empirical determination; and second, utility is highly personal and varies from person to person. Patterns of purchases have been postulated as a substitute for the utility measure and assumed to be invariant in utility. This is a generalization that is not perfectly applicable to any particular case. The degree of applicability varies inversely with the degree of deviation from the postulated pattern of purchases.

These two problems, and particularly the second, must mitigate any conclusions about the use of index numbers. In view of the criterion of relevance, however, it is imperative that the present price valuation be presented and that the adjustments be made to the past valuations. This procedure will leave the informational content of the latest report intact. Further, it will allow each individual to calculate his personal price index, if he has the ability and desire.

In spite of these serious problems, an index-adjusted time series is a desideratum. As a generalization it is conceptually useful, although its limitations are rather severe. The decision presents us with the problem of postulating a pattern of purchases, i.e. selecting an index.

In light of our earlier observations on the chain of motivation for the enterprise, we conclude that the Consumer Price Index is appropriate. Admittedly, this is not a perfect index, but it is superior to its competitors. The other general indices include intermediate goods, and their use requires some rather odd assumptions about the nature of the enterprise's motivation. The use of specific indices reverts to the replacement cost argument and shifts the valuing agent from money to the specific commodity. In short, the alternatives lead to absurdity, and this strengthens our conclusion that the Consumer Price Index is appropriate.

XIV

EPILOGUE

The principal problem of this study has been the determination of the proper or best way to measure income. Given the generally accepted definition of income as the difference between wealth at two points in time plus consumption or dividends, the problem may be reduced to the proper method of measuring wealth. Under the assumption that the components or individual commodities are to be valued and summed in order to get the value of the whole, as opposed to directly valuing the whole, the problem is reduced to the appropriate method of valuing each commodity class. There are many diverse and complex methods of valuation in complex situations. In order to reduce the problem to manageable proportions and get at what we believe to be the fundamental issues, a highly simplified firm model was postulated—a wheat trader in a perfect market with a stable price level. In this model the problems are abundantly clear and may be cast in strong relief.

The value of the commodity class in such a model is given by the product of a valuation coefficient and a quantity. We assume that there is no difficulty in determining or deciding on the quantity. Four valuation coefficients have been suggested in the literature, and thus the problem is reduced to the selection of the appropriate valuation coefficient.

Boulding and others have argued that the valuation is arbitrary and therefore a constant valuation coefficient is as appropriate as any other. The other valuation coefficients that have been advanced are all transformation coefficients—prices—which are distinguished by their temporal location. The Accounting Tradition uses a past (purchase) price; Present Market uses a price current at the time the report is prepared; and the Fisher Tradition uses a discounted future (sale) price.

We noted that it was possible to measure the stock of goods (and the changes in that stock) in many dimensions—e.g. weight—and that there was no a priori reason for the selection of any of those dimensions. Thus, we did not start from a completely naive position, because we restricted our considerations to the specified valuation and transformation coefficients. Even this restriction requires some preliminary decisions, because of the dispute and confusion over whether physical capital or monetary capital should be measured. One of the commodities must be "transformed to," or "measured in terms of," the other. Many proponents of lifo and replacement cost argue that the money held or received should be valued on the basis of the number of units of inventory that the money can purchase. This procedure in effect makes the physical quantity the basic unit of measure or the valuing agent. The alternative is to value the physical quantity in money terms. Shifting from one valuing agent to the other leads to apparent paradoxes and disputes that cannot be resolved. Selection of the valuing agent required that we consider the nature of the enterprise, and we concluded that the motivation of the enterprise was provided by the trader-owner. In turn, the trader's motivation is the maximization of utility, which varies in the same direction as the command over goods. Therefore, we selected money as the appropriate valuing agent.

The fact that income is a temporal concept, being defined as the difference in wealth at two points in time, and the fact that reports of income and wealth are prepared periodically led us to decide to measure at a point in time, as opposed to an event. The impetus of such a measurement is to provide information at a point in time about the current state of the enterprise and about the events that have occurred since the last report was received.

THE CRITERIA

Informational Content

Because "information" is desired, one possible criterion for selection is the "informational content" of the various valuation coefficients. We isolated two attributes of information: verity and relevance.

Verity. Information, as opposed to misinformation, must be "veritable." The goal is to describe "reality" by forming certain propositions which must correspond in some way to that reality. The difficulty is that reality is subject to different perceptions by different perceivers and that the same perceptions by the same perceivers are subject to different interpretations. Tests of which perceptions and interpretations are erroneous are hard to come by, because, among other reasons, the tester is subject to perception and interpretation errors. The ultimate test for both is agreement among qualified observers. Thus, there is (1) a "democratic" assumption that the modal perception and interpretation is the true one and (2) an "authoritative" assumption that a certain group of people has superior perception and interpretation abilities.

In addition, the intent of the informant may be either to inform or misinform. Thus, the proposition about reality may not be veritable if the informant intends to deceive.

One attribute of verity that is implied by these considerations is that the propositions are contingent as opposed to analytic. Analytic propositions refer to the rules of logic being employed and may be valid or invalid. Contingent propositions refer to reality and are testable by observation.

Relevance. An infinite number of empirical observations can be made, and thus an infinite number of veritable contingent propositions may be formulated. The problem is to select the appropriate veritable contingent propositions.

All veritable contingent propositions may be said to be "valuable information," since they all provide knowledge of the world and one may simply be curious about the world. If one is faced with a situation that requires selection from alternative courses of action and a particular proposition or set of propositions is thought to bear on those alternatives, then those propositions may be said to be "more valuable" than others. Such a state is referred to as a "problematic situation," and the partciular proposition is said to be "relevant information."

Thus, relevance refers to a particular problematic situation. The problematic situation itself does not specify the relevant information. A "decision theory" is required. A decision theory is a set of inter-related generalized analytic and contingent propositions, the specific values of which are undefined. It is used to select from among alternative courses of action by manipulating the propositions in accordance with certain rules. The outcomes of the manipulations are expected to correspond with the empirical consequences of selecting different alternatives. Thus, the decision theory may be said to "predict" the empirical consequences of various alternatives. This is said to be a "solution" of the problematic situation.

Communications. When the object about which information is desired is spatially and/or temporally separated from the person who is faced with the problematic situation, a communication system is required. In a communication system a person ("transmitter") at the transmission source makes the observations and formulates the contingent propositions ("message") and transmits that message to the persons faced with the problematic situations ("receivers"). Thus, the transmitter acts as a proxy for the receivers in that he must make the observations and formulate the contingent propositions. In order for the message to be informative (a) the transmitter's perceptions and interpretations must be accurate; (b) he must intend to inform rather than deceive; and (c) he must decide which contingent propositions are relevant. Given (a) and (b), the problem is reduced to the selection of the relevant information by the transmitter.

Difficulties arise because different receivers may be faced with different problematic situations and because different receivers may employ different decision theories for the solution of the same problem. Thus, the transmitter must know the problems and decision theories of the receivers in order to decide which information is relevant to them. Given no constraints, it is conceivable that the transmitter could satisfy all of the receivers. Unfortunately there are constraints: resources are scarce and costly. We call these constraints "channel capacity." Given that the capacity of the channel is less than the capacity required to satisfy all of the receivers, the transmitter must select certain information to be transmitted from a set of information, all of which is relevant to at least one receiver.

Further difficulties become apparent when it is recognized that (1) the receiver may not be aware of a problematic situation until a message is received; (2) the classification by the receivers of data into relevant and irrelevant categories is likely to have been influenced by the data included and not included in previous messages; and (3) some receivers may be employing erroneous decision theories. For these reasons, reverse direction messages ("feedback" or surveys) cannot be relied on to provide a satisfactory solution. Feedback is usually concerned with the clarification or elaboration of information already received which was relevant to a problem. Because of (1), the receiver may not be aware of a problem. Surveys may turn out to be circular because of (2); and they may not be adequate to improve the quality of decisions because of (3). Therefore, the transmitter cannot be neutral. Instead he must be actively engaged in the evaluation and refinement, if not construction, of decision theories.

The decision theory specifies which data is relevant, and therefore the problem of selecting the relevant information reduces to the selection of the appropriate decision theory. The appropriateness of a decision theory depends upon the existing problematic situation and the relative ability of that decision theory to predict empirical consequences of alternative courses of action. The transmitter's task may be broken down into three parts:

(1) Empirical: The determination of the perceived problems and decision theories now being employed by the receivers.
(2) Theoretical: (a) Comparison of the receivers' perceived problems to the "actual" (theoretically determined) problems. This provides an indirect evaluation of the adequacy of the messages now being transmitted; (b) evaluation of the decision theories now being employed for the solution

of the perceived problems; (c) construction of better decision theories for the solution of present perceived problems; and (d) anticipation of future problems and decision theories.

(3) Educational: The instruction of the receivers in the relevance (or lack thereof) of the previously transmitted data and the reasons for converting (or not converting) to different data, including instruction on decision theories.

Measurement

The preference for measurements is subsumed under the criterion of relevance. To use Churchman's language, measurements *are* "precise information" that "can be used in a wide variety of problems." In our terms, measurements are likely to be relevant to more problematic situations, and they are more amenable to manipulation in the decision theories. To speak loosely, then, measurements may be said to be "more informative" than other kinds of information.

Sometimes essentially the same requirement is stated in terms of "theoretical import" for "systematic purposes." These are Hempel's terms, and he means that certain properties are specified by theories because they are related to other properties via that theory. Some properties, such as "hage," are curiosities because they are *not* specified by *any* theory. These other properties, in our terms, would be said to be completely irrelevant, because they do not bear upon any problematic situation.

The problem is that the items of wealth ("commodities" or "goods") may take different forms. This is sometimes stated as the problem of heterogeneity. From a measurement point of view this formulation is not strictly correct. All objects are "heterogeneous" to some degree, if for no other reason than that they occupy different spatial locations. We do not compare objects per se. Instead we compare properties or characteristics of objects. Thus, the problem is to discover the property or characteristic that is common to the goods. However, there are many such properties (e.g. weight, hardness, color), and therefore the problem reduces to discovering the particular property (or properties) that is relevant to the particular decision theories being employed.

In addition to relevancy, there are specific measurement criteria that are pertinent because of the peculiarities of the problem at hand.

Additivity. Since we have postulated that we will add to get wealth and subtract to get income, the criterion of additivity or extensivity must be met. This narrows the set of properties or characteristics that are appropriate. Hardness, for example would be excluded on these grounds.

Temporal Consistency. Since we have accepted the definition of income as being the difference between wealth at two points in time, the requirement that wealth be measured at a point in time, as opposed to an event, is established. The fact that we are adding commodity classes to get wealth implies that each commodity class be measured at some point in time. The fact that a commodity class's value is a product of two coefficients implies that both coefficients be determined at the same point in time.

Decisions

In general, a decision is the process of selection from among currently available alternatives. One predicts the outcome of each alternative and then selects the alternative that yields the preferred predicted outcome. Given the decision-maker's preferences or maximand, there are two problems.

Determination of Currently Available Alternatives. In every decision one selects from among alternatives that are *available currently*. One may reflect on alternatives that are not available or hypothesize about what would have happened had other alternatives been selected in the past. Such reflection may be useful in formulating a decision theory. However, by definition, one is restricted to the selection from among currently available alternatives in each decision.

In matters of economics the alternatives are to hold certain goods or claims against goods. Each combination of goods and claims against goods can be said to be one alternative. Goods may be exchanged via a transformation coefficient or price. Prices relate all goods to each other, and therefore current prices delineate all available alternatives. Thus, the set of all current prices is relevant to all decisions, because those prices define the currently available alternatives and one must know his currently available alternatives in order to decide.

Prediction of Consequences of Alternatives. Prediction of specific consequences, as opposed to if-then or *ceteris paribus* consequences, is notoriously difficult. Many different methods of predicting are in use. It is impossible to prove that any predictive method is superior to another, because all of the evidence confirming or disconfirming a particular method lies in the past and predictions are concerned with the future. Thus, one can demonstrate that a particular method *has been* superior to another, but to allege that it *will be* superior to another requires a prediction about predictive methods which leads to an infinite regress.

Thus, there are disagreements about prediction models that are not subject to ultimate resolution. Different people may use different prediction models, and therefore different information is relevant to their decisions.

Valuation. Valuation is a decision process. A person is presented with certain available courses of action, and he must select. In commerce and economics these courses of action are usually mutually exclusive. Thus, the valuation process requires that one sacrifice one course of action in order to obtain or maintain another. Since the selection is an individual matter that varies from one person to another and varies over time for the same person, one cannot measure value directly. However, it is possible to measure the sacrifice that one incurs. To measure the current sacrifice requires that one measure the amount of funds that is not acquired because one holds a good in addition to measuring the funds exchanged when the good was obtained. Thus, for all goods possessed, the current money sacrifice is the immediate sale price of the goods. When that magnitude is added to the stock of money held, the command-over-goods dimension is measured.

APPLICATION OF THE CRITERIA

The criterion of relevance reduces to the specification of the problematic situation and the decision theory applicable to that situation. That decision theory then specifies the particular bits of empirical information that are needed to make the decision. One requirement of all decision theories is that the available alternatives be specified. The available alternatives pertinent to this study are the kinds and quantities of goods that can be held. This information is given by the present prices of the goods offered in the market. Thus, the present market price is relevant to all decision theories.

The trader needs to know the present price in order to know what alternatives are available to him. Then he needs to predict the future in order to choose. The other interested receivers need to know the present value (present sale price times present quantity) in order to compare that value with their predictions of future values, regardless of how they predict the future. Also both the trader and other receivers need to know the present value in order to know whether or not the enterprise can meet present obligations.

The future prices and values are also relevant to the decision process. In fact, knowledge of the future is *the* most valuable information in the sense that people would be willing to pay more for it than any other kind of information. However, the reason why it is so valuable is that it is so scarce. Different people use different methods for predicting the future, and different data is required for those different methods. Different people predict different future outcomes, including, in our case, exactly opposite outcomes, since there is a long for every short. Most predictions in matters of commerce are not precisely formulated. For these reasons, we concluded that the reporting of present values should have precedence over the reporting of predicted future values. In addition we noted that the trader's current position, valued in current prices, gave information about the direction of his expectations. Thus, the present values yield information about the currently available alternatives *and* the predictions of the trader.

Past (purchase) prices have no relevance to any well-formulated decision theory that we are aware of. Such values are sunk and therefore cannot specify the currently available alternatives. One *may* use a series of past prices as a basis for predicting future prices, but such a series may or may not include the price at the event of the exchange. Thus, a series of past prices may be relevant to some prediction methods, but the elements of that series are more likely to be chosen on the basis of their temporal location than on the basis of a particular exchange.

Regarding the other criteria, we argued that present values met all the requirements but that past and future values failed many of the requirements. In a perfect market it is likely that observer agreement would be perfect in respect to present prices; but the very nature of the market prohibits observer agreement on future prices, and the different accounting procedures allow for many different historical costs. Therefore, present prices are "objective and verifiable," while discounted expectations and historical costs are not.

We specified the sacrifice or command-over-goods dimension which present prices measure. That dimension has a clear empirical meaning, and in a perfect market the individual prices are additive within the commodity class as well as among commodity classes. We are not aware of the dimension being measured in the Accounting Tradition. The empirical significance of the sum of a present quantity of wheat multiplied by a past price added to a present quantity of money is not clear to us. Any of the accounting procedures used to allocate the costs may be considered to be analytic, as opposed to contingent, propositions. Fifo *means* that one is to exhaust the earlier purchase prices as the goods are sold. The only empirical variable in such cases is the quantity sold. Although we were able to describe such figures in a fairly precise manner, we are not aware of the theoretical import of those figures. Until the theoretical import is known, we would put them in the same class as "hage"—a figure that may have high precision and uniformity of usage, but is of no use for systematic purposes.

In short, the Present Market method of valuation is (1) relevant to all receivers, because it specifies the currently available alternatives and the ability to perform current obligations; (2) veritable, in the sense that all observers would agree to the value; (3) a measurement of an empirically meaningful dimension; (4) additive, in the sense that the sum of the parts is equal to the independent measurement of the whole; (5) temporally consistent, in that the measurement is made at a point in time as opposed to an event and as opposed to a prediction; (6) a valuation, in that we can infer that the trader prizes his selected position more than the other available positions; and (7) more informative than any other single figure, because it indicates the direction of the trader's expectation.

When the market is imperfect, there will be disagreement among observers, and there will be questions about the additivity of the parts. When the price level is unstable, the measure will not reflect the changes in the command over goods and sacrifice (although it will still reflect the sacrifice and command-over-goods at a point in time), and the procedures for correcting this are imperfect. Despite these limitations, the Present Market is the superior valuation method. It still meets the criteria better than the other suggested valuation methods. Therefore, for this type of firm, we conclude that the periodic reports ought to show the current (exit) values at the time the report is prepared, and the subsequent reports should adjust the previous reports by the Consumer Price Index.

These conclusions are restricted to the trading assets in a trading firm. Given that restriction, we think the conclusions of this study are incontrovertible. We invite the reader to demonstrate that they are not.

We also think that these conclusions can be extended with minor modifications to other types of firms. However, since we have not demonstrated their extensibility and since Braithwaite (p. 93) has warned that "the price of the employment of models is eternal vigilance," we will offer the extension of these conclusions to other firm models as an unsupported conjecture that requires further research.

WORKS CITED

Abbott, Lawrence. *Economics and the Modern World*. New York: Harcourt, Brace and World, Inc., 1960.

Alexander, Sidney S. "Income Measurement in a Dynamic Economy," revised by David Solomons, in *Studies in Accounting Theory*, eds. W. T. Baxter and Sidney Davidson, pp. 126-200. 2nd ed.; Homewood, Illinois: Richard D. Irwin Press, 1962.

American Institute of Certified Public Accountants. *Accounting Trends and Techniques*. New York: American Institute of Certified Public Accountants, Periodical.

American Institute of Certified Public Accountants. *Reporting the Financial Effects of Price Level Changes*. ("Accounting Research Study No. 6.") New York: American Institute of Certified Public Accountants, 1963.

American Institute of Certified Public Accountants. *Restatement and Revision of Accounting Research Bulletins*. ("Accounting Research and Terminology Bulletins," final edition.) New York: American Institute of Certified Public Accountants, 1961.

Andersen (Arthur) and Company. *The Postulate of Accounting*. Chicago: Arthur Andersen & Co., 1960.

Baxter, W. T. "Accounting Values: Sale Price Versus Replacement Cost," *Journal of Accounting Research*, V (Autumn, 1967), 208-14.

Bergmann, Gustav. "The Logic of Measurement," in *Proceedings of the Sixth Hydraulics Conference, June 13-15, 1955*, pp. 19-33. ("State University of Iowa Studies in Engineering.") Iowa City: State University of Iowa, 1956.

———, and Spence, Kenneth W. "The Logic of Psychophysical Measurement," in *Readings in the Philosophy of Science*, eds. Herbert Feigl and May Brodbeck, pp. 103-22. New York: Appleton-Century-Crofts, Inc., 1953.

Berle, Adolph A., Jr. *Power Without Property: A New Development in American Political Economy*. New York: Harcourt, Brace and Co., 1959.

Boulding, Kenneth E. *Economic Analysis*. 3rd ed.; New York: Harper and Bros., 1955.

————. *A Reconstruction of Economics.* New York: John Wiley and Sons, Inc., 1950.

————. *The Skills of the Economist.* Cleveland: Howard Allen, Inc., 1958.

————. "Contemporary Economic Research," in *Trends in Social Science,* ed. Donald P. Ray, pp. 9-26. New York: Philosophical Library, Inc., 1961.

————. "Economics and Accounting: The Uncongenial Twins," in *Studies in Accounting Theory,* eds. W. T. Baxter and S. Davidson, pp. 44-55. Homewood, Illinois: Richard D. Irwin, Inc., 1962.

Bowers, Russell. "Tests of Income Realization," *Accounting Review,* XVI (June 1941), 139-55; reprinted in *An Income Approach to Accounting Theory,* eds. Sidney Davidson *et al.* Englewood Cliffs, New Jersey: Prentice-Hall, Inc., 1964.

Bows, Albert J. "The Urgent Need for Accounting Reform," *The National Association of Accountants Bulletin,* XLII, No. 1 (September 1960), pp. 43-52.

Braithwaite, Richard Bevan. *Scientific Explanation: A Study of the Function of Theory, Probability and Law in Science.* Cambridge: The Cambridge University Press, 1953.

Bridgman, Percy William. *The Logic of Modern Physics.* New York: Macmillan Co., 1927.

Broad, C. D. "On the Relation Between Induction and Probability," Part I, *Mind,* XXVII (October 1918), 389-404.

————. "The Relation Between Induction and Probability," Part II, *Mind,* XXIX (January 1920), 11-45.

Bruner, Jerome Seymour, and Postman, Leo. "On the Perception of Incongruity: A Paradigm," *Journal of Personality,* XVIII (1949-1950), 206-23.

Burnham, James. *The Managerial Revolution: What is Happening in the World.* New York: The John Day Company, Inc., 1941.

Butterfield, Herbert. *The Origins of Modern Science 1300-1800.* New York: Free Press, 1957.

Butters, J. Keith. *Effects of Taxation: Inventory Accounting and Policies.* Boston: Division of Research, Graduate School of Business Administration, Harvard University, 1949.

Campbell, Norman R. *Account of the Principles of Measurement and Calculation.* London: Longmans, 1928.

————. *Physics: The Elements.* Cambridge: Cambridge University Press, 1920. Reprinted as *Foundations of Science: The Philosophy of Theory and Experiment*. New York: Dover Publications, Inc., 1957.

———. "Measurement and Its Importance to Philosophy," *Aristotelian Society Supplement*, XVII (1938).

Canning, John B. *The Economics of Accountancy*. New York: The Ronald Press Co., 1929.

Carr, Edward Hallett. *The New Society*. Boston: Beacon Press, 1957.

Caws, Peter. "Definition and Measurement in Physics," in *Measurement: Definitions and Theories*, eds. C. West Churchman and Philburn Ratoosh, pp. 3-17. New York: John Wiley and Sons, Inc., 1959.

Chambers, Raymond J. *Accounting, Evaluation, and Economic Behavior*. Englewood Cliffs, New Jersey: Prentice-Hall, Inc., 1966.

———. "Measurement and Objectivity in Accounting," *Accounting Review*, XXXIX (April 1964), 264-74.

Cherry, Colin. *On Human Communication: A Review, a Survey, and a Criticism*. Cambridge: The Technology Press of Massachusetts Institute of Technology, 1957.

Churchman, Charles West. "A Materialist Theory of Measurement," in *Philosophy for the Future*, eds. Roy Wood Sellars, V. J. McGill, and Marvin Farber, pp. 476-94. New York: Macmillan Co., 1949.

———. "Why Measure?" in *Measurement: Definitions and Theories*, eds. Charles West Churchman and Philburn Ratoosh, pp. 83-94.

Cohen, Morris R., and Nagel, Ernest. *An Introduction to Logic and Scientific Method*. New York: Harcourt, Brace and Co., 1934.

Corbin, Donald A. *Accounting and Economic Decisions*. New York: Dodd, Mead and Co., 1964.

Davidson, Donald, and Marschak, Jacob. "Experimental Tests of a Stochastic Decision Theory," in *Measurement: Definitions and Theories*, eds. C. West Churchman and Philburn Ratoosh, pp. 233-69. New York: John Wiley and Sons, Inc., 1959.

Devine, Carl Thomas. "Loss Recognition," in *An Income Approach to Accounting Theory*, eds. Sidney Davidson *et al.*, pp. 162-72. Englewood Cliffs, New Jersey: Prentice-Hall, Inc., 1964.

Dewey, John. *The Quest for Certainty: A Study of the Relation of Knowledge and Action*. New York: Minton, Balch & Company, 1929.

———. "Theory of Valuation" (*International Encyclopedia of Unified Science*, Foundations of the Unity of Science, Vol. II, No. 4). Chicago: The University of Chicago Press, 1939.

Dicksee, Lawrence Robert. *Auditing*. London: Gee and Co., 1892.

Duhem, Pierre Maurice Maric. *The Aim and Structure of Physical*

Theory, tr. Phillip P. Wiener. Princeton: Princeton University Press, 1954.

Dun's Quarterly Failure Report.

Edwards, Edgar O., and Bell, Phillip W. *The Theory and Measurement of Business Income.* Berkeley: University of California Press, 1961.

Einstein, Albert. *Relativity: The Special and General Theory.* 15th ed.; New York: Crown Publishers, Inc., 1961.

Eisner, Internal Revenue Collector, v. *Macomber* 252 U.S. 189, 1920.

Evans, Ralph Merrill. *An Introduction to Color.* New York: John Wiley and Sons, 1948.

Ferguson, A., *et al.* "Quantitative Estimates of Sensory Events," *British Association for the Advancement of Science,* 1938, pp. 277-334; January 1940, pp. 331-49.

Finney, Harry A. "Principles and Conventions," *Accounting Review,* XIX (October 1944), 361-66.

————, and Miller, Herbert E. *Principles of Accounting: Intermediate.* 4th. ed.; Englewood Cliffs, New Jersey: Prentice-Hall, Inc., 1951.

————. *Principles of Accounting: Introductory.* 6th ed.; Englewood Cliffs, New Jersey: Prentice-Hall, Inc., 1963.

Fisher, Irving. *The Theory of Interest.* New York: The Macmillan Co., 1930.

————. *The Nature of Capital and Income.* New York: The Macmillan Co., 1906.

Furubotn, Eririk G. "Investment Alternatives and the Supply Schedule of the Firm." Unpublished paper presented at the Annual Conference of the Southern Economic Association, Roanoke, Va., November 15, 1963.

Geiger, George R. "Toward an Integrated Ethics," in *The Cleavage in Our Culture,* ed. Frederick Henry Burkhardt, pp. 105-18. Boston: Beacon Press, 1952.

Gibson, W. I. "On the Nature of Total Perception." Unpublished manuscript, Cornell University, Ithaca, New York.

Goldberg, Louis. "The Present State of Accounting Theory," *Accounting Review,* XXXVIII (July 1963), 457-69.

Goldman, Stanford. *Information Theory.* New York: Prentice-Hall, 1953.

Goodman, Nelson. "The Problem of Counterfactual Conditionals," *Journal of Philosophy,* XLIV (February 1947), 113-28, reprinted as chapter 1 in Nelson Goodman, *Fact, Fiction, and Forecast* (2nd ed.; New York: Bobbs-Merrill Company, Inc., 1965).

Gordon, Myron J. "Scope and Method of Theory in Research in the Measurement of Income and Wealth," *Accounting Review*, XXXV (October 1960), 603-18.

Grady, Paul. *Inventory of Generally Accepted Accounting Principles for Business Enterprises.* ("Accounting Research Study No. 7.") New York: American Institute of Certified Public Accountants, 1965.

Greenwald, William I. "Some General Limitations of the Consumer Price Index," *Labor Law Journal*, April 1956.

Grünbaum, Adolf. *Philosophical Problems of Space and Time.* New York: Alfred A. Knopf, 1963.

Guilbaud, Georges T. *What is Cybernetics?* tr. Valerie MacKay. New York: Criterion Books, 1959.

Guilford, Joy Paul. *Psychometric Methods.* 2nd ed.; New York: Mc-Graw-Hill Co., Inc., 1954.

Haig, Robert Murray. "'The Concept of Income—Economic and Legal Aspects," in *American Economic Association Readings in the Economics of Taxation*, IX, eds. Richard R. Musgrave and Carl S. Shoup, pp. 54-76. Homewood, Illinois: Richard D. Irwin, Inc., 1959.

Hansen, Palle. *The Accounting Concept of Profit.* Amsterdam: North Holland Publishing Co., 1962.

Hanson, Norwood Russell. *Patterns of Discovery.* Cambridge, England: Cambridge University Press, 1958.

Hayek, Friedrich A. *Pure Theory of Capital.* London: Macmillan & Co., Ltd., 1941.

Hempel, Carl G. "Fundamentals of Concept Formation in Empirical Science" (*International Encylcopedia of Unified Science*, II, No. 7). Chicago: The University of Chicago Press, 1952.

Hicks, John Richard. *Value and Capital.* 2nd ed.; London: Oxford University Press, 1946.

Hill, Thomas M., and Gordon, Myron J. *Accounting: A Management Approach.* Rev. ed.; Homewood, Illinois: Richard D. Irwin, Inc., 1959.

Hölder, O. "Die Axiome der Quantität und die Lehre vom Mass," *Leipzig: Berichte, Königl. Sächseschen Gesellschaft*, 1001.

Ijiri, Yuji. *The Foundations of Accounting Measurement.* Englewood Cliffs, New Jersey: Prentice-Hall, 1967.

Johnson, Arnold W., and Kriegman, Oscar M. *Intermediate Accounting.* 3rd ed.; New York: Holt, Rinehart and Winston, 1964.

Kerr, Jean St. G. "Three Concepts of Business Income," in *An Income Approach to Accounting Theory,* eds. Sidney Davidson *et al.,* pp. 40-48. Englewood Cliffs, New Jersey: Prentice-Hall, Inc., 1964.

Keynes, John Maynard. *A Treatise on Money.* Vol. I: *The Pure Theory of Money.* London: Macmillan and Co., Ltd., 1930.

————. *A Treatise on Probability.* London: Macmillan and Co., Ltd., 1921.

————. *The General Theory of Employment, Interest and Money.* New York: Harcourt, Brace and Co., 1936.

Keynes, John Neville. *The Scope and Method of Political Economy.* London: Macmillan and Co., 1891.

Koivisto, William A. *Principles and Problems of Modern Economics.* New York: John Wiley and Sons, Inc., 1957.

Kuhn, Thomas S. *The Structure of Scientific Revolutions.* Chicago: University of Chicago Press, 1962.

Ladd, Dwight R. *Contemporary Corporate Accounting and the Public.* Homewood, Illinois: Richard D. Irwin, Inc., 1963.

Lamont, William D. *The Value Judgment.* Edinburgh: University of Edinburgh Press, 1955.

Lassiter, Roy. "A Note on the Effects of Skewness and Kurtosis on Present Value." Unpublished manuscript, University of Florida, Gainesville.

Lester, Richard A. "Shortcomings of Marginal Analysis for Wage-Employment Problems," *American Economic Review,* XXXVI (March 1946), 63-82.

Lewis, Clarence Irving. *Mind and the World-Order: Outline of a Theory of Knowledge.* New York: Charles Scribner's Sons, 1929.

Life, XVII (September 18, 1964), 32.

Lindahl, Erik. "The Concept of Income," in *Economic Essays in Honour of Gustav Cassel,* pp. 399-407. London: George Allen & Unwin Ltd., 1933.

Littleton, Ananias Charles. *Structure of Accounting Theory.* ("American Accounting Association Monograph No. 5.") Urbana, Illinois: American Accounting Association, 1953.

McDonough, Adrian M. *Information Economics and Management Systems.* New York: McGraw-Hill Book Co., Inc., 1963.

Machlup, Fritz. "Operational Concepts and Mental Constructs in Model and Theory Formation," *Giornale degli Economisti e Annali di Economia,* XIX (September-October 1960), 553-82.

MacNeal, Kenneth. *Truth in Accounting.* Philadelphia: University of Pennsylvania Press, 1939.

Margenau, Henry. "Philosophical Problems Concerning the Meaning of Measurement in Physics," in *Measurement: Definitions and Theories,* eds. C. West Churchman and Philburn Ratoosh, pp. 163-76. New York: John Wiley and Sons, 1959.

Marple, Raymond P. "Value-itis," *Accounting Review,* XXXVIII (July 1963), 478-82.

Marshall, Alfred. *Money, Credit and Commerce.* London: Macmillan & Co., Ltd., 1923.

Mason, Perry. *Price-Level Changes and Financial Statements.* Columbus: American Accounting Association, 1956.

May, George O. *Financial Accounting.* New York: The Macmillan Company, 1943.

Merton, Robert K. *Social Theory and Social Structure.* Rev. and enl. ed.; Glencoe, Illinois: Free Press, 1957.

Mill, John Stuart. *Principles of Political Economy,* ed. Sir W. J. Ashley. London: Longmans, Green and Co., 1921.

Mitchell, E. T. "Values, Valuing, and Evaluation," in *Value: A Cooperative Inquiry,* ed. Ray Lepley, pp. 190-210. New York: Columbia University Press, 1949.

Montgomery, Robert H. *Auditing.* 2nd ed., rev. and enl.; New York: The Ronald Press, 1916.

Moonitz, Maurice. *The Basic Postulates of Accounting.* ("Accounting Research Study, No. 1.") New York: American Institute of Certified Public Accountants, 1961.

———, and Jordan, Louis H. *Accounting: An Analysis of Its Problems.* Rev. ed., Vol. I; New York: Holt, Rinehart and Winston, 1963.

Nagel, Ernest. "On the Logic of Measurement." Unpublished Ph.D. dissertation, Columbia University, 1930.

———. *The Structure of Science: Problems in the Logic of Scientific Explanation.* New York: Harcourt, Brace & World, Inc., 1961.

Ogden, C. K., and Richards, I. A. *The Meaning of Meaning. A Study of the Influence of Language Upon Thought and the Science of Symbolism.* 8th ed.; New York: Harcourt, Brace and Co., 1946.

Pap, Arthur. *An Introduction to the Philosophy of Science.* New York: Free Press of Glencoe, 1962.

Paton, William A. "Measuring Profits Under Inflation Conditions: A Serious Problem for Accountants," *The Journal of Accountancy,* LXXXIX (January 1950), 16-27.

———, and Littleton, A. C. *An Introduction to Corporate Accounting Standards.* Chicago: American Accounting Association, 1940.

———, and Paton, William A., Jr. *Asset Accounting.* New York: Macmillan Co., 1952.

Peirce, Charles S. S. *Essays in the Philosophy of Science.* New York: The Liberal Arts Press, 1957.

Pigou, Arthur Cecil. *The Economics of Welfare.* 4th ed.; London: Macmillan and Co., Ltd., 1932.

Poincaré, H. *The Foundations of Science.* Lancaster: The Science Press, 1946.

Reese, Thomas Whelan. "The Application of the Theory of Physical Measurement to the Measurement of Psychological Magnitudes, with Three Experimental Examples," *Psychological Monographs,* LV, No. 3 (1943), 1-89.

Robnett, Ronald H., Hill, Thomas M., and Beckett, John A. *Accounting: A Management Approach.* Homewood, Illinois: Richard D. Irwin, Inc., 1951.

Rogers, Hartley, Jr. "Information Theory," *Mathematics Magazine,* March 1964, pp. 63-78.

Russell, Bertrand. *Human Knowledge: Its Scope and Limits.* New York: Simon and Schuster, 1948.

———. *The Problems of Philosophy.* New York: Oxford University Press, 1959.

Schindler, James S. *Quasi-Reorganization.* Ann Arbor: Bureau of Business Research, School of Business Administration, University of Michigan, 1958.

Schlaifer, Robert. *Probability and Statistics for Business Decisions.* New York: McGraw-Hill Book Co., Inc., 1959.

Schumpeter, Joseph A. *Economic Doctrine and Method,* tr. R. Avis. New York: Oxford University Press, 1954.

Seligman, Edwin R. A. "Are Stock Dividends Income?" *American Economic Review,* IX (September 1919), 517-36.

Shannon, Claude E., and Weaver, Warren. *The Mathematical Theory of Communication.* Urbana, Illinois: The University of Illinois Press, 1949.

Simon, Herbert A. "Theories of Decision-Making in Economics and

Behavioral Science," *American Economic Review*, XLIX (June 1959), 253-83.

Simons, Harry, and Karrenbrock, Wilbert E. *Intermediate Accounting*. 4th ed.; Cincinnati: South-Western Publishing Co., 1964.

Simons, Henry C. *Personal Income Taxation*. Chicago: The University of Chicago Press, 1938.

Smith, Adam. *Inquiry Into the Nature and Causes of the Wealth of Nations*, ed. Edwin Cannan. New York: Random House, Inc., 1937.

Spacek, Leonard. "The Need for an Accounting Court," *Accounting Review*, XXXIII (July 1958), 368-79.

Sprouse, Robert T. "Historical Costs and Current Assets—Traditional and Treacherous," *Accounting Review*, XXXVIII (October 1963), 687-95.

———, and Moonitz, Maurice. *A Tentative Set of Broad Accounting Principles for Business Enterprises*. ("Accounting Research Study, No. 3.") New York: American Institute of Certified Public Accountants, 1962.

Stevens, Stanley Smith. "Mathematics, Measurement, and Psychophysics," in *Handbook of Experimental Psychology*, ed. S. S. Stevens, pp. 1-49. New York: John Wiley and Sons, 1951.

———. "Measurement, Psychophysics, and Utility," in *Measurement: Definitions and Theories*, eds. C. West Churchman and Philburn Ratoosh, pp. 18-63. New York: John Wiley and Sons, 1959.

———. "On the Theory of Scales of Measurement," *Science*, CIII (June 7, 1946), 677-80.

———, and Volkmann, J. "The Relation of Pitch to Frequency: A Revised Scale," *American Journal of Psychology*, LIII (July 1940), 329-53.

Stigler, George J. *The Theory of Price*. Rev. ed.; New York: Macmillan Co., 1952.

Stonier, Alfred W., and Hague, Douglas C. *A Textbook of Economic Theory*. London: Longmans, Green and Company, Ltd., 1953.

Suppes, Patrick. "Measurement, Empirical Meaningfulness, and Three-Valued Logic," in *Measurement: Definitions and Theories*, eds. C. West Churchman and Philburn Ratoosh, pp. 129-43. New York: John Wiley and Sons, 1959.

———. "A Set of Independent Axioms for Extensive Quantities," *Portugaliae Mathematics*, X, Fasc. 4 (1951).

Tunick, Stanley B., and Saxe, Emanuel. *Fundamental Accounting*. 3rd ed.; Englewood Cliffs, New Jersey: Prentice-Hall, Inc., 1963.

Vatter, William J. *The Fund Theory of Accounting.* Chicago: The University of Chicago Press, 1947.

Walras, Leon. *Elements of Pure Economics,* tr. William Jaffé. Homewood, Illinois: Richard D. Irwin, Inc., 1954.

Whorf, Benjamin L. *Language, Thought, and Reality.* New York: John Wiley and Sons, 1956.

Wueller, Paul H. "Concepts of Taxable Income," *Political Science Quarterly,* Part I, LIII (March 1938), 83-110; Part II, LIII (December 1938), 557-83; Part III, LIV (December 1939), 555-76.

INDEX

PERSONS

Abbott, Lawrence, 32n

Alexander, Sidney S., on accounting objectivity, 15-16; definition of income, 10-11; on market value, 16

Andersen (Arthur) and Company, 297

Aristotle, 185, 309

Baxter, W. T., vii, xi

Beckett, John A., operationalist views quoted, 84; on valuation and going-concern assumption, 300

Bell, Phillip W., and entry-price vs. exit-price measurement, 328-30; on Fisher Tradition, 13; on future assumption, 99, 100; and market value, 17; mentioned, ix; on static economy, 181n

Bergmann, Gustav, on arithmetical and descriptive relations, 102; mentioned, 89n, 107n

Berle, Adolph A., Jr., on profit and power, 34

Blodgett, Ralph, vii

Boulding, Kenneth E., on accountants' rituals, 194; apparent loss of, 199-202; apparent paradox of, 199-202, 270; concern with futurity, 99; firm model used by, 21; and heterogeneous assets, 27; on information for decision-making, 196-97; transformation coefficient of, 22; on utility, 33; on valuation coefficient, 25n; on variant definitions of profit, 9n, 11; *see also* Boulding's Constant in subject index

Bowers, Russell, on stock dividends and liquidity, 293-94

Bows, Albert J., criticism of current accounting, 15

Braithwaite, Richard Bevan, on employment of models, 361; mentioned, 49n

Bridgman, Percy William, mentioned, 49n; on operation, 195n; operationism of, 110

Brillouin, Léon, on information, 61-62

Broad, C. D., 96n

Brogan, A. P., and good, 119

Bruner, Jerome Seymour, on perception, 113

Burnham, James, 33

Butterfield, Herbert, on observation, 44, 114; on perception and mental transposition, 309-10

Butters, J. Keith, on changing accounting practice, 268

Campbell, Norman R., on definition of measurement, 66, 69; mentioned, 89n, 102n-103n, 107n

Canning, John B., influence of, 254

Carr, Edward Hallett, on propaganda, 54n

Cassirer, Ernst, Caws on, 48; on measurements, 74

Caws, Peter, on analysis and metaphysics, 191-92; on Cassirer and conception, 48; on measurement theory, 74n; mentioned, 15n; on operationism, 195n

Chambers, Raymond J., xi, xii, 301n

Cherry, Colin, on observation, 44

Churchman, Charles West, on communications and measurement, 40n; on decision problem of measurement, 60; on measurements, 356; on precision, 71-73; on prediction, 96n; on standardized data, 86

Cohen, Felix, on good, 119

Cohen, Morris R., 89n, 102n

Copernicus, 44

Corbin, Donald A., on objectivity, 106

Crane, Stephen, quoted, vi

Davidson, Donald, 124n

373

SUBJECTS